Designing for Emerging Technologies

UX for Genomics, Robotics, and the Internet of Things

Edited by Jonathan Follett

Beijing · Cambridge · Farnham · Köln · Sebastopol · Tokyo

Designing for Emerging Technologies
Edited by Jonathan Follett

Published by O'Reilly Media, Inc.,
1005 Gravenstein Highway North, Sebastopol, CA 95472.

O'Reilly books may be purchased for educational, business, or sales promotional use. Online editions are also available for most titles (*safaribooksonline.com*). For more information, contact our corporate/institutional sales department: (800) 998-9938 or *corporate@oreilly.com*.

Editors: Jonathan Follett, Mary Treseler, and Angela Rufino	**Cover Designer:** Ellie Volckhausen
Production Editor: Kara Ebrahim	**Interior Designers:** Ron Bilodeau and Monica Kamsvaag
Copyeditor: Dianne Russell	**Illustrator:** Rebecca Demarest
Proofreader: Charles Roumeliotis	**Compositor:** Kara Ebrahim
Indexer: Ginny Munroe	

November 2014: First Edition.

Revision History for the First Edition:

2014-10-30	First release
2015-05-08	Second release

See *http://www.oreilly.com/catalog/errata.csp?isbn=0636920030676* for release details.

ISBN: 978-1-4493-7051-0

[LSI]

[*List of Contributors*]

Chapter 1: *Designing for Emerging Technologies*
Jonathan Follett, Principal—Involution Studios

Chapter 2: *Intelligent Materials: Designing Material Behavior*
Brook Kennedy, Associate Professor, Industrial Design—Virginia Tech

Chapter 3: *Taking Control of Gesture Interaction*
Gershom Kutliroff, Principal Engineer—Intel
Yaron Yanai, Creative Director—Omek Studio at Intel

Chapter 4: *Fashion with Function: Designing for Wearables*
Michal Levin, Senior User Experience Designer—Google

Chapter 5: *Learning and Thinking with Things*
Stephen P. Anderson, Independent Consultant—PoetPainter, LLC

Chapter 6: *Designing for Collaborative Robotics*
Jeff Faneuff, Director of Engineering—Carbonite

[Contents]

[*Foreword*]

Buckle up fellow design and innovation junkies! We are the proverbial kids in the candy store, invited to peer into the gray area between brain-exploding stories about emerging technologies, any one of which alone could change the world. Resist the temptation to gorge on any one story before sampling the full cross section offered in these pages. Perhaps a better metaphor—particularly after appreciating the full breadth of possibility contained in *Designing for Emerging Technologies*— is that you will feel like a kid in a sandbox; a sandbox filled with nascent technologies beckoning design and innovation junkies like us to come play together to unleash the *adjacent possible*. To combine and recombine emerging technologies in new ways to change the way we solve the important social challenges we face in the twenty-first century. You know what I'm talking about: the little system challenges, like education, healthcare, energy, and government. Jon Follett has beautifully curated a sandbox that will inspire you, make you think, and most importantly enable you to act to help design a better future.

"Nascent" is a beautiful and optimistic word. The stories about to grab you in this book are about emerging technologies. These are stories of capabilities in their formative stage, when they are most malleable and offer the greatest possibility frontier. Nascent technologies are the stem cells of society's future. There's a reason why so much biology research focuses on stem cells. Stem cells are undifferentiated; they have the potential of becoming differentiated into most other kinds of cells. The hopes of human regenerative medicine lie on stem cell research and application. I've always been fascinated by the salamander, the highest order animal capable of regeneration. When a salamander loses or injures a body part stem cells rush to the cite enabling it to regenerate the body part. It's amazing. The nascent technologies described in this book are undifferentiated, they have unlimited potential for regeneration to unleash incredible value. We live in a magic time when technology is no longer a limiting factor in solving the big social challenges we face. It's on us humans to unleash our inner newts!

The real superpower of *Designing for Emerging Technologies* is in enabling us to connect the dots across emerging technologies. Stuart Kaufman first described the untapped potential of what could be as the adjacent possible. Most innovation isn't about inventing new technology but merely the recombination of existing parts assembled in new ways to solve a problem or deliver value. Everything we need to innovate is in our sandbox and can be found at the edges between our sectors, disciplines, and technological silos. Innovation is all about exploring the adjacent possible. Author Stephen Johnson says it well: "Ideas are works of bricolage. They are, almost inevitably, networks of other ideas. We take the ideas we've stumbled across, and we jigger them together into some new shape. The adjacent possible is a kind of shadow future, hovering on the edges of the present state of things, a map of all the ways in which the present can reinvent itself."[1]

The most important applications for the emerging technologies described in this book haven't been imagined yet. Designers have an important role to play in helping us to unleash the adjacent possible. Design helps us focus on outputs rather than just inputs. Invention is great, but innovation is a better way to deliver value. It isn't an innovation until it solves a problem and value is actually delivered in the real world. Far too many conflate invention and innovation. They are different. Design is crucial to getting the promise of these nascent technologies out of the lab, off of the whiteboard, and into the real world. It's time for designers to stop trying to make the argument that design thinking and process is important. We stipulate that design is important. It's time for designers to create the conditions and tools enabling everyone to design. It's time to move the design conversation to a new, actionable, place. Welcome to the sandbox of adjacent possibilities. Grab your pail and shovel. Let's design a better future together.

—Saul Kaplan
Founder and Chief Catalyst
Business Innovation Factory

---

1   "The Genius of the Tinkerer." *Wall Street Journal* September 25, 2010.

[*Preface*]

Why We Wrote This Book

In this collection of essays, you will discover designers, engineers, researchers, and scientists working with groundbreaking technology, discussing their approaches to experience design. This compilation spans the technological spectrum from robotics to connected environments, 3D printing to synthetic biology, genomics to wearables. It is neither definitive nor all encompassing but rather a rare combination of vision and hard-won experience, identifying nascent domains of user experience and getting down into the primordial ooze.

Consider that when the Internet first began to proliferate in the mid-to-late 1990s, there was little definition or agreement around how design should intersect with it, the emerging technology of the time. Today, we have the panoply of design subpractices that cater to very specific areas of web creation from interaction designers to usability experts, visual designers to frontend coders. The path has been laid; the trail blazed.

If this collage of ideas around emergent technology seems diverse, it is deliberate. As designers, we must cross-pollinate, drawing our inspiration from fields we've never before considered, breaking down boundaries to create something new and humane. New forms of design will emerge from this multidisciplinary brew.

Who Should Read This Book

The philosopher and writer Isaiah Berlin in his work "The Hedgehog and the Fox," described the people who excel in this type of multivariate environment, looking at many different things and approaching each situation in a new way, as "foxes." Those who wanted to focus on only one thing, who sought orderly specialization, he referred to as "hedgehogs."

If you're a UX designer or engineer interested in a multidisciplinary practice, are flexible in your outlook, accepting of complexity and dissonant ideas, and never completely satisfied with the status quo, this is the book for you. We hope that you will use this book, both as a source of inspiration to look beyond the screen to the rich world of interactions and user experiences that need to be designed, and as a preliminary resource for approaches to the unique problem sets presented.

How This Book Is Organized

There are many paths through this book. The most direct route provides a diversity of technology and perspective but also moves quickly from one topic to the next, which will suit some readers, but certainly not all. If you fall into the former category, the list of chapters and summaries that follow will provide a broad and intriguing array of topics to explore. If you fall into the latter category, and prefer your reading to be focused on a particular technology or practice area, we've organized the chapters by category in the next section, so you can choose your own adventure through *Designing for Emerging Technologies*.

Here are the luminaries from whom you will hear in this book:

- Jonathan Follett, on design for disruption and the ways in which designers can approach the power of emerging technologies, in *Designing for Emerging Technologies*

- Brook Kennedy, on future materials that will enable physical products and environments to exhibit new behaviors and interactions, in *Intelligent Materials: Designing Material Behavior*

- Gershom Kutliroff and Yaron Yanai, on the promise of gesture recognition, and the tricky problem of enabling our devices to understand us in the same way that other people do, in *Taking Control of Gesture Interaction*

- Michal Levin, on the user experience of wearable technology, and the ecosystem for innovation inherent in an increasingly device-rich world, in *Fashion with Function*

- Stephen P. Anderson, on how we might improve our learning abilities through tangible interfaces, when the physical objects with which we play are endowed with new digital properties, in *Learning and Thinking with Things*

- Jeff Faneuff, on the profound challenges in the design of interaction, emotion, culture, and technology frameworks, as robots start to work side-by-side with people, in *Design for Collaborative Robotics*

- Hunter Whitney, on how visualization design can help us understand things that are at seemingly impossible scale, such as neuroscience and cosmology, in *Design Takes on New Dimensions*

- Andy Goodman, on the intriguing idea of embeddables throughout history as body modification, and in the future as mental and sensory prosthetics, increasing our knowledge and perception of the world around us, in *Embeddables*

- Scott Sullivan, on the UX designer's need for understanding computer science and electrical engineering, in order to achieve a level of mastery over emerging interfaces for the Internet of Things, in *Prototyping Interactive Objects*

- Barry Kudrowitz, on how emergent technology might be incorporated into future playthings, and the difficulties of creating robust, low-cost products that appeal to a broad audience, in *Emerging Technology and Toy Design*

- Camille Goudeseune, on the product design of musical interfaces and the deep parallels to experience design for emerging technologies, in *Musical Instrument Design*

- Juhan Sonin, on the convergent technological and societal trends pushing design to the forefront of health, in *Design for Life*

- Erin Rae Hoffer, on the transformation of the built environment into a networked set of data-enabled elements and devices, where interconnected and intelligent spaces will impact how people live and work, in *Architecture as Interface*

- Matt Nish-Lapidus, on the core skills for designing modern networked objects and the role of the designer in shaping the future, in *Design for the Networked World*

- Martin Charlier, on the necessity of being critical about new technology, in *New Responsibilities of the Design Discipline*

- Scott Stropkay and Bill Hartman, on the growing influence and capabilities of robots in our work and personal lives, in *Designing Human-Robot Relationships*

- Marco Righetto and Andy Goodman on the possible future manifestations of synthetic biology and the side effects produced along the way, in *Tales from the Crick: Experiences and Services When Design Fiction Meets Synthetic Biology*

- Steven Keating, on the future possibilities for 3D printing technologies, including printing buildings and structurally engineering and altering color on a nano-scale, in *Beyond 3D Printing: The New Dimensions of Additive Fabrication*

- Lisa deBettencourt, on ways for user experience practitioners to satisfy the need to rapidly acquire domain knowledge, in *Become an Expert at Becoming an Expert*

- Dirk Knemeyer, on the evolution of the design field, in *The Changing Role of Design*

Chapters Organized By Subject Area

3D printing/additive fabrication

The evolution of the design field

Genomics and synthetic biology

The Internet of Things/connected environments

Product design

Robotics

Visualization

Wearable Technology

Safari® Books Online

Safari Books Online (*http://safaribooksonline.com*) is an on-demand digital library that delivers expert *content* in both book and video form from the world's leading authors in technology and business. Technology professionals, software developers, web designers, and business and creative professionals use Safari Books Online as their primary resource for research, problem solving, learning, and certification training.

Safari Books Online offers a range of *product mixes* and pricing programs for *organizations*, *government agencies*, and *individuals*. Subscribers have access to thousands of books, training videos, and prepublication manuscripts in one fully searchable database from publishers like O'Reilly Media, Prentice Hall Professional, Addison-Wesley Professional, Microsoft Press, Sams, Que, Peachpit Press, Focal Press, Cisco Press, John Wiley & Sons, Syngress, Morgan Kaufmann, IBM Redbooks, Packt, Adobe Press, FT Press, Apress, Manning, New Riders, McGraw-Hill, Jones & Bartlett, Course Technology, and dozens *more*. For more information about Safari Books Online, please visit us *online*.

How to Contact Us

Please address comments and questions concerning this book to the publisher:

O'Reilly Media, Inc.
1005 Gravenstein Highway North
Sebastopol, CA 95472
800-998-9938 (in the United States or Canada)
707-829-0515 (international or local)
707-829-0104 (fax)

We have a web page for this book, where we list errata, examples, and any additional information. You can access this page at:

http://bit.ly/emerging-tech

To comment or ask technical questions about this book, send email to:

bookquestions@oreilly.com

For more information about our books, courses, conferences, and news, see our website at *http://www.oreilly.com*.

Find us on Facebook: *http://facebook.com/oreilly*

Follow us on Twitter: *http://twitter.com/oreillymedia*

Watch us on YouTube: *http://www.youtube.com/oreillymedia*

Acknowledgments

This book has been a great collaborative experience—one that has spanned multiple continents and time zones, companies, and professions—Its diversity more resembles a multidisciplinary conference than a publication. Yet, this collection simply would not exist without the efforts of all the contributors and editors who worked tirelessly over the past 16 months to produce something so unique and forward looking.

I'd like to acknowledge the following people for their invaluable contributions:

- The visionary team of editors at O'Reilly for pushing this forward: Mary Treseler, Brian Anderson, and Angela Rufino

- The unsung contributing editors for their advice, outreach, and evangelism: Lisa deBettencourt, Erik Dahl, Matthew Holm, Dirk Knemeyer, and Scott Sullivan

- The peer reviewers for their feedback, critique, and helpful suggestions, especially Karl Fast

- The team at Involution, past and present: Juhan Sonin, Danielle Monroe, and Quentin Stipp for his lovely illustrations for my chapter

- Saul Kaplan for writing the Foreword and inspiring others to innovate

- And, most important, for her endless encouragement, my wife Jennifer

The adventure is just beginning...

—Jonathan Follett
@jonfollett

[1]

Designing for Emerging Technologies

A Call to Arms

Since the dawn of technology, humanity has lived with both its benefits and burdens. The fire that cooks our food also burns our hands; the mills and factories that produce our clothes often pollute our water and air; the computers that process our data sometimes crash and send our mission-critical records into oblivion. From the Agricultural to the Industrial to the Information Revolution, humanity has enjoyed great advantages from technology, but we have suffered the consequences of flawed thinking regarding its use, resulting in wasteful consumption of our world's resources, problems for our environment, and social disruption. Humanity enters the new millennium struggling with the challenges we've created for ourselves in areas from energy to infrastructure, transportation to healthcare, and manufacturing to agriculture. To address these challenges, we will no doubt turn once again to technology: in the coming century, we'll be able to hack our DNA, embed computers in our bodies, and print replacement organs. The question is, what will we do when we find ourselves with the capability to do just about anything we can dream of?

To explore that question—at least from a design perspective—let's consider the implications of four significant emerging technologies whose growth, maturation, and widespread commercial adoption has the potential to disrupt the current economic order:

- A networked, intelligent world connected by the Internet of Things (IoT)

- More efficient and effective manufacturing, healthcare, and disaster relief aided by advanced robotics

- Custom, just-in-time manufacturing, driven by additive fabrication/3D printing

- Medicine, food, and fuel created by altering the code of life itself, through genomics and synthetic biology

Through the lens of these disruptive technologies, we'll look at what designing products, services, and experiences for people might require and examine some of the high-level user experience (UX) tenets practitioners might consider when approaching the design for such new fields.

Today, we're on the cusp of a significant technological period, not unlike the Second Industrial Revolution that occurred in America from the end of the Civil War until World War I, when major discoveries and inventions completely transformed the economic, social, and political fabric of the United States. During this particularly prolific era, inventors, innovators, and scientists such as Alexander Graham Bell, Thomas Edison, Henry Ford, and Nikola Tesla introduced the world to technologies that would define modern life in the twentieth century. These included the light bulb, the telephone, and the mass-produced automobile, among many others. The light bulb and basic electrical service provided the cornerstones of the electric age, while the telephone started a communication revolution, and the automobile began an era of personal transportation that would alter the landscape of America itself. Historically, this period provides a powerful example of the systemic disruption that occurs when multiple technological innovations emerge, mature, and reach popular adoption along roughly the same timeline. Just as the inventions of the Second Industrial Revolution transformed the United States on almost every level, robotics, additive fabrication, the IoT, and synthetic biology similarly have the potential to define and shape our next era.

As these technologies evolve, they will influence humanity's progress as a species, making the tumult of our current Information Revolution look like a minor blip by comparison. Although the miracles of our age are many, computers, the Internet, and mobile devices primarily serve to *accelerate* human communication, collaboration, and commerce. Without dismissing their importance, we observe that many existing models of interaction have been enhanced, rather than transformed, by moving from the physical to the digital realm—becoming cheaper, faster and, perhaps, better in the process. Email is an accelerated version of the postal service, e-commerce, a more convenient and efficient version of the brick-and-mortar store, and so on. Conversely, in technologies such as synthetic biology and additive fabrication, we can see the potential to remake our current order in substantial fashion, with the formation of entirely new industries and the birth of new markets.

A May 2013 McKinsey Global Institute report titled "Disruptive technologies: Advances that will transform life, business, and the global economy," identifies the global markets ready for disruption and describes the potential economic value of this transformation. Genomics has the potential to alter the $6.5 trillion healthcare and $1.1 trillion agriculture industries through products such as personalized medicines and genetically modified foods. Additive fabrication/3D printing and advanced robotics will upend the global manufacturing industry—affecting the $6 trillion in labor expenditures and $11 trillion in global manufacturing GDP, respectively. And, the IoT will disrupt the manufacturing, healthcare, and mining industries to the tune of $36 trillion.[1]

Design for Disruption

Let's look briefly at the disruptive potential of each of these emerging technologies—the IoT, advanced robotics, 3D printing, and synthetic biology—and the need for design thinking in their formation.

---

1 James Manyika, Michael Chui, Jacques Bughin, Richard Dobbs, Peter Bisson, and Alex Marrs. "Disruptive technologies: Advances that will transform life, business, and the global economy." May 2013; McKinsey Global Institute Report (*http://bit.ly/1CJ2q8v*).

THE IOT, CONNECTED ENVIRONMENTS, AND WEARABLE TECHNOLOGY

The IoT is a popular shorthand that describes the many objects that are outfitted with sensors and communicating machine-to-machine. These objects make up our brave, new connected world. The types and numbers of these devices are growing by the day, to a possible 50 billion objects by 2020, according to the Cisco report, "The Internet of Things: How the Next Evolution of the Internet Is Changing Everything."[2] Inexpensive sensors providing waves of data can help us gain new insight into the places in which we live, work, and play, as well as the capabilities to influence our surroundings—passively and actively—and have our surroundings influence us. We can imagine the possibilities of a hyper-connected world in which hospitals, factories, roads, airways, offices, retail stores, and public buildings are tied together by a web of data.

In a similar fashion, when we wear these sensors on our bodies, they can become our tools for self-monitoring. Combine this capability with information delivery via Bluetooth or other communication methods and display it via flexible screens, and we have the cornerstones of a wearable technology revolution that is the natural partner and possible inheritor of our current smartphone obsession. If we consider that the systems, software, and even the objects themselves will require design input on multiple levels, we can begin to see the tremendous opportunity resident in the IoT and wearables.

ROBOTICS

In 2013, Google's purchase of eight robotics companies (which are to be consolidated into a new division led by Andy Rubin, the former head of its successful Android operating system) was publicly heralded as an inflection point for the robotics industry. Not coincidentally, the stocks of competitors such as iRobot rose dramatically.[3]

---

2 Dave Evans. "The Internet of Things: How the Next Evolution of the Internet Is Changing Everything." April 2011; Cisco White Paper (*http://bit.ly/1CJ2sNE*).

3 John Markoff. "Google Puts Money on Robots, Using the Man Behind Android." December 4, 2013; The New York Times (*http://nyti.ms/1CJ2tkR*).

More so than any other emerging technology, robotics has captured the imagination of American popular culture, especially that of the Hollywood sci-fi blockbuster. We're entertained, enthralled, and maybe (but only slightly) alarmed by the legacy of *Blade Runner*, *The Terminator*, *The Matrix* and any number of lesser dystopian robotic celluloid futures. It remains to be seen if robot labor generates the kind of societal, economic, and political change depicted in the more pessimistic musings of our culture's science fiction. Ensuring that it does not is a design challenge of the highest order.

In the near term, robots are ideal for taking care of jobs that are repetitive, physically demanding, and potentially hazardous to humans. As such, immediate opportunities for advanced robotics lie in areas where human labor is still intensive, such as manufacturing and logistics.

3D PRINTING

Additive manufacturing—more popularly known as 3D printing—is a process of creating a three-dimensional object by printing one miniscule layer at a time, based on a computer model. This flexible technology can use a wide variety of substrates including plastic, metal, glass, and even biological material. Custom production using additive manufacturing techniques promises to disrupt many industries, from construction to food to medicine. Possibilities for this technology range from immediately practical applications such as printing new parts just-in-time to fix a broken appliance; to controversial, uncomfortable realities, including generating guns on demand; to hopeful and futuristic methods, perhaps the ability to create not just viable human tissue, but complete, working organs, which could be used in transplants or for the testing of new drugs and vaccines.

Today, additive manufacturing is already changing architecture and construction. In April 2014, WinSun, a Chinese engineering company, reported that it can construct 10 single-story homes in a day by using a specialized 3D printing technology that creates the main structure and walls using an inexpensive combination of concrete and construction waste materials.[4]

---

4 "China: Firm 3D prints 10 full-sized houses in a day." April, 25 2014; BBC News (*http://bbc.in/1CJ2rJE*).

In the field of health, the work of roboticist Easton LaChapelle represents the change made possible by additive fabrication in medical-device prototyping and production processes. The 17-year-old wunderkind has created an ultra-light, fully functioning prosthetic arm whose parts can be 3D-printed for about $500. Traditionally manufactured prosthetic arms that are currently available can cost upward of $80,000. LaChapelle's prosthetic arm is controlled using an EEG headset, which measures brainwaves and communicates with the arm wirelessly via Bluetooth.

At the Business Innovation Factory BIF9 conference in Providence, Rhode Island, held in September 2013, LaChapelle demonstrated his invention and discussed his amazing progression through the design and prototyping phases. The first generation of the product LaChappelle created was a robotic hand, made of Lego bricks, surgical tubing, and five servo motors. He created the second-generation robotic arm by using 3D-printed parts and a Nintendo Power Glove. Now in its third generation, the arm is made almost entirely of 3D-printed parts, and most dramatic of all, it has human strength. While LaChapelle has not made the leap from prototype to a manufacture-ready device, it's easy to imagine the potential for disruption in the market it represents.

From a process standpoint, LaChappelle's methods in designing and engineering the prosthetic demonstrate the speed at which ideas can move from a designer's imagination to becoming something real and testable. Even though prototyping has always been a part of the designer's toolkit, additive fabrication makes it possible to apply the same rapid and flexible process of ideation, creation, testing, validation, and iteration to physical products that used to be reserved for the realm of digital development.

GENOMICS AND SYNTHETIC BIOLOGY

In April 2003, the publicly funded Human Genome Project completed the sequencing of the entirety of our human DNA, providing the blueprint for building a person at a price of $3 billion. At the time, this scientific achievement was heralded as one of the greatest in history, with far-reaching implications for health and medicine. Then-President Bill

Clinton, in announcing the working draft sequence of the Human Genome in 2000, said "Without a doubt, this is the most important, most wondrous map ever produced by human kind."[5]

Fast forward just slightly more than a decade, and the cost of sequencing a human genome has dropped to roughly $1,000—an exponential reduction in price far exceeding what Moore's Law would predict. A host of companies are racing to introduce technology to make even more rapid and inexpensive sequencing possible. With the widespread affordability of this sophisticated test quickly becoming reality, genomics can provide the map for a new wave of personalized therapies: highly targeted drugs for fighting cancer, cardiovascular disease, diabetes, and other hereditary illnesses.

As with genomic sequencing, the price of DNA synthesis continues to drop. It now approaches 25 cents per base pair or less via services such as GenScript, DNA 2.0, and others. Writing the code of life is the cornerstone of the science of synthetic biology; the intentional design and engineering of biological systems will make incredible things possible. In his book *Regenesis*, George Church, geneticist, Harvard professor, and perhaps the most well-known scientist in this field, outlines some of the inventive solutions offered by this future potential, including biofuels, targeted gene therapies, and even virus-resistant human beings. In Church's expansive vision, we see a future in which humans have the capability to design nature itself, changing the fabric of biology and human evolution.[6]

If advanced robotics, additive fabrication, synthetic biology, and other emerging technologies extend humanity's grasp, making it possible for us to achieve our goals in manufacturing, health, energy, and other industries rapidly and efficiently, they also will place their own set of demands upon us. The fields of graphic design, industrial design, and software UX design have all evolved in response to the unique demands of new technologies. It's a classic human characteristic to relate to and interact with our latest tools. Graphic design makes information

---

5 "Breaking News—President Clinton, British Prime Minister Tony Blair Deliver Remarks on Human Genome Milestone." June 26, 2000; CNN.com Transcripts (*http://bit.ly/1CJ2xky*).

6 George Church and Edward Regis. *Regenesis: How Synthetic Biology Will Reinvent Nature and Ourselves.* 2012; Basic Books.

depicted in printed media clear, understandable, and beautiful; industrial design makes products elegant, usable, and humane; and UX design makes the interaction with our digital products and services efficient and even pleasurable.

Historically, bridging this gap between man and disruptive technology has not been an easy task. In addition to the positive outcomes of the Industrial Revolution, the political, societal, and economic change across the globe also engendered negative responses by people whose lives and livelihoods were displaced. Most famously, the Luddites in England sabotaged machines in the factories, preferring to destroy the technology they felt would ruin man's existence, rather than proceed forward in concert with it. Mass production similarly had its tensions with traditional craftsman—from woodworkers to painters to architects—who responded by creating the influential Arts and Crafts movement in the late 1800s. And, in the literature of the time, industrialization faced one of its most enduring critiques in Mary Shelley's *Frankenstein*, which articulated most eloquently the idea that science left unchecked and pursued for its own sake was not to be trusted. We, too, can expect that the road to adopting the emerging technologies of our time will be subject to societal tensions and negative reactions, critiques, and counter-movements, which is all the more reason for designers to involve themselves early.

Eight Design Tenets for Emerging Technology

As we face a future in which the definition of what it is to be human might be inexorably changed, we will need design to help frame our interactions with technologies, from skin-top embeddable computers to bioprinted organs to swarming robots, which often seem to be racing ahead of our ability to process and manage on an emotional, ethical, and societal level. Designers have an opportunity to help define the parameters of and sculpt the interactions between man and technology, whether we're struggling with fear and loathing in reaction to genetically altered foods, the moral issues of changing a child's traits to suit a parent's preferences, the ethics guiding battlefield robots, or the societal implications of a 150-year extended lifetime. At its best, not only can design provide the frame for how technology works and how it's used, it can also situate it within a broader context: incorporating system thinking, planning for a complete technological lifecycle, and evaluating the possibility of unintended consequences.

Our field of practice will be transformed, as well, and we must prepare for it by moving from design as facilitation, shaping the interface and workflow, to design as the arbiter, driving the creation of the technology itself and applying our understanding of interaction, form, information, and artistry to new areas. To balance those asking, "How can this be done?" we should ask, "Why should we do this, to what end, and for whose benefit?" We must move from being passive receptors of new technology to active participants in its formation. As design thinkers and practitioners we're called to be explorers. And, although it's true that not every designer will want or be able to follow this path, those who do will have an opportunity to contribute in significant fashion.

Today, design work is changing at an unprecedented pace, and we are all too aware of the need to constantly evolve our skills to match the demands of the marketplace. With this uncertainty comes opportunity: the design positions of the future are not yet defined. Just as there was no industrial, graphic, or interaction designer at one time, so too the designer of emerging technologies has, at least for now, a broad canvas to explore. How we bring our current skills to bear on new problems, how we determine new subjects to learn, and how we integrate with burgeoning new industries will all play a part in the way our emerging design practices form.

What competencies will be most important for the designer in these new areas? What approaches will be most effective for managing the disruptive power of emerging technologies? What thinking processes will help the designer negotiate the technical, social, and ethical complexities that emerging technology will inevitably present? As a first attempt at answering these questions, the tenets that follow articulate some high-level guidelines for creative thinking and process development, drawing broad-based inspiration from related professional fields, including architecture, art, ethnography, engineering, and most of all, user experience. Although these tenets are certainly also applicable to knowledge work in a general sense—for the scientist, technologist, or entrepreneur—we will consider them in the context of design for emerging technology.

1. IDENTIFY THE PROBLEMS CORRECTLY

The gap between the problems we face as a species and the seemingly unlimited potential of technologies ripe for implementation begs for considered but agile design thinking and practice. Designers should be problem identifiers, not just problem solvers searching for a solution to a pre-established set of parameters. We must seek to guide our technology, rather than just allow it to guide us.

On the cover of the November/December 2012 issue of MIT Technology Review, the shortcomings of the past decade's technological achievements are expressed in the damning headline dramatically superimposed in white type over the bemused portrait of astronaut Buzz Aldrin: "You Promised Me Mars Colonies. Instead I Got Facebook." The subhead elaborates tellingly: "We've stopped solving big problems. Meet the technologists who refuse to give up." The accompanying article "Why We Can't Solve Big Problems"[7] details some of the current limitations in American culture, finance, and politics that, since the Apollo moonshot, have relegated big thinking and technical aspirations to the sidelines. The author, however, concludes the following:

---

7 Jason Pontin. "Why We Can't Solve Big Problems." MIT Technology Review, October 24, 2012 (*http://bit.ly/1CJ2zJ9*).

It's not true that we can't solve big problems through technology; we can. We must. But all these elements must be present: political leaders and the public must care to solve a problem, our institutions must support its solution, it must really be a technological problem, and we must understand it.

We are on the cusp of a new technological age, saddled with the problems of the previous one, demanding that as we step forward we do not make the same mistakes. To do this, we must identify the right challenges to take on: the significant and valuable ones. Chief among our concerns must be the environment, not only in reducing the carbon we release as a result of consumption and seeking new sources of energy, but also in understanding the effects of a growing global population, against the backdrop of limited resources. We must also improve human health and consider the ramifications as humans live longer lives. And, we must find new ways to manufacture goods and produce food and clean water for a planet currently with 7.2 billion inhabitants—a population that is projected to explode in the next 35 years by an additional 2.4 billion, reaching 9.6 billion by 2050, according to the UN report, "World Population Prospects: The 2012 Revision."[8] Recognizing these major challenges for humanity in the twenty-first century and seeking proactive solutions, even in significant areas such as the environment, energy, health, manufacturing, agriculture, and water usage, will not be an obvious or easy task.

We can see an example of this in the tragic events of the Fukushima meltdown. On March 11, 2011, a 9.0 magnitude earthquake and subsequent tsunami damaged the Fukushima Daiichi nuclear reactors in Japan. Over the course of 24 hours, crews tried desperately to fix the reactors. However, as, one by one, the backup safety measures failed, the fuel rods in the nuclear reactor overheated, releasing dangerous amounts of radiation into the surrounding area. As radiation levels became far too high for humans, emergency teams at the plant were unable to enter key areas to complete the tasks required for recovery. Three hundred thousand people had to be evacuated from their homes, some of whom have yet to return.

---

8   United Nations, Department of Economic and Social Affairs, Population Division (2013). World Population Prospects: The 2012 Revision (*http://esa.un.org/wpp/*).

The current state of the art in robotics is not capable of surviving the hostile, high-radiation environment of a nuclear power plant melt-down and dealing with the complex tasks required to assist a recovery effort. In the aftermath of Fukushima, the Japanese government did not immediately have access to hardened, radiation-resistant robots. A few robots from American companies—tested on the modern battle-fields of Afghanistan and Iraq—including iRobot's 710 Kobra (formerly Warríor) and 510 PackBot were able to survey the plant.[9] The potential for recovery-related tasks that can and should be handled by advanced robotics is far greater than this. However, for many reasons, span-ning political, cultural, and systemic, before the Fukushima event, an investment in robotic research was never seriously considered. The meltdown was an unthinkable catastrophe, one that Japanese officials thought could never happen, and as such, it was not even acknowl-edged as a possible scenario for which planning was needed.

The Fukushima catastrophe inspired the United States Defense Advanced Research Projects Agency (DARPA) to create the Robotics Challenge, the purpose of which is to accelerate technological devel-opment for robotics in the area of disaster recovery. Acknowledging the fragility of our human systems and finding resilient solutions to catastrophes—whether it's the next super storm, earthquake, or nuclear meltdown—is a problem on which designers, engineers, and technologists should focus.

In the DARPA competition mission statement, we can see the framing of the challenge in human terms.

> History has repeatedly demonstrated that humans are vulnerable to natural and man-made disasters, and there are often limitations to what we can do to help remedy these situations when they occur. Robots have the potential to be useful assistants in situations in which humans cannot safely operate, but despite the imaginings of science fiction, the actual robots of today are not yet robust enough to func-tion in many disaster zones nor capable enough to perform the most basic tasks required to help mitigate a crisis situation. The goal of the DRC is to generate groundbreaking research and development

---

9 Marina Koren. "3 Robots That Braved Fukushima." Popular Mechanics (*http://bit. ly/1CJ2DZu*).

in hardware and software that will enable future robots, in tandem with human counterparts, to perform the most hazardous activities in disaster zones, thus reducing casualties and saving lives.[10]

The competition, so far, has been successful in its mission to encourage innovation in advanced robotics. In the competition trials held in December 2013, robots from MIT, Carnegie Mellon, and the Google-owned Japanese firm, Schaft, Inc., competed at a variety of tasks related to disaster recovery, which included driving cars, traversing difficult terrain, climbing ladders, opening doors, moving debris, cutting holes in walls, closing valves, and unreeling hoses.

2. LEARN CONSTANTLY

Designers will need to understand the implications of science and technology for people. To do this effectively, we must be able to immerse ourselves in new technical domains and learn them quickly. Just as our understanding of and empathy for people allows us to successfully

---

10 "DARPA Robotics Challenge." DRC. *http://www.theroboticschallenge.org/* (accessed June 10, 2014)

design with a user's viewpoint in mind, understanding our materials, whether they be pixels or proteins, sensors or servos, enables us to bring a design into the world. To achieve this, designers need to be early adopters of technology, learning constantly.

The ability to quickly learn new materials and techniques has always been one of the most important of a designer's core competencies. However, the speed at which this is expected and at which technological change occurs is the critical difference today. *How* we learn will soon become as important a consideration as *what* we learn. To prepare designers for the new roles that emerging technology will bring, schools will need to develop curricula that emphasize continuous learning as a core competency and provide tools and methods to enable it.

AIGA, the professional association for design, and Adobe Systems, Inc., the design software giant, released research, "Defining the Designer of 2015," based on the input of 2,500 designers and a variety of experts and focused on the future of the field.[11]

> In order to fulfill the expectations placed upon designers in the future, they will need to employ a set of skills that include some beyond today's typical scope. No single designer is likely to have all the skills required, yet this research revealed the range of competencies that a studio or design department, among its full complement of staff, will need in order to meet the demands of the future.

Although the AIGA/Adobe survey results focus largely on communication-related design, it acknowledges that among the competencies needed by the designer of 2015, the need for "understanding of and ability to utilize tools and technology" and the "ability to be flexible, nimble and dynamic in practice." Ultimately, designers will need to be lifetime learners.

---

11 "Defining the Designer of 2015." AIGA. *http://www.aiga.org/designer-of-2015/* (accessed June 10, 2014)

3. THINK SYSTEMICALLY

Increasingly, designers will also need to be system thinkers. As we consider the fields of advanced robotics, synthetic biology, or wearable technology, the design of the ecosystem will be just as important as the design of the product or service itself.

A good example of such a product is Mimo, a next-generation baby-monitoring service that goes far beyond the usual audio and video capabilities in soothing the anxieties of new parents. A startup company led by a group of MIT engineering grads called Rest Devices has created an ingenious baby "onesie." It's a connected product that delivers a stream of data including temperature, body position, and respiration information, ensuring that mom and dad are fully versed in the minutiae of their offspring. What at first glance might seem like the enablement of over-parenting paranoia, could, in fact, also provide valuable scientific data, particularly given that crib death or SIDS (Sudden Infant Death Syndrome) is a phenomenon that is still not fully understood.

From a design perspective, a company such as Rest Devices has a range of needs typical of those startups in the budding wearable technologies industry. The onesie itself must be designed for both functional and aesthetic elements—a mixture of industrial design for the "turtle" on-body device that houses the sensor and the fashion design of the garment itself. The mobile software application that provides the data interface requires interaction design and visual design—not to mention the UX design of the total system, which must be optimized for setup and navigation by nervous parents. Whether one person or many provide these different design skills for Rest Devices, it's clear that at every point at which people touch the technology, there is ample opportunity for the interaction to be carefully examined and optimized in relation to the entire ecosystem. In this way the Mimo is a good example of the first wave of wearable technology. Like the Nike FuelBand, the Fitbit, and even the Recon heads-up ski display, these wearables represent technology embedded into the infrastructure of our lives in a way never before seen. But the magic of the consumer experience of these products is only possible through the design of a complete, and hopefully seamless, ecosystem.

4. WORK AT A VARIETY OF SCALES

Designers should be able work at a variety of scales, from the aforementioned overall system view, to the nitty-gritty details. Moving between these levels will be important, too, as each one informs the other—the macro view informs the micro, and vice versa.

At the highest level, designers can work proactively with politicians and policy makers to effectively regulate new technology. As one example of this, in September 2013, the FDA released final guidance on mobile medical apps, which was crafted with input from industry experts. From bioethics to industrial regulations governing the use of robotics, designers will want and need to have input into the realm of policy. Just as free markets cannot exist without effective and enforceable contract law, so, too, technological advancement cannot exist without sensible, effective, and enforceable regulation with a long-term view. Designers will need a seat, not just at the computer or the lab bench, but at the policy-making table, as well.

At Involution Studios, an experience design firm, we've worked with healthcare industry clients on emerging technology projects such as genomics research software and connected medical devices. As one depiction of how design thinking can be utilized at the organizational level, one engagement we recently completed for the Personal Genome Project (PGP) at Harvard University exemplifies how design research tools and techniques can help cutting-edge organizations focus on human-centered problems.

Founded in 2005 by George Church, the mission of the Personal Genome Project (PGP) is to sequence and publicize the genomes of 100,000 volunteers for use by the scientific community in the improvement and management of human health and disease. When Involution first engaged with the PGP, however, everyone on the team saw the organization functioning slightly differently, with different objectives.

It was clear that the volunteer members—those who were donating their genome and medical histories—were the type of people who were willing to take on great risk to help advance scientific discovery. The PGP had done a good job of educating their members on the possible perils that could come with publishing their genomic data for the world to see. However, the members received little to no feedback on whether their information was being used by the scientific community, how it was being used, or the potential impact of their contributions. Because members could reclaim their contributions at any time, the PGP needed to find a way to better nurture these relationships so that the project could continue striving toward its goal of 100,000 participants.

Involution and the PGP collaboratively mapped the organization's ecosystem to better visualize how it was functioning. "It was time for us to step back and talk about what that overarching goal was, and we did that through this workshop. It was very helpful," said Jason Bobe, executive director of the PGP, who believes the workshop gave his team members a forum to tease out their big ideas as well as their roles within the organization. As a result of sketching, brainstorming, and mapping exercises, the PGP team members were able to see the risks and benefits of their organizational model through the lens of the many different users they were serving. "We had a team where we had a bunch of ideas about what we were doing, but we didn't have a cohesive, shared understanding of how we were going to do everything we wanted to do," said Bobe. With Involution's help, the team was able to uncover multiple challenges that were holding the PGP back. The result from the workshop was significant: a complete reimagining of the PGP's organizational model, separating member recruitment efforts from data collection and sequencing, and truly focusing on member relationships.

5. CONNECT PEOPLE AND TECHNOLOGY

Design should provide the connective tissue between people and technology. The seamless integration of a technology into our lives is almost always an act of great design, coupled with smart engineering; it's the "why" that makes the "what" meaningful. It is through this humane expression of technology that the designer ensures a product or service is not just a functional experience, but one that is also worthwhile. We must consider the outputs of these technologies—what people need and want. The designer should ask: "Why are we doing these things? How is humanity represented against what's possible with technology?" It is the designer's duty to be a skeptic for the human side of the equation.

For instance, as robots take a greater role in the fields such as manufacturing by automating repetitive and dangerous tasks, as well as augmenting human abilities, we can see that even though there are many benefits, there remains a question as to how such robotic optimization can coexist with meaningful work for people in the long term. At first glance, the combination of collaborative robotics and agile manufacturing seems to be one potential answer to this problem. Rethink Robotics' Baxter, Yaskawa Motoman's Dexter Bot, and Universal Robotics' UR are examples of collaborative robots designed with human-like characteristics, flexibility regarding the tasks they can execute, and ease of programming, opening up new possibilities for working in tandem with human workers on the factory floor. In this model, human labor is augmented by, not replaced with, the robotic technologies.

Advanced collaborative robotics could readily provide the flexible systems required to meet the demands of agile manufacturing. A key advantage to robotic manufacturing is its adaptability: robotic production lines can be easily modified to accommodate shorter-run, customized products. We could soon see robots replace expensive dedicated industrial machinery made for specific production processes, which can be extremely difficult to repurpose when changes to a process are required. As a part of this agile manufacturing paradigm, robots with the ability to work in collaboration with human beings—in factories, warehouses, and other industrial settings—will be a critical component. Human workers will be responsible for programming, monitoring, supervising, and otherwise interacting with a robotic workforce that is repurposed regularly to handle the creation of custom, short-run production.

6. PROVOKE AND FACILITATE CHANGE

It is not only the designer's responsibility to smooth transitions and find the best way to work things out between people and the technology in their lives; it is also the designer's duty to recognize when things are not working, and, rather than smooth over problems, to provoke wholesale change. Technological change is difficult and disruptive. Even today, there are countless examples of technologies outpacing the frameworks for controlling them, resulting in a sense of unease in people about the seemingly unprecedented and unchecked advances, from digital surveillance encroaching on our privacy to genetically modified foods filling our grocery stores. Designers can start the discussion and help lead the process of transformation.

As one illustration of this, despite the seemingly unlimited potential of genomics, or perhaps because of it, the tension between those who wish to move the science forward and those cautioning restraint is palpable. Take the example of 23andMe, a company that provides inexpensive personal DNA sequencing. In November 2013, the United States Food and Drug Administration (FDA) shut down the service for supplying medical interpretation of the DNA data in the reports the company issued to its customers.[12] Here's the notice that appeared on the 23andMe website:

> At this time, we have suspended our health-related genetic tests to comply with the U.S. Food and Drug Administration's directive to discontinue new consumer access during our regulatory review process. We are continuing to provide you with both ancestry-related genetic tests and raw genetic data, without 23andMe's interpretation. … We remain firmly committed to fulfilling our long-term mission to help people everywhere have access to their own genetic data and have the ability to use that information to improve their lives.

The FDA's action brings into question the future regulatory environment that scientists, entrepreneurs, designers, and engineers could encounter in the realm of personalized medicine. The regulator's dilemma for emerging tech is that the rules governing familiar industries might not apply to technology likely to be disruptive to those industries. In the case of 23andMe, regulators must balance the benefits of customers learning about diseases they carry or are at risk for with the dangers of false positives, misuse, or misinterpretation of the data. 23andMe is disruptive because it provides personal genomic testing at a low price point. It also ventures into territory never before seen by an industry familiar with expensive testing regimes typically administered in a reactive, rather than proactive, manner.

In December 2013, the Presidential Commission for the Study of Bioethical Issues released its report, "Anticipate and Communicate: Ethical Management of Incidental and Secondary Findings in the Clinical, Research, and Direct-to-Consumer Contexts." This document provides guidance on how to manage the issues of incidental and secondary findings.

> How clinicians, researchers and direct-to-consumer companies manage incidental and secondary findings will likely touch all of us who seek medical care, participate in research, or send a cheek swab to a company for a peek at our own genetic make-up," said Amy Gutmann,

---

12 Chris Welch. "FDA orders 23andMe to halt sales of DNA test kit." The Verge. *http://bit.ly/1CJ2GEt* (accessed June 10, 2014)

Ph.D., Commission Chair. "The reality is that we might find out more than we bargained for. Yet practitioners are getting conflicting advice about how to manage such findings across contexts and modalities such as genetics, imaging, and biological specimen testing. We all need to know how to better manage health information we did not expect.[13]

As designers, we need to be engaged in proactive, society-wide conversations such as this so that we can help define safe boundaries and people-centric policies ahead of time, rather than trying to figure things out—and spend time defending our industries' very existence—after the horse has left the gate.

7. WORK EFFECTIVELY ON CROSS-DISCIPLINARY TEAMS

The challenges inherent in much of emerging technology are far too great for an individual to encompass the requisite cross-domain knowledge. For this kind of work, then, the team becomes paramount. It is a multidisciplinary mix of scientists, engineers, and designers who are best positioned to understand and take advantage of these technologies. And, it is crucial that these creative disciplines evolve together.

---

13 "Bioethics Commission on Incidental Findings: Anticipate and Communicate." December 12, 2013; Presidential Commission for the Study of Bioethical Issues (*http://bioethics.gov/ node/3186*).

From such collaborations new roles will be created: perhaps we will soon see a great need for the synthetic biological systems engineer or the human-robot interaction designer. This cross-pollination of science, design, and engineering is already happening at organizations such as the Wyss Institute at Harvard, whose mission is to develop materials and devices inspired by nature and biology. Wyss structures itself around multidisciplinary teams. Forward-thinking design firms such as IDEO have also added synthetic biology to their established practices of industrial and digital design.

As an example of this cross-pollination, in a presentation, "Life is what you make it," given at a Friday Evening Discourse at The Royal Institution of Great Britain in London, esteemed scientist and Imperial College professor Paul Freemont described how biological design could take its cues from computer software engineering, using an abstraction hierarchy for biological design.[14] In the design of complex systems, an abstraction hierarchy makes it possible for engineers to focus on solving the problems at hand because they don't necessarily need to understand the complexity of the lower levels of the hierarchy. In software development, for example, engineers can code in Java or C++ and not need to understand the machine-level code that ultimately executes the program. In the coming revolution in biological design, such an abstraction hierarchy will offer bioengineers the capability to operate similarly.

Although programming might be an apt analogy for that manipulation of nature, there are fundamental differences between the writing of computer code and genetic code. Even if we know the outcome of the genetic code we write, the environment into which it is released is far more complex than the controlled operating system of a computer or mobile device. There is so much unknown about biological systems that prototyping and testing will be critical steps for responsible innovation. Even though designers won't necessarily need to become genetic engineers to contribute to the field of synthetic biology, they'll need to understand the materials just as deeply.

---

14 Paul Freemont. "Life is what you make it." November 29, 2013; The Royal Institution, Friday Evening Discourse. (*http://bit.ly/1CJ2Mfj*).

At Boston University, the Cross-Disciplinary Integration of Design Automation Research (CIDAR) lab is creating bioCAD tools such as Clotho, an open source software framework for engineering synthetic biological systems. The larger goal for Clotho—named for the Greek goddess of Fate who was responsible for spinning the thread of human life—is to create standardized data, algorithms, and methodologies for synthetic biology. Other software tools such as Genome Compiler and Gene Designer aim to improve the process of genome creation from design to quality assurance to fabrication. At the intersection of software design and genome design, these tools for automating aspects of the synth bio process are cross-disciplinary efforts.

8. TAKE RISKS, RESPONSIBLY

To find our way forward as designers, we must be willing to take risks—relying upon a combination of our education, experience, and intuition—which can be crucial to innovation. We must always keep in mind both the benefits and consequences for people using these new technologies, and be prepared for mixed results.

The Glowing Plant Kickstarter project is a good example of such inspired risk taking in action. There is perhaps no technology more fraught with perceived peril than genomics and synthetic biology. Seeing the opportunity to both inspire and educate the public, a team of biochemists started a project to generate a bioluminescent plant, which they touted as "the first step in creating sustainable natural lighting." Financed on the crowd-funding website Kickstarter, the Glowing Plant project generated so much grassroots excitement that it raised $484,013 from 8,433 backers, far exceeding its initial goal of $65,000.

However, soon after the Glowing Plant project finished its campaign, Kickstarter, without any explanation, changed its terms for project creators, banning genetically modified organisms (GMOs) as rewards for online backers.[15] Glowing Plant, with its project financing already in place, might be the last example of crowd-funded synthetic biology for a while. Although this incident, in and of itself, might seem minor, it's worth remembering that Kickstarter is the primary resource for crowd-funding in the United States. Removing this financial option for synthetic biology startups, in a seemingly arbitrary decision, will have a chilling effect on future innovators.

The results of the Glowing Plant crowd-funding project illustrate the promise and perils of designing for such a disruptive technology as synthetic biology. How do we evaluate the risk and reward, in this case, knowing the outcome? Even though the team initially received immense grassroots enthusiasm and financial backing, they also caused the Kickstarter ban, as an established corporate entity reacted with fear. During this transition time between fear and acceptance, designers of genetically modified organisms, like the team behind the Glowing Plant project, will continue to push the envelope of what companies, regulators, and the government find acceptable. It's safe to say

---

15 Duncan Geere. "Kickstarter bans project creators from giving away genetically-modified organisms." August 2, 2013 (*http://bit.ly/1CJ2QvH*).

that until synthetic biology is better understood, policy decisions such as this ban will continue to happen. It might be that a willingness to push forward and to take risks will be important to making the transition, to reach public acceptance and ultimately help move the technology forward.

Changing Design and Designing Change

People are less interested in the science and engineering, the mechanisms that make emerging technologies such as advanced robotics, synthetic biology, and the IoT possible, but they are deeply concerned with the outcomes. As these technologies emerge, grow, and mature over the coming years, designers will have the opportunity to bridge human needs and the miraculous technological possibilities.

It will be a great and even intimidating challenge to involve design early in the process of defining new products and services, but it will be critical as we establish the practices of the twenty-first century—from the design of technology policy, to systems, to tactical interaction frameworks and techniques. Policy design will involve advising regulators and politicians on the possibilities and perils of emerging tech; system design will demand clear understanding of the broader interactions and implications that surround the immediate details of a product; and framework design will benefit our day-to-day tactical work, providing a foundation for designers and design practice to come. What all of these technologies will create, as they evolve together, remains to be seen. But, the most interesting discoveries will be at the intersections.

Understanding new technologies, their potential usage, and how they will impact people in the short and long term will require education and collaboration, resulting in new design specializations, many of which we have not yet even considered. In the coming years, as the boundaries between design and engineering for software, hardware, and biotechnology continue to blur, those who began their professional lives as industrial designers, computer engineers, UX practitioners, and scientists will find that the trajectory of their careers takes them into uncharted territory. Like the farmers who moved to the cities to participate in the birth of the Industrial Revolution, we can't imagine all of the outcomes of our work. However, if history is any indicator, the convergence of these technologies will be greater than the sum of its parts. If we are prepared to take on such challenges, we only have to ask: "What stands in the way?"

Intelligent Materials: Designing Material Behavior

BROOK KENNEDY

Bits and Atoms

Will bits eventually control atoms? It is certainly tempting to think so—digital tools mediate ever-increasing parts of our physical environment. Walk down any urban street these days and you will see droves of people glued to their devices—checking their messages, posting photos, even turning their heat down at home, all digitally—while being completely oblivious to the world of atoms around them. And, this is only the beginning. Sure, the physical design of our gadgets might earn our admiration and devotion, but isn't it what happens on the screen that really commands our attention? Just as the iPhone represents iconic industrial design now, it could just as easily be remembered one day as a milestone in the inevitable shift to bits from atoms. After all, who needs a wallet, a clock, a map or even a flashlight when "there's an app for that"?

Science fiction films such as *Minority Report* present future visions of digital experiences integrated into our lives to such an extent that the physical object disappears altogether—from hardware-free interfaces that we control by waving our hands through the air to Google Glass. Pervasive computing of this kind will certainly continue to expand into all of the activities around us in the home, at the office and in the public domain. But what would happen if digital technology were to reenter the physical world at the most basic material level? What if changing the wallpaper on the walls of your home were just as easy as changing the wallpaper on your computer desktop? Could the materials of products and environments themselves actually "behave" more like the dynamic screens with which we interact? At some point in the not-so-distant future, the answer will be yes. Converging knowledge at the intersection of biology, additive manufacturing, and computing are driving new research frontiers such as *adaptive materials* and *programmable matter* that might bring about this future. For the purpose of this chapter, we will call these new fields *Intelligent Materials*—when combined, the outcome of these emerging research areas will have a huge impact on physical design.

In traditional physical design disciplines such as architecture and industrial design, understanding materials has always been an important foundation in learning the craft. Materials have unique properties that are employed to construct buildings or mass-manufacture the products we have traditionally relied on in our daily lives. Stone, wood, metals, plastics, and composites are harvested, quarried, forged, and synthesized in a chemical facility, or a combination thereof. When delivered, physical designers will then shape, mill, mold, and manipulate these materials into an assembly of other parts to create a finished product. Materials are selected for their inherent properties whether those properties are appearance, strength, elasticity, translucency, or any other combination of desired qualities that are suitable for the intended use case of a designed object. Materials frequently perform a specialized function by means of their chemical properties but often with an undesirable trade-off of toxicity or recyclability. The resounding pattern here is that materials are basically static and designers have to accept their properties and limitations and compromise accordingly.

In coming decades, we will see a fundamental evolution in the meaning of the word material. Materials will be able to be optimized to a particular purpose by fine-tuning the microscopic physical surface structure rather than by altering their chemistry. More to the point, we will also see the introduction of more materials that can change on demand through devices or computer control to fit our needs. Just as screen technologies such as LCD and E-Ink can change quickly to display moving images, physical material properties like color, translucency, the ability to repel or attract water, and even the ability to change shape will be controllable by the user, mediated by embedded sensors and computers. These new advances are beginning to be brought about by accomplishments in the sciences and engineering that would not be possible without their deep interdisciplinary collaboration. The outcome of this work will have considerable implications on what the world looks like in the coming decades. At that time, physical designers will have a greater ability to design the materials themselves, not just the physical artifacts that the materials are used to make.

We will also see fields of design continue to evolve beyond their traditional silos. Just as physical designers have crossed the boundary into digital experiences from atoms to bits to create broader, richer user experiences (UX), digital and interaction designers will similarly be able to design the UX of changeable physical materials and products. Bits will control atoms.

INSPIRED BY NATURE AT A SMALL SCALE: MATERIAL PROPERTIES FROM MICROTEXTURES

In recent decades, life scientists around the world have made astonishing discoveries about how nature endures in the most challenging environments by evolving high-performance physical "technologies" that operate on a microscopic and even molecular level—and all without damaging the environment. As recently as the past decade some researchers have uncovered how these microtextures on the skins and bodies of living organisms in the plant and animal kingdoms can be adapted or applied to human problems. Let me give you a few examples.

Sharklet Technologies, a startup company based in Aurora, Colorado, has discovered that shark skin is often composed of microundulating scale structures called *denticles* that perform two remarkable functions at once: they prevent bacterial colonization and improve hydrodynamic performance. At the outset of Sharklet's breakthrough research for the United States Navy, founder Dr. Anthony Brennan of the University of Florida was exploring alternative solutions for cleaning algae from the hulls of warships.[1] This was a huge concern because buildup of algae impacts cruising-speed performance and is costly and time consuming to remove in dry dock. Additionally, toxic biocidal chemical treatments are frequently used to remove the algae, which the Navy was under increasing pressure to abandon. Dr. Brennan discovered that shark skin has a microtexture that bacteria and other microorganisms could not stick to, and as a result, bacterial colonies could not form. This helps reduce drag and increase swimming performance, which give sharks an advantage over their prey while also helping them to

---

1 Sharklet (*http://www.sharklet.com*)

dodge predators. When this phenomenon was translated into a proto-type of a new type of material, it not only met the Navy's goals, but it also offered the promise of an additional, more significant application: antifouling of this sort could be useful in hospitals where infectious diseases are frequently spread. Sharklet Safe Touch was born, proving advantageous over chemical spray solutions that had been traditionally used in healthcare environments by *preventing* bacterial colonization rather than killing it after the fact. Killing bacteria with germicides has the distinct disadvantage of creating resistant super bugs such as MRSA and others.

Lotusan paint, developed by STO in Germany, is another example of a product for which microscopic texture yields a specific benefit based on a biological model. As the name suggests, Lotusan was inspired by the intricate surface texture of Lotus leaves, which have long been known for their ability to shed water and dirt. Reproducing the small, imperceptible hydrophobic texture drove the design and development of a paint, which naturally repels dirt from surfaces, an attribute that is very useful in public spaces that need to be cleaned and maintained, usually with toxic chemical detergents and monkey grease. Lotusan also reduces the amount of water and energy exerted to maintain sur-faces, which is a welcome quality for cash-strapped municipalities.

Unfortunately, the production of Lotusan paint is also complex and expensive due to the scale of the physical features required to enable the hydrophobic effect.[2] At Harvard's Wyss Institute for Biologically Inspired Engineering, a team of researchers led by Dr. Joanna Aizenberg has developed a potential improvement in a material called SLIPS (Slippery Liquid-Infused Porous Surfaces), which is able to do many of the things Lotusan can and more.[3] In addition to water, SLIPS can repel oils and other liquids. It is modeled after the surfaces of a Nepenthes Pitcher Plant flower, which captures insect prey (and eats them!) by causing them to slip and fall into a chamber where they are unable to escape. Just as with Lotusan, when used on fabrics, proto-types of coatings that use a microscaled porous, textured solid—in this case infused with lubricating film—have demonstrated the ability to repel wine, blood, and every other imaginable liquid that could stain or

---

2 Lotusan (*http://www.lotusan.com*)

3 Wyss Institute of Biologically Inspired Engineering (*http://wyss.harvard.edu*)

congregate on a surface. Imagine children's clothing that would never stain! Another advantage of SLIPS, according to Aizenberg, is that the effect can be created by using existing materials and continues to function even after being scratched or abused.

In contrast, other examples of microtextures and features have been found that promote "dry adhesion" or stickiness without a chemical substrate. Biologist Robert Full of the University of California, Berkeley studied how geckos can climb flat walls without falling as humans would. At the core of this superhuman ability are nanometer scale keratin hairs (setae) on their toes that adhere to surfaces by means of intermolecular forces. To substantiate this hypothesis, Dr. Full asked Stanford engineering professor Mark Cutkowsky to develop a robot and subsequently a human climbing suit based on the principles of gecko toes. The demonstrations of this remarkable technology (which you can see on YouTube) have inspired other research teams to investigate other superhuman animal qualities for their potential commercial application. However, later follow-up articles about the gecko technology have suggested that the robots only work on clean surfaces and would require greater finesse to work on more uneven or textured surfaces. Smaller hairs like those actually on the gecko's feet would help, but again the tiny scale and reliability of these hairs are difficult to reproduce and maintain. In the meantime, the technology is being translated into a potential reusable dry adhesive.

Maintenance is certainly a concern with microscopic-scale features that are delicate and potentially broken. Whereas complex natural organisms have the biological means to regrow fine hairs on a gecko toe, regenerative materials are an entirely new level of complexity to challenge human ingenuity. Notwithstanding, successful experiments have been made to create regenerative materials such as self-healing concrete that is able to fill its own small cracks with resin to prevent fractures from becoming bigger problems requiring costly maintenance.

These are only a few of a growing library of examples of biologically inspired microtextures and features that could spur on innovative materials and design in exciting and impactful ways. But before this can happen, in many cases economical manufacturing capability needs to catch up with the discoveries being made. Biological function frequently operates at a smaller (microscopic), more intricate scale, which is difficult to reproduce reliably in large quantity using current methods of manufacturing. Traditional production methods—plastic injection molding, casting, milling, and machining—are limited to a certain level of scale, detail, and resolution, but the technology is changing quickly. With recent rapid advancements in the scale and resolution of additive manufacturing, the potential to emulate these biological properties will likely soon be feasible.

Emerging Frontiers in Additive Manufacturing

Popular media coverage about additive manufacturing—or as it's more commonly known, 3D printing—has produced tremendous excitement and speculation about what it will mean in the future when everyone has access to it. The current reality is that consumer 3D printing is just in its infancy with limited capabilities. Complex shapes can be created, but only out of a few solid and elastomeric-based materials at a time and at a low resolution. This might help you custom design and print a plastic smartphone case but it is far from being able to print a smartphone itself, with a display, battery, printed circuit board, and other materials layered and assembled together. But, what if 3D printers could use a wide assortment of different materials, from plastics and electronics to living cells and semiconductors, mixing and matching the materials with microscopic precision? The ability to print all of these materials is currently being explored in labs across the world, and the abilities of the technology are changing with increasing rapidity.

Materials scientists, such as Dr. Jennifer Lewis at Harvard's Wyss Institute, are developing the chemistry and machines to make this kind of multimaterial 3D printing possible. She prints intricately shaped objects from "the ground up," precisely adding materials that are useful for their mechanical properties, electrical conductivity, or optical traits. This means 3D printing technology could make objects that sense and respond to their environment. As Lewis says, "Integrating form and function is the next big thing that needs to happen in 3D printing."[4]

Others are taking a different approach by trying to use the process of additive manufacturing itself to create a variety of performance properties from one material through the arrangement, topography, and structure of a single material. Neri Oxman, a veritable Renaissance

---

4 Jennifer Lewis, Wyss Institute (*http://wyss.harvard.edu/viewpage/412*)

woman at MIT with degrees spanning Architecture and Computational Design, has been exploring the synergy of biological approaches to creating structure and 3D printing. Rather than relying only on different material chemistries to produce desired properties, some of her work is placing the onus on surface topography to produce the desired material properties. Carpal Skin, an experimental carpal tunnel therapy glove, is 3D printed for a patient according to the "pain map" that individual is experiencing. The pain map then corresponds to the surface geometry of the glove, offering flex and support tailored to the user's condition.[5]

Also at MIT, Dr. Markus Buehler has been investigating how different material properties can be encoded at a molecular scale by using basic chemical building blocks. In his words:

> Proteins are the main building blocks of life—universally composed of merely about 20 distinct amino acids—realize a diversity of material properties that provide structural support, locomotion, energy and material transport, to ultimately yield multifunctional and mutable materials. Despite this functional complexity, the makeup of biological materials is often simple and has developed under extreme evolutionary pressures to facilitate a species' survival in adverse environments. As a result, materials in biology are efficiently created with low energy consumption, under simple processing conditions, and are exquisite as they often form from a few distinct, however abundantly available, repeating material constituents.[6]

The significance of Dr. Buehler's work here lies in understanding how material properties could eventually be designed through their molecular arrangement and then fabricated to meet a desired human application. Being able to create materials in this manner from chemically benign building blocks could revolutionize material science.

Micro Manufacturing

So far, we have shown how science has advanced considerably in understanding how materials can deliver remarkable performance properties, but this is only half of what will lead to creating new materials.

---

5 Neri Oxman, Mediated Matter Group (*http://www.media.mit.edu/research/groups/ mediated-matter*)

6 *http://web.mit.edu/mbuehler/www/*

Additive manufacturing at a nano scale is still very experimental, so the kinds of material construction that Dr. Buehler's work suggests is still far from being feasible to produce in any mass volume. But, the ability to manufacture at a smaller scale continues to develop. Newer additive manufacturing techniques such as Micro Laser Sintering (MLS) are pushing the boundaries of small-scale production to the level of micrometers and smaller. These have been used to produce insect-sized flying robots and microfluidic medical devices, but they also have been used to experiment with microtexturing and self-assembled structures. Going back to the example of shark skin, researchers under Dr. George Lauder at Harvard's Wyss Institute have just recently managed to scan and recreate the shark skin's denticles for the purpose of hydrodynamic performance. Different from Sharklet, the goal was to re-create an array of the denticles' geometry at actual scale to see if it would perform. Using a state-of-the-art 3D printer that is capable of printing multiple materials simultaneously at a tiny scale, Dr. Lauder's team succeeded in achieving a 6 percent efficiency increase with their prototype when compared against a control model without the texture.

Dynamic Structures and Programmable Matter

On an architectural scale, designers have been keenly interested in the ability to change the shape or properties of a building in some manner to respond to environmental conditions. Sun load in particular is a large source of interior heat generation and is usually counteracted with mechanical air conditioning systems, at enormous energy cost. This inspired architects such as Achim Menges (University of Stuttgart)[7] and Doris Sung (University of Southern California)[8] to explore passive dynamic facades that open and close in response to humidity and heat load, respectively, to allow (or prohibit) water and air from passing through. Yet there have not been widely successful efforts yet to control external façade systems like these with automated intelligent systems—although many are trying.[9] One example developed by kinetic

---

7 Achim Menges, Center for Design Computation, University of Stuttgart (*http://icd.uni-stuttgart.de/?cat=6*)

8 Doris Sung, USC (*http://arch.usc.edu/faculty/dsung*)

9 French architect Jean Nouvel's celebrated Arab Institute in Paris (1988) employed a façade system composed of an array of electronically controlled oculi, like camera lenses, to control the heat gain in the building from daily sunlight (*http://www.imarabe.org*).

sculptor Chuck Hoberman's Adaptive Building Initiative called *adaptive fritting* hints at least at the possibilities of this kind of dynamic intelligent control.[10] Many more projects like these are undoubtedly in the works and are bound to become more prevalent with the accessibility of electronic prototyping tools such as Arduinos and Raspberry Pis.

It is especially exciting to think about the possibilities of creating dynamic computer control of physical materials at the micrometer scale. Again, biology has provided some of the vision of what these kinds of complex dynamic materials could do. Biologists have been fascinated by the changeable behaviors of certain organism's bodies and skin. Bioluminescent organisms from the deepest parts of the ocean are able to control their luminescence on demand for communication and protection. Similarly, several organisms, including the octopus, have the ability to change the appearance of their skin entirely for the purpose of camouflage. Roger Hanlon and David Gallo, scientists at the Woods Hole Oceanographic Institution, along with other researchers, have begun to learn how these underwater creatures are able to achieve this effect.[11] It is a complicated system, but one that the United States Defense Department and fashion designers alike would be interested in emulating: the ability to change the color, texture, and shape of your clothing to match your environment or to change your appearance to fit any occasion.

Similar to the processes of an octopus, technology giant Qualcomm developed a digital screen technology called Mirasol based on the controllable light reflectance behaviors of butterfly wings. Unlike energy intensive LCDs, Qualcomm explored how reflecting light using micromirrors could produce color. In this case, electric charge is used to control the angles of these "mirrors." After several years of development, Qualcomm made the decision to shelve the technology for a familiar reason: the challenges involved in production made the cost too high and unreliable. But, just as we saw in the examples earlier, rapid advancements in additive manufacturing scale and resolution combined with programmability will reduce the barriers to producing such a technology.

---

10 Chuck Hoberman, Adaptive Building Initiative (*http://www.adaptivebuildings.com*)

11 Woods Hole Oceanographic Institution (*http://www.whoi.edu*)

At present, there are numerous experimental frontiers in *program-mable matter*, which we will begin to see realized and manufactured. Research teams at MIT, Carnegie Mellon University, Cornell, and other universities have been pushing the boundaries in this field. Part science fiction (think of the T-1000 model android in *Terminator 2*) but also a tangible reality, these efforts endeavor to build structures from the micro scale and up that can fold, shape-shift, and otherwise reconfigure their form from the bottom up to fit any number of applications. There are many new efforts in this area: at Carnegie Mellon, a programmable matter proposal called "Claytronics" (*http://www.cs.cmu. edu/%7Eclaytronics/movies/carDesign_12_vo_H264.mov*) is being explored for collaborative design visualization applications. In this wild concept, physical objects themselves would be able to transform into different shapes according to human or environmental input.[12] Teams working in product development could use this tool to collaborate in the refinement of a physical design. One possible near-term application for this kind of technology is so called "morphing wings," which are being researched by NASA. This technology explores the flight control potential of airplane wings that respond to flight conditions by transforming fluidly from one airfoil form to another. Rather than pivoting like a swept wing, morphing wings could optimize their form in limitless ways.

In a similar defense-related contract, but with a more tangible result, an interdisciplinary team of researchers from MIT and Harvard, working in conjunction with the United States Defense Advanced Research Projects Agency (DARPA) have been developing folding origami structures that self-fold and assemble into different physical configurations under computer control. The significance of projects like these suggests a future wherein human-made structures could dynamically fold and change shape—imagine a dynamic building façade with embedded solar panels that can simultaneously track the sun while changing shade levels to control heat gain. This is the future of intelligent matter.

---

12 Claytronics, Carnegie Mellon University (*http://www.cs.cmu.edu/~claytronics/*)

Connecting the Dots: What Does Intelligent Matter Mean for Designers?

As we have just seen, many of these developments between biology, manufacturing, and computing lead toward a new era and new definition of what it could mean to be a designer of "physical things." Just as societies have progressed through ages based on mastery of materials—the Stone Age, Bronze Age, and more recently, the Plastic Age—perhaps we are seeing even more evidence that we stand at the dawn of a new age. Instead of being defined and constrained by a material, in the decades to come we stand to define the materials that will be all around us. Could this be the dawn of the Intelligent Materials Age? If this is so, where does the designer fit into this new age, especially the designer of physical artifacts? Let's consider some possible scenarios about how the designer might approach their field.

DESIGNING MATERIAL BEHAVIORS

Imagine buildings with dynamic structures and programmable, functional material properties such as the aforementioned Lotusan or SLIPS being applied throughout the structure's environment at every scale. Let's examine a couple of potential applications.

Rainwater management in civic spaces and building exteriors

What if every expansive surface on a building could be optimized to control how water behaves? Depending on how much it has rained or snowed, buildings might want to adapt dynamically to how they react to water. If rain has been sporadic, perhaps a building would want to capture the water and store it for internal use. Maybe the roof and gutters could mechanically expand or unfurl, similar to a morphing wing, to collect more water. On the other hand, if it has been raining normally or perhaps excessively, roof materials would be designed to shed the water quickly by increasing the hydrophobicity to minimize leaks. Wall surfaces could repel water and dirt and never need cleaning; subway stations and underpasses could be lower maintenance and (mostly) graffiti-free. Indoors, some of the most reviled rooms could also be lower maintenance or even maintenance free, such as the bathroom.

Building interior spaces and water management

Imagine maintenance-free bathroom surfaces for showers, tubs, sinks, and even toilets! By maintenance-free, I mean surfaces that would not need to be scrubbed: vertical surfaces or tiles would be manufactured with hydrophobic microtextures to deter water minerals, soap, and other residue from collecting. Other banes such as tile grout mildew would have a harder time growing if these surfaces would dry more easily on their own. Toilets and sinks could maintain their clean appearance with less water use to clean them. Think about what it would mean for our health and watershed if we could drastically cut down on the harsh chemistry and water required to clean a bathroom.

Shower floors would present a slightly different challenge. A shower floor would need simultaneous or changeable properties—the ability to shed water on one hand, but also provide grip for safety. By rearranging the microtexture of the floor, grip level might be something that could "turn on" the same way you turn on the hot water or the lights. Perhaps the floor's "grip mode" would activate when a sensor detected a person in the shower space.

Because these textures are so small and invisible, how would a designer communicate the presence of these attributes? Although advanced additive manufacturing will be able to custom texture materials to control these performance qualities, the designer's task in this case would be to communicate that grip is "on" or "off." Rather than using an obvious indicator like a red light to communicate that a floor is slippery, how could a programmable material communicate physically that it is slippery even if you cannot "see" slipperiness?

Similar programmable intelligent materials with on-off modes could find practical applications in the kitchen. Consider, for example, the design of dishware, flatware, and cookware that is often cleaned in dishwashers. Many types of plastic, metal, and ceramics (such as ceramic tile in the shower) retain residual water on their surfaces. After a dishwasher cycle is complete these products sometimes need to be hand dried, which could be a time-consuming extra step. Commercial chemical rinse agents such as Jet-Dry solve this issue but have not been tested conclusively for toxicity. In the age of intelligent matter, this variable of hydrophobicity or water dispersal might be able to be tuned in or turned on, and design decisions will have to be made to balance or find the right places to do this. If placed on the outside of a bowl, water could disperse, but the designer might not want to coat the inside of the bowl in order to avoid liquid foods such as soup or cereal sloshing out and making a mess. Perhaps a dishwasher might be able to activate a hydrophobic texture in a wash cycle using a magnetic field, which would allow residue to disperse in the washer without interfering with the eating experience during mealtime.

DESIGNING MODES FOR PHYSICAL PRODUCTS

Beyond water management, physical products of all kinds will have the opportunity to adopt dynamic behavior. More than the bimodal scenarios discussed in the last section, products could have multiple, if not limitless, states and modes. Like the shape-shifting ability of the octopus, what if our shoes could "adapt" to different weather conditions, seasonal activities, and social occasions, freeing us to own fewer pairs? If it were raining heavily outside, perhaps your shoes could adapt to be impermeable to water like a rubber boot or perhaps be hydrophobic to drive water away. If it were hot out, the shoe could become structurally more porous to allow your feet to breathe better. Perhaps the color and texture could also change to reflect the context and formality of the social environment. If it were to snow, the sole of your shoes could change texture to provide traction on slick surfaces.

DESIGNING PHYSICAL BEHAVIORS IN PHYSICAL PRODUCTS

Thomas Heatherwick, principle of Heatherwick Studio, has a distinct body of work along with some other pioneering firms that have begun to explore the unique considerations involved in designing physical design behavior. One of his iconic commissions, Rolling Bridge (2004), a pedestrian drawbridge in London, is unremarkable in its open and closed states, but when it moves, it all changes. Watching the lobster-shell design roll up or unroll is both surprising and remarkable to behold. As design and architecture become more expressively dynamic such as this bridge, designers will need to consider how a structure like this opens, not just that it opens, and how it needs to look or be constructed. You can make a bridge appear friendly and trustworthy in form and materials, but how can the motion of its unfurling build confidence in a user? How can you make the nuances of motion appear friendly or inviting? Could the bridge make you laugh? Could it slowly accelerate, or speed up and then decelerate to a gentle stop?

In the same way that interaction designers create digital experiences that behave in context or brand-appropriate ways (think of the slow, "breathing" pulse of an Apple power indicator light when a computer is sleeping), product designers will also be faced with the opportunity to bring these dynamic behaviors to the physical world. This is where the act of being a physical designer will surely evolve. In designing the personality with which a transition is made between modes, physical designers will have to think more like animators, choreographers, or any other design field involving motion.

One area in which motion plays a critical role today is in the behavioral design of safety lighting, such as that on trains, planes, and emergency vehicles. In the 1950s, the average police car had a single, slowly revolving light indicating engagement in a pursuit—hardly urgent in its behavior and not terribly good at attracting attention. Today, police cars and ambulances use fast moving, abrupt, pulsating LEDs and sound bursts to capture your attention. Beyond the bright lights and loud sounds, it is the motion and transition of these cues that define a behavior suitable for emergencies.

In a recent industrial design studio, I challenged my students to create a piece of safety equipment for bicyclists to help promote better visibility on the road. Of the many different approaches the students took, one concept emerged that I believe forecasts considerations designers will face in the near future. Called the "puffer jackets," the student envisioned a vest that would emulate the behavior of a puffer fish, which uses physical parts of its body to startle and repel predators. The design proposed electronically controlled mechanics as used in experimental fashion design by Studio XO and Hussein Chalayan. The design would inflate an area of the jacket on command with reflectors, thereby making the cyclist look bigger and more noticeable (this was a short conceptual user experience project). In the ensuing development of this idea, the class reached a significant conclusion: what really mattered in the design was less the visual quality of the vest and more the motion behavior transitioning from a normal state to the attention-grabbing mode. In a future of dynamic intelligent matter, these kinds of considerations will only continue to grow in importance.

Conclusion

Much of what I've been discussing has focused on technical possibility and, to a lesser extent, ecological implications of the future of materials and what it means for design. Of course, no design should proceed just because it is simply novel and feasible—design should always be concerned with what *should* be done. Is it desirable? Does it fulfill a need? Is the world going to be better off with it? That said, altogether the implications ahead of these technologies are huge. In an age of intelligent matter, physical design will no longer be three-dimensional and static. The fourth dimension, time, and behavior will come to the physical tactile world just as it has existed in the digital realm to date, and designers will need to think about the possibilities and opportunities to create meaningful user experiences driven by these new parameters.

[3]

Taking Control of Gesture Interaction

GERSHOM KUTLIROFF AND YARON YANAI

Reinventing the User Experience

For those of us old enough to remember a world before iPods, the computer we used when we were 15 years old looked very similar to the computer we were using when we were 35. There was a (generally boxy) console, a monitor for display, and a keyboard and mouse for input. Now, it seems we have a new class of devices every other year—smartphones, tablets, Google Glass, and now smartwatches (not to mention "phablets," "two-in-ones," and the various other hybrids). Many factors are driving this rapid introduction of new products, among them cheap (and plentiful) processing, new display technologies, and more efficient batteries, to name a few.

One commonality shared by all of these devices is the critical role user interaction plays in their design. Indeed, today the size of a portable device is largely limited by input/output considerations—the screen size and keyboard—and no longer by the requirements of the different technology components. As devices are further integrated into our daily activities (think "wearables"), the importance of reinventing the way we communicate with them increases.

Gesture control is an intriguing solution to this problem because it promises to enable our devices to understand us the way other people understand us. When we want to indicate an object (virtual or real), we point at it; when we want to move something, we pick it up. We don't want to be constrained to a keyboard or a mouse or a touchscreen to communicate. This potential has begun to be realized over the past few years as gesture control technology reaches end users in the forms of Microsoft's Kinect sensor, Samsung's Galaxy smartphone, and Intel's RealSense initiative.

As with many emerging technologies, gesture control has enjoyed some early successes as well as some clumsier, less successful attempts at reinventing the user experience (UX). The challenging aspect of the problem is all the more evident when we pause to consider the complexity (and early nature) of the different technology components that must work together smoothly: the sensor, the camera, middleware solutions, and, of course, the applications that must bring all these elements together to create a great user experience.

Moreover, the general difficulty of working with early technology is compounded by the specific design challenges inherent to gesture recognition interfaces: how can a user understand the effects of his actions when there is no tactile feedback? How can false positives be avoided? What can be done to address user fatigue?

Thus, for all of its promise, the futuristic dream of ubiquitous gesture control remains... well, futuristic. Yet, there is a growing sense that although many of the technical challenges will be solved, perhaps the most important question of all remains a riddle: what will designers do with this technology?

In our former company, Omek Interactive, we developed middleware to accurately and robustly track hand and finger movements in real time, by interpreting the data generated by 3D cameras (see Figure 3-1). 3D cameras compute the distance between objects in front of the camera and the camera itself; this "depth" data is very effective in solving many hard problems in computer vision and is therefore a key enabler of the tracking algorithms. Our objective was to enable a compelling gesture-based interaction driven by our hand and finger tracking solution.

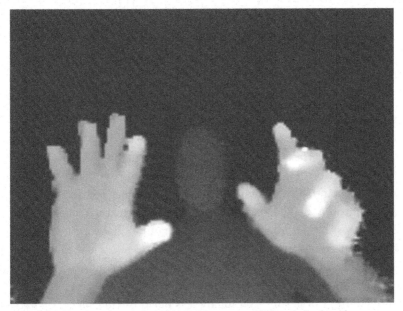

Figure 3-1. Depth map generated by a 3D camera (different shades of gray indicate proximity to the camera) (Omek Interactive Ltd. © 2013)

Gesture-based interaction can be supported by other technologies such as conventional (2D) cameras and ultrasound signals. However, we believed that the fully immersive, natural, and intuitive user experience we envisioned required robust and finely nuanced skeleton tracking, possible only with 3D camera technology. Concurrent with the development of the skeleton tracking middleware, the Omek Studio worked with early versions of the technology to realize a new paradigm for human-machine interaction. In this chapter, we discuss how we approached this challenging task, the inherent usability issues we faced, and especially the tactics we employed to resolve these difficulties. In particular, we describe in some detail how we progressively evolved the gesture-based experience through an iterative prototyping process that made it possible for us to take advantage of the benefits of gesture-based interaction and to compensate for its flaws. We submit that our specific experience of designing a next-generation gesture interface and the lessons we learned are broadly applicable to a range of design problems, characteristic of many emerging technologies.

Analysis

We began by performing a clear-headed analysis of the relative strengths and weaknesses of gesture interaction. What are the disadvantages of the technology, which we want to avoid, and what are the concomitant advantages, which we will try to adopt.

Several disadvantages of gesture interaction are self-evident. By its nature, gesture lacks the ability to incorporate tactile feedback. With traditional interfaces, the user receives information about the gesture he's performing; for example, in the form of keys that depress, or touchscreens that feel solid, or mouse buttons that he can feel click. Another common (and justified) criticism of gesture interaction is user fatigue, resulting from the need to move in unfamiliar ways to perform even simple interactions. The term "gorilla arm" refers to the fatigue in a user's shoulder and biceps from maintaining his arm in a horizontal position for an extended period, as he reaches toward the screen. Other shortcomings of gesture control are less obvious. One such drawback is the difficulty users have in orienting themselves in the 3D world to understand how the space in which they are moving maps to the projected 2D space they see on the display screen.

On the positive side, the promise of gesture-based interaction is its ability to provide a user experience that is at once "natural, intuitive, and immersive." In the early design phase, we worked to translate these high-level principles into tactical directions that would guide our development.

By *natural* interaction, we mean movements that are comfortable and easy for the user to perform. The touchscreen and mouse both require the user to extend his hands away from the body, in a way that he would not do in the course of his natural interactions. Ideally, a user would be able to communicate with his device through movements next to his body, in the user's own space.

An *intuitive* interaction is one in which the user's interactions with a device closely correlate to those in daily life. To the extent that UX designers succeed in replicating real-world interactions, users understand more quickly what is expected of them and what the response will be. In this regard, the interface is often a limiting factor. Thus, for example, we double-click an icon to activate an application, when other movements—grabbing with two fingers, for example—might be more intuitive for the user. We move a mouse on a table, when the intuitive action would be to simply point at the screen where we want the cursor to be positioned. Designing more *intuitive* interactions requires the richness of movements in 3D space as well as the ability to capture the broad range of expression in a user's movements that gesture interaction offers. A critical element in allowing the user to move freely and intuitively is to place the onus of understanding his intentions on the technology.

Finally, we wanted the user to be *immersed* in the experience, free from thinking consciously about how to manipulate the virtual objects presented to him. We identified two ways to realize this goal:

- The results of the user's actions should be predictable and deterministic, so as not to break the flow between the real world and the virtual.

- We decided to incorporate anticipatory elements in our design. Standard interactive technologies have no way to predict the user's next action.

A touchscreen and a mouse react immediately to any user interaction and don't provide any information about his behavior at other times. By contrast, gesture-based technology tracks the user's movements persistently, even while he is not directly engaged with his device. The designer can utilize this expanded knowledge of the user's actions to clarify his intentions, and preemptively guide his movements. These principles of a natural, intuitive, and immersive experience guided the design of our gesture-based interaction, and were critical in delivering an engaging and fun experience.

Prototyping

After we sketched out the overarching principles to motivate and guide our design work, we began implementing various concepts to test their viability. The prototyping work we did was extensive and spanned a wide design spectrum, from "sandboxing" individual gestures, to implementing a full multilevel experience, complete with graphics and sounds. Many questions had to be researched during this process. Do the individual gestures meet the necessary quality requirements? Even if individual gestures are clear and well defined, are there conflicts among multiple gestures? How do the different contexts of the application integrate with the gesture and tracking interactions? How does the player know where the interaction area begins and ends? What happens when there are multiple users visible—which one should control the experience? How is control passed from one user to another?

Notably, the process of implementing these prototypes was itself quite challenging. The dependence of the prototypes on such an early technology, lacking maturity and robustness, placed real obstacles on the ability to run user testing programs that generated authentic feedback about the experiences. To make matters worse, it was not only the 3D camera hardware that was still in development during the prototyping phases, but the tracking middleware and system specifications, as well.

There is a school of thought that in the case of early and immature technologies, the prototyping process should be abandoned, with the design done instead "on paper." In this way, designers are free to push the limits of their creativity without being constrained by the current state of the technology, which they would have to consider to build prototypes. Following this line of reasoning, prototyping on early technology can even result in compromises of the design goals, ratcheting them down to meet the current, early state of the technology at the expense of the final design.

We subscribe to a contrasting approach, in which the design and the technology development happen concurrently, throughout the development process. Admittedly, there is a clear price that is paid, both in terms of the risks (as just discussed), and the additional effort required due to the early state of the technology. Nonetheless, we believe that the knowledge gained from prototyping, even limited by the technology, justifies this cost. As our designers became intimately familiar with the technology, the cycle of prototyping and user testing exposed many nonintuitive and surprising aspects of gesture-based interaction design.

The prototypes we developed were not simply "bare bones" demonstrations. By definition, a user interaction experience is composed of two components: the sensing technology that captures the user's actions, and the display (including graphics and sounds) that provides the user feedback. In designing an experience meant to be immersive and intuitive, we felt it was important to incorporate both the sensing and the display elements to maximize the knowledge gained from the prototyping activities. Moreover, our prototypes spanned the full scope of interactions, from narrow, individual elements, all the way up to system-level demonstrations, containing graphics and sounds, changing contexts in the application, mechanisms to make the user aware of the interaction area, elegant recovery in the case of errors, and any other considerations that might affect the holistic user experience.

Early experiments revealed serious flaws in several concepts that we considered. One example of this is the "invisible wall," which projects gesture control into the context of touchscreen interaction. As the user's fingers approach the device's screen, she crosses a virtual barrier at some fixed distance from the screen, at which point the 2D positions of her hands and fingers are projected directly onto the display in front of her, for as long as her fingers "touch" the invisible wall. Although simple to understand and straightforward to implement, this approach fails to provide a compelling gesture-based experience. The absence of an actual physical touchscreen means that the user doesn't have a clear indication of where this virtual wall is located, resulting in a high prevalence of false positives and a lack of responsiveness. Moreover, this paradigm limits the gesture interaction to a 2D plane, thus failing to take advantage of a key benefit of gesture control: the additional dimension of depth.

Another unsuccessful technique we tested was the "push-to-click" mechanic. A user interacts with a mouse by moving the mouse with her hand, positioning the cursor over the item to be selected and then clicking a button to select. Analogously, we implemented the "push-to-click" gesture mechanic by using the hand, or a finger, to move the cursor on the display screen over the item to be selected and then moving the hand or finger closer to the screen to actually select the item. Again, this technique does not translate well to gesture interaction, primarily because it is very difficult for the user to move only in the "Z" (depth) direction. Inevitably, the hand also moves slightly two dimensionally, as well, inadvertently positioning the cursor over an adjacent item immediately prior to "click"ing, such that the adjacent item is selected more often than not. Indeed, the design flaw in this case is the reliance on the same control for two distinct functions. If the hand is being used to move the cursor, any movement required of the hand to select an item will necessarily also move the cursor. Mouse interaction differs in this regard because clicking the button does not affect the mouse position.

A Case Study: Gesture Control

We turn now to explore, in some detail, several prototyping experiments we conducted on gesture control, the problems we encountered, and the solutions we implemented.

FEEDBACK

Initially, we wrestled with the fundamental problem of how to enable the user to select one of several icons displayed on a screen. A key focus of this early effort was to discover an effective feedback mechanism, one which would reassure the user that his intentions are understood, and convey the sense that the system is responsive to his actions. The obvious approach was to map the hand movements to a mouse-like cursor on the display, and use a gesture such as a grabbing motion to select an icon. An advantage of this mechanic is that users find themselves in familiar territory and orient to it almost immediately. After some brief testing, however, we quickly discarded this approach, as its shortcomings became evident straightaway: the jittery feel of the cursor mapped to a point on the finger—fingers are rarely still—and the difficulty of performing the "select" gesture without also moving the cursor.

For our second attempt, we drew inspiration from touchscreen user interface (UI) design: we relied on large buttons for the UI control elements, which are far more natural in the context of finger interactions. To this interface, we added one important enhancement which takes advantage of the technology's ability to anticipate the user's movements. Specifically, when the hand hovered above an element, the icon expanded slightly, indicating to the user which item he was about to select. This second design was more forgiving of small variations in the hand and finger movements, and the selection was more fluid and predictable. However, user testing revealed that the experience was not as immersive as we hoped. We concluded that the problem was in the way the feedback was provided, in discrete steps, by highlighting each icon as the hand passed over it. This is in contrast to a constant feedback mechanism, such as that generated by continuous mouse cursor rolling, which continuously reassures the user that the system is "aware" of him.

We liked the technique of preemptively providing feedback to the user based on predicting his next move. Indeed, the persistent knowledge of the user's hand movements is a differentiating feature of gesture control. Both of our initial feedback designs exposed only part of the information available to the system. Therefore, for our next attempt, we abandoned the concept of mapping the hand onto elements of the 2D display; instead, we tried projecting a render of the actual hand directly onto the screen, as depicted in Figure 3-2.

Figure 3-2. AR-hand feedback (Omek Interactive Ltd. © 2013)

We refer to this concept as the *augmented reality* (AR) feedback approach, and it proved to be a great success. Users appreciated the sense of immediacy and responsiveness, and the learning curve was negligible; there was an almost immediate sense of identification with the rendered hand on the screen. We readily embraced this AR-hand mechanism, but subsequently went through several iterations to adapt and further improve upon the experience.

For example, to maintain the sense of persistence, the rendered hand must be visible on the screen at all times. If screen elements such as a button or a menu are rendered on top of the hand, the feedback becomes discontinuous. Alternatively, if the hand is rendered above the UI elements, it blocks the user's view of these objects. An elegant solution is to render the hand twice: an opaque hand behind the UI elements, and the hand's outline in front of the UI elements.

We were pleased with how the AR mechanic allowed us to move easily around the screen. We were also satisfied with the responsiveness of the rendered image when performing a grab gesture to select an element. Next, though, we were confronted with a subtle problem. The rendered hand can cover a large part of the screen. Which part of the hand should be used to actually indicate which icon is of interest? Is it the index finger? Is it the palm of the hand? Is it an average of these two points? We will revisit this question further on.

SCROLLING AND ZOOMING

Encouraged by the immersive feel of our AR hand, we next broadened our focus to the general problem of searching through a collection of objects, some of which might not be visible within the current view. Traditional mouse-keyboard-touch interactions rely on UI controls such as scroll bars and lists to provide this functionality. We wanted to avoid these elements, aiming instead for a more intuitive experience that would replicate real-world interaction.

This time, one of our first attempts yielded a promising approach; we imagined the hand as a small, portable video camera, able to move freely in all three axes. We mapped the virtual camera to the center of the hand, so that the perspective view of the application changes according to the movements of the user's hand. When the user's hand moves closer to the screen, the collection zooms in, providing a closer look at the content; when her hand moves to the side, the collection scrolls. We liked the fluid, always-on feel of this interaction as well as its seamless integration of the depth ("Z") dimension.

We began to integrate these concepts into the wider context of a real application, building a prototype experience for browsing and select-ing books from a library. This brought us naturally to our next design challenge: how should the user actually select the book she wants, and then how should she open it, read it, and turn its pages? After some experimentation, we decided to further employ our ability to anticipate the user's next move. As the user moves her hand horizontally over the books, the books react as if the user's touch slightly moved them. When her hand stops moving, remaining stable over a specific book, the book falls slightly off the shelf, toward the user, as if she had pulled it closer with her finger (see Figure 3-3). This "falling-towards-me" animation invites the user to pick up and open the book. Then, a text balloon appears, instructing the user to perform a pinch gesture to select the book. This behavior is inspired by a classic UI mechanic: the book tipping forward is immediate, like the hover highlight of a mouse, whereas the text balloon is like a tooltip, appearing a few sec-onds after the action is available. In our case, however, these mechanics were translated to a 3D interface, where the interaction can be done directly with the objects themselves, rather than through the medium of a mouse (Figure 3-3).

Figure 3-3. Anticipating the user's action by tipping the book forward (Omek Interactive Ltd. © 2013)

The techniques of browsing a shelf of books and then allowing a single book to tip forward are strongly influenced by analogous real-world interactions. However, we also discovered that there are limits to this strategy of reflecting real-world behaviors. In an early prototype, the user had to physically move her hand backward in order to take a book off the shelf, which is, of course, what she would do in the real world. However, when we tested this mechanic with users, it surprised them and disrupted the continuity of their experience. Thus, in a successive implementation, the book is pulled off the shelf automatically when it is grabbed (Figure 3-4). When the book has been selected, the user can do the following, as she would with a real book:

- Move it toward her to have a closer look

- Rotate her hand to turn it around and look at the back side of the cover

- Open it by grabbing the cover with one hand and then moving her hand toward the center of the screen

Figure 3-4. The book rotates off the shelf when selected (Omek Interactive Ltd. © 2013)

As we continued to expand the prototype to provide a more holistic application-level experience, additional issues arose that required attention. One worth noting is the need for "soft landings" when switching contexts. In our design, user interaction varies based on the context of the application. Sometimes, the hand moves over static objects, and sometimes the objects scroll or zoom, according to the movements of the hand. Transitions from one context to another can catch users off-guard, resulting in false positives and disoriented users. It is therefore important to implement a gradual transition ("soft landing") at these points, in which the new interaction becomes active only after a few seconds, allowing the user to understand and adapt to the change.

SELECTION: THE SMART POINTER

Initially, and likely prejudiced from designing for mouse and touch experiences, we controlled the cursor movement by mapping it to a single point on the hand, such as the tip of the index finger. (We use "cursor" here in a very general sense, as anything that indicates a position on the display. It might be, for example, the action of highlighting a UI element, rather than a specific graphical element.) Unexpectedly, user testing revealed that people don't actually use their hands in this way. Sometimes, they point with the index finger; other times, they use two or three fingers together to gesture toward an object, or even the center of the palm. It became evident that relying on a single, predefined point of the hand produced a disconnect between the user's free and natural movements and the result he expected. As an example, refer to Figure 3-5, which demonstrates three different ways in which users select objects with their hands.

Figure 3-5. Alternative ways to select an element (Omek Interactive Ltd. © 2013)

One of our guiding principles was that the interface should understand people's natural movements, rather than forcing the user to adapt himself to the limitations of the technology. In this spirit, we implemented a mechanic we called a *smart pointer*, which aggregates the data from multiple regions of the user's hands to compute a single point of interaction with the display. The smart pointer is flexible enough to model multiple ways in which people use their hands to point at objects.

The data from the multiple regions is captured by assigning each of these regions an "interest point," and an associated weight. We also added some virtual interest points, which themselves are weighted averages of additional points on the hand. We tested many different locations and weights for these actual and virtual interest points before coming up with the configuration that you can see in Figure 3-6.

The smart pointer works by calculating a score for the UI control elements, based on the interest points. This score is computed for each element at every frame; it is simply the weighted sum of all the interest points currently positioned over the UI element. The "cursor" then shifts to the UI element with the highest score, and this element is highlighted to provide feedback for the user. Figure 3-7 shows the hand hovering over a group of buttons. The button corresponding to the highest score is highlighted.

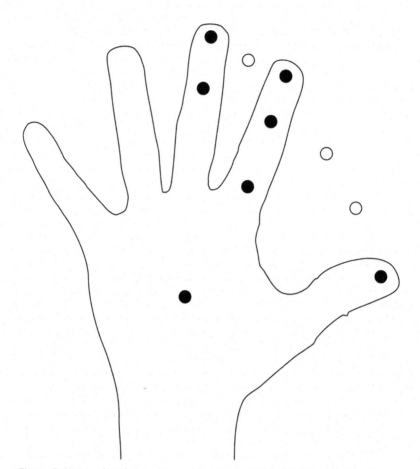

Figure 3-6. Actual and virtual interest points on the hand (Omek Interactive Ltd. © 2013)

Through sustained prototyping, we continued to refine the smart pointer in some important ways. To avoid jittering when the scores of adjacent elements are similar, we enlarge the highlighted element on hover, and reduce it when it is no longer highlighted. We also realized that users almost never rely on nonextended fingers to point to an object, and so we allow the interest point weights to vary. In particular, the weights for each interest point on a given finger are functions of the finger's extension, with the weights decreasing to 0 as the finger folds completely over the palm (Figure 3-7).

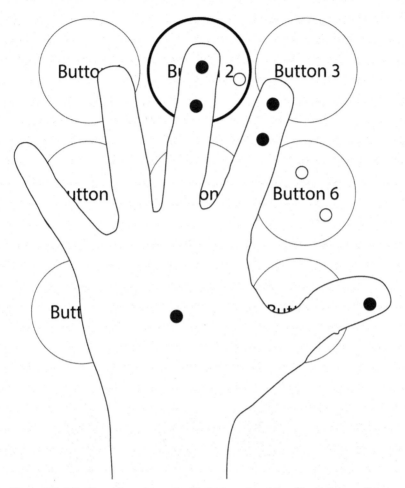

Figure 3-7. Selection of an element with the smart pointer (Omek Interactive Ltd. © 2013)

When implemented well, the effect of the smart pointer is quite subtle. Users were not explicitly aware of how this mechanic was assisting them in selecting objects more intuitively. However, the interaction itself was far more natural for them, and the experience felt smooth. There was a strong preference for the smart pointer selection method over other methods we tested.

USER FATIGUE AND THE ARC MENU

At this point, we were feeling pretty good about our feedback system as well as our selection mechanic. We now turned to one of the more challenging aspects of gesture control: user fatigue. Fatigue is often among the main complaints that users have when discussing gesture interaction. However, because the user's movements are dictated by the design of the interface, we were optimistic that we could address the problem of fatigue through careful design considerations.

The first design of our menu system contained four buttons, each large enough to be easily selected, and evenly spaced along a horizontal line across the screen, as illustrated in Figure 3-8. There were several problems with this design, which quickly became evident:

- Fatigue was high, even though the necessary movements were much finer than what is required for long-range gesture control systems such as Kinect.

- When the hand is on the right side of the screen, it blocks the user's line-of-sight to part of the menu.

- It was very difficult for right-handed people to select items on the far left side of the screen, and vice versa for left-handed people.

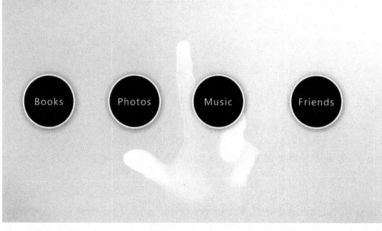

Figure 3-8. UI elements spread evenly across the screen in a horizontal line (Omek Interactive Ltd. © 2013)

To mitigate these problems, we tried limiting the menu to only the right half of the screen and made another round of tests. The results were a bit better, but fatigue was still a major concern. After some consideration, we determined that the best way to deal with fatigue was to make it possible for the user to rest her elbow on the tabletop, or on the arm of a chair. When users tried to operate the menu while their elbows were resting on the table, the results were good for the two buttons on the right side of the menu. However, they were unable to comfortably reach the left-side buttons without lifting their elbow, inducing fatigue after just a few minutes.

We experimented with different configurations of the menu buttons, placing them in a square formation, and then in a stack formation on the righthand side of the screen. Still, users were compelled to raise their elbow off the surface, or to uncomfortably bend the wrist to reach all the menu buttons. Trying to approach the problem more creatively, we realized that the natural motion for the body's joints is in the shape of an arc. So we hypothesized that the best way to build a menu would be to position the menu items such that they mimic the shape of an arc. We tested this hypothesis by asking several people to move horizontally and vertically, without raising their elbow, or moving in any awkward way. The results of these experiments are plotted on the graph in Figure 3-9.

Figure 3-9. The hand naturally moves in an arc (Omek Interactive Ltd. © 2013)

Finally, we created our *Arc Menu* modeled on these natural movements and tested the new menu again (see Figure 3-10). The results were very positive. The interaction was intuitive and fun, and, more important, fatigue was low even after several minutes. All of the buttons on the menu were equally accessible, selection was reliable, and there was a very low rate of false positives.

Figure 3-10. Final design of the Arc Menu (Omek Interactive Ltd. © 2013)

We added an additional element, simplifying the design by hiding the Arc Menu when it is not needed. By default, the arc is folded into the Home button, and it unfolds only when the user hovers above it, as shown in Figure 3-11.

Figure 3-11. Hiding the Arc Menu when it is not needed (Omek Interactive Ltd. © 2013)

Integrating the individual components together—the Arc Menu, smart pointer, and AR-hand feedback mechanism—allowed us to experience the interaction holistically. We found that the sum was indeed greater than its parts. The individual efforts complemented one another at creating a more immersive and natural interaction. Removing fatigue from the equation resulted in crisper, better-defined movements by the user, and the deterministic, predictable reactions of the UI instilled confidence in the interface as a whole. Most important, the experience itself was fun and engaging.

The goal of our design efforts was to create a compelling experience that realized the promise of gesture interaction, showcasing its benefits while overcoming its limitations. To this end, we employed methodologies that emphasized the user experience first and foremost, and we encouraged creative approaches to solving some weighty design problems. We have described several techniques that we developed through these methodologies. However, we hope our primary contribution is less the specific solutions that we have presented, and rather the overall approach to designing for gesture interaction, and emerging technologies in general.

Trade-offs

Gesture control remains a nascent field. Although recognizing its promise, the industry continues to wrestle with the unique mix of challenges it presents. Indeed, there is still a vigorous debate about which core technology is best able to power a compelling gesture interaction experience. Different companies have placed their bets on conventional "2D" cameras, 3D cameras, or ultrasound signals. Even within the realm of 3D cameras, there are passive stereo, active stereo, time-of-flight, and various flavors of coded light technologies, all with their own characteristics and assorted trade-offs. Notably, the first Kinect camera was based on coded light technology, whereas the second version relies on a time-of-flight solution. When the question of which core technology to utilize is settled, the debate shifts to finding the right balance among the various parameters—which include power consumption, range, resilience to fast movements, and sensitivity to ambient lighting. No solution is perfect, of course, and each decision must weigh multiple trade-offs against one another.

In our previous company, we developed middleware solutions to power next-generation UIs. Like others in the industry, we struggled with the question of which core technology would best support our product vision, and which associated set of parameter values would provide the optimal balance. Naturally, cost, time-to-market, and corporate strategy—among other factors—each play a role in these decisions.

However, it was our conviction that the user experience would ultimately drive this emerging technology to market. Cognizant of the challenges in providing such an experience, we invested considerably in its development, through a program of early and iterative (and often painful) prototyping and design. As a result, we well understood the implications of the technology trade-offs, and could empower design considerations to drive our decision making.

Thus, our design efforts served a dual purpose. On the one hand, they produced experiences that are natural and intuitive, and also compelling—realizing the potential of gesture interaction. At the same time, these prototyping activities also generated critical early feedback, which was then channeled to the development teams, anchoring the requirements in realistic and relevant usages. Our efforts ensured that the requirements of the product—even including selection of the underlying sensor technology—were guided primarily by considerations of user experience.

Here is one more takeaway for working with emerging technologies: in every development cycle, product maturity necessitates certain trade-offs, and when choices must be made, it is all too easy to allow these decisions to be made by considerations other than how they impact the final experience. To the extent that the designer understands these trade-offs, he is also able to influence the decisions. A persistent program of iterative design activities that coexists with the product development—while demanding to support—offsets the competing interests and can be the critical factor in the overall success of the product.

Looking Ahead

The emphasis on innovation in the consumer electronics industry is evident in the accelerated pace at which new device form factors and capabilities are released. At the same time, companies are compressing the product development cycle, pushing to bring products to market before consumer interest wanes. UX continues to be a driver of this innovation, and this is reflected in several ways. One is a consistent focus on improving the user experience, granting designers an increasingly central role in the product development process. A second is the effort to cultivate new sensing and display capabilities, to capture more data on the user's behavior, and to provide him more useful feedback.

Emerging technologies such as gaze detection, 3D face tracking, emotion recognition, and even detecting the level of user engagement are being integrated into consumer devices. On the display side, we can include 3D displays at one end of the spectrum, and wearables—with limited displays, or no displays at all—at the other end. In each case, carefully considered design will determine whether these core technology capabilities are translated into a successful user experience. For each modality, what are its respective strengths and weaknesses, and what types of interactions engage the user in a compelling way that adds value to his experience? In this chapter, we have addressed some of the challenges in working with a single UI technology: gesture control. Integrating multiple modalities together into a unified, seamless interaction introduces yet another layer of complexity to the design problem. How can these various inputs be combined to deliver an experience that is more—and not less—than the sum of its parts?

This confluence of factors—the rate at which emerging technologies are being developed and introduced to the market, the persistent demand for user experiences that are engaging yet intuitive, and the synthesis of multiple elements together to yield superior experiences—will challenge designers in unique ways in the coming years. It will be fascinating to watch talented designers tackle and solve these problems, to deliver ever more natural, intuitive, and immersive experiences.

Fashion with Function: Designing for Wearables

MICHAL LEVIN

The Next Big Wave in Technology

Wearables, also referred to as body-borne computers, are small electronic or sensor devices that are worn on the physical body—either on the bare skin or on top of clothing. They do not include computing devices that are implanted *within* the body (a medical domain that I expect will grow over the next decade); rather they are attached *to* the body.

Wearable computing is not a new concept—it has been around for more than half a century,[1] mostly used for military purposes, assisting soldiers and aviators in the battlefield. Over time, as technology advanced and computer components increased in power while shrinking in size, the range of wearable technology applications grew, expanding into the consumer market. From healthcare, fitness, and wellness, which have already started blooming, to gaming, entertainment, music, fashion, transportation, education, finance, and enterprise, wearable technology is creating a massive new mobile market, with the power to transform the way people behave and interact with devices, the environment, and one another.

Today, wearable devices span the gamut from smart rings, bracelets, and necklaces, to smart glasses and watches, to smart gloves, socks, and t-shirts. Moreover, wearables don't stop at humans. There are

---

1 The first wearable computer was invented in 1961 to predict winning roulette numbers.

already smart collars for dogs, cats, and even cows,[2] monitoring their activity, health, and behavior 24/7, while keeping owners connected to their four-legged friends at all times.

The wearable device market is still in its infancy, but it's growing fast. According to IMS Research,[3] the number of units shipped is expected to grow from 14 million in 2011, to 171 million devices shipped by 2016. ABI Research forecasts a much stronger penetration with 485 million annual device shipments by 2015. BI Intelligence estimates annual wearables shipments crossing the 100 million milestone in 2014, reaching 300 million units by 2018.

In terms of revenue, Transparency[4] anticipates that the global wearables market, which stood at $750 million in 2012, will reach $5.8 billion in 2018 (a compound annual growth rate of 40.8 percent). According to IMS research,[5] the wearables market will already exceed $6 billion by 2016.

Regardless of whether the $6 billion line will be crossed in 2016 or 2018, all these market estimations point to the same conclusion: *wearables are the next big wave in technology.*

The Wearables Market Segments

Looking at the wearables market today—in its infancy—we can see four dominant segments emerging:

Sports and fitness trackers
> Wristbands or clip-on trackers that collect activity data such as steps taken, calories burned, stairs climbed, distance traveled, and hours slept. Figure 4-1 presents a few examples in this device-rich market segment, which includes Fitbit Flex, Jawbone UP, Misfit Shine, and Nike+ FuelBand.

---

2 A few examples of the emerging Pet Tech domain include *http://www.fitbark.com/*, *http://www.eyenimal.com/en/*, and *http://tnw.co/1CJ2V2o*.

3 *http://www.businessinsider.com/wearable-devices-create-a-new-market-2013-8*

4 *http://www.transparencymarketresearch.com/wearable-technology.html*

5 *http://bit.ly/1CJ2YeG*

Figure 4-1. Popular sports and fitness trackers (from left to right): Nike+ FuelBand and Basis (top); Jawbone UP, Fitbit Flex, and Misfit Shine (bottom)

Health and medical sensors

A variety of devices (i.e., bracelets, clip-ons, bands, and patches) that monitor physiological status, including heart rate, respiration rate, ECG, temperature, emotional stress, dehydration, glucose level, and even posture. Lumo Back, Zephyr's BioHarness, and Nuubo's nECG are a few examples of this promising domain (see Figure 4-2).

Smartwatches

These are typically wrist watches operating in collaboration with a smartphone (through a Bluetooth connection). Smartwatches offer an alternative display for some of the smartphone's existing features in a more accessible fashion as well as dedicated functionalities and apps. The Pebble watch and Samsung's Galaxy Gear are two prominent examples of this category. Motorola's Moto 360 smartwatch, launched mid-2014, is another popular player in this category (see Figure 4-3).

Figure 4-2. Examples of health and medical sensors (from upper left to lower right): Zephyr's BioHarness, Metria IH1, Lumo Back, and Nuubo's nECG

Figure 4-3. Examples of smartwatches (from upper left to lower right): the Samsung Galaxy Gear, Pebble watch, Sony SmartWatch, and Moto 360

Smartglasses

The fourth market segment, as the name implies, are eyewear devices, offering a computer display projected against the lens. Smartglasses allow for hands-free interaction for actions such as checking notifications, taking a photo, running a search, and more. In addition, smartglasses can offer an augmented reality (AR) experience while interacting with the real world. Examples include Google Glass, the Vuzix M100 and GlassUp AR (see Figure 4-4).

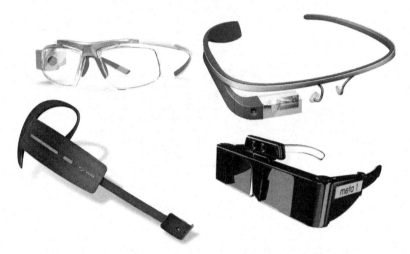

Figure 4-4. A variety of smartglasses (from upper left to lower right): GlassUp AR, Google Glass, Vuzix M100, and Meta AR

A distinct group within the smartglasses category is that of virtual gaming devices. Two dominant examples are the virtual reality (VR) headset Oculus Rift (acquired by Facebook in March 2014) and CastAR (see Figure 4-5). These devices offer a new type of video game experience, expanding the interaction possibilities beyond (the limited) keyboard, mouse, and handheld gamepad interfaces. The VR/AR capabilities make it possible to establish immersive real-life sensation, and scale the game experience far beyond what the flat display can provide. The player becomes an integral part of the virtual game environment and actually needs to look up to see the top of hundred-foot jungle trees, for example, or use his hands to move objects in space to pick up a sword.

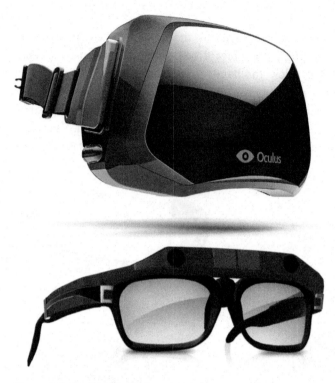

Figure 4-5. Oculus Rift (top) and CastAR (bottom)

These four segments, while reflecting a market that is still evolving, serve as a foundation of inspiration for wearables user experience (UX).

Before we dive into the details of the UX (and human) factors to be considered when designing for wearables, it's important that we step back and look at these devices as part of the broader ecosystem to which they belong. Remember that wearables are joining an increasingly device-rich world. In this world, people already own multiple connected devices—computers, smartphones, tablets, TVs, and more—which they use together in various combinations to access and consume data. This existing ecosystem of devices and the relationships between them carry an immense impact on the way wearables are used and the role they play in people's lives.

Discussion: Event-Based Wearables

Although wearables are commonly envisioned as devices that people wear *all the time*, it's not necessarily their only usage model. Wearable devices can also serve contextual use cases, in which the functionality needs are bound to specific time and place. One great example is Walt Disney Parks' creative wristband wearable called "MagicBand," introduced as part of their larger initiative ("MyMagic+") to create "a more immersive, more seamless, and more personal experience" (*http://bit.ly/1wdgy8b*).

MagicBand provides guests with access to their hotel room, theme park, FastPass+ selections, and PhotoPass, and can also be linked with a payment account, serving essentially as a personal identifier while visiting the resort.

This wearable works in collaboration with the bigger Disney Park ecosystem, specifically the My Disney Experience website (*http://bit.ly/1CHjhsj*) and mobile app (*http://bit.ly/1CHjzzp*), with which guests can plan their trip and access the latest information on Walt Disney World Resort.

Looking ahead, the opportunities are vast: visitors could use wristbands such as these as a tool for tracking lost kids, communicating with others, posting social updates, paying for practically anything on site (including food and drinks, souvenirs, and so on), and receiving real-time alerts on upcoming shows and other events taking place in the park—maybe even providing directions there. And as an added bonus, the wearable itself serves as a souvenir of the visit.

Wearables Are Not Alone

In my book *Designing Multi-Device Experiences* (O'Reilly), I describe how since 2007 an ecosystem of connected devices has gradually formed, beginning with the proliferation of smartphones, tablets, and the plethora of apps that truly brought these devices to life. In this ecosystem, multiple connected devices interact with one another and wirelessly sharing data. These interactions are shaped by the different ways in which individuals use the content and services that flow between devices, along different contexts.

As a result, whenever new devices join the ecosystem (such as wearables), they change that grid of connections by introducing new ways to connect devices, content, and people to one another. I call this phenomenon the *Interaction Effect*. People's behaviors and usage patterns with their existing device(s) change depending on the availability of other (often newer) devices. This change can manifest in using the devices more, using the devices less, or using them differently, for example in conjunction with one another.

Tablets are a good example of these dynamic changes: their increasing use led to a gradual decline in the purchase of older media and device usage (printed magazines and books, desktop computers, laptop computers, and dedicated e-readers). Simultaneously, tablets introduced a new usage pattern in conjunction with the TV, serving as a *second-screen*[6] device providing an enhanced viewing experience.

In a similar manner, when you think about wearables, it's important to consider their role as part of the existing—and future—ecosystem of devices[7] and the ways they could impact interactions with all these devices. For example, owners of the Pebble watch get their smartphone notifications (text messages, phone calls, tweets) directly on their watch, which is accessible at a glance. In addition, with the new Mercedez-Benz Digital DriveStyle app, the Pebble watch complements the automotive experience. When outside of their car, Mercedez owners can see vital information about their cars, such as fuel level, door-lock status, and vehicle location. When driving, the watch provides a vibratory alert for real-time hazards such as accidents, road construction, or stalled vehicles.

These examples reinforce the premise that as wearables spread into the mainstream, they will change habits and usage patterns with existing devices as well as relationships between devices. Certain functionalities, commonly associated with smartphones (or other devices) today, might be replaced, complemented, or augmented by wearables, side by side, introducing the wearer to new capabilities and connections.

Here are two fundamental questions that you should constantly keep in mind:

---

6 Second screen refers to the use of a computing device (usually a smartphone or a tablet) to provide an enhanced viewing experience for content on another device (commonly a TV). This enhanced experience often includes complementary information about the TV program currently being viewed as well as interactive and social features, such as voting, sharing moments, answering questions, and more.

7 With special emphasis on the Internet of Things, predicted to connect around 40 billion devices and things by 2020 (source: *http://onforb.es/1CJ2ZiS*). These "things" can be any physical objects, from home appliances and medical devices, to roads and bridges, to toasters, coffee machines, and milk cartons—even microchipped pets and people.

Wearables as substitutes for existing device experiences

In which cases are wearables superior compared to other devices, and when are they inferior or just as good?

Remember that people usually have alternative devices. In most cases, they have already formed habits with respect to using those devices. If you want them to change their behavior, the wearable experience needs to clearly win over consumers and make them want to abandon their existing device. The crucial elements are simplicity, benefit, and time. As Russell Holly accurately articulates:[8] *"Plain and simple, there are exactly zero times when it is acceptable for a task on your watch to take longer than the time needed to pull your smartphone out and complete the task."* And this doesn't apply just for smartwatches.

Wearables as complementary devices for existing device experiences

Which new ecosystem connections can you create between devices to enhance wearables' benefits for people? Which can better integrate these devices as part of the overall experience en route to their goal? For example, can the wearable device complement other devices (such as a smartphone)?

These questions will accompany us through the remainder of this chapter as we dive into the detailed set of wearables UX factors.

UX (and Human) Factors to Consider

When designing for wearables, there are several aspects to take into account in order to ensure an effective, well-considered, scalable user experience, both in terms of the product's industrial design and the interface design. These factors involve the actor (the person wearing the device[9]), its surroundings, the device itself, the context of use, feature sets, interaction models, and any relationships with other devices.

---

8 *http://bit.ly/1CJ31ar*

9 In certain cases, the person wearing the device doesn't necessarily control it or even interact with it (for example, a parent controlling a wearable on a child, or a caregiver tracking wearable data on an elderly patient). In this case, there are actually two actors—the one wearing the device and the person controlling it.

TABLE 4-1. UX factors and their corresponding design options

FACTOR	DESIGN OPTIONS
Visibility	• Visible to others • Invisible
Role	• Tracker • Messenger • Facilitator • Enhancer

Display on-device	• No display
	• Minimal output display (LED-based)
	• Full interactable display
	  – Physical screen
	  – Projected display

Interaction model	• Multimodal interaction:
	  – Visual: display
	  – Audio: voice and sound
	  – Tactile: touch and vibration
	  – Physical keys
	• Multi-device interaction

Table 4-1 lists the main UX factors and their corresponding design options that you need to address when designing for wearables. As you look through them, keep in mind the following:

- The different factors are intertwined and impact one another to different degrees. For example, wearable visibility is closely connected to design decisions about the display and interaction model: a wearable attached to a body part that is invisible to others (such as the ankle or back) and thus not immediately accessible to the wearer either, doesn't need a dedicated display, and definitely not one with which the wearer has full interaction. In terms of the interaction model, tactile feedback is critical for the ongoing communication between the wearer and the device (more on that next).

- A single wearable experience can integrate multiple design options associated with one factor. For example, a wearable device can incorporate both tracker and messenger roles, which enhance each other and/or address different contexts of use (more on that next).

Next, we will take a deep dive into these factors and discuss what each one means, the design options involved, and the affordances to consider. We accompany it all with product examples. Together, these factors provide you with a comprehensive UX framework when designing for wearables that accounts for all the core experience components.

VISIBILITY

The way a wearable device is designed to be worn—specifically, if it's an accessory visible to others—carries a critical impact on the balance between function and fashion in the design process. While aesthetics play a role in the desirability of almost any product, when it comes to apparel that decorates the body, attractiveness moves up on the priority list. It has long been demonstrated that the articles people wear are a form of self-expression, a way for individuals to show the world their identity, uniqueness, and personality. As such, for wearables to move beyond the early, tech-savvy adopters into the open arms of the mass market, designers of those wearables must consider fashion. In other words, they need to consider how the wearable looks, how it looks on people, and how it makes them feel when they're wearing it. The latter also includes investigating how to personalize the wearable and make people feel unique when wearing it, even if many others wear the same (or similar) wearables.

The importance of fashion and beauty in wearable design is beginning to sink in. The consumer wearables industry is driving the convergence of tech and fashion, with an increasing number of technology companies collaborating with fashion and jewelry designers to build their product. At CES 2014, Intel Corporation announced that is was teaming up with cutting-edge fashion design house and retailer, Opening Ceremony, to make a bracelet that will be sold at Barneys. Similarly, Fitbit announced a collaboration with Tory Burch to design fashionable necklaces and bracelets for its activity trackers. CSR, the chip manufacturer, already launched a slick-looking Bluetooth pendant (see Figure 4-6), which was developed in collaboration with jeweler Cellini. The device has a single customizable light for receiving notifications, and can also be configured to release perfume throughout the day. Figure 4-7 shows another example, the Netatmo June bracelet, designed in collaboration with Louis Vuitton and Camille Toupet, which measures sun exposure throughout the day. In Figure 4-7, note how the advertisement follows the jewelry industry spirit.

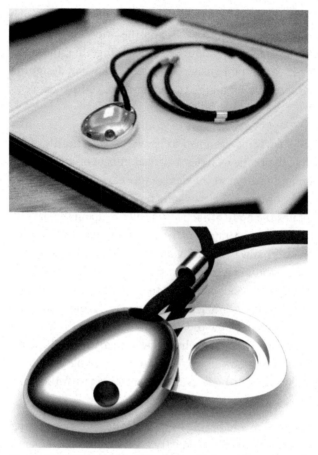

Figure 4-6. CSR's Bluetooth necklace, designed as an item of jewelry

Figure 4-7. Netatmo June, made with jewels designed by Louis Vuitton and Camille Toupet

From a product design perspective, this new fashion-function relationship suggests a few important imperatives:

- From the very early stages of the product inception, you should focus not only on the user interface design and the feature set (software side), but also put an emphasis on the wearable design itself (hardware side). This means that you'll need to manage two core design efforts side by side: user interface (UI) design and industrial design (ID). Each effort requires dedicated attention, resources, and expertise, but at the same time they are tightly integrated and dependent on each other, functionally and visually. ID decisions in areas such as form factor, size, shape, display, ergonomics, texture, and colors directly impact the universe of possibilities (and constraints) of the UI, from layout, interaction, and flows, to art and visual language. This is especially prominent if the wearable offers an on-device display, which we discuss later in the chapter.

  At the end of the day, from a consumer's standpoint, both the UI and ID design create the overall experience. Thus, the two design groups need to work closely together to ensure ongoing conversation and collaboration, creating together a holistic user experience that feels like a synergy.

- When defining your Minimal Viable Product (MVP) as well as in the ongoing process of setting the product roadmap and milestones, fashion attributes should be an integral part of the prioritization process. This means that if you're building a smartwatch, for example, you might prefer to wait with some functional features in favor of launching it with a larger variety of wristband designs that appeal to wider target audience groups. Pebble demonstrated this approach with their release of Pebble Steel, a higher-end version of its popular smartwatch. Although we're not privy to complete information about its product considerations, it's probably safe to assume that Pebble has a long list of features in the pipeline. Still, the company chose for its second major product milestone (a year after their initial launch) to keep the same feature set of the original Pebble and offer instead a new fashionable stainless-steel body design, which you can see alongside the black-matte finish in Figure 4-8.

Figure 4-8. Pebble Steel, a premium version of the Pebble watch, made of stainless steel, with a screen protected by a layer of Corning Gorilla Glass

- When characterizing your target audience(s), it's not enough to consider just the "traditional" attributes in the digital sphere, such as demographics, skills, behavior patterns, usage habits, and so on. You also need to understand your users' attitudes and preferences in terms of fashion, accessories, and jewelry. In that respect, just considering the gender already plays an important role. Looking at the selection of wearables today, most of them are still characterized with a very masculine design—dark colors, hard corners and edges, heavier, and more sturdy looking. This is a look and feel that appeals mostly to men. If you wish to attract the female audience, you'll need to adopt a different design approach that corresponds with their fashion preferences. Better yet, go beyond the gender stereotypes and learn your specific audience preferences.

Discussion: Where Should the Wearable Be Worn?

When considering the wearable's industrial design and where it should be worn, you might want to consider how "saturated" with accessories (wearables or regular fashion accessories) certain body parts already are. For example, there's only so much that people are willing to wear on their wrists at any given moment. Humans only have two arms, and most people would probably wear no more than one or maybe two items on each wrist. The wearables market is already filled with bracelets, wristbands, and wristwatches that offer a variety of functionalities. Introducing yet another bracelet—even if it offers a new functionality—would need to directly compete on the same limited body space that is already occupied by a large set of existing wearables and fashion bracelets.

One way to deal with this challenge is to consider a different body location (if possible), which is exactly what Flyfit did (*http://www.myflyfit.com/*). The company offers an ankle tracker (see Figure 4-9) for fitness, cycling, and swimming.

Figure 4-9. Flyfit's ankle wearable

As technology progresses, the flexibility in terms of body placement will probably grow, which will open up additional opportunities for body parts to which wearables can be attached.

Another approach is to offer a modular wearable that can be attached to the body in various ways, as was the case with Misfit Shine. Figure 4-10 demonstrates how the circular tracker can be worn as a wristband, pocket clip-on, or shirt clip-on.

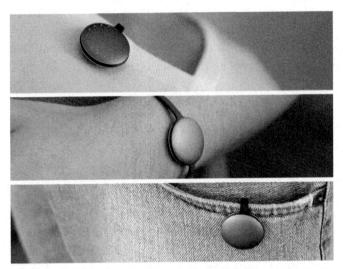

Figure 4-10. Various locations where the Misfit Shine can be worn

Such a wearable provides more wearing options, potentially accommodating more diverse user preferences. However, it comes with its own set of challenges.

First, you need to ensure that your wearable does indeed have flexibility: can the user attach it to the skin as well as on top of clothing? Second, even if the answer is yes, manufacturing a modular wearable that needs to fit different constellations doesn't usually allow the same level of finesse and polish as when focusing on just a single accessory, head to toe. Third, offering a variety of wearing options along with multiple accessories takes something away from the straightforward simplicity of "just wearing it."

In any case, whether you provide a modular wearable, or one that can only be worn on a specific body part, you need to consider people's different body sizes and types. There are several ways to address this issue. Fitbit delivers its product with two wristband sizes: small and large. Nike+ FuelBand offer several wristband sizes that the consumer chooses during the purchase process. Jawbone designed its UP wristband in a flexible one-size-fits-all way. Users can wear the Misfit Shine by using "clip-ons" that are size-agnostic. Whichever strategy you choose to adopt, make sure your design accommodates the human heterogeneity.

ROLE

Looking at the current wearables landscape, these devices often take one or more of the following roles:

Tracker

The wearable collects data about the wearer activity or physiological condition. This data can be used to monitor the user's state as well as to encourage her to improve her fitness, movement, and other health factors. Jawbone UP is an example of such a wearable.

Messenger

The wearable device, often being more readily accessible to the user than his smartphone, displays selected alerts and events from that device, such as a phone call, incoming message, or meeting reminder. The user can then decide whether to pick up the phone and act upon it or respond later.

Note that most wearables acting as "Messenger" today rely on a Bluetooth connection with the smartphone for their operation.[10] Through this connection, they essentially mirror selected event notifications, so users are alerted more quickly. The Pebble watch functions as such a device. Another is Moto 360, which displays a variety of on-time alerts and notifications to users, as shown in Figure 4-11.

Figure 4-11. Examples of alerts and notifications on the Moto 360

---

10 As technology advances, I expect we will see more independent wearables, which don't require connection to another device for their activity. Along with that, alerts (and other actions) could go beyond mirroring notifications, and get triggered based on various contextual signals (like getting to a certain location, being in proximity to certain people or devices, and others).

Facilitator

The wearable facilitates certain communication, media, or other activities that are already available on the smartphone (or other devices) by offering a simpler, more convenient experience. For example, capturing a video by using Google Glass is much easier compared to a smartphone. Instead of the user having to turn on the screen, unlock the device, launch the camera app, change to video mode, and then hold the camera device in front of the body to take the video, Google Glass allows the user to immediately trigger the camera (via a voice command/button click), right in the moment, to capture the video seamlessly, still remaining an integral part of that experience (rather than holding a device that places a "wall" between her and the scene).

Enhancer

The wearable device augments the real world with information that is overlaid on the environment and its objects, potentially with the capability to interact and digitally manipulate that information. The film *Minority Report* is a popular culture reference for this type of AR technology. In the iconic scene shown in Figure 4-12, agent John Anderton (Tom Cruise) is manipulating—in a perfect orchestral fashion—a heads-up AR display interface at the Justice Department headquarters.

Figure 4-12. An image from the famous movie *Minority Report*, directed by Steven Spielberg (Paramount Home Entertainment)

AR-equipped wearables open up a wide array of use cases that these devices can enhance and optimize (from gaming, navigation, shopping, and traveling, to communication, education, medicine, search, and more). It is clearly a promising direction toward which the industry is advancing, one which could offer a more natural, unmediated, immersive interaction with the world. I expect that AR technologies along with their implementation in consumer products will significantly mature and grow over the next 5 to 10 years, leading to a tremendous change in the way we perform daily tasks, engage with content and media, and interact with the environment (and each other).

At the same time, it's worth noting that currently very few devices are actually able to deliver such experiences (especially when referring to the interaction layer, on top of the information overlay), let alone for broad daily consumer use cases. Recall at the beginning of this chapter, I mentioned Oculus Rift and CastAR as two smart-glass devices that integrate AR/VR technology focused on gaming. Another example is Meta's Pro AR eyewear, which is one of the pioneering devices to introduce an interactive holographic UI. As of this writing, this wearable is on the cusp of becoming available, with an anticipated price tag of $3,650 (which is still far beyond mass market reach).

If you look carefully at these different roles, you'll notice that they greatly impact other UX factors as part of the design, further stressing the interconnectedness between all these factors. For example, Facilitator and Enhancer both require the wearable to have a display—physical or projected—so that users can view the information and potentially interact with it, as well (we talk more about the types of wearable displays in the next section). This also means that the device needs to be located in an area that is easily reachable for the user (within touch, sight, and, preferably, hearing). These requirements essentially restrict you to the upper front part of the body (from the hips up). The head, arms, hands, and neck, as well as pockets are usually the most convenient locations.

A Tracker usually requires that it be placed on a specific body location and/or have direct contact with a certain body part in order to reliably record the desired data. This narrows down the location options yet still leaves room for creativity. For instance, if the device needs to be in touch with the chest, you could design it as a chest band, a necklace, or even as a smart t-shirt. The preferred route depends on the type of data you want to collect, the technology used, the target audience, and the use cases in focus.

Discussion: From Wearable Devices to Smart Clothing

Athos is one of the pioneers in smart workout gear (*https://www.liveathos.com/*). The company's athletic clothing is equipped with sensors that measure muscle exertion from the chest, shoulders, arms, back, quads, hamstrings, and glutes, plus heart rate and breathing—all rolled up into a single piece of clothing, as illustrated in Figure 4-13.

Figure 4-13. Athos smart workout gear, equipped with sensors throughout

With its clothing, Athos demonstrates an important principle of wearable design: keep it simple and single. In other words—it's better to design the wearable experience based on a single unit, rather than break it down to multiple components, such as a set of multiple trackers to wear or a smartglass that comes with a separate touchpad for interaction.

Multiple components are much harder to manage on a day-to-day basis, they are more cumbersome to wear and remove, and people are more likely to lose pieces along the way. As a result, they could be a significant barrier for adoption and ongoing use. Athos cleverly packaged all of its sensors in a single clothing unit, so that as a consumer, you need only to wear a shirt (a daily, familiar behavior), and the rest is done seamlessly.

Looking ahead, touchscreen t-shirts, which allow interaction on the clothing itself (through projected display) appear to be just a few years away (*http://mashable.com/2013/02/15/armour39/*).

As the wearable market and technology continue to develop, we will see the list of wearable roles enriched, both in terms of the functional and interaction possibilities within each role and additional new roles (probably more tailored to specific domains/market segments and needs).

In any case, remember that these roles are not necessarily mutually exclusive. Some wearables do choose to focus on a specific role only; consider, for example, MEMI (see Figure 4-14), an iPhone-compatible smartbracelet that serves as a messenger wearable. The bracelet uses light vibrations to notify the user of important phone calls, text messages, and calendar alerts.

Figure 4-14. MEMI smartbracelet, designed as chic jewelry that looks nothing like a "technological device"

Others, however, integrate multiple roles within the same device. Samsung's Galaxy Gear smartwatch is an example of a wearable that serves as a tracker, messenger, and facilitator, all in one device. It has a pedometer that tracks step data; it is linked with the smartphone and displays notifications on the watch screen; and it facilitates actions such as calling, scheduling, and taking a voice memo by speaking to the Gear device (which is immediately accessible).

Deciding which route to take with a wearable (single role or multifunctional) goes back to the design fundamentals: your users, use cases, and the broader ecosystem of devices. As with any UX design, there's a trade-off between simplicity and functionality; the more features you add to the product, the more complex it is to use. Therefore, make certain that you focus on your users and try to determine what they *really* need by looking across the entire experience map (with all its touch points) before adding more features.

Also, wearables are very small devices; thus, they are very limited in terms of display and interaction (which we discuss in the upcoming sections). Additionally, you have other devices in the ecosystem that people are using (smartphones, tablets, and so on), and these can either work in conjunction with the wearable or take care of some of the functionality altogether, thereby relieving the wearable of the burden.

[NOTE]

Remember the discussion about the need to consider gender in fashion preferences and the current masculine-dominated wearable industry?

The MEMI smartbracelet shown in Figure 4-14 is focused on changing exactly this status quo. It is designed and branded as "Wearable Technology Made by Women for Women." On their Kickstarter page, the founders explain, "Our friends don't want to wear big, black, bulky tech devices. In fact, they don't wear 'devices,' they wear jewelry. So, we set out to create a bracelet that is both stylish and functional" (*http://kck. st/1phgyxX*). The MEMI design is definitely a refreshing change in the wearables landscape, and the project has already exceeded its funding goal of $100,000.

DISPLAY ON-DEVICE

The concept of *display on-device* is crucial to wearable design, both in terms of the physical design of the device and the experience it engenders.

The three core questions you should ask yourself to determine the right display treatment for your wearable are these:

- Should the wearable inform the wearer of something, and how often?

- What level of interaction is needed with the wearable (none, view information, browse information, add/edit information, other)? Does it need to be visual?

- Can the wearer use a smartphone (or other device) as an extension of the wearable, together providing an engaging experience for the user?

With these questions in mind, let's review the range of options and their implications on the experience design.

No display

Having no display means more industrial design flexibility in terms of the wearable size (specifically, it can be much smaller), the shape, thickness and overall structure. It's also cheaper and technologically simpler to build. On the other hand, no display also means no visual interface, and thus less user interaction with the device. It doesn't necessarily mean no interaction at all (as the wearable might still have physical buttons, a touch surface, sound, vibration, or voice interaction), but still, having no active visual communication with the wearable limits the scope and level of user interaction with it.

Keep in mind, though, that having no display doesn't necessarily mean the wearable has no *display channel* at all. This is where the power of the ecosystem comes into play: the wearable device can send the data it collected to another connected device the user owns such as a smartphone or tablet, and the interaction takes place on that device, which offers a comfortable display.

The most common usage for wearables without display is data trackers, which measure physical and/or activity data. These wearables are often hidden—worn under clothes, or attached to them seamlessly. Here are a few examples:

Notch

A tiny movement and activity tracker designed to be hinged on or concealed within clothing such as a jacket sleeve, as depicted in Figure 4-15, or sport wristband. It tracks and captures precise body movement and sends the data to a complementary iOS app for tracking and review. Furthermore, this wearable can provide haptic feedback through its vibration motors, and thus can be set to trigger motion-based notifications in the smartphone app.

Figure 4-15. Notch activity tracker attached seamlessly to a jacket sleeve

Notch is a good example of the design advantages (mainly size and shape) of having no display to support. Each sensor is only 30 x 33 x 8 millimeters in size and weighs less than 10 grams.

Lumo Back

A smart posture sensor that fits around the waist and vibrates to alert the user if he slouches. It works in coordination with a smartphone app, which provides visual feedback regarding the user's posture, and tracks progress over time, as demonstrated in Figure 4-16.

Figure 4-16. The Lumo Back posture sensor and its companion smartphone app

In addition, given the growing role of wearables in the healthcare industry, for cases in which the wearer is not the one interacting with the data (for example, pets, babies, the elderly, or ill people), having no display on the device would probably be the preferred route. It affords greater flexibility in the wearable design. Consequently, it can be more easily customized for their specific purpose, and the data collected can be sent to a caregiver's device. See Figure 4-17 for three examples of such wearables.

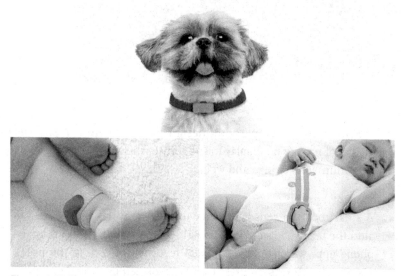

Figure 4-17. Three examples of wearables with no display: Fitbark (top), Sproutling (bottom left), and Mimo (bottom right)

Minimal output display (LED-based)

Similar to the no-display wearables but with a little bit more visual feedback are the minimal-display wearables. These devices incorporate a small LED or OLED display, which displays on-device selected information that is critical to the experience. This display is not interactive: it's one-directional, outputting information for the user to view, but the user doesn't actively interact with it nor can the user enter any input.

Activity and health trackers currently dominate this wearables group, as well, offering to the wearer visual feedback on their progress. This feedback can take several forms:

Rough progress

A set of lights that provide a rough indication to the user about her daily activity progress. Figure 4-18 shows Fitbit Flex and Misfit Shine, two examples of this kind of minimal display. The lights illuminate automatically when the user reaches her daily goal (all lighting up festively, usually accompanied by vibration feedback). Additionally, the user can manually ask to see her progress status by clicking a button or performing a gesture (for instance, a double-tap on the wearable surface), which turns on the relative number of lights, based on the progress.

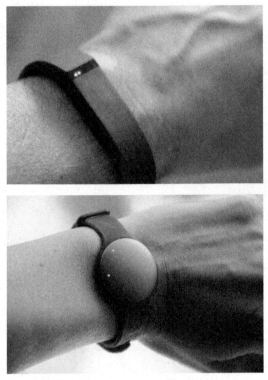

Figure 4-18. Fitbit Flex (top) and Misfit Shine provide light-based visual feedback on the wearable device

Similarly, you can also use a single light (turning on/off, or changing colors) to reflect different key experience states. One good example is CSR's Bluetooth smart necklace, mentioned earlier in the chapter. It uses a smart LED which illuminates when a smartphone notification arrives. In fact, the user can customize the light to display different colors for different kinds of notifications. Figure 4-19 shows another example, the Mio LINK, a heart rate monitor, which offers just a single status LED.

Figure 4-19. Mio LINK, which uses a single on-device LED to provide feedback about the heart rate state

Mio LINK comes with a complementary smartphone app, Mio GO, which offers extended data as well as a second-screen companion during indoors workout by re-creating landscapes and trails via video footage on the tablet screen.

The LED-based wearable UI keeps the display minimal and clean. Such a display is limited in terms of data, but it facilitates designing more fashionable, elegant-looking wearables. In other words, in the fashion-function balance, more weight is put on the design. Additional data and functionality is provided on the companion apps, similar to the no-display wearables.

Concrete numbers

An OLED display can present selected numbers to provide more concrete data about the user's activity, such as calories burned, number of steps taken, distance walked, and so on. The activity trackers LG Lifeband and Withings Pulse are two products that use this display (see Figure 4-20). To keep the display as small as possible, the metrics are rotating on the same display area, either automatically every few seconds or by using a gesture or clicking an on-device button to switch between the numbers displayed.

Figure 4-20. The Withings Pulse (top) and LG Lifeband activity trackers

Discussion: Minimal Display Is Not Just for Activity Trackers

Minimal-display wearables are not limited to activity and health trackers alone. For example, the Razer Nabu shown in Figure 4-21 uses an OLED display to present a variety of notifications (which the user can customize), including call, email, text messages, and social network notifications, calendar alerts, and more.

Figure 4-21. The Razer Nabu shows selected notifications by using an OLED display

The Razer Nabu is similar to the Pebble watch in terms of its value proposition. The main differentiator is its focus on privacy and discreteness, which is also manifested in its unique UI design. The Razer Nabu is built with a dual screen, as shown in Figure 4-22—the one on the top is visible to the surroundings ("Public icon screen"), and the second display on the bottom is visible only to the wearer ("Private message screen").

PUBLIC ICON SCREEN   PRIVATE MESSAGE SCREEN

Figure 4-22. The Razer Nabu's dual-screen operation

When a call, message, or notification arrives, the public part of the wrist-band shows only the event category (for example, a call or message icon). To view the actual content—which could be private—the wearer rotates his arm to reveal the details of the event (for example, the caller ID or message text).

Even though this design cleverly addresses privacy concerns, I can't help but wonder if this use pattern, which requires the user to repeatedly rotate his arm back and forth, will quickly lead to ergonomic issues, especially given the variety of notifications Razer Nabu integrates, and the increasing frequency with which people receive (and check) these notifications.

Minimal display wearables can also combine both types of visual feedback, lights and numbers, as in the case of the Nike+ FuelBand, which is depicted in Figure 4-23.

Figure 4-23. The Nike+ FuelBand provides both exact numbers (such as numbers of steps) along with a visual indication about the progress in relation to the daily goal

With this combined approach, the user gets more comprehensive data about her status, accomplishments, and goal completion, which could contribute to her ongoing engagement with the device. However, it comes with a visual cost: the display becomes busier and less slick. Some of it has to do with the specific visual design applied (font size, colors, and so on). However, it is mainly tied to the amount of information that is displayed on the device.

This aesthetics-functionality trade-off emphasizes a fundamental question that wearables raise: *how much information do people need to see on a wearable device versus viewing it on other ecosystem devices (a smartphone, for instance) to stay engaged with the experience?*

This question doesn't have a simple answer—especially given the novelty of this industry and that it hasn't penetrated the mass market just yet. Also, as with most UX issues, the behavior depends on multiple factors, such as the type of wearable, the use case, the specific user group, the context, use patterns, and more. We still need a lot more user data and research to understand this aspect.

With that having been said, when I look at the case of the combined displays shown previously, I lean towards a single indicator (preferably a simple visual cue) for overall progress. It not only establishes a cleaner interface, but also offers a much simpler flow for users to grasp, follow, and act upon. The famous premise "less is more" is becoming practically sacred when it comes to wearables. Given their small size, interaction limitations, and interruption-based use pattern (more on this in a moment), keeping the UI clean, clear, and glanceable is key to their usability.

[NOTE]

Looking ahead, I think a projected display can help minimal-display wearables in addressing the fashion-function trade-off. Instead of the device itself having a physical screen component, it could project the info using some gesture/button click on an adjacent surface, whether it's some body part (like the dorsal of the hand), a physical object, or even thin air. This way, rough progression indication (using lights, for example) can be immediately accessible on-device, but concrete numbers will be projected on an external surface. This will still permit quick access to this data directly from the wearable while keeping the device design more aesthetic, clean, and elegant.

Full interactive display

The third category of wearables in the Display On-Device factor is one that offers a full display. This allows for rich interaction with the device, which usually comes with a much broader feature set. Smartwatches and smartglasses are most common in this category, with an important distinction between them:

- Smartwatches have an actual physical screen on-device with which users interact.

- Smartglasses use a projected display that emulates a screen, but there is no actual physical one on-device.

Still, these devices share some key UX design challenges, mainly the small display size and mix of interaction patterns.

Small display size. Both smartwatches and smartglasses today offer a very small display area to present and interact with information and actions. For example, Samsung's Galaxy Gear screen size is 1.6" with 320 x 320 pixel resolution; Sony's SmartWatch offers a 1.6" screen, too, but with resolution of 220 x 176 pixels. Google Glass offers a display resolution of 640 x 360 pixels, which is the equivalent of a 25" screen viewed from eight feet away.

From a UX perspective, this means the design needs to be very sharp—clear contrast, stripped down to the core essence of information—and to rely on large visual elements that are easy to scan and process at a glance. In that respect, surprisingly enough, the design principles for full display wearables share a lot more in common with designing for TV, compared to devices such as smartphones or tablets. Although TV screens are significantly larger, the information is consumed and interacted with from a distance, and thus require a simplified design, as demonstrated in Figure 4-24.

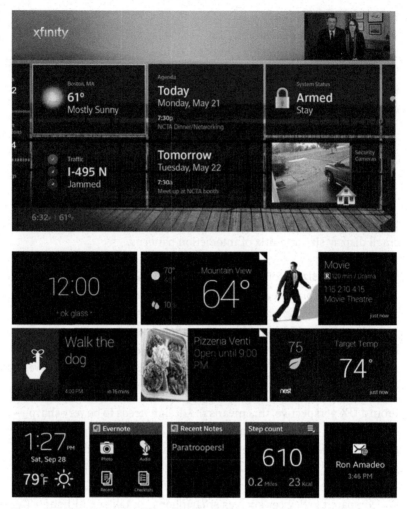

Figure 4-24. Comparison of interface design between TV and wearables: at the top is a TV dashboard by Comcast, followed by screen examples from Google Glass, and Samsung Galaxy Gear

In case the wearable display is not focused on information consumption only, but also allows touch interaction (as with smartwatches), the screen layout needs to accommodate the size of a human finger. Contrary to smartphones, for which interaction is often done using the thumb,[11] when it comes to smartwatches, the index finger is the one most people use. The thumb is often needed to use physical keys on-device, or to help stabilize the device while using the index finger to press keys, as illustrated in Figure 4-25.

Figure 4-25. A comparison view between a common one-thumb operation interaction on a smartphone versus a common smartwatch use

Looking ahead, comparing the two display types used by smartwatches and smartglasses today (physical screen and projected display, respectively), the latter seems to have better scaling prospects.[12] In fact, there

---

11 One-thumb operation in smartphones is feasible and convenient as long as the device size affords enough room for stable grip and free thumb movement using one hand. With larger smartphones (2.5-inch width and larger), it's becoming harder to hold and operate them steadily with one hand only. In these cases, the typical grip is one hand holding the device (usually the nondominant hand) and the index finger of the other hand interacting with the touch interface.

12 A potential future direction for enabling expanded display in physical screens is a newly discovered material that allows electronics to stretch. You can read more about this at http://mashable.com/2012/06/28/stretchable-electronics/.

are already several prototypes for smartglasses that offer a much bigger display area.[13] Still, when considering the display size, it's important to keep in mind—especially with smartglasses—that bigger displays mean masking a bigger part of the visual field, as the displays are overlaid. We'll discuss this more in the section "Separate Versus Integrated Visual Field Display."

Mix of interaction patterns. There are multiple input methods that you can use (and are often needed, partly due to the limitations of the display size just described) to establish a comprehensive interaction model on these devices. These include voice, touch, and physical keys.

These channels are all applicable ways to interact with these wearables. In fact, in most cases of full interactive displays—especially as the feature set and available apps expand (along with their respective use cases and contexts of use)—no one method can cover the entire interaction spectrum required. Finding a way to take advantage of the strengths of each method while establishing a clear structure around the interaction model throughout the system is a challenging task, as discussed in the section "Interaction Model."

Discussion: Beyond the Standard Rectangular Screens

Having a full interactive screen doesn't necessarily mean it has to be the standard rectangular screen shape to which we're accustomed. Wearables open up new ground for innovation, with the opportunity to rethink both industrial design and interface design practices as we know them today. Two creative concepts for iOS wearable devices that spur the imagination and encourage exploring new design approaches were created by Todd Hamilton and Federico Ciccarese, which you can see in Figure 4-26 and Figure 4-27, respectively.

---

13 One example is Meta's Pro glasses, which offer a display area 15 times larger than Google Glass.

Although both of these concepts raise various questions around their usability, scalability, and usage patterns, their important value is in breaking out of existing paradigms and exploring new design approaches that can better meet this new wearables space.

Figure 4-26. iWatch concept by Todd Hamilton: envisioning how Apple's smartwatch could be designed on a thin wristband wearable

Figure 4-27. A spider-like design concept for a wearable iOS device that grips the hand, by Federico Ciccarese

Along with the similarities between smartwatches and smartglasses, there are also a few important differences between the two display types, which impact their design considerations.

Direct versus indirect manipulation. Smartwatches encompass a physical display that can easily support direct manipulation on-screen by using touch (similarly to the familiar interaction model on smartphones and tablets). The majority of smartglasses, however, at least at this point cannot offer a parallel experience.[14] Users cannot simply reach out and interact with the projected display; they need to rely on indirect manipulation using separate input methods, such as external touchpad, physical keys, or voice commands. This makes the interaction model somewhat more challenging for users because they need to make the cognitive leap between what they see and seems within reach, and the actual input methods they can use to interact with the display. This requires building and forming habits around a set of logical connections between the display and the available means to manipulate it. In our current digital world, where a vast portion of the daily interaction with devices is direct (touch-based smartphones, tablets, media players, kiosks, and so on), getting users to learn a new interaction model that relies on indirect manipulation, introduces a certain stumbling block. As a result, investing design resources in the onboarding experience as well as ongoing in-product education is very important to help people ramp up quickly.

Separate versus integrated visual field display. Interacting with smartwatches—which are worn on the wrist and are therefore out of the main visual field—is essentially a separate, independent experience. The user's attention needs to actively turn away from the direction he is looking to focus instead on the smartwatch screen (which receives the full attention for the interaction duration). When using smartglasses, however, the display is integrated into the main field of vision. Wherever the person's attention is and in whichever direction he is looking, the display is right there, overlaid on top of the visual field; it cannot be separated from it. The user's attention

---

14 MetaPro AR Smartglass is the first to introduce a holographic interface, allowing spatial control using the fingers. This is an important step in advancing us towards making the *Minority Report* interaction model a reality.

inevitably spans both—an additional UX challenge when designing for these devices. Furthermore, at this point in time (and probably for the next few years), most smartglasses don't provide a seamless AR integration with the environment; rather, they project a small screen-like display within the field of vision. As a result, this virtual screen covers a portion of the background information. Finding the sweet spot where the overlaid display is integrated effectively in the visual field, visible enough to the user when needed but not in his way, requires careful handling (and continuous testing) in terms of display location, size, shape, colors, opacity, and so on. Currently, different smartglass providers take different approaches along these dimensions. Additional testing with larger populations is required to determine the optimal settings for such wearables.

Level of control on the display. With smartwatches, users can control—at the least—the angle of the screen and how close they are to it; therefore, they can increase legibility and facilitate usage.

With the displays for smartglasses, until they can be digitally manipulated (for example, the ability to zoom in/out), users are constrained to a fixed screen (in terms of size, angle, and location). This further enhances the need, discussed earlier, to keep the design very simple, clean, and focused on the very essence. As you add more visual elements to the display, you will face a more pressing need to use smaller font sizes, add colors/shades, decrease spacing, and so on to accommodate all the elements and establish visual prioritization between them. This in turn increases the cognitive load on the users, cluttering the display and harming legibility.

THE INTERACTION MODEL

For the most part, users' interaction with wearables is based on *microinteractions*.[15] Microinteractions are defined as *contained product moments that revolve around a single use case—they have one main*

---

15 This behavior pattern might change when fully AR-equipped smartglasses/lenses become widespread. In the future, where people can digitally manipulate the display, the interaction might become a longer one, focusing the entire user's attention on completing a more complex task.

task.[16] Every time a user answers a call, changes a setting, replies to a message, posts a comment, or checks the weather, she engages with a microinteraction.

Microinteractions can take three forms of operation:

Manual
> Initiated by the user; for example, double-tapping the Fitbit bracelet to get the information on goal completion status.

Semi-automatic
> The user is alerted by the system to take an action. For example, consider Lumo Back vibrating when the wearer is slouching, signaling him to straighten up. These alerts can be triggered as a result of manual user configuration or contextual signals (for instance, location, proximity, the presence of other people/devices, body physiological metrics, and more).

Fully automatic
> Performed by the system, in the same manner as the Nike+ FuelBand synchronizes activity data automatically to Nike+.

When it comes to wearables, all three forms of operation come into play, though in different degrees based on the wearable role and the context of use. Trackers, for example, rely heavily on system automation to synchronize the data collected. In addition, many of them also incorporate semi-automatic operation by displaying notifications to users (for example, achieving the daily goal or running out of battery). Messengers work almost solely in semi-automatic mode, focusing on alerting the user whenever an event is taking place on the smartphone (for example, an incoming call or incoming message), based on whether the user chooses to take an action. Facilitators and enhancers, which facilitate richer interactions (and usually offer a richer feature set) incorporate all three.

Still, the largest share of user interaction is generated semi-automatically, as a result of interruptions triggered by the wearable device, or on behalf of the smartphone. The semi-automatic dominance shouldn't come as a surprise, though. First, wearables are meant to be

---

16 *http://microinteractions.com/what-is-a-microinteraction/*

unobtrusive, and mostly "sit there" (hopefully looking pretty), keeping out of the way when not needed. Second, most wearables rely on just delivering information to the users, with minimal input, if at all. Third, given the wearable constraints in terms of display size and often inter-action, too, the engagement pattern with them is mostly quick, focused microinteractions for a specific purpose, on a need basis.

From a UX perspective, this use pattern further emphasizes the impor-tance of "less is more":

- The repeated short interactions, along with the limited attention span allocated to them, require that a special emphasis be placed on simple glanceable UI and fast response times.

- Learning is a function of the time spent on a task and the time needed to complete it. Short, scattered interactions, like those that place with wearables, make it harder to promote learning com-pared to longer, more continuous engagements (as are often done on the desktop, for example). This means that you need to keep the core UX building blocks—mainly, navigation structure, informa-tion architecture, and interaction model—as simple and consistent as possible. Deep navigation hierarchies, or diversified interaction patterns along the product will make it harder to use and form habits.

- The wearable experience needs to be focused on what the device does absolutely best, while always considering the broader ecosys-tem. It's important to crystalize the wearable role in this bigger constellation of devices, and define the relationship between the different devices. Part of designing for wearables is also under-standing what the wearable device should handle versus the parts that other devices should take on, together providing an optimized experience for the user.

Multimodal interaction

When going into the detailed interaction design for wearables, you need to consider three relevant human senses: sight, hearing, and touch.

These senses can be communicated with through several main interac-tion channels (multimodal interaction):

- Visual (display)

- Audio (sound/voice)

- Tactile (touch/vibration)

- Physical keys

These interaction channels serve two main information flows: *output* (user feedback) and *input* (data entry). Let's explore each one through the lens of the main interaction channels.

Output. As discussed throughout this chapter, most wearable devices today focus on the output information flow—providing feedback to the user (based on data these devices collect seamlessly).

Given that wearable devices are by definition worn on the body and thus come in direct (or close) contact with the skin, *tactile feedback becomes a primary interaction channel.*

In some cases, tactile is even more important than the visual. Why?

Let's analyze this by going back to the wearable display types, which handle the visual feedback:

- *Wearables that have no display* cannot rely on visual feedback at all. Consequently, tactile feedback becomes the main communication channel.

  Audio (whether as a sound effect or voice output) is also an option that might be an effective feedback channel in certain contexts. However, it carries several caveats:

  - It can be heard publicly-, and thus takes away the advantage of discreteness many wearables provide.

  - To set audio feedback to a minimum (to keep it private), the device needs to be located in close proximity to the ears. This puts a significant constraint regarding the device placement.

○ Incorporating sound requires adding a way (setting/button/gesture) to turn it on and off, for cases in which it might disturb the user or her surroundings (work meetings, cinema, going to sleep, and so on)[17]

Furthermore, between the tactile and audio channels, the tactile one (vibration) is often much more salient than sound, which brings up the question whether an additional feedback channel is even needed. Be aware that both vibration and sound are interruptive—they immediately grab the user's attention and disrupt what she's doing. For the sake of simplicity and delight, if you can have a single feedback channel, one that is subtle yet effective, you should prefer it and avoid any added disruptions (especially where with some wearables, the frequency of alerts can become pretty high).

- *Wearables that have minimal display* should definitely utilize the visual feedback channel. However, visual clarity should also be accompanied by tactile feedback that is more immediate and noticeable. This is especially important when the feedback is a result of a system-triggered alert, and not initiated by the user. Remember that in many cases, the wearable is peripheral to or completely out of the user's visual field; therefore, the feedback could be easily missed, without actively drawing the user's attention to it.[18]

- *Wearables that have full interactive displays* have less clear-cut guidelines with regard to the feedback channels and require closer analysis on a per-case basis. In smartglasses, for example, the visual display is obviously the primary feedback channel, as it's integrated into the user's field of vision. In this case, there is no real need to add yet another feedback channel in the form of vibration. Also, the head area—and especially around the eyes—is not the

---

17 It would be helpful to establish an intelligent context-aware mechanism for automatically changing the sound state. For example, consider turning the sound off when the device detects the user is in the cinema based on data signals such as location, time, motion, calendar, ticket reservations, and so on. But even then, you would probably still need to provide a manual option as well to give users control when the autosound mechanism doesn't capture the context.

18 In case the display includes expanded information (e.g., concrete numbers rather than just light-based feedback), a physical button might be needed to allow easy paging between the different metrics. Alternatively, if the wearable is based on a touchpad, this action could also be implemented as a gesture (a tap, double-tap, or long press). The latter, though, is less discoverable.

best area for tactile feedback. In addition, because smartglasses are placed close to the ears, the audio channel becomes an effective channel, as well. You can use this channel for sound effects indicating certain events as well as for voice output (reading the information presented on the screen, for example).

With smartwatches, however, both visual and tactile feedbacks are important for information output. Similar to minimal-display wearables, the device is generally away from the visual field, and although a visual effect in a full-screen display draws more attention compared to a minimal display, it can still be easily missed.

Input. When it comes to a full interactive display, which offers not only information display but also input entry by the user, the interaction model becomes more complex—especially as the feature set and interaction spectrum expands. Still, there are several UX guidelines to keep in mind:

- Voice is a great input channel for users to express their intent; it's flexible, based on natural language, and easy to do. However, there are certain considerations to take into account:

  - If you allow voice input in one part of the interface, users will naturally try to continue using it across the system. This means that you should strive to support voice interaction across the board.

  - In case full voice support is not possible, and depending on the importance of voice interaction in your experience, you can still provide partial voice support (rather than none at all). In that case, identify first the user flows that would benefit most from speech input. Then, try to have voice support integrated throughout these flows, from start to end rather than only in a few screens within a user flow. Also, it's highly recommended to provide a clear UI indication as to where speech input is supported, to establish predictability and confidence among users.

  - Preferably, the voice interaction should be available for use at any time (that is, the device is in constant listening mode), without requiring the user to first turn on the screen or unlock the device.

- Remember, voice interaction cannot fit all use contexts. Due to its "loud" nature, publicly available to the surroundings, it has to be backed up with a way to operate the UI silently (for example, using the visual display).

- Although voice recognition technology has improved immensely, it's still experiencing significant challenges in languages other than English or when used by people with heavy foreign accents. This means that users who are not native English speakers (or non-English speakers) might face problems using that input method. This is yet another reason to provide an alternative interaction channel.

- Popular actions that users are expected to use often would benefit greatly from quick access. You can provide this access in a number of ways:

  - Dedicated gesture (similarly to the "shake" gesture on Moto X, which immediately launches the camera app)

  - Dedicated physical key (such as the back button on the Pebble watch)

  - Shortcut(s) in the home screen

  - Direct voice command

- You can use physical keys methodologically in two main ways:

  - *Main navigation*: Keys are used for an ongoing operation of the device, such as navigating up/down in menus and lists, select ingitems, going back, and skipping to home. This type of physical keys usage is much more suited to a smartwatch than smartglasses.

  - *Peripheral/dedicated actions*: Keys are used for very specific actions, such as launching specific apps, power on/off, and mute. This model can fit both smartwatches and smartglasses.

    When using physical keys for dedicated actions, you may notice you need to offer access to some of the actions via the visual interface as well, in order to prevent friction. An example could be when a physical key provides quick access to an app on the device, or to contacting a specific person. In such a case, you should also include that app (or person) as part of the dedicated UI area (apps section or contacts list), so users can easily get to them when their interaction is focused on the visual interface.

Note that given the small size of these wearable devices (and until projected displays mature), trying to incorporate physical or virtual keys for typing in text is not recommended. This action will be extremely cumbersome, time consuming, and error prone. You should probably reconsider offering text-heavy features on those devices in the first place, and if there's a pressing need for text entry, using voice would be a better approach.

- If a touchscreen is used for main navigation (as in smartwatches), be sure you accommodate the "fat finger" syndrome, allowing for a big enough touch area and keeping a simple and clean display. If you use a touchpad that requires indirect manipulation (as in smartglasses, for example):

  ○ Try to stay loyal to the familiar swiping patterns and directions people are already accustomed to from using other devices like smartphones, tablets, and laptops.

  ○ Be sure to align as much as possible the visual interface transitions and animations with the swiping movements done on the touchpad, to enhance the logical connections between them.

- Sound can be a useful feedback channel to provide reassurance to users during their interaction with the device interface (for example, when navigating through screens, making a selection, confirming an action, and so on).

  ○ This channel is beneficial when the wearable is placed close to the ears so that the sound can be kept subtle and nonintrusive.

  ○ When the wearable is far from the ears—thus sound feedback becomes less effective—you can replace it with tactile feedback (such as subtle vibration)

- If your product is open for third-party integrations (external apps that can be developed for the wearable), provide a clear specification of the UI framework, rules, and principles so that developers can more easily follow that UI and help establish a consistent experience.

Multi-device Interaction

As discussed throughout this chapter, wearables are part of a broader ecosystem of connected devices. As such, when designing for wearables, you have to think about them in the context of the bigger constellation, along the user journey. Wearables are not small smartphones, nor can they replace them. They complement them in different ways, along a variety of contexts and functionalities:[19]

- In some cases, wearables provide a superior experience compared to smartphones due to the sensory information they can track, being more readily accessible, or allowing hands-free operation. Getting directions on smartglasses or tracking body movement using a smart shirt are a few examples. In other cases, however, the smartphone is still more convenient to use due to its bigger screen size and embedded keyboard (for example, when sending a text message or making a call).

- It's not always about one device's superiority over the other but rather their joint operation providing an overall better experience to the user. One set of important use cases here is using the wearable as a personal identifier. Given the highly personal nature of wearables, and their physical attachment to the body, these devices can be used as "identity devices," allowing the wearer to seamlessly authenticate to and activate other devices. One good example is Walt Disney's MagicBand, described earlier in the chapter. Another example is Moto X's trusted-device feature. A user can set a connected Bluetooth device (such as a Pebble watch) as a "trusted device" for the phone. From that point on, when the phone is connected to that trusted device, the lock screen is bypassed. Pressing the power button takes the user directly to the home screen, as shown in Figure 4-28. Given the number of times a day people go through their lock screen having to enter their password/PIN to access the phone's content, this feature significantly streamlines the experience.

---

19 For more information about types of relationships between multiple devices (for instance, Consistent, Complementary, and Continuous), see my book *Designing Multi-Device Experiences* (O'Reilly, *http://bit.ly/design_multidevice_exp*).

Figure 4-28. The Pebble watch added as a trusted device to Moto X, which enables unlocking the phone as long as the two devices are in Bluetooth connection proximity (source: AndroidCentral[20])

- The wearable can sometimes start the user flow, which then continues onto the smartphone.[21] A good example is the Pebble watch or MEMI bracelet, which alerts the user about important events immediately, even if the phone is in her bag or silent. The user can then act upon these alerts using the smartphone (e.g., answering a call or replying to a message). Another example is passing on content from one device to the other (e.g., starting a hangout on smartglasses during the taxi ride to work and then continuing it on the desktop when getting to the office).

- Wearables can also control and/or be controlled by the smartphone (or other devices). Going back to the wearables as personal identifiers, they can serve as "keys" to other devices, like unlocking the car, opening the home doors, or controlling the alarm system. The Nymi bracelet, which uses your unique cardiac rhythm to verify your identity, is an example of such a wearable device (see Figure 4-29).

---

20 *http://bit.ly/1CJ3glM*

21 You can read more about continuous experience in *Designing Multi-Device Experiences*, Chapter 3.

Figure 4-29. The Nymi bracelet

In addition, fully interactive display wearables can also take on the remote control capabilities that smartphones offer today, perhaps controlling the thermostat, or TV. Their greater accessibility can be beneficial in such use cases.

The challenge—and opportunity—is in identifying these different cases, and designing the wearable user experience accordingly, not replicating the smartphone (or any other device), but really understanding a wearable's role in the broader ecosystem, and as part of people's daily lives, as they go through their tasks.

Summary

- Wearable computing has expanded into the consumer market and is growing fast. Four market segments gained early adoption: sports and fitness trackers, health and medical sensors, smartwatches, and smartglasses.

- Wearables are joining an already device-rich world in which people already own multiple connected devices and use them together. This existing ecosystem of devices carry an immense impact on the way wearables are used, and the role they play in people's lives.

- When designing for wearables, there are four main UX and human factors to consider: visibility, role, display on-device, and interaction model. These factors are closely tied to each other and impact one another.

- *Visibility*: The way a wearable device is designed to be worn—specifically, if it's visible to others—demands special attention to the balance between function and fashion. Aesthetics play a critical role in advancing to the next level of mass adoption.

- *Role*: In the current wearables landscape, wearables take one or more of the following roles: tracker, messenger, facilitator, and enhancer. As the industry matures, we will see more roles added, especially as AR (and the ability to project displays) advances.

- *Display on-device*: Display on-device is crucial to wearable design, ranging between no display on-device, minimal OLED-based display, and fully interactive display.

  Each option carries different implications on the experience design, and should be determined based on the following questions:

  - Should the wearable inform the wearer of something, and how often?

  - What level of interaction is needed with the wearable? Does it need to be visual?

  - Can the smartphone (or other device) be used as an extension of the wearable, together providing an engaging experience for the user?

- *Interaction model*: For the most part, users' interactions with wearables are based on microinteractions, which can be manual, semi-automatic, or fully automatic. In addition, the interaction model involves 2 dimensions:

  - *Multimodal interaction* via four main channels: visual, audio, tactile, and physical keys. These channels serve two information flows: output and input.

  - *Multi-device interaction*: Wearables are part of a broader ecosystem of connected devices, and thus they need to be considered in the bigger constellation, along a variety of contexts and functionalities.

- "Less is more" is a key guideline when designing for wearables. Focusing on the essence and delivering it through a simple, glanceable UI is critical to the experience design.

[5]

Learning and Thinking with Things

STEPHEN P. ANDERSON

Tangible Interfaces

The study of how humans learn is nothing new and not without many solid advances. And yet, in the rush to adopt personal computers, tablets, and similar devices, we've traded the benefits of hands-on learning and instruction for the scale, distribution, and easy data collection that's part and parcel to software programs. The computational benefits of computers have come at a price; we've had to learn how to interact with these machines in ways that would likely seem odd to our ancestors: mice, keyboards, awkward gestures, and many other devices and rituals that would be nothing if not foreign to our predecessors. But what does the future hold for learning and technology? Is there a way to reconcile the separation between all that is digital with the diverse range of interactions for which our bodies are capable? And how does the role of interaction designer change when we're working with smart, potentially shape-shifting, objects? If we look at trends in technology, especially related to tangible computing (where physical objects are interfaced with computers), they point to a sci-fi future in which interactions with digital information come out from behind glass to become things we can literally grasp.

One such sign of this future comes from Vitamins, a multidisciplinary design and invention studio based in London. As Figure 5-1 shows, it has developed a rather novel system for scheduling time by using... what else... Lego bricks!

Figure 5-1. Vitamins Lego calendar[1]

Vitamins describes their Lego calendar as the following:

> ...a wall-mounted time planner, made entirely of Lego blocks, but if you take a photo of it with a smartphone, all of the events and timings will be magically synchronized to an online digital calendar.

Although the actual implementation (converting a photo of colored bricks into Google calendar information) isn't in the same technical league as nanobots or mind-reading interfaces, this project is quite significant in that it hints at a future in which the distinctions between physical and digital are a relic of the past.

Imagine ordinary objects—even something as low-tech as Lego bricks—augmented with digital properties. These objects could identify themselves, trace their history, and react to different configurations. The possibilities are limitless. This is more than an "Internet of Things," passively collecting data; this is about physical objects catching up to digital capabilities. Or, this is about digital computing getting out from behind glass. However you look at this, it's taking all that's great about being able to pick up, grasp, squeeze, play with, spin,

---

1 http://www.lego-calendar.com

push, feel, and do who-knows-what-else to a thing, while simultaneously enjoying all that comes with complex computing and sensing capabilities.

Consider two of the studio's design principles (from the company's website) that guided this project:

- It had to be *tactile*: "We loved the idea of being able to hold a bit of time, and to see and feel the size of time"

- It had to work both *online and offline*: "We travel a lot, and we want to be able to see what's going on wherever we are."

According to Vitamins, this project "makes the most of the tangibility of physical objects, and the ubiquity of digital platforms, and it also puts a smile on our faces when we use it!"[2] Although this project and others I'll mention hint at the merging of the physical and the digital, it's important to look back and assess what has been good in the move from physical to digital modes of interaction—and perhaps what has been lost.

KANBAN WALLS, CHESS, AND OTHER TANGIBLE INTERACTIONS

Oddly enough, it is the software teams (the folks most immersed in the world of virtual representations) who tend to favor tangibility when it comes to things such as project planning; it's common for Agile or Scrum development teams to create *Kanban* walls, such as that shown in Figure 5-2. Imagine sticky notes arranged in columns, tracking the progress of features throughout the development cycle, from backlog through to release. Ask most teams and they will say there is something about the tangibility of these sticky notes that cannot be replicated by virtual representations.

There's something about moving and arranging this sticky little square, feeling the limitations of different size marker tips with respect to how much can be written, being able to huddle around a wall of these sticky notes as a team—there's something to the physical nature of working with sticky notes. But, is there any explanation as to "why" this tangible version might be advantageous, especially where understanding is a goal?

---

2 *http://www.special-projects-studio.com*

Figure 5-2. Kanban walls[3] and chess[4]

Before answering that question, first consider this question: where does thinking occur?

If your answer is along the lines of "in the brain," you're not alone. This view of a mind that controls the body has been the traditional view of cognition for the better part of human history. In this view, the brain is the thinking organ, and as such it takes input from external stimuli, processes those stimuli, and then directs the body as to how to respond.

Thinking; then doing.

But, a more recent and growing view of cognition rejects this notion of mind-body dualism. Rather than thinking and then doing, perhaps we think through doing.

Consider the game of chess. Have you ever lifted up a chess piece, hovered over several spots where you could move that piece, only to return that piece to the original space, still undecided on your move? What happened here? For all that movement, there was no pragmatic change to the game. If indeed we think and then do (as mind-body dualism argues), what was the effect of moving that chess piece, given that there was no change in the position? If there is no outward change in the environment, why do we instruct our bodies to do these things? The likely answer is that we were using our environment to extend our thinking skills. By hovering over different options, we are able to more clearly see possible outcomes. We are extending the thinking space to include the board in front of us.

Thinking through doing.

This is common in chess. It's also common in *Scrabble*, in which a player frequently rearranges tiles in order to see new possibilities.

Let's return to our Kanban example.

Even though many cognitive neuroscientists (as well as philosophers and linguists) would likely debate a precise explanation for the appeal of sticky notes as organizational tools, the general conversation would shift the focus away from the stickies themselves to the role of our bodies in this interaction, focusing on how organisms and the human mind organize themselves by interacting with their environment. This perspective, generally described as *embodied cognition*, postulates that thinking and doing are so closely linked as to not be serial processes. We don't think and then do; we think through doing.

But there's more to embodied cognition than simply extending our thinking space. When learning is embodied, it also engages more of our senses, creating stronger neural networks in the brain, likely to increase memory and recall.

Moreover, as we continue to learn about cognition ailments such as autism, ADHD, or sensory processing disorders, we learn about this mind-body connection. With autism for example, I've heard from parents who told me that learning with tangible objects has been shown to be much more effective for kids with certain types of autism.

Our brain is a perceptual organ that relies on the body for sensory input, be it tangible, auditory, visual, spatial, and so on. Nowhere is the value of working with physical objects more understood than in early childhood education, where it is common to use "manipulatives"—tangible learning objects—to aid in the transfer of new knowledge.

MANIPULATIVES IN EDUCATION

My mother loves to recall my first day at Merryhaven Montessori, the elementary school I attended through the sixth grade. I recall her asking, "What did you learn today?" I also remember noticing her curiosity at my response: "I didn't learn anything—we just played!"

Of course "playing" consisted of tracing sandpaper letters, cutting a cheese slice into equal parts, and (my favorite) counting beads; I could count with single beads, rods consisting of 10 beads, the flat squares of 100 beads (or 10 rods, I suppose), and the mammoth of them all: a giant cube of 1000 beads! (See Figure 5-3.) These "manipulatives" are core to the Montessori method of education, and all examples—dating back to the late 1800s—of learning through tangible interactions. Playing is learning, and these "technologies" (in the anthropological sense) make otherwise abstract concepts quite, concrete.

But why is this so?

Jean Piaget, the influential Swiss developmental psychologist, talks about stages of development, and how learning is—at the earliest ages—physical (sensorimotor). As babies, we grasp for things and make sense of the world through our developing senses. At this stage, we learn through physical interactions with our environment. This psychological theory, first proposed in the 1960s, is supported by recent advances in cognitive neuroscience and theories about the mind and body.

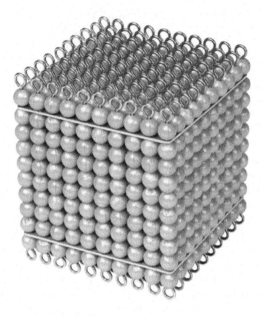

Figure 5-3. Montessori beads[5]

Essentially, we all start off understanding the world only through physical (embodied) interactions. As infants, even before we can see, we are grasping at things and seeking tactile comforts. We learn through our physical interactions with our environment.

Contrast this with the workbooks and photocopied assignments common in most public schools. These pages represent "what" students should be learning, but ignore the cognitive aspects of "how" we learn, namely through interactions. Much of learning is cause and effect. Think of the young child who learns not to touch a hot stove either through her own painful experience or that of a sibling. It is through interactions and experimentation (or observing others) that we begin to recognize patterns and build internal representations of otherwise abstract ideas.

Learning is recognizing or adding to our collection of patterns.

---

5 As featured on Montessori Outlet (*http://www.montessorioutlet.com*)

In this regard, computers can be wonderful tools for exploring possibilities. This is true of young children playing with math concepts, to geneticists looking for patterns in DNA strands. Interactive models and simulations are some of the most effective means of sensemaking. Video games also make for powerful learning tools because they create possibility spaces where players can explore potential outcomes. Stories such as *Ender's Game* (in which young children use virtual games to explore military tactics) are a poignant testimony to the natural risk-taking built into simulations. "What happens if I push this?" "Can we mix it with...?" "Let's change the perspective." Computers make it possible for us to explore possibilities much more quickly in a playful, risk-free manner. In this regard, physical models are crude and limiting. Software, by nature of being virtual, is limited only by what can be conveyed on a screen.

But, what of the mind-body connection? What about the means by which we explore patterns through a mouse or through our fingertips sliding across glass? Could this be improved? What about wood splinters and silky sheets and hot burners and stinky socks and the way some objects want to float in water—could we introduce sensations like these into our interactions? For all the brilliance of virtual screens, they lack the rich sensory associations inherent in the physical world.

VIRTUAL MANIPULATIVES

For me, it was a simple two-word phrase that brought these ideas into collision: "virtual manipulatives." During an interview with Bill Gates, Jessie Woolley-Wilson, CEO of DreamBox, shared a wonderful example of the adaptive learning built in to their educational software. Her company's online learning program will adapt which lesson is recommended next based not only the correctness of an answer, but by "capturing the strategies that students [use] to solve problems, not just that they get it right or wrong." Let's suppose we're both challenged to count out rods and beads totaling 37. As Wooley-Wilson describes it:

> You understand groupings and you recognize 10s, and you very quickly throw across three 10's, and a 5 and two 1's as one group. You don't ask for help, you don't hesitate, your mouse doesn't hesitate over it. You do it immediately, ready for the next. I, on the other hand, am not as confident, and maybe I don't understand grouping strategies. But I do

know my 1's. So I move over 37 single beads. Now, you have 37 and I have 37, and maybe in a traditional learning environment we will both go to the next lesson. But should we?

By observing how a student arrives at an answer, by monitoring movements of the mouse and what students "drag" over, the system can determine if someone has truly mastered the skill(s) needed to move on. This is certainly an inspiring example of adaptive learning, and a step forward toward the holy grail of personalized learning. But, it was the two words that followed that I found jarring: she described this online learning program, using a representation of the familiar counting beads, as virtual manipulatives. Isn't the point of a manipulative that it is tangible? What is a virtual manipulative then, other than an oxymoron?

But this did spark an idea: what if we could take the tangible counting beads, the same kind kids have been playing with for decades, and endow them with the adaptive learning properties Woolley-Wilson describes? How much better might this be for facilitating understanding? And, with the increasing ubiquity of cheap technology (such as RFID tags and the like), is this concept really that far off? Imagine getting all the sensory (and cognitive) benefits of tangible objects, and all the intelligence that comes with "smart" objects.

EMBODIED LEARNING

You might wonder, "Why should we care about tangible computing?" Isn't interacting with our fingers or through devices such as a mouse or touchscreens sufficient? In a world constrained by costs and resources, isn't it preferable to ship interactive software (instead of interactive hardware), that can be easily replicated and doesn't take up physical space? If you look at how media has shifted from vinyl records to cassette tapes to compact discs and finally digital files, isn't this the direction in which everything is headed?

Where learning and understanding is required, I'd argue no. And, a definite no wherever young children are involved. Piaget established four stages of learning (sensorimotor, pre-operational, concrete operational, and formal operational), and argued that children "learn best from concrete [sensorimotor] activities." This work was preceded by American psychologist and philosopher John Dewey, who emphasized firsthand learning experiences. Other child psychologists such as Bruner or Dienne have built on these "constructivist" ideas, creating materials used to facilitate learning. In a review of studies on the use of manipulatives in the classroom, researchers Marilyn Suydam and Jon Higgins concluded that "studies at every grade level support the importance and use of manipulative materials." Taking things one step further, educator and artificial intelligence pioneer Seymour Papert introduced constructionism (not to be confused with constructivism), which holds that learning happens most effectively when people are also active in making tangible objects in the real world.

OK. But what of adults, who've had a chance to internalize most of these concepts? Using Piaget's own model, some might argue that the body is great for lower-level cognitive problems, but not for more abstract or complex topics. This topic is one of some debate, with conversations returning to "enactivism" and the role of our bodies in constructing knowledge. The central question is this: if learning is truly embodied, why or how would that change with age? Various studies continue to reveal this mind-body connection. For example, one study found that saying words such as "lick, pick, and kick" activates the corresponding brain regions associated with the mouth, hand, and foot, respectively. I'd add that these thinking tools extend our thinking, the same way objects such as pen and paper, books, or the handheld calculator (abacus or digital variety—you choose) have allowed us to do things we couldn't do before. Indeed, the more complex the topic, the more necessary it is to use our environment to externalize our thinking.

Moreover, there is indeed a strong and mysterious connection between the brain and the body. We tend to gesture when we're speaking, even if on a phone when no one else can see us. I personally have observed different thinking patterns when standing versus sitting. In computer and retail environments, people talk about "leaning in" versus "leaning back" activities. In high school, I remember being told to look up, if I was unsure of how to answer a question—apparently looking up had, in some study, been shown to aid in the recall of information! Athletes, dancers, actors—all these professions talk about the yet unexplained connections between mind and body.

As magical as the personal computer and touchscreen devices are, there is something lost when we limit interactions to pressing on glass or clicking a button. Our bodies are capable of so much more. We have the capacity to grasp things, sense pressure (tactile or volumetric), identify textures, move our bodies, orient ourselves in space, sense changes in temperature, smell, listen, affect our own brain waves, control our breathing—so many human capabilities not recognized by most digital devices. In this respect, the most popular ways in which we now interact with technology, namely through the tips of our fingers, will someday seem like crude, one-dimensional methods.

Fortunately, the technology to sense these kinds of physical interactions already exists or is being worked on in research labs.

(Near) Future Technology

Let's consider some of the ways that physical and digital technologies are becoming a reality, beginning with technologies and products that are already available to us:

- In 2012, we saw the release of the Leap Motion Controller, a highly sensitive gestural interface, followed closely by Mylo, an armband that accomplishes similar *Minority Report*-style interactions, but using changes in muscles rather than cameras.

- When it comes to touchscreens, Senseg uses electrostatic impulses to create the sensation of different textures. Tactus Technologies takes a different approach, and has "physical buttons that rise up from the touchscreen surface on demand."

- To demonstrate how sensors are weaving themselves into our daily lives, Lumo Back is a sensor band worn around the waist to help improve posture.

- We've got the Ambient umbrella, which alerts you if it will be needed, based on available weather data.

- A recent Kickstarter project aims to make DrumPants (the name says it all!) a reality.

- In the wearables space, we have technologies such as conductive inks, muscle wire, thermochromic pigments, electrotextiles, and light diffusing acrylic (see Figure 5-4). Artists are experimenting with these new technologies, creating things like a quilt that doubles as a heat-map visualization of the stock market (or whatever dynamic data you link to it).

Figure 5-4. A collage of near-future tech (from left to right, top to bottom): Ambient umbrella, DrumPants, the Leap Motion Controller, Lumo Back, Mylo armband, Senseg, and Tactus tablet

If we look a bit further out:

- Sites such as Sparkfun, Parallax, or Seeed offer hundreds of different kinds of sensors (RFID, magnetic, thermal, and so on) and associated hardware with which hobbyists and businesses can tinker. Crowdfunding sites such as Kickstarter have turned many of these hobbyist projects into commercial products.

- Smartphones have a dozen or more different sensors (GPS, accelerometer, and so on) built in to them, making them a lot more "aware" than most personal computers (and ready for the imaginative entrepreneur). And while most of us are focused on the apps we can build on top of these now-ubiquitous smartphone sensors, folks like Chris Harrison, a researcher at Disney Research Labs, have crafted a way to recognize the differences between various kinds of touch—fingertip, knuckle, nail, and pad—using acoustics and touch sensitivity; the *existing* sensors can be exploited to create new forms of interaction.

- Indeed, places such as Disney Research Labs in Pittsburgh or the MIT Media Lab are hotspots for these tangible computing projects. Imagine turning a plant into a touch surface, or a surface that can sense different grips. Look further out, and projects like ZeroN show an object floating in midair, seemingly defying gravity; when moved, information is recorded and you can play back these movements!

- How about a robotic glove covered with sensors and micro-ultrasound machines? Med Sensation is inventing just such a device that would allow the wearer to assess all kinds of vital information not detectable through normal human touch.

There is no shortage of exciting technologies primed to be the next big thing!

We live in a time full of opportunity for imaginative individuals. In our lifetime, we will witness the emergence of more and varied forms of human-computer interaction than ever before. And, if history is any indication (there's generally a 20-year incubation period from invention in a laboratory to commercial product), these changes will happen inside of the next few decades.

I can't help but wonder what happens when ordinary, physical objects, such as the sandpaper letters or counting beads of my youth, become endowed with digital properties? How far off is a future in which ordinary learning becomes endowed with digital capabilities?

THINKING WITH THINGS, TODAY!

Whereas much of this is conjecture, there are a handful of organizations exploring some basic ways to make learning both tangible and digital.

Sifteo Cubes

The most popular of these technologies is, of course, the Sifteo Cubes (see Figure 5-5). Announced at the February 2009 TED conference, these "toy tiles that talk to each other" have opened the doors to new kinds of play and interaction. Each cube, aside from having a touchscreen, has the added ability to interact with other cubes based on its proximity to a neighboring cube, cube configurations, rotation, and even orientation and gesture. In various games, players essentially reposition blocks to create mazes, roll a (virtual) ball into the next block, and do any number of other things accomplished by interacting with these blocks the way you would dominoes. They've been aptly described as "alphabet blocks with an app store." Commenting on what Sifteo Cubes represent, founder Dave Merrill has said "What you can expect to see going forward are physical games that really push in the direction of social play."

Motion Math

Similar to Sifteo Cubes, in that interaction comes through motion, is the fractions game Motion Math (Figure 5-5). This simple app for the iPhone and Android uses the accelerometer to teach fractions. Rather than tapping the correct answer or hitting a submit button, as you would with other math software, players tilt their devices left or right to direct a bouncing ball to the spot correctly matching the identified fraction; you learn fractions using hand-eye coordination and your body (or at least your forearm). And, rather than an "incorrect" response, the feedback loop of a bouncing ball allows you to playfully guide your ball to the correct spot.

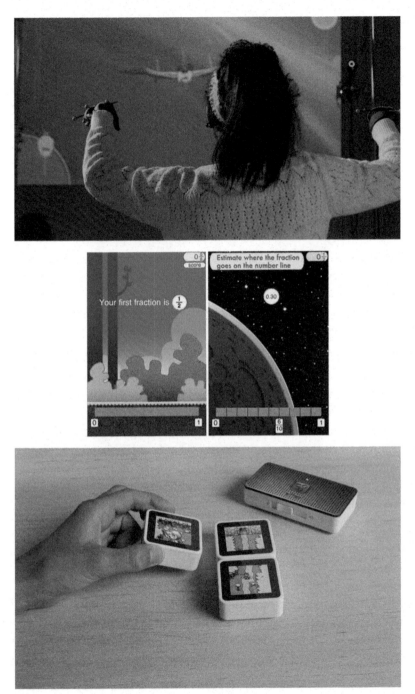

Figure 5-5. Edu tech (from top to bottom): GameDesk's Areo, the Motion Math app, and Sifteo Cubes

GameDesk

As exciting as Sifteo and Motion Math are, some of the best examples of whole body learning with technology would be the learning games developed by GameDesk. Take Aero, as an example. Codesigned with Bill Nye the Science Guy, Aero teachers sixth graders fundamental principles in physics and aerodynamics. How? According to GameDesk founder Lucient Vattel:

> In this game, you outstretch your arms and you become a bird. It's an accurate simulation of bird flight. And through that you get to understand the vectors: gravity, lift, drag, thrust. These concepts are not normally taught at the sixth grade level...

Vattel goes on to add that "a game can allow the concepts to be visualized, experienced..." And this is what is remarkable: that students are *experiencing* learning, with their entire body and having a blast while they're at it—who doesn't want to transform into a bird and fly, if only in a simulation?

GameDesk also works with other organizations that are exploring similar approaches to learning. One of those organizations is SMALLab Learning, which has a specific focus on creating embodied learning environments. SMALLab uses motion-capture technology to track students' movements and overlay this activity with graphs and equations that represent their motions in real time. In a lesson on centripetal force, students swing an object tethered to a rope while a digital projection on the ground explains the different forces at play. Students can "see" and experience scientific principles. "They feel it, they enact it," says David Birchfield, co-founder of SMALLab Learning.

The technology in these examples is quite simple—for Aero a Wiimote is hidden inside each of the wings—but the effect is dramatic. Various studies by SMALLab on the effectiveness of this kind of embodied learning show a sharp increase as evidenced by pre-, mid-, and post-test outcomes for two different control groups.

Timeless Design Principles?

Technology will change, which is why I've done little more here than catalog a handful of exciting advancements. What won't change, and is needed, are principles for designing things with which to think. For this, I take an ethnographer's definition of technology, focusing on the effect of these artifacts on a culture. Based on my work as an educator and designer, I propose the following principles for designing learning objects.

A good learning object:

Encourages playful interactions

Aside from being fun or enjoyable, playfulness suggests you can play with it, that there is some interactivity. Learning happens through safe, nondestructive interactions, in which experimentation is encouraged. Telling me isn't nearly as effective as letting me "figure it out on my own." Themes of play, discovery, experimentation, and the like are common to all of the learning examples shared here. Sifteo founder Dave Merrill comments that "Like many games, [Sifteo] exercises a part of your brain, but it engages a fun play experience first and foremost."

Supports self-directed learning (SDL)

When learners are allowed to own their learning—determining what to learn, and how to go about filling that gap in their knowledge—they become active participants in the construction of new knowledge. This approach to learning encourages curiosity, helps to develop independent, intrinsically motivated learners, and allows for more engaged learning experiences. Contrary to what is suggested, SDL can be highly social, but agency lies in hands of the learner.

Allows for self-correction

An incorrect choice, whether intended, unintended, or the result of playful interactions should be revealed quickly (in real time if possible) so that learners can observe cause-and-effect relationships. This kind of repeated readjusting creates a tight feedback loop, ultimately leading to pattern recognition.

Makes learning tangible

Nearly everything is experienced with and through our bodies. We learn through physical interactions with the world around us and via our various senses. Recognizing the physicality of learning, and that multimodal learning is certainly preferable, we should strive for manipulatives and environments that encourage embodied learning.

Offers intelligent recommendations

The unique value of digital objects is their ability to record data and respond based on that data. Accordingly, these "endowed objects" should be intelligent, offering instruction or direction based on passively collected data.

Each of these principles is meant to describe a desired quality that is known or believed to bring about noticeable learning gains, compared to other learning materials. So, how might we use these principles? Let's apply these to a few projects, old and new.

CYLINDER BLOCKS: GOOD LEARNING OBJECTS

In many ways, the manipulatives designed by Maria Montessori more than a century ago satisfy nearly all of these principles. Setting aside any kind of inherent intelligence, they are very capable objects.

Consider the cylinder blocks shown in Figure 5-6. You have several cylinders varying in height and/or diameter that fit perfectly into designated holes drilled into each block. One intent is to learn about volume and how the volume of a shallow disc can be the same as that of a narrow rod. Additionally, these cylinder block toys help develop a child's visual discrimination of size and indirectly prepare a child for writing through the handling of the cylinders by their knobs.

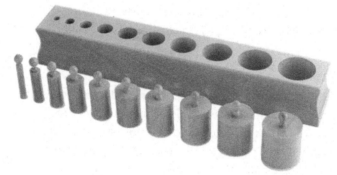

Figure 5-6. Montessori cylinder blocks[6]

How do these blocks hold up?

---

6 As featured on Montessori Outlet (*http://www.montessorioutlet.com*)

As with nearly all of Maria Montessori's manipulative materials, these objects are treated like toys, for children to get off the shelf and play with, satisfying our first principle, playful interactions. Because children are encouraged to discover these items for themselves, and pursue uninterrupted play (learning) time with the object, we can say it satisfies the second principle: self-directed learning. Attempting to place a cylinder into the wrong hole triggers the learning by either not fitting into the hole (too big), or standing too tall and not filling the space; students are able to quickly recognize this fact and move cylinders around until a fitting slot is found, allowing for self-correction, our third principle. As you play with wooden cylinders, using your hands, we can safely say this satisfies our fourth principle: tangibility. As far as intelligence, this is the only missing piece.

With this kind of orientation in mind, I'd like to share a personal project I'm working on (along with a friend much more versed in the technical aspects).

Case Study: An appcessory for early math concepts

When my kids were younger, I played a math game that never ceased to amuse them (or me, at least). The "game," if you can call it that, consisted of grabbing a handful of Teddy Grahams snack crackers (usually off of their plate) and counting them out, one by one. I'd then do simple grouping exercises, moving crackers between two piles or counting by placing them into pairs. The real fun kicked in when we'd play subtraction. "You have seven Teddy Grahams. If Daddy eats one Teddy Graham, how many do you have left?" I think I enjoyed this more than my kids did (to be fair, I'd also make a few additional Teddy Grahams appear out of nowhere, to teach addition). All in all, this was a great way to explore early math concepts such as counting, grouping, subtraction, and addition.

So, how does this game stack up on the design principles? The learning is playful (if not downright mischievous). And the Teddy Grahams are tangible. On these two attributes my game is successful. However, the game doesn't fare so well on the remaining principles: although my presence is not a bad thing, this doesn't encourage self-directed learning, and the correction comes entirely from me and is not discovered. As for the intelligence, it's dependent on my presence.

This left me wondering if this simple game, not all that effective without my presence, could be translated into the kinds of experiences I'm describing here? Could this be improved, to satisfy the identified five design principles?

Here's my concept: what if we combined my pre-math Teddy Graham game with an iPad? As depicted in Figure 5-7, what if we exchanged the crackers for a set of short cylinders (like knobs on a stereo), and what if we figured out how to get these knobs talking to the iPad. Could that work? Is that possible? Even though this could be accomplished with a set of Sifteo blocks, the costs would be prohibitive for such a singular focus, especially where you'd want up to 10 knobs. I'm treating these as single-purpose objects, with the brains offloaded to the device on which they sit (in this case the iPad). Hence, the "appcessory" label.

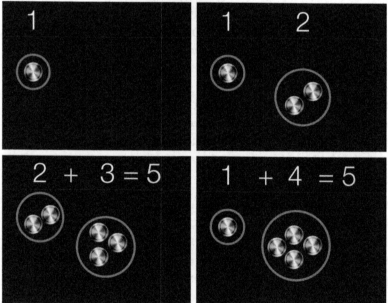

Figure 5-7. Appcessory concept and walkthrough

Here's a walkthrough of how the interactions might work:

- Placing one of these knobs onto the surface of the iPad would produce a glowing ring and the number 1.

- Adding a second knob in close proximity would make this ring larger, encircling both knobs (and changing the number to 2).

- Let's suppose you added a third knob farther away, which would create a new ring with the corresponding number 1.

- Now you have two rings, one totaling 2, the other totaling 1. If you slide the lone knob close to the first two, you'd end up now with one ring, totaling 3. In this manner, and as you start to add more knobs (the iPad supports up to 10, double that of other platforms), you start to learn about grouping.

- In this case, the learning is quite concrete, with the idea of numeric representations being the only abstract concept. You could then switch to an addition mode that would add up the total of however many groups of knobs are on the surface.

I could go on, but you get the idea. By simply placing and moving knobs on a surface the child begins to play with fundamental math concepts. As of this writing, we have proven out the functional technology, but have yet to test this with children. Although the app I'm describing could be built very quickly, my fundamental thesis is that by making these knobs something you can grasp, place, slide, move, remove, and so on, learning will be multimodal and superior to simply dragging flat circles behind glass.

How does this stack up on the five principles?

As with the earlier Teddy Grahams version, it is interactive and tangible. Moving this game to a tablet device allows for self-directed learning and feedback loops in the form of the rings and numerical values. As far as intelligence goes, there is no limit to the kinds of data one could program the iPad to monitor and act upon.

So where might this thinking lead, one day?

Farther Out, a Malleable Future

In the opening scenes of the Superman movie *Man of Steel*, one of the many pieces of Kryptonian technology we see are communication devices whose form and shape is constantly reshaping—a tangible, monochromatic hologram, if you will. Imagine thousands of tiny metal beads moving and reshaping as needed. Even though this makes for a nice bit of sci-fi eye candy, it's also technology that MIT's Tangible Media Group, led by Professor Hiroshi Ishii, is currently exploring. In their own words, this work "explores the 'Tangible Bits' vision to seamlessly couple the dual world of bits and atoms by giving physical form to digital information." They are creating objects (the "tangible bits") that can change shape!

Even though the team's vision of "radical atoms" is still in the realm of the hypothetical, the steps they are taking to get there are no less inspiring. Their latest example of tangible bits is a table that can render 3D content physically, so users can interact with digital information in a tangible way. In their video demonstration, a remote participant in a video conference moves his hands, and in doing so reshapes the surface of a table, rolling a ball around. The technology is at once both awe-inspiring and crude; the wooden pegs moving up and down to define form aren't that unlike the pin art toys we see marketed to children. Having said that, it's easy to imagine something like this improving in fidelity over time, in the same way that the early days of monochromatic 8-bit pixels gave way to retina displays and photorealistic images.

I mention this example because it's easy to diminish the value of tangible interactions when compared to mutability of pixels behind glass; a single device such as a smartphone or tablet can become so many things, if only at the cost of tangibility. Our current thinking says, "Why create more 'stuff' that only serves a single purpose?" And this makes sense. I recall the first app for musicians that I downloaded to my iPhone—a simple metronome. For a few dollars, I was able to download the virtual equivalent of an otherwise very expensive piece of hardware. It dawned on me: if indeed the internal electronics are comparable to those contained in the hardware, there will be a lot of companies threatened by this disruption. This ability to download for free an app that as an object would have cost much more (not to mention add clutter) is a great shift for society.

But...

What if physical objects could reshape themselves in the same way that pixels do? What if one device, or really a blob of beads, could reshape into a nearly infinitesimal number of things? What if the distinctions between bits and atoms become nearly indistinguishable? Can we have physical interactions that can also dynamically change form to be 1,000 different things? Or, at a minimum, can the interface do more than resemble buttons; perhaps it could shape itself into the buttons and switches of last century and then flatten out again into some new form. How does the role of interaction designer change when you're interface is a sculpted, changing thing? So long as we're looking out into possible futures, this kind of thinking isn't implausible, and should set some direction.

Nothing New Under the Sun

While much of this looks to a future in which physical and digital converge, there is one profession that has been exploring this intersection for some time now: museums.

Museums are amazing incubators for what's next in technology. These learning environments have to engage visitors through visuals, interactions, stories, and other means, which often leads to (at least in the modern museum) spaces that are both tangible and take advantage of digital interactions. The self-directed pace that visitors move through an exhibit pressures all museum designers to create experiences that are both informative and entertaining. And, many artists and technologist are eager to, within the stated goals of an exhibit, try new things.

Take for example the Te Papa Tongarewa museum, in Wellington, New Zealand. Because New Zealand is an island formed from the collision of two tectonic plates, you can expect volcanoes, earthquakes, and all things geothermal to get some attention. As visitors move about the space, they are invited to learn about various topics in some amazing and inventive ways. When it comes to discussions of mass and density, there are three bowling ball–sized rocks ready for you to lift; they are all the same in size, but the weight varies greatly. When learning about tectonic shifts, you turn a crank that then displaces two halves of a map (along with sound effects), effectively demonstrating what has happened to New Zealand over thousands of years, and what is likely to happen in the future. Visitors are encouraged to step into a house in which they can experience the simulation of an earthquake. The common denominator between these and dozens more examples is that through a combination of technology and tangible interactions, visitors are encouraged to interact with and construct their own knowledge.

Closing

Novelist William Gibson once commented that future predictions are often guilty of selectively amplifying the observed present. Steam power. Robots. Many of us are being handed a future preoccupied with touchscreens and projections. In "A Brief Rant on the Future of Interaction Design" designer and inventor Bret Victor offers a brilliant critique of this "future behind glass," and reminds us that there are many more forms of interaction of which we have yet to take advantage. As he says, "Why aim for anything less than a dynamic medium that we can see, feel, and manipulate?"

To limit our best imaginings of the future, and the future of learning, to touching a flat surface ignores 1) a body of research into tangible computing, 2) signs of things to come, and 3) centuries of accumulated knowledge about how we—as human creatures—learn best. Whether it's the formal learning of schools or the informal learning required of an information age, we need to actively think about how to best make sense of our world. And all that we know (and are learning) about our bodies and how we come to "know" as human beings cries out for more immersive, tangible forms of interaction. I look forward to a union of sorts, when bits versus atoms will cease to be a meaningful distinction. I look to a future when objects become endowed with digital properties, and digital objects get out from behind the screen. The future is in our grasp.

[6]

Designing for Collaborative Robotics

JEFF FANEUFF

Introduction

Robots are starting to work side by side with people and present profound new challenges for interaction, emotion, culture, and technology frameworks. Collaboration is defined as "the action of working with someone to produce or create something." Robots can only collaborate with us if they are designed for that purpose with safety, communication, and responsiveness in mind. Previously, highly trained technicians and programmers were the only ones allowed to interact with robots that cost hundreds of thousands of dollars. Even technically savvy people were not allowed near the robots when they were running, and safety regulations required the robots to be caged off. New technology is enabling robots to be safer, cheaper, and to work in a wider variety of environments performing new tasks. They are helping doctors, police, fireman, farmers, factory workers, disabled patients, soldiers, cleaners, and warehouse employees. The huge increase in deployed robots means they will interact with millions of untrained and unprepared people.

In the 1970s, computers were locked in big rooms and only computer scientists had the knowledge and access to program them. The general population was not impacted by computers and was even somewhat unaware of their presence. By 2010 computers were in virtually every workplace and in most homes in the developed part of the world. It took computers about 40 years to explode in numbers, and new interaction design frameworks resulted. Bill Gates said during a 2013 hosted Reddit interview that "Robots, pervasive screens, and speech interaction will all change the way we look at computers." Unfortunately, design for human-robot interaction (HRI)[1] is lagging and is currently comparable to the first version of Microsoft Windows or even DOS. People interact with robots via programming languages, command-line prompts, and complex dialogs with dozens of variables that they don't completely understand.

Two robots, Kuka and Fanuc, have made it easier for engineers to program their robots by providing application libraries, operating systems, and control panels.[2] To be fair, these companies are designing with a technical person in mind and are well-respected industry leaders. However, Figure 6-1 and Figure 6-2 demonstrate how complex it can be to train a robot, and make clear one measure of the challenges that must be overcome to enable the average person to do it.

Figure 6-1. The Kuka control panel[3] (© 2014 KUKA)

Today's robots are smart and adaptable, but are nowhere near good enough to completely replace people, and, in fact, only work best when collaborating with them. One example is the da Vinci Surgical System that helps doctors perform surgery but cannot navigate complex procedures independently. This necessary interdependent relationship forces robots and people to work in close concert together. A second example is the manufacturing and packaging tasks done by Baxter from Rethink Robotics and UR5 from Universal Robots. Each of these robots picks and places parts alongside human line workers. A third example is the robotic tractors by John Deere and driverless cars by Audi and BMW.[4] Lastly, we can say the future is here now with some robots taking over

1 http://humanrobotinteraction.org/1-introduction

2 http://www.kuka-robotics.com/en/products/software

3 http://www.kuka-systems.com/usa_nao/en/products/industrial_solutions/arc_welding

4 http://www.cnn.com/2014/01/09/tech/innovation/self-driving-cars-ces

the kitchen and waiting at restaurants. At Robot Restaurant in Harbin in the Heilongjiang province in China, 20 robots deliver food to the table, cook dumplings and noodles, usher diners, and entertain them.[5] Figure 6-3 shows a waiter robot on the job.

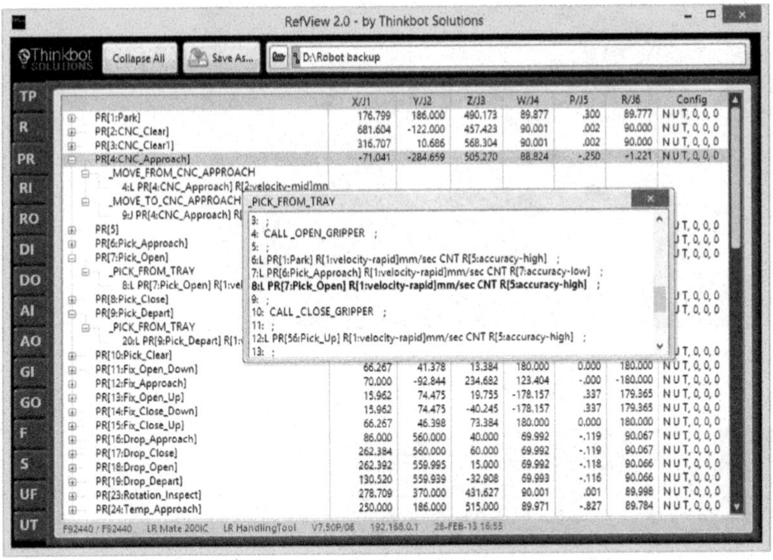

Figure 6-2. Programmer interface for the Fanuc Robot[6] (© 2014 Thinkbot Solutions)

Chef Cui is a noodle-slicing robot developed by Cui Runguan, a Chinese restaurateur. It is now being mass-produced and sold in China at a cost of around $2,000, whereas the average worker would make about $4,700 a year working at a Chinese noodle shop.[7] The robot warehouse in Figure 6-4 looks like a scene from a futuristic movie, but it is real and in the present time.

---

5 *http://dailym.ai/1nTw2x3*

6 *http://www.thinkbotsolutions.com/refview*

7 *http://www.geekosystem.com/meet-chef-cui*

Figure 6-3. A waiter robot delivering dinner in China (© Reuters 2013)

Figure 6-4. The Chef Cui noodle-slicing robot (© 2012 Geekosystem, LLC)

However, some people fear the new experience of interacting with robots and the possibility of them stealing jobs. These negative perceptions might cause some companies to require password protection to prevent people from erasing programs on the robot. Recent books such as *Jobocalypse: The End of Human Jobs and How Robots Will Replace Them* by Ben Way fuel fears already primed by science-fiction movies such as *The Terminator*.

Creative design frameworks are needed to support the coming exponential growth of robots in the workplace. Here are some that we will need to consider:

1. Design for safety needs to be redefined because the new generation of robots can sense their environment and people are required to be close to them.

2. The designed interaction must include social cues to help robots fit in with people in the workplace, learn and master new interaction paradigms, and build initial trust with regard to safety.

3. Designs must enable collaboration instead of following the old model of programming the machine and then leaving it alone.

4. Hardware and software platforms are needed to facilitate learning how people best interact with robots. Robotics designers and developers can then rapidly evolve how the robot presents itself, interacts, and behaves.

The most successful user experience (UX) designers in the robotics field actively engage with the many experts required to build a robot. Mechanical engineers, controls engineers, robotics engineers, computer vision scientists, and software engineers help define what is possible and suggest simplifying abstractions. Product marketing can focus the project goals on the addressable target customer market because it is easy to wander off course with the many possibilities in robotics development.

This chapter describes examples of collaborative robots created for factories, for work in the home, and for medical assistance. These robots are leading the field in practical deployments that will eventually see exponential growth and provide a rich set of designs to explore. There are simply too many robots and applications to cover in this short chapter, but the design concepts presented here can be applied to the broader industry. Discoveries are still being made every day in the rapidly advancing robotics field and the best HRI designs are still to be found. The applications are limitless, so HRI designers will need to build on these concepts to keep pace and continue to amaze the world. People must first have confidence in robot safety before they will accept this leap forward in technology.

Designing Safety Systems for Robots

Accidents with a robot would naturally frighten people and cause investors to worry about lawsuits. One such accident happened in June 2007 at a Swedish factory in which an industrial worker was attempting to perform maintenance tasks on a large excavation robot that he thought was powered down. The robot surprised him by activating, grabbing his head, and eventually breaking four of his ribs.[8] The company was fined, but the prosecutor also laid some of the blame on the worker for not double-checking that the power was indeed cut off. Carelessness is part of the human condition, so the burden of safety has to be mainly with the robot system. The Swedish robot passed regulations, but the interface and safety mechanisms were not enough to prevent injury to the worker.

The standards for safety are being actively updated to address the concerns and enforce compliance. The United States Department of Labor Occupational Safety and Health Administration (OSHA) publish regulatory standards based on the type of robot and application.[9] The American National Standards Institute (ANSI) and Robotic Industries Association (RIA) created a new American national robot safety standard ANSI/RIA R15.06-2012 in May 2013 that is similar to the International ISO 10218:2011 standard.[10]

THE SAFETY FRAMEWORK

Designers should be aware of applicable safety standards that might apply to the product requirements, and they can learn lessons from the experience gained by robots deployed in the field. Awareness, fault tolerance, and explicit communication are the three areas of the robotic safety framework that will replace the need for cages.

Awareness

Awareness can be enhanced by the use of inexpensive computing power and sensors that monitor the work environment. Human proximity detection has been accomplished by using video cameras, sonar, weight sensing mats, lasers, infrared detectors, 3D sensors using structured light, and time-of-flight sensors. Robotic self-awareness of the task being performed, speed, angles, and forces on the moving parts enables it to know if something goes wrong such as bumping into the person next to it. Designers can use any combination of the

---

8 http://www.thelocal.se/19120/20090428/

9 https://www.osha.gov/SLTC/robotics/

10 http://bit.ly/1nTwdbL

aforementioned technologies and strategies, but the best mix has yet to be discovered. Cost, reliability, and the added complexity present tremendous challenges that will be dependent upon the application and customer. The 2007 Swedish factory worker might not have been hurt at all if the robot was aware that he was there.

Erik Nieves, technology director at Yaskawa Motoman, demonstrated a robotic arm slowing down when he entered a work zone defined by a laser measurement system (see Figure 6-5). It is an example of *speed and separation monitoring* for collaborative robots by which the robot slows down if a person enters the danger zone. In speed and separation monitoring, you might use a traditional robot connected to safety-rated controllers/sensors and essentially keep the human and robot separated during full-speed operation and then slow to a speed of 250 mm/s when a worker moves within the collaborative space. The installation can claim compliance with the safety standards if it is certified by an integrator.

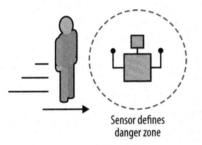

Sensor defines
danger zone

Figure 6-5. Speed and separation monitoring

The approach employed by Rethink Robotics' Baxter and Universal Robots' UR5 is that of *power and force limiting* (see Figure 6-6), and both companies state compliance with the applicable sections of the safety standard. This approach is inherently safe because the robot does not move too fast and does not exert excessive force when bumping into an object or person; thus, the requirement for external sensors is negated. Users are free to approach the robot and only need to perform their own safety assessment to identify and mitigate any potential hazards present in the environment and application.

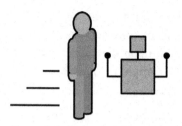

Figure 6-6. Power and force limiting

In the Motoman example, a laser scanner points vertically to create a virtual wall at the front edge of the robot's work area. SICK is one of the more well-known manufacturers of laser scanners and other sensors.[11] Specifications to consider are the range of detection, viewing angle, resolution, sensitivity, and robustness of the interference. Figure 6-7 presents SICK's LMS400 measurement system, which has a range of 0.7 to 3.0 meters and 99 degrees of view.

Figure 6-7. LMS400 laser scanner (© 2013 SICK AG)

Fault tolerance

Fault tolerance becomes even more critical as the number of sensors increases because each one represents a possible point of failure. If a camera stops sending valid video to the human detection algorithm, somebody could wander into a robot arm operating at full speed and be at danger for potentially serious injury. The rule of thumb must dictate the graceful stopping of the robot when sensors are compromised

---

11 *http://www.sick.com/us/en-us/home/products*

in any way. A carpenter would not keep hammering nails if somebody pulled a bag over his head. During the design phase, keep in mind that not all sensors are rated for use in human safety applications, so use caution when selecting them.

A power outage is a special type of failure because a robot's intelligent awareness capabilities disappear when the electricity is terminated. Redundant backup batteries are often too costly and bulky for most applications. Passive resistance is an option to slow the descent of mechanical arms being held up by motors and gears. Strategies are required to accommodate the possibility of heavy objects held in the hand of a robot that loses power. Latching mechanisms are a commonly used method to avoid dropping a heavy chunk of metal on somebody's foot.

Designers have the responsibility to prevent the user from entering in control parameters that could cause dangerous robotic behaviors. For example, fast arm speeds and rapid changes in direction could exceed the gripping force of a robot's hand and result in parts being thrown. A user should be prevented from setting force detection thresholds too high, so the arm will not bump into somebody harshly.

Explicit communication

Explicit communication is necessary because humans can be easily distracted and forget the robot is working next to them. Before starting a task or new motion the robot should signal a warning through sounds, lights, or gestures, which provides an extra layer of safety. Think of the loud beeping signal made by a large truck when it is shifted into reverse. Avoid the perception of unexpected behaviors, which would catch a person off guard and put them into compromised situations. Several robots have practice modes of operations that give people an opportunity to observe the task and learn what to expect. The same lights, graphics, and sounds should be repeatedly used so that the user becomes familiar with the signals that precede the robot's movement. The mode of communication must be suitable for the environment; for example, sound is less effective in a noisy factory, and light might not be seen when the user's gaze is occupied by the task in front of her. Again, the Swedish factory worker would have been safe if the robot actually warned him before engaging into action.

DEVELOPING SOCIAL SKILLS

Human social interaction has many cues that could be adopted by robots to explicitly communicate with their coworkers. Consider how people monitor and calculate the speed of other cars when merging onto a highway or even how we make minute adjustments to our pace when walking into a line of pedestrians. Each driver or pedestrian speeds up or slows based on their observation of the others surrounding them. They will often exchange a gaze and nod to signal their intentions.

There are three design areas to consider when developing social cues for the HRI. Appearance can speed learning and adoption during the crucial first impression by conveying a friendly form that is suitable to the task. People feel more confident in that first impression when the robot acknowledges their proximity and responds to their movements. Body language has the potential to increase communication and create a more effective collaboration between human and robot. Essential trust is built when the robot responds in an obvious manner that the user expects. Design considerations can be categorized into the following three areas.

- Physical appearance

- Acknowledgement of people

- Behavior and body language

Let's take a closer look at each of these areas.

Physical appearance

Physical appearance is a mix of form, contours, color, texture, lights, and expression, all of which play an important role in how a robot is perceived. The Baxter robot from Rethink Robotics, pictured in Figure 6-8, is a factory robot that was designed with all these elements in mind. The humanoid form and smooth contoured features signal this machine is meant to be among people. The abundant LEDs bring it to life and big eyes convey a friendly countenance. The warm red color and smooth texture add to the human feeling and sets Baxter apart from cold metallic machines often found around it on the factory floor. The physical appearance was designed to create the impression that Baxter is a member of the team, just like any other line worker in the factory, and it succeeded beyond expectations. Watching people meet Baxter for the first time is a real treat because they usually express a high level of comfort, wonder, and even joy.

Figure 6-8. Baxter (© 2013 Rethink Robotics)

The Mahru research robot created by Samsung Electronics goes even further than Baxter in mimicking humanoid form with more exact proportions and a round head. Figure 6-9 demonstrates how the bright blue eyes give it a cute appearance similar to toy robots, but the conventional silver and gray body colors are less welcoming.

Figure 6-9. Mahru (© 2013 IEEE Spectrum)[12]

---

12 Mahru, by the Korean Institute of Technology and Samsung Electronics (2007), *http://bit. ly/1xGONXB*.

Figure 6-10 presents FRIDA[13] (Flexible Robot Industrial Dual Arm) from ABB. This robot uses soft colors and smooth contours but does not include a head. This limits the robot's ability to provide feedback and diminishes its attempt at a friendly humanoid form. FRIDA is a very capable robot, and its creators made a design choice to sacrifice physical appearance for a reduction in cost. The ergonomics of the design allow an average-sized person to interact with FRIDA for setup and programming.

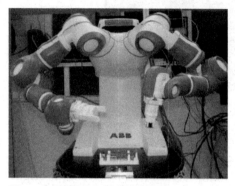

Figure 6-10. FRIDA (© 2013 ABB)

There will always be cost constraints during the design process, so designers will need to justify the added benefits of appearance. The appearance and form are often decided early in development and designers must then turn to the challenge of communication that begins with the robot being aware that somebody is nearby.

Acknowledgement of people

A human workmate's confidence in a robot will increase if the robot acknowledges her presence. It requires addressing two separate design challenges: detection and then communication. Many different sensors can detect the presence of a person, such as cameras, lasers, infrared, sonar, capacitive, time-of-flight, and pressure sensitive resistors. The choice of sensors to employ depends on the application, environment, and cost. Decisions on what combination of sensors to use are driven by cost, precision, and environment. Table 6-1 provides a high-level description of the trade-offs.

---

13 *http://bit.ly/1CJ3yJo*

TABLE 6-1. Sensors and use factors

SENSOR	PRECISION	CHALLENGE	COST
Lasers (LIDAR)*	Very high	Limited reflections	Very high
3D Kinect	High	Noise interference	High
3D via stereo 2D	High	Combine multiple views	High
2D camera	High	Position and lighting	Medium
Sonar	Medium	Noise interference	Low
Infrared	Medium	False detection	Low
Weight pressure mat	Low	Stationary	Low

* Light Detection and Ranging, *http://www.lidar.com/*

The Multisense-S7 camera shown in Figure 6-11 is an example of a 3D sensor that combines multiple 2D views and color processing, but each unit costs more than a thousand dollars.

Figure 6-11. Multisense-S7, 3D sensor[14] (© 2013 Carnegie Robotics LLC)

A robot's responses to human presence are dictated by its physical platform, but they can include sounds, speech, lights, gaze, head nods, change in speed, and gestures. Some effective acknowledgements include slowing down or stopping movement, gazing in the direction of the person, and head nods, which are common social cues between people. Lights are more startling and typically indicate a status specific to the particular robot. Beeping sounds might not be heard in a noisy environment, but they can be appropriate for urgent situations if loud enough. If the robot speaks, it should also meet the expectation that it can understand human speech. Gestures require movements from a

14 *http://carnegierobotics.com/multisense-s7/*

part of the robot that is not occupied in an actual task, which might not always be the case. Anything beyond a simple wave is subject to interpretation and thus might not be clear.

The Baxter robot communicates a range of social cues via common facial expressions (look ahead to Figure 6-13). Notice how clearly the message is conveyed by using eyes and eyebrows. Excluding a mouth does not sacrifice clarity of communication and avoids any false implication that the robot can speak. This is further evidence that robots communicate better when they have heads.[15, 16]

Behavioral cues and body language

This area goes beyond just acknowledging the proximity of people. Visible cues that consistently precede expected behaviors build trust and cadence between a person and a collaborative robot. For example, the robot's head and eyes can look at an object before picking it up and then look where it intends to place it. A mobile robot should look where it intends to travel and signal a change in direction before turning. Figure 6-12 shows how the WorkerBot from pi4 in Germany uses a smile to indicate things are running fine and occasionally shifts its eyes to the objects it is manipulating.[17]

Figure 6-13 depicts the range of Baxter's expressions, which are derived from a long history of research at MIT and other institutions.[18] Experimental research robots such as Kismet helped ground the theory in real human experiences, which have been proven further by Baxter.

Baxter's behavioral programming enables it to do intelligent things. For example if an object is pulled from its hand, Baxter will go back to get another one instead of trying to do a placement with an empty hand. Baxter can also detect when there are no more objects to pick from a pile and wait for more material. A simple bump into Baxter's arm or grabbing the cuff of its arm will cause the arms to stop. These intuitive cues make it possible for natural communication and interaction to occur with people.

15 *http://robohub.org/ajung-moon-on-do-robots-need-heads/*

16 *http://robohub.org/mark-stephen-meadows-on-do-robots-need-heads/*

17 *http://www.pi4.de/english/products/pi4-workerbot.html*

18 *http://www.ai.mit.edu/projects/sociable/facial-expression.html*

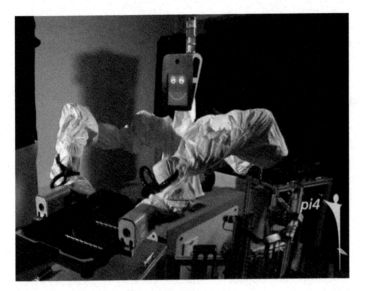

Figure 6-12. WorkerBot[19] (© 2013 pi4)

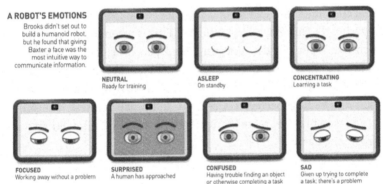

Figure 6-13. Baxter's expressions (© 2013 Rethink Robotics)

Robots that work in the home require even more behavioral cues because they operate in a less structured environment and have informal interactions that can include children. Social cues are also important to establishing trust and rapport with the humans around it. The Hoaloha robot is designed to assist the elderly and disabled in their

19 http://www.pi4.de/typo3temp/pics/93b831a88d.jpg

homes. It uses facial expressions and body posture to make its intentions known.[20] Unfortunately, as of this writing there are no pictures available of the Hoaloha because it is still under development.[21]

Humanlike Robots

Toyota's Robina incorporates head tilt and hand gestures when it speaks, which affords much richer communication. Proximity sensors enable Robina to politely allow others to pass before it while it's moving. Robina is one of the Toyota's Partner Robots that can help provide medical and nursing care or perform housework. It is able to think and move for itself, carry objects, and converse with people.[22]

PAL Robotics REEM-C[23] robot, shown in Figure 6-14, has similar capabilities to Robina, but it can also walk. REEM-C has speech recognition and text-to-speech support for multiple languages. Designers will notice the friendly rounded edges with a simple black and white color pattern.

When creating humanoid robots, designers need to be cautious to avoid triggering the *uncanny valley*[24] effect.[25] This is when the robot looks so much like a person, it's "uncanny," and people usually become very uncomfortable around it because of unknown expectations. The graph depicted in Figure 6-15, which was first shown by Masahiro Mori, describes the full spectrum of reaction to human likeness. For example, a person may feel more familiarity with a stuffed animal than with a prosthetic hand.

---

20 http://spectrum.ieee.org/img/hoa_concept-1378276598979.jpg

21 http://www.hoaloharobotics.com

22 http://www.toyota-global.com/innovation/partner_robot/family_2.html#h201

23 http://www.pal-robotics.com/en/robots

24 The term was coined by Masahiro Mori as Bukimi no Tani Genshō in 1970.

25 MacDorman, K.F. (2005). Androids as an experimental apparatus: why is there an uncanny valley and can we exploit it? CogSci-2005 Workshop: Toward Social Mechanisms of Android Science, 106–118.

Figure 6-14. The REEM-C from PAL Robotics (© 2013 PAL Robotics)

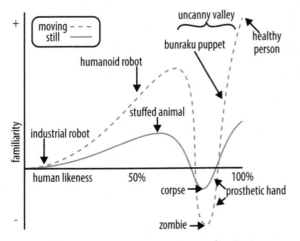

Figure 6-15. Plot of human likeness versus familiarity

Some robots are pushing past the uncanny valley effect as illustrated in Figures 6-16, 6-17, and 6-18, in which human likeness and familiarity are reaching new heights. The HRP-4C[26] is a feminine-looking humanoid robot, created by Japan's National Institute of Advanced Industrial Science and Technology (AIST), which has a friendly and familiar appearance. The Repliee Q2 is another very humanlike robot being tested for different social interactions at the Intelligent Robotics Laboratory at Osaka University (*http://bit.ly/1xGQJiS*).

Figure 6-16. A Bunraku puppet

Figure 6-17. The HRP-4C[27]

---

26 *http://www.aist.go.jp/aist_e/latest_research/2009/20090513/20090513.html*

27 Courtesy of AIST, *http://www.aist.go.jp*.

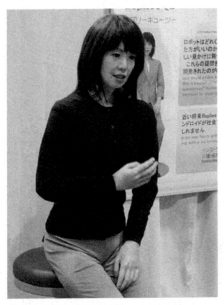

Figure 6-18. Repliee Q2

The uncanny valley is not a simple pass/fail test, and the framework lacks an accurate system to measure the effects.[28] Consistency in facial representation is another important factor to consider when designing humanlike robots. For example, you should avoid glowing computer eyes in a face with realistic flesh tones.

Toyota's Human Support Robot (HSR)[29] is functional and compact. HSR is similar in form to the UBR-1 from Unbounded Robotics pictured in Figure 6-19. The single arm can pick up a dropped remote control or other household objects. The computer screen on the head offers a rich display while the robot can be instructed from common mobile computing devices that are touchscreen enabled such as smartphones, tablets, or laptops. Users can command it by using a speech interface and it responds by voice, as well.

28 http://www.popularmechanics.com/technology/engineering/robots/4343054
29 http://www.toyota-global.com/innovation/partner_robot/family_2.html

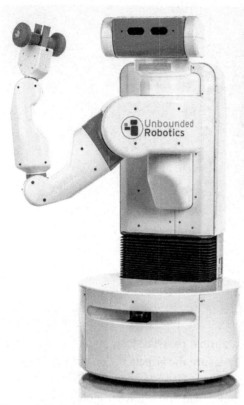

Figure 6-19. Unbounded Robotics' UBR-1 (© 2013 Unbounded Robotics)

The HSR could possibly collaborate with people to carry out tasks such as carrying a basket of laundry that a person had folded. It could fetch the newspaper, medicines, or a book—without complaining.

Human-Robot Collaboration

Robots can work tirelessly at well-defined repetitive tasks, apply brute strength, provide a steady hand, and perform tasks with submillimeter accuracy. Human contextual awareness, reasoning, memory, and decision-making abilities far surpass even the most advanced robots. Emerging technologies will enable human-robot collaboration to do things neither could accomplish alone but only if designers create the right communication channels. "The future challenge for designers is to find a natural way for robots and people to understand what each other is going to do and change their behaviors accordingly," said Rodney Brooks, the founder of both iRobot and Rethink Robotics.

DEVELOPING REAL-WORLD COLLABORATION SOLUTIONS

Design principles based on the latest robotics research and development are an excellent place to start. It is important to trust data from field deployments much more than experiments done in artificial environments with limited sample sizes. The four areas in the list that follows are the foundation of several deployed solutions helping people in real world situations:

1. Fit to task and customizable

2. Consistent behavior and fluid motion

3. Natural feedback and adaptive behavior

4. Environmental awareness

Fit to task and customization

This is one of the first things to consider in general robot design that naturally has implications on the human-robot interaction. iRobot's Roomba 880[30] is a perfect example of a robot designed for a specific task. They rejected initial suggestions of a humanoid robot pushing around a conventional vacuum cleaner. As is evident in Figure 6-20, the flat, round design makes it hard to image the Roomba doing anything but clean floors. The large button on top simply says "Clean."

Figure 6-20. The Roomba 880 (© 2013 iRobot)

---

30 http://www.irobot.com/en/us/learn/home/roomba.aspx

Robot arms with grippers are a fit for tasks that require it to pick things up and manipulate them. The Kuka LWR 5 in Figure 6-21 is an example of a pick-and-place capable robot[31] that is used for tasks in a factory for lightweight industrial duty. For example, it can position a piece over a pin to precisely assemble two parts. The company describes the LWR 5 as follows on its website: "Relatively slim and low-weighted, it can work in tight spaces and it can be integrated on assembly lines quite easily. It is the first lightweight robot that can handle a payload of over 10 kg. Because it is presented as a collaborative robot, no fences are needed for its implementation."[32] Custom grippers give these robots the ability to grasp objects of different shapes and sizes. Designing this type of easy extensibility is important because technology has not provided robots with a universally dexterous hand yet. Customization also provides a sense of ownership and pride to customers.

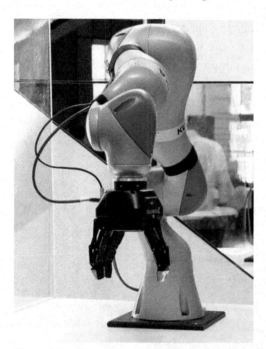

Figure 6-21. The KUKA LWR 5 (© 2013 KUKA Roboter GmbH)

---

31 http://blog.robotiq.com/bid/65588/Collaborative-Robot-Series-KUKA-s-New-IIWA-LWR-5
32 http://blog.robotiq.com/bid/65588/Collaborative-Robot-Series-KUKA-s-New-IIWA-LWR-5

Consistent behavior and fluid motion

Smooth motion conveys a sense of predictability, safety, and intelligence in the robot. Sudden changes in direction, shaking, or erratic motion makes people feel apprehensive and gives the appearance that the robot is out of control. The UR5 from Universal Robots is an example of fast, smooth motions with submillimeter accuracy.[33] Fluid motion is achieved by paying attention to overall system design that incorporates selection of motors, gears, mechanical design, and controls algorithms, which typically increases the total cost substantially.

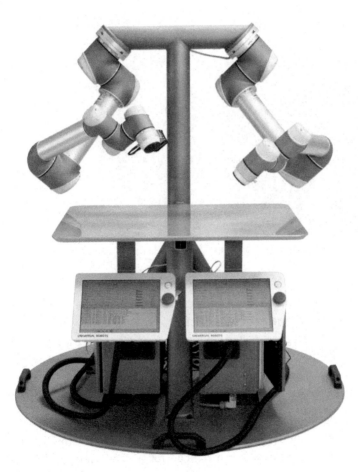

Figure 6-22. UR5 © 2013 Universal Robots

---

33 *http://www.universal-robots.dk/DK/Presse/Multimedia/Videos.aspx*

Natural feedback and adaptive behavior

This is where the real connection is made between human and robot. Rethink Robotics' Baxter (Figure 6-23) is a forerunner in collaboration with its force sensing to detect when a human bumps into it or grabs the cuff on its wrist. Haptic feedback tells the user where the arms can be trained without colliding into any part of the robot. The robot also gazes at a location that it intends to move toward, so people can anticipate its next move. Baxter is trained by demonstration, which is a natural way that people teach each other a new task.

Figure 6-23. Getting up close and personal with Baxter (© 2013 Rethink Robotics)

The point about human-robot communication is even more compelling when you consider the driverless car from Google, which you can see in Figure 6-24. Imagine you are stopped in your car and see a driverless Google car stopped at the opposite side of an intersection. When do you move forward? The safest decision is to wait for the Google car to go first because you have no idea what it will do next.[34]

Speech recognition is a viable interface for in-home assistive robots because their mobility gives them the capability to overcome the big challenge of microphone acoustics. The robot can bring the microphone closer to the talker, which increases the strength of the received

---

34 *http://on.wsj.com/1nTxwr9*

signal. The robot can also directionally point the microphone at the person speaking to focus on their speech and ignore noises coming from other parts of the room. The Kompai robot from Robosoft shown in Figure 6-25 uses speech recognition as its main interface.[35]

Figure 6-24. The Google driverless car © 2013 Google

Figure 6-25. Robosoft's Kompai (© 2013 Robosoft)

---

35 *http://bit.ly/1xGSdcS*

The da Vinci Surgical System[36] depicted in Figure 6-26 is a tremendous example of collaborative robotics. On a personal yet related note, my father-in-law underwent surgery to remove a cancerous tumor on the base of his tongue. The procedure was performed by a doctor at the Boston Medical Center using the da Vinci system. The da Vinci system made it possible for the doctor to access the base of my father-in-law's tongue without needing to break his jaw open. The robot gave visibility and provided precise movement to minimize damage and recovery time. The human in this collaboration (the doctor) observed data, made decisions, and controlled the motions.

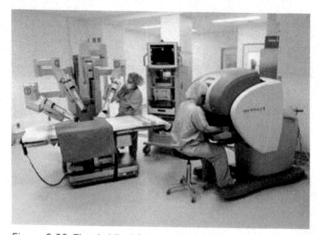

Figure 6-26. The da Vinci Surgical System (© 2013 Intuitive Surgical, Inc.)

Environmental awareness

The Robonaut[37] shown in Figure 6-27 is a joint development of NASA and General Motors. It can detect when somebody is reaching for an object in its grasp and release the object when the person tugs it. Robotnaut stops when somebody puts his hand in the way of its motion and continues when the hand is removed.

---

36 http://www.davincisurgery.com/
37 http://robonaut.jsc.nasa.gov/default.asp

Figure 6-27. Robonaut, developed by NASA and GM (courtesy of GM and NASA and Marty Linn)

Figure 6-28. Robonaut demonstrating a familiar human gesture (courtesy of GM and NASA and Marty Linn)

Testing Designs by Using Robotics Platforms

Robots and people exist in the physical world, so simulations are insufficient tools for evaluating user experience and performance. The robot's ability to complete tasks well depends on the human setting up the task, teaching or programming the instructions, and collaborating interactions. A robotics platform consists of hardware, software, programmability, tools, and interchangeable parts with which it can carry out multiple different tasks. Research robots such as the PR2, Baxter, and Robonaut are examples of these types of robotics platforms.

Hardware and software platforms are required for testing designs in real environments with target users. Flexibility and extendibility are important because it takes more than two years to build a new robot, given the complexity that's involved. Robotics platforms must integrate all aspects of emerging technologies in the real-world environment to be effective. Researchers continue to explore sensors, multiple degrees of freedom arms, specialized hands, artificial intelligence, and advanced mechanical structures. The applications and user experience is where all these things come together to create a useful and astonishing robot.

Criteria to consider when choosing a robotics platform for design research include the following:

1. Capabilities

2. Integrated hardware and software

3. Programmable software interfaces

4. The ability to add customer grippers, sensors, and displays

5. Use of open standards to enable switching robots and reusing software

6. Cost

Table 6-2 lists the range of potential robot capabilities.

Low-cost robotics platforms are very much in need because previous models, such as the PR2 from Willow Garage (see Figure 6-29), used to cost in excess of $300,000. Although it is no longer manufactured,[38] the PR2 is still widely used for research. In one experiment it was able to demonstrate how difficult it is for a robot to perform the seemingly simple task of folding a towel, as illustrated in Figure 6-30. Folding the towel was indeed an accomplishment even it if it took the robot 25 minutes to achieve. Low-cost robots do not need to completely replace human workers; instead, they can help people complete tasks faster and not tire as easily. The platforms would enable researchers to explore interactions that maximize this collaborative productivity.

---

38 *http://www.willowgarage.com/pages/pr2/order*

TABLE 6-2. Possible robot capabilities

Arm degrees of freedom, weight, and speed	Sensors: sonar, radar, infrared, laser
Grippers and degrees of freedom	Contextual awareness
Mobility	Artificial intelligence, rules, pattern matching, and so on
Computer vision	Networked communication to other local devices, sensors, or other robots
Cameras and resolution	Networked communication to remote devices—potentially on other side of the planet
Audible cues	Head display with motion
Speech recognition	
Collision/force detection	
Sense position of itself and objects	
Access to data and quickly searching	

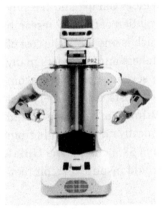

Figure 6-29. The PR2 from Willow Garage (© 2013 Willow Garage)

Tasks that have a large number of uncontrolled variables are most difficult for robots to perform. The size and flexibility of the towel along with the influence of air on its shape make it a difficult object to handle in a repeatable fashion.

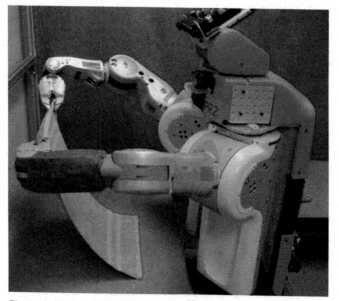

Figure 6-30. The PR2 folding a towel[39] (© 2013 Willow Garage)

Unbounded Robotics[40] is a spinoff from Willow Garage and recently introduced the UBR-1 (Figure 6-31) as the evolution of the PR2 research robot. The price of the UBR-1 is $35,000, which is one-tenth the cost of the PR2.[41] The rich feature set offers researchers and designers many options to explore. The robot has a single seven-degrees-of-freedom arm, mobile base, 2D laser scanner to detect obstacles, a battery that lasts more than 5 hours, charging dock, a PrimeSense 3D sensor, and 180 degrees of head movement. It can dynamically raise its height from a minimum of 38 inches up to a maximum of 58 inches.[42] The UBR-1 is only a research robot at this point, but it could inspire new commercial applications in the home or factory.

39 *http://bit.ly/ZBRlIw*

40 *http://unboundedrobotics.com/press/*

41 *http://www.engadget.com/2013/10/21/unbounded-robotics-ubr-1-robot/*

42 *http://unboundedrobotics.com/ubr-1/specification/*

Figure 6-31. Unbounded Robotics' UBR-1 research robot (© 2013 Unbounded Robotics)

EVALUATING DESIGNS BY USING REAL PLATFORMS

During my time at Rethink Robotics,[43] using the real Baxter robot platform was essential for evaluating designs to visually recognize an object and then pick it up from a moving conveyor. The original design was for the user to position the arm with a camera over the object and then press a button to capture the image. Clever visual feedback from a bounding box around the image informed the user when the arm was in a position where the object could be recognized. This approach was simple, but several problems were revealed when attempting to train the robot for real tasks:

---

43 *http://www.rethinkrobotics.com/*

- The visual background when learning objects should be similar to the background for detection while performing a task.

- The rotation of the wrist changed the view, which impacted accuracy.

- Lighting impacted detection results.

- The height of the camera needed to be different depending on the object and environment.

- Grippers sometimes partially occluded the object.

As a result of these difficulties, only a few people acquired the skills and knowledge to make visual object training and recognition work well for our demonstrations. Armed with information from user studies on the fully functional robot, we redesigned the entire object training experience.[44] The user put the object in the robot's gripper at the desired pick location and then pressed the Learn button. The robot released the object and took several pictures while slowly raising the arm. An algorithm next filtered the best images onto a list for the user to choose the best among them. Background, wrist rotation, lighting, height of arm relative to object, and grippers were all accounted for in the visual object learning.

Another example of the need to verify behaviors with the physical world is the representation of obstacles. The default trajectory planning will work fine in simulation and move the arm correctly on the real robot. However, the robot needs to be trained with paths and waypoints to avoid obstacles. Training by demonstration on a live robot is much easier than programming all the various joint positions and entering coordinates for obstacles.

Rethink Robotics offers a research and development version of the Baxter Robot (see Figure 6-32) with an extendible software development kit for $22,000. It builds on the open source industry standard Robot Operating System (ROS) and the Universal Robot Description File (URDF), which is also used by the PR2 robot.

---

44 *Object Learning Design* by Bruce Blumberg, Yuri Ivanov, and Noelle Dye

Figure 6-32. The research and development version of Baxter[45] (© 2013 Rethink Robotics)

MICROSOFT ROBOTICS DEVELOPER STUDIO

Microsoft released Robotics Developer Studio in 2007 to build on the strengths of its Windows operating system and Visual Studio software development tools. However, its environment failed to gain wide adoption over the past six years because it lacked accessible hardware platforms to complement the software. The Microsoft robotics platform got a boost with the Kinect 3D sensor that was developed in 2010 for the Xbox game platform because it was also a great sensor to help robots be more aware of their surrounding environments. Microsoft did publish a reference hardware design to use with its software tools and partnered with Parallax to create a hardware kit, depicted in Figure 6-33.[46]

The Microsoft robotics software platform[47] is good for running simulations, using the Parallax robot for mobility, and doing research with the Kinect sensor. One example from Microsoft research is a way to map force sensing and haptic feedback to an on-screen image in which the haptic feedback is accomplished by motors moving the entire display. However, Microsoft has not announced anything new in robotics for over a year and it might switch to individual technologies.

45 http://www.rethinkrobotics.com/products/buy-baxter/buy-baxter-research-robot

46 http://www.parallax.com/robots/robots-overview

47 http://www.microsoft.com/robotics/

Figure 6-33. The PC Robot (© 2013 Parallax)

Every year, more robotics platforms are emerging that are being used in hundreds of universities and many companies. "Presently, there are over 1,000 robotics companies around the world," notes Frank Tobe of The Robot Report.[48] Rodney Brooks said, "When I look out to the future, I can't imagine a world, 500 years from now, in which we don't have robots everywhere."

Future Challenges for Robots Helping People

Dr. Tessa Lau[49] gave a talk recently at MIT Media Lab titled "End-User Programming Robots,"[50] which described the challenges for everyday people to train a robot to perform a task.[51] "From an HCI researcher's perspective, robotics is a very rich field: incredibly complex systems which are sorely in need of good design and usable interfaces. Because of their complexity, merely using robots requires precise specification of what they should do: in short, programming. Yet how can we expect mere mortals to program robots?"[52]

Here are the three approaches she suggested to meet this challenge:

48 http://www.wfs.org/blogs/james-lee/investing-future-robotics

49 Dr. Tessa Lau is chief robot whisperer and cofounder at Savioke, where she is creating a new generation of usable robots for the service industry. Previously, Dr. Lau was a research scientist at Willow Garage.

50 http://media.mit.edu/events/2013/11/22/tessa-lau-media-lab

51 http://tlau.org/research

52 http://www.savioke.com/blog/2014/1/21/tessa-lau-gives-talk-at-mit-media-lab

1. Use a graphical language instead of computer programming

2. Physically interact with the robot by demonstrating the task

3. Simplify the environment and task

A graphic language can be made more intuitive by using familiar pictures and concepts. Explicitly showing the robot what to do by physically interacting with it comes natural to people who see a robot for the first time, if that robot is designed with the appropriate hints.

Emerging technology for gesture-based commands used for the Xbox and Wii video game platforms are worth exploring for HRIs. Combining voice commands and gestures to instruct the robot could be another rich area of advancement for designers to tackle in the future. Imagine being able to tell your personal assistant robot to "get me the red book over there," and gesture to where it is, and the robot responds accordingly.

The details of the real world show up in robot logic as special cases in their underlying programming, which requires user input to make the correct decisions. The burden and complexity placed on the user increase dramatically as more input is demanded from them. The number of decisions a robot must make to "get the notebook from my room" when the room is messy versus clean and orderly, as show in Figure 6-34. A robot's ability to independently reason about an unstructured world is not much better than a two-year-old child, and about as difficult to instruct. A valid approach toward making the HRI easier to use is to simplify the environment in which it is required to operate.

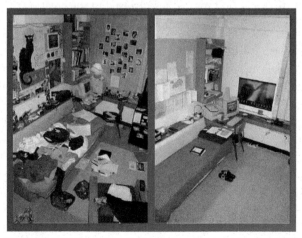

Figure 6-34. Messy versus clean room: even a human would find it hard to make sense of the cluttered environment

What if the book is orange or not there? Informative failure modes are another broad area of improvement for the user experience with robots. By today's standards the robot could look for the book, come back empty handed, and blankly stare at you. For how long should it search for the book before giving up? Is it OK to move obstacles out of the way? Should it just grab any orange book? Robots will need innovative designs to communicate and resolve failure conditions to effectively collaborate in our messy human world.

Conclusion

A robotic arm from Universal Robotics rang the closing bell of the Nasdaq stock exchange on November 12, 2013. This action was a symbolic gesture that coincided with the launch of a stock index, Robo-Stox, comprised of companies working on robotics and automation technologies.[53] Big companies such as Amazon, Apple, and Google are investing billions into robotics, which adds even more momentum to its rising popularity.[54] Apple is interested in having robots manufacture their iPhone and other devices. Apple acquired 3D sensor maker Primesense. Amazon purchased Kiva Systems, which makes mobile robots that move products in its warehouses. Google bolstered its San Francisco robotics division by acquiring seven robotics companies, including Redwood Robotics, Holomni, and Industrial Perception. Sales of medical robots increased by 20 percent worldwide in 2012.[55] Siemens, Mazor Robotics,[56] and other large companies are quickly following the lead of Intuitive Surgical's da Vinci Surgical System. As of this writing, there are over 2,000 companies involved in the creation of robots,[57] so they will arrive in overwhelming numbers in coming years!

Emerging technologies are making robots faster, cheaper, and more capable. Designers like you have the opportunity to make our robotics experience truly collaborative and satisfying.

---

53 *http://bit.ly/1nTzbwP*

54 *http://robohub.org/apple-amazon-and-now-google-its-a-pretty-exciting-day-for-robotics/*

55 *http://www.worldrobotics.org/index.php?id=home&news_id=268*

56 *http://mazorrobotics.com/*

57 *http://www.therobotreport.com/index.php/site/TRR-Global-Map/*

Robotics Resources

- Business of Robotics—*http://thebusinessofrobotics.com*
- Human-Robot Interaction (HRI)—*http://humanrobotinteraction.org*
- Robobusiness Conferences—*http://www.robobusiness.com*
- Robohub—*http://robohub.org*
- The Robot Report—*http://www.therobotreport.com*
- Robotics Online—*http://www.robotics.org*
- Social Robots Project—*http://www.cs.cmu.edu/~social*
- World Robotics—*http://www.worldrobotics.org*

Design Takes on New Dimensions: Evolving Visualization Approaches for Neuroscience and Cosmology

HUNTER WHITNEY

The Brain Is Wider Than the Sky

The Brain—is wider than the Sky—
For—put them side by side—
The one the other will contain
With ease—and You—beside—
—EMILY DICKINSON, FROM *THE BRAIN IS WIDER THAN THE SKY*

The ability to perceive and understand the words you're currently reading is made possible by signals flowing across synaptic junctions in your brain. In total, you have about 100 *trillion* of these synapses—a figure that exceeds all of the stars in the Milky Way galaxy. For most of us, that's just an interesting statistic; for neuroscientists and cosmologists, those kinds of numbers are a part of their work environment. Both fields share other commonalities, as well. Whether it's the activity patterns among nerve cells or the interactions of stars and black holes, both disciplines explore physical objects and systems that don't easily lend themselves to direct observation and experimentation.

Increasingly, interactive visualizations[1] such as that shown in Figure 7-1 can help people involved in these areas explore, analyze, and test the unimaginable.

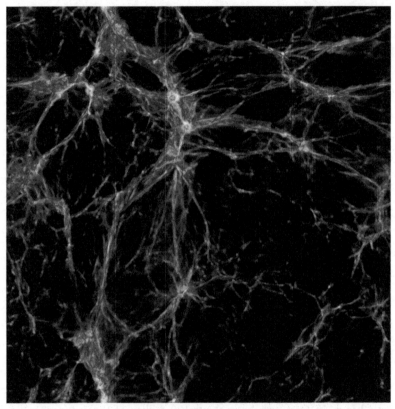

Figure 7-1. A cosmic web of galaxies in a region of space 140 million light years across from a cosmological simulation run on NICS Kraken (courtesy Britton Smith)

Within the past few years, emerging technologies are starting to redefine what can be seen, simulated, and explored in both neuroscience and cosmology. Whether it's mapping the neural circuitry that drives

---

1 There are many definitions and labels for visualizations of various kinds. Here's one version that's compact but encompassing and captures the meaning intended for this chapter:

"The use of computer-generated, interactive, visual representations of data to amplify cognition."

—Card, Mackinlay, and Shneiderman. *Readings in Information Visualization Using Vision to Think.* Morgan Kaufmann, 1999.

thought or modeling the formation of galaxies, new tools are making it possible to see otherwise hidden processes at work. Advances in low-cost, high-performance computing hardware, including graphical processing units (GPUs), combined with distributed and parallel computing software are providing the vehicles and fuel propelling new design forward.

Meaningful visualizations depend on far more than just good visual design. They are the result of a process that integrates ideas and expertise from many different sources. To exemplify that point, the following three sections look at visualizations from a range of angles. The first section presents some visual and interaction design approaches, including using 2D and 3D representations. The second section examines the creation of simulations and models. The third explores the need for cross-disciplinary collaborations and drawing design inspiration from unexpected sources. This chapter includes examples showing the range of considerations that go into a display.

Section 1: An Expanding Palette for Visualization

You are about to enter another dimension. A dimension not only of sight and sound, but of mind.
—ROD SERLING, "THE TWILIGHT ZONE"

ENTERING ANOTHER DIMENSION

What color is ≥75%? What is the hue and saturation of ≥25%? The answers to these questions—and countless more like them—come from conscious and unconscious design choices. Data visualization involves applying selected graphical approaches to represent data to make it faster and easier to see meaningful patterns. These choices are called *visually encoding* data (that is, representing data with selected visual attributes such as color, shape, and size). Effective encoding makes it possible for people to maximize their perceptual and cognitive strengths to discover the meaning in the measurements. But, there can be many measurements, each with complex relationships to others. How many dimensions should be displayed at the same time and how are they all visually represented? The palette of visualization is quickly expanding to offer more ways to represent and engage with complex problems. That's good for disciplines for which the flood of measurement is rising particularly fast.

Paul King, a software product strategist and computational neuroscientist says, "Just recording the rapid-fire signaling by neurons for relatively brief periods of time can quickly generate gigabytes of data." Characterizing processes that occur in very short or long intervals can be equally challenging. King observes, "Simulations in astronomy often try to speed things up to see the cosmic forces at work, whereas neuroscientists often try to slow things down to understand properties of living neurons in action." He adds that, "Filtering and summarizing signal information is necessary to keep things manageable."

Along with the challenges of time scales, King observes that people try to come up with "creative approaches to represent the data in ways that summarize the n-dimensional information structures and complex surfaces." For example, he states, "There are many interesting things going on within the neural sheet that makes up the cerebral cortex, but this sheet has to be in a crumpled form to fit inside the skull. The creases give it a highly irregular three-dimensional shape that makes it difficult to study and visualize." To put this into context, just imagine trying to read something printed on a scrunched-up piece of paper. One novel approach, he says, to address this was to create "a simulation that shows what the cortex would look like if you inflated it with air, turning it into a balloon to uncrumple it." Then, just as a globe of Earth can distinguish countries by color overlays, different hues can be used on the surface of the brain sphere to differentiate regions.[2] This mind-blowing idea (pun intended) can be an easier way to perceive aspects that would otherwise be obscured. The approach enables the viewer to see features of a single brain, and the spherical representation enables the aggregation of data from multiple brains to show commonalities in a single place. Essentially, the spherical representation provides a convenient mathematical space to represent multiple individual brains, as is demonstrated in Figure 7-2.

King points out that this kind of approach can be extended to help make various imaging data such as functional magnetic resonance images (fMRIs) easier to visually analyze.

---

2 *ftp://surfer.nmr.mgh.harvard.edu/pub/articles/fischl99b-recon2.pdf*

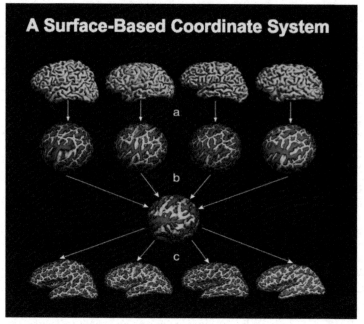

A Surface-Based Coordinate System

a

b

c

Figure 7-2. Inflated cortex visualization

PIXELS AND VOXELS

Consider a teakettle sitting on a stovetop. Some of its attributes will be immediately apparent—including its physical dimensions as well as its position in space at a given moment. Many other important properties of the kettle might not be perceptible without employing other senses and additional information. Is it full of water and heavy or empty and light? Are the surfaces and handle hot or cool? The way I interact with the object will be based on a combination of my perception of the physical shape and knowledge of other key attributes. A good or bad experience using the kettle depends on an accurate and timely understanding of a combination of cues. How are these types of attributes visualized for other kinds of less readily accessible objects such as a network of neurons or a cluster of galaxies?

For both the brain and celestial objects, form and function are deeply connected. This means that "true" 3D displays can provide an important vehicle for discovery in both neuroscience and cosmology. Thinking about design from the perspective of both 2D representations with pixels ("picture" and "element") and 3D voxels ("volume" and "pixel"—a basic visual unit used for medical and scientific visualization as well as some game engines) is important. 3D displays have been making progress, moving away from a common perception of being problematic novelties toward viable visualization tools. However, there's ongoing work to be done to solve design challenges for 3D visual interfaces. Achin Bhowmik, the general manager and chief technology officer of the Perceptual Computing group at Intel Corporation, says there are three key ingredients to making life-like 3D visualizations.

Stereopsis

This display shows different content to your left and right eye (if you've ever looked at a 3D movie with, and without, a sporty pair of polarized glasses, you're already familiar with this idea.)

Motion parallax

When we move in daily life, our eyes and heads are in constant motion. When you move, you want to see the content of the picture change. However, as Bhowmik points out, "This doesn't happen on a vast majority of the 3D displays currently in the market." He adds, "This is part of the reason why we can experience discomfort with current 3D interfaces."

Accommodation/convergence

The lenses of your eyes are not rigid but rather flexible. They change shape so that you can focus objects that are close or far away. Your brain sends signals to muscles that increase or decrease the curvature of the lenses to focus light appropriately (accommodation). At the same time, your two eyeballs are rotating to look at the same object in space (convergence). Hold up a finger and then move it closer to your face and notice your eyes will cross a little. Bhowmik says, "Today's 3D displays result in a mismatch between the accommodation and the convergence points, because the lenses of the eyes have to bring the light emanating from the display's surface to focus on the retina." However, he adds, "the eyes are trying to converge on objects shown in 3D that are away from the display surface." This mismatch causes eye fatigue and discomfort for the viewer.

"Beyond stereopsis, there is progress in addressing motion parallax issues," Bhowmik says. However, he cautions, "there's work to be done in resolving the accommodation-convergence mismatch issue, though some promising research is being done." In the real world, we've evolved to have synchronized accommodation and convergence.

As for the need for voxels versus pixels in specific applications, Bhowmik says, "Let's look at a complete computed tomography (CT) model of the brain based on imaging data where you have real voxels. In the volume of the object, you have real physical data for every point. If you take a virtual slice through this brain, you can see the details of any particular point." He says to compare that with a visualization of the 3D surface structure. "I can move around it virtually and create a 3D print-out, but there's nothing inside the structure. There is only information about the surface." In the former example, Bhowmik says the use of voxels makes sense, whereas in the latter, pixels can be used. He adds, "Let's say in astronomical simulation where we just want to see the relationships of different objects in space, you may not necessarily care what's on the interior of these objects, but you can still fly around surface representations."

Despite the challenges with current 3D display technologies, Bhowmik says that in the longer term, screens with 3D visualization capabilities will be ubiquitous. It's not a matter of whether, but when. Just as technological limitations at one time meant that silent movies were the only form of cinema or that films could only be shot in black and white, times do change. He notes, "We now look back at those forms as the things of the past, while enjoying the brilliant full-color screens with surround sound."

3D FLUENCY

Making the best practical use of interactive 2D and 3D visualization tools requires more than just good visual images. There's also a need for thoughtfully designed interfaces and workflow strategies with which actual users can utilize the images effectively. Ron Schilling and Sergio Aguirre, who started a company called Echopixel, are working on protocols to help physicians work more effectively by using 3D medical visualization tools that have a computer-aided design (CAD) quality to them.

The sequence of images shown in Figure 7-3 illustrates the steps of using 3D visualization software to use neuroimaging data to create a precise virtual 3D model of a patient's brain tumor. Although the process employs advanced technologies, elements of it are akin to an ancient technique in art of making a statue from a cast. Here's a short synopsis of the steps:

1. The neuroimaging data is loaded into the system.

2. The image of the brain is rotated and cut to expose the location of the tumor.

3. The tumor is isolated, measured, and magnified.

4. Segmentation markers are laid down.

5. The space that surrounds the tumor is filled in with a 3D visual representation (a "cast" of the tumor contour surface).

6. The tumor can then be interacted upon as well as viewed in the context of the full image.

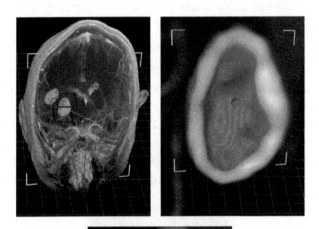

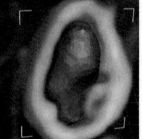

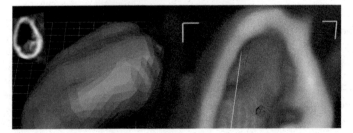

Figure 7-3. A sequence of images showing the process of brain casting

Ron Schilling says creating well-defined and easily executed steps in a process with these kinds of tools can help shorten the time it takes to solve visual-spatial problems in medical settings.

VISUALIZING VASTNESS

"You've been lied to by textbooks that have to squeeze the Earth and the Moon into the same page," exhorted astrophysicist and director of the Hayden Planetarium, Neil deGrasse Tyson (Figure 7-4), during his packed SXSW 2014 keynote presentation. He made this comment to a volunteer from the audience who was trying to figure out how far away to stand with a model of the Moon in relation to Tyson, who was holding a beach ball Earth.

Figure 7-4. Neil deGrasse Tyson during his packed SXSW 2014 keynote speech (photo by Hunter Whitney)

The brave volunteer stood a foot away from deGrasse Tyson—far too close. He noted that in our schoolbooks, the Moon is shown extremely close to Earth, but added there's a practical reason for this representation. If the scaled images were shown properly, he said there'd be about an eight-page gap between the two bodies. Even as we move away from static, paper-based representations of the cosmos, there are still challenges for practically conveying appropriate senses of scale and distance as well as the ability to move from large to small while maintaining context.

From the subatomic to the galactic, the range of scale needed to think about the universe is vast. So too, representing the way the brain works requires thinking in terms of big shifts in scale from the molecular to the anatomical. Familiar frames of reference can help users maintain orientation, even in extremely large information spaces.

Randal Jackson is the manager of Internet communications at NASA's Jet Propulsion Laboratory. Figure 7-5 shows an interactive visualization called "Eyes on Exoplanets," for which Jackson says a primary goal was to give the general public a way to understand the growing database of exoplanet discoveries (*http://eyes.nasa.gov/exoplanets*). "We want lay users to develop a sense of the scale of the deep space 'search bubble' for exoplanets within 10,000 light years of our solar system," he says. To ensure that viewers would not get lost in space, the interface offers navigational frames of reference including a label for our sun and a "Home button for Earth." With almost 1,600 exoplanetary systems in the database, the interface lets people see how long it would take to get to each system by automobile traveling at 60 miles per hour. For one star he randomly selected, it would take about five billion years. If you conceptually traveled by commercial jet, the journey would last around 528,000,000 years. At the unachievable rate of light speed, it would take *only* 473 years. The strategy is to relate things to a familiar context. Another way the interface allows for this is that for every exoplanetary solar system, the user can compare the size of it with out solar system as an overlay. Jackson says the visualizations are powered by NASA's Exoplanet Archive—the same database that the scientists use as the official repository. The key for creating the public interface, he says, is "filtering for the data that we believe lay users would find the most interesting and relatable."

Figure 7-5. NASA's "Eyes on Exoplanets" interactive visualization tool

EMBRACING UNCERTAINTY AND CONSTRAINTS

Knowledge is an unending adventure at the edge of uncertainty.
—JACOB BRONOWSKI

Some of the most important considerations about any visualization are the limits, constraints, and assumptions behind the data that drives what we see. The aesthetic purity of a graphical representation can belie the fact that what it's conveying doesn't really represent the truth. The power of the visual image in general—and the credibility we might unconsciously invest in polished charts and graphs—can overshadow the fact that the underlying data or assumptions are incorrect. An essential but often easily overlooked question is: what about any potentially problematic data behind the chart? How do we address that? The data might not be bad in and of itself. It might be meticulously collected and categorized but still be problematic. Can the graphical perfection of a visualization be counterproductive for the purposes of knowledge, discovery, or even simply communicating an idea?

In neurobiology and cosmology, grappling with uncertainty in measurements, assumptions, and knowledge is a fundamental concern. This uncertainty can come in many forms and combinations, including various kinds of gaps in the data, limitations of statistical approaches, artifacts from the tools and methods of collection, and other issues. Visually representing uncertainty is another crucial element for helping people ask the right questions and draw the most accurate conclusions about the data. But showing uncertainty requires visual techniques that can jostle with the other encoding of data dimensions. In the visualization, what represents the data and what represents the level of uncertainty about them?[3]

We can solve some of the practical problems of displaying uncertainty by using interactivity. For example, we can provide sliders or buttons so that users can select the amount of uncertainty for a given visualization. For clarity purposes, they might begin with an idealized presentation and then adjust the controls to see how the picture changes when various statistical factors, sample sizes, or competing assumptions are introduced into the mix.

Section 2: Visualizing Scientific Models (Some Assembly Required)

The purpose of models is not to fit the data, but to sharpen the questions.
—SAMUEL KARLIN[4]

TINKERING IN THE MODEL SHOP

Whether it's gaining a better understanding of brain function or galaxy formation, scientists increasingly employ data-intensive simulations based on a combination of observations and theories. Visualizations of these models (which we'll explore in a few moments) don't need to embody every possible aspect of a system to be valuable investigative tools. For example, in one visualized model example that follows, you can see some effects on a star that is undergoing the gravitational tug of a black hole. These visualizations just need to capture elements of complex systems and dynamics that people can probe, test, and predict. Some of the uses include:

- Investigating theories that are very difficult, if not impossible, to observe directly

---

3 E.A. Allen, E.B. Erhardt, V.D. Calhoun. "Data visualization in the neurosciences: overcoming the curse of dimensionality." Neuron, 2012. Elsevier.

4 Delivered at the Eleventh R. A. Fisher Memorial Lecture, Royal Society (20 April 1983). In Carl C. Gaither and Alma E. Cavazos-Gaither, *Statistically Speaking: A Dictionary of Quotations* (1996), 140 (*http://bit.ly/1CJ3Ik6*).

- Accelerating the probing and testing of a hypothesis and its parameters (for example, how much dark matter is required to give a galaxy its observed shape?)

- Providing a way for scientists to use visual representations to explore complex systems

- Highlighting different aspects of a system by using different kinds of visualizations

- Revealing the potential missing pieces and hidden connections in the data

- Enabling better collaborations between researchers

- Conveying scientific concepts to general audiences

- Providing literal "hands-on" experience with conceptual models

Yet, how can scientists be certain their simulations truly represent reality rather than capturing quirks of code or faulty assumptions? Perhaps the simulations are revealing something completely new, true, and unexpected. Well-constructed visual simulations can be compared with like representations displaying alternate models. When possible, the simulations can also be matched against direct observations of the actual subjects of investigation.

Making model visualizations that encourage exploring, testing, and even playing with scientific hypotheses demands paying attention to various details of the users' experience. Think about it: who would want to spend much time playing with a toy train that continually falls off the track or a toy plane that crashes back to the ground? An interactive visual model of a scientific concept that was glitchy or frustrating would not invite engagement or the kind of exploration that leads to important insights.

In general, that means the responsiveness of the visualizations needs to be crisp and the interactions easy. They need to be fast and simple enough to encourage pushing and probing of the data. Given the typical scope and scale of data in neuroscience and cosmology, that's no mean feat. Decisions have to be made about how and where the numbers are crunched and the manner in which images are served up and rendered. There's often an ongoing tinkering and tuning of code and hardware. For example, how much work will be demanded of the user's own device versus the machines serving up the simulation? Mapping the data, in terms of their relationships and the organizational structures in which they reside, is an integral part of the process.

Morgan MacLeod, a graduate student at the Department of Astronomy and Astrophysics at the University of California, Santa Cruz, has been working with visualizations of physics models to help researchers—and the general public—develop a sense of what happens during certain interactions between stars and supermassive black holes (SMBHs). For example, if a star strays too near to an SMBH, gravitational forces can rip it apart and the stellar material can be stretched into two tails. These are big, but rare, events that occur very far from Earth, so scientists can benefit from models and simulations to get a good view of these epic encounters.

One of the choices that astrophysicists have to make regularly, MacLeod says, is whether to use representative or exact system models and simulations. He explains that in an exact system approach, the scientist tries to re-create the entire system with every known element included. However, this might not always be the best and most direct road to gain a clear understanding. "There are many times when people can only show or digest one slice at a time," MacLeod says. He adds, "It should not be the ambition of a visualization to always be complete." It just needs to be able to clarify a point. You want to show the constraints of the information but also convey something.

There can be obvious differences in the approach to designing a targeted visualization for focused researchers versus one geared for lay audiences. Some kinds of visualizations can be tuned to show a highly specific aspect of a system that will be meaningful only to people steeped in the subject matter. With that said, it can be easy to fall into the trap of assuming great knowledge of a scientific area necessarily translates into proficiency with other kinds of technology.

For example, a group of scientists might have very deep knowledge about their subject area but be unfamiliar with the nuances of how to work with a certain kind of interactive chart. Crucially, they might not be able to gauge how much to trust the representation they are looking at or what to do next to evaluate it. Lay users might be proficient at working with the software but not have enough context to understand what they are seeing. Many subtle differences can emerge between different types of users and these should be considered in the design process.

"There's trade-off in the people who are willing to invest a minute versus the people who are only willing to invest a few seconds. I often ask myself whether I should throw in x, y, z aspects of a model into the visualization. Even with scientific graphs there's a certain degree of salesmanship, in that you want to make a point and have people see and believe it," MacLeod says. Simplifying models that isolate specific aspects of the data and turning this into visual and physical forms is not a new impulse. Centuries ago, people created clockwork embodiments of the solar system to help give the viewer a sense of the relative positions and motions of bodies in the solar system with the heliocentric orientation (the Sun rather than Earth as the center of the system.) In some respects, MacLeod, who at the time of this writing is living in Rome, traces a lineage between the visualizations of the dynamics of black holes he's helped to create and the orreries (an example is shown in Figure 7-6) he's seen at the Museo Galileo at the Pellazo Castellani.

Figure 7-6. An example of an orrery[5]

Although these orreries are not built even remotely to scale or entirely representative of planetary motion, they still serve a useful function to convey the best understanding of the time.

---

5   Photo by raneko (*http://www.flickr.com/photos/24926669@N07/5163898181*) CC-BY-2.0 (*http://creativecommons.org/licenses/by/2.0*).

SIMPLICITY AND PREDICTION

Concerns about piling on too many elements into models, which can easily arise when representing the cosmos, also arise in the world of neuroscience. Gully Burns is project leader in biomedical knowledge engineering with the University of Southern California's Information Sciences Institute. He has spent a lot of time thinking about the organization and presentation of neuroscience data. Burns has seen visualizations that might be spectacularly ornate and arresting, but that very quality can short-circuit their main purpose and value. "Sometimes people tend to revel and get lost in the complexity," he points out. Burns recalls a paper describing cerebral function that was formative in his own career. The authors were showing connections in the brain that were beautiful and complicated. Burns thinks what was lost in the image was a larger point about a hierarchical pattern; it was obscured by the complexity. The value of simplicity in design is certainly not a new idea. However, with the increasing use of interactive visualized models and simulations, being able to look past complexity can make it possible for underlying patterns in the data to emerge and give new kinds of displays more predictive power.

EXAMPLES FROM THE YT PROJECT

What I cannot create, I do not understand.

—RICHARD FEYNMAN

Simulations are, in a sense, re-creating parts of the universe. No matter how you slice it, virtually re-creating galaxies or brain dynamics is a tall order. The yt Project[6] is a visualization and analysis platform to help researchers in areas ranging from cosmology to neuroscience to explore simulation-based data and models (*http://yt-project.org*). Matt Turk, an associate research scientist at Columbia Astrophysics, is the original author of the project, which he began as a graduate student. "We found that researchers feel this is a good place to collaborate without direct competition," Turk says. Sam Skillman, a postdoctoral stu-

---

6 Matt Turk, the author of the project, explains that the name "yt" comes from the Neal Stephenson book *Snow Crash*. (He had Neal Stephenson sign his thesis, which included a chapter on yt.) In the book, "YT" stands for "Yours Truly." The spelling is lowercase because he wanted the module name to match the name of the project. "And, I made it fixed width so it would stand out from other text," says Turk. There's more to the story but those are the basics.

dent at Stanford, started working on the yt Project as a means to ask more simple and direct questions of the data he was using. He has since become involved in the development of the platform for working on large data sets in volume rendering. yt is a framework and analysis of data that was originally focused on astrophysical data, but is beginning to branch out into other domains in nuclear engineering and seismology and is just starting to include a neuroscience project called "Neurodome."

Turk says, "At some level there is a crossover in concepts between astrophysics and neuroscience in some of the ways you approach data, including segmentation and feature identification." One of the very early visualizations of astrophysical data was *isosurfaces*; that is a very common way of representing neuroscience data, as well. Skillman says another similarity is that both disciplines are entering the era of giant surveys. He elaborates, "You've got new technologies that can probe the brain in different ways that generate disjointed but associated data-sets. Both fields are really trying to grapple with taking data from many different places and then trying to put it together." For example, a yt Project called AGORA (Assembling Galaxies of Resolved Anatomy) is focused on investigating galaxy formation with high-resolution numerical simulations. It then compares the results across different platforms as well as with observations of the real thing (see Figure 7-7).

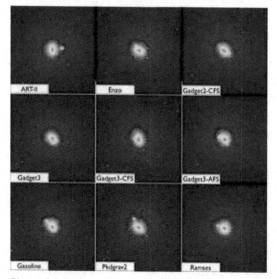

Figure 7-7. Project AGORA (Assembling Galaxies of Resolved Anatomy)

Section 3: Evolving Tools, Processes, and Interactions

OBSERVATORIES OF THE BRAIN

A simple glance up at a clear night sky can show much, including the current positions of stars and planets as well as indicating where you are on Earth at that moment. If you use a telescope, even more details come into view. Quantum theory aside, viewing the universe does not prevent it from going about its regular business. Observing the real-time activities of a living brain is a very different story.

Although there are many properties of the universe that are not directly available to our eyes, there's still an innate visibility to stars. Not so the processes of the brain—the myriad activities occurring within the skull must be rendered visible. Imaging tools such as magnetic resonance imaging (MRI) that are commonly used to do this have an obvious impact on the range of actions that a subject can do while being observed. Our brains are constantly generating electrical impulses in specific patterns that define who we are and what we do. But, these vital patterns, generated when neurons transmit electrochemical signals (called *firing*), are completely hidden inside our heads. Brain wave mapping with electroencephalographs (EEGs) and imaging technologies, such as fMRIs (the "f" stands for "functional"), can reveal much useful information, but the resolution is not fine enough to reveal the interaction and networks of individual neurons that hold the crucial keys to decipher the workings of the mind.

Neuroscientists routinely employ genetic methods to make individual nerve cells in specific brain regions literally light up when they are firing. The process involves genetically engineering neurons in living mice by using a special type of virus to insert additional coding instructions into the DNA. A related approach is taken in gene therapy. These modified nerve cells are now programmed to express a protein that fluoresces green when the neuron fires, thereby temporarily "lighting it up."

Inscopix, a Palo Alto–based neuroscience company, has created a small digital microscope that attaches to the head to capture these flashes of light as they occur in thousands of individual neurons—reminiscent of stars twinkling in the night sky. The patterns of flashes are translated to familiar types of scientific plots and then analyzed. This technology is being honed by using mice, but it ushers in new ideas and applications to the human brain.

Pushkar Joshi, a neurobiology research scientist at Inscopix, describes it as decoding the patterns of optical signals and then translating them into meaningful representations of neural activity. Joshi says, "The goal of this work is to improve the human condition." As a practical example of this, he notes, "Many neurological and psychiatric disorders have been described as 'chemical imbalances,' but these imbalances are more a result of neural circuit activity dysfunction." That is, many problems are primarily due to faulty wiring in the brain. That could mean that, in the future, visual representations of patterns of neuronal activity can show the root cause and potential treatment of the problem.

Joshi adds that the fact the flash-detecting devices are small and mass producible means, that in principle, "you could run experiments with 100 mice in parallel and over substantial periods of time." That volume of comparative data can bring new insights into neuroscience, but it will also require effective measures to manage and work with the influx.

The work, Joshi says, "necessarily involves the collaboration of a highly cross-disciplinary team." The approach requires the involvement of neuroscientists, data scientists, developers, designers, hardware engineers, software engineers, and others. This way of working will play an increasingly important role in helping to create brand new forms of visualization.

KICKING THE TIRES OF CONVERGENCE

It's tough to make predictions, especially about the future.
—YOGI BERRA

The adoption of emerging technologies in the real world can take both predictable and surprising turns. Trying to integrate diverse new kinds of capabilities, such as interactive 3D visualizations and voice interfaces, into one seamless user experience (UX) can add even more twists as shown in Figure 7-8. In thinking through how new technologies converge, the basic UX design tools such as personas, scenarios, and prototypes can be useful guides. For example, can data about the brain that is in different formats and from different sources be more effectively explored with multimodal interfaces that include a mix of voice input, gesture control input, and 3D visualization output?

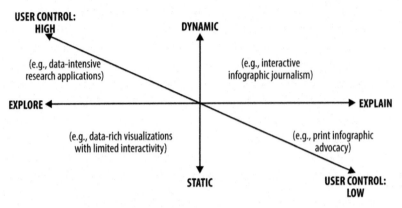

Figure 7-8. UX options for data visualization

I had the opportunity to work with Jeff Chang, an emergency room radiologist and startup founder, on a design concept for a multimodal interface used for an analysis of patients with traumatic brain injury. We created a prototype of a 3D neuroimaging system that we named NEAAL, which stands for NeuroElectric and Anatomic Locator. The system facilitates a fast, fluid investigation of heterogeneous data about the brain from the population level down to a specific neural pathway in an individual patient (see Figure 7-9). We had these goals in mind when thinking about the visualization:

- Incorporating 3D anatomical visualizations with related nonphysical data in a simple, elegant display

- Making the most of visual display and gestural input for specific work goals (for example, localizing a specific point of injury in the brain) and employing verbal input for functional tasks (such as calling up specific kinds of neuroimaging or patient history files)

- Helping users maintain context and orientation as they move through an analytic process while still not overloading the display (ephemeral context)

- Allowing users to quickly and easily zoom in on, and tag, points of interest

- Accelerating workflows and enabling more rapid, iterative hypothesis testing

Figure 7-9. The NEAAL (NeuroElectric and Anatomic Locator) 3D neuroimaging system

What are the ways visualization tools can integrate medical imaging data with other kinds of related patient information? The area of medical image fusion is gaining increased traction.[7] Obtaining more insights from data is not just about new and better sets of tools and techniques; it also depends on the ways people on a team assemble data and how they enable users to interact with each of the different elements. Chang says, "You can help users get a better understanding of the connections between data by letting them automatically flip through layered imagery, fly through, and sift through both primary and secondary visualizations, and supporting gestural and voice control." Chang believes, "The adoption of new technologies at the consumer level—whether in eye tracking, gestural control, voice recognition, projected displays or immersive augmented reality—forms the basis for many new use cases in more narrowly targeted applications, whether neurobiological research, medicine, or our understanding of the cosmos." He adds, "People work with what they are used to—and developers will build around the technologies they recognize."

---

7 A.P. James, B.V. Dasarathy, Medical Image Fusion: A survey of the state of the art. Information Fusion, 2014.

The project provided a framework to investigate many questions—including which kinds of interactions are best supported by gesture, and which by voice. For example, voice can be a great way to call up a particular kind of imaging data (for example, "Let's start with the VTA, T2 Flair... overlay EEG... show me the DTI..."). Gestures can be a far more efficient and intuitive way to manipulate and position a virtual 3D object, particularly compared to a voice command such as, "a little more to the right." Hand motions, if implemented well, remove the ambiguity inherent in many different kinds of voice commands.

It also provided an opportunity to think through the transitions between views and the interactions that best supported the analysis of a particular type of imaging data. For example, Chang says, "In the current practice of radiology, we most commonly move through images in the axial plane (up and down through horizontal slices), whether for CT or MRI." He adds, "Once image resolution allows for more fine-tuned evaluation of microscopic regions of the brain, it will become particularly useful to overlay other types of data on user request—localized electrical potentials, white matter tracts, estimated concentrations of neurotransmitters, scouting for iron deposits, and differentiating among multiple layers of cells." In the NEAAL prototype, the ability to "fly along" the course of a particular white matter tract introduces another way to interact with and understand the full context of the data. Chang says, "We might then figure out ways to treat injuries that are far beyond the reach of current medical science."

The best way to think through these design issues is by storyboarding, prototyping, getting people of many backgrounds into the same room, working closely with key stakeholders and users, and being completely open-minded about the possibilities. Chang says, "Even though new technologies may take some time to catch up, they each have a lot of potential."

MACHINE LEARNING AND HUMAN COMMUNICATION

With the challenges presented by the increasing volume and complexity of data, people will need to rely on data mining and machine learning (ML) as supporting tools. As important and refined as these approaches may become, human conceptual frameworks and communication will continue to be an essential component of science. Nick Ball is a data scientist with a background in astronomy who works at Skytree, a company that does predictive analytics by using ML methods.

Ball says that the relationships and linkages between the data points are formed in the context of the language in which they are described. For example, he says, "There can be an entire semantic infrastructure that develops around a particular kind of data collection technique." He adds, "At the end of the day, it comes down to the assertions someone is making—a person who is a specialist in one domain may be looking at the same kinds of questions and data as someone else, but there's a divide between the language they are using. Therefore, the understanding that they might share is lost." Ball continues, "There's often not a lot of cross-over between paradigms; it's something I've seen as a general principle throughout my career."

The techniques people use are very different because they have to be in order to look at detailed aspects of a system. As a result, he says, fields fragment into various subdomains that don't talk to one another. "I'm interested in how to create encompassing models in a fractured scientific landscape. If you start by different paradigms and try to bring them together in a single knowledge space, how do you scale up and automate that infrastructure?" He believes that visualizations can help reveal patterns in the data, but also show the fault lines between disciplines. Seeing the contours of these disconnects is a necessary step in addressing them. As we've seen earlier in this chapter, there are examples such as Inscopix as shown in Figure 7-10, wherein new data imaging and analysis tools require breaking down silos between disciplines.

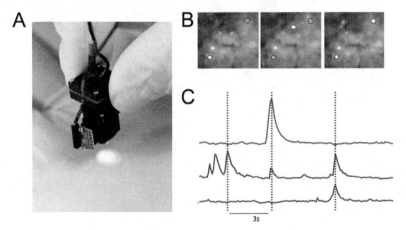

Figure 7-10. Inscopix miniaturized microscope system enables the gathering of unprecedented data sets

LATERAL THINKING AND CROSS-DISCIPLINARY TEAMS

In many of the discussions about data visualizations I've had over the years, there's often so much focus on what goes into making things happen on the screen that what might being going on inside the head of the person looking at it is all but forgotten. That's understandable. Programming environments, software libraries, and off-the-shelf charting and visualization tools are relatively straightforward topics for comparison and have a somewhat limited set of answers.

Human perception and cognition can be a little more complex and variable. But, that doesn't mean those conversations should be avoided. Although questions about specific development environments and tools to create visualizations are certainly important, considering how they might be perceived is even more crucial. Two people looking at the same display can derive very different ideas from it. Figure 7-11 illustrates that a biologist and a physicist can look at the same display of data and yet ask very different but equally relevant questions about it, based on their backgrounds and perspectives.

Comparing "Perspectives"

Physicist

- How much energy is needed to do this?
- How much force does it take to cross this barrier?
- Are reaction rates altered during this process?
- How much time does it take?
- What are the spatial effects?

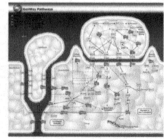

Biologist

- What cell, molecule, tissue is it?
- What changed?
- Where does this fit?
- Do I see the same thing in several tumors?

Both 'view' the same picture differently, but having both perspectives yields a more comprehensive (clearer) picture of what cancer is and how it functions at all levels – especially at the sub-molecular/atomic scales

Figure 7-11. The differing perspectives of physicists and biologists[8]

---

8 Courtesy Ann Barker from the presentation "Physical Sciences-Oncology Centers (Integrating and Leveraging the Physical Sciences to Open a New Frontier in Oncology)."

GAME MECHANICS AND WINNING TEAMS

Differences in subject matter expertise are not the only kind of cross-disciplinary thinking that we can use to make visualizations more robust and effective. There are also various perspectives from the world of design itself that we can apply to data-intensive displays. For example, key ideas in game design can help guide data representation and interaction level decisions. Applying a few basic ideas from game play to human-computer interactions might help people solve some of the biggest puzzles of neuroscience and cosmology. Dan Kaufman, director of the Defense Advanced Research Projects Agency (DARPA) Information Innovation Office, has spent years thinking about various facets of game mechanics and applying those ideas to addressing hard problems. He says, "The core of software has always been levels of abstraction—that's what empowers us." He continues, "The question is how do we find ways to create levels of abstraction and rules that allow more people to play?" The catch is accomplishing this goal without stripping away the actual value of the data being studied. "It's a fine line," he says, "but if you can hit it, you get amazing results."

As an example, Kaufman mentioned Foldit,[9] an online game involving protein folding that he managed. The game made a splash with the general public and resulted in generating genuinely useful scientific insights. He said it worked because, "It turned out to be a very complex biological problem that was boiled down to a basic set of rules that could be codified." He continues, "This removed the need for special knowledge of biochemistry to participate in the work and allowed some people to have an impact by exploring the problem in a design space and play a game involving minimum and maximum energy. I can translate something that is esoteric and complex into something where different skill sets can be applied."

For Kaufman, drawing lessons from even simple games such as Pickup Sticks® can be more than just child's play. He believes that designs can help people make more use of senses, rather than vision alone, to analyze data and use other modalities to explore the information space. As an example, he notes that humans are well-attuned to detecting motion. He says to imagine a large pile of Pickup Sticks in which

---

9 *https://fold.it/portal/*

many of the sticks are connected to another. Kaufman continues, "If I wiggle one stick, those connected closer to it will move more than those connected farther away. The unconnected ones won't wiggle at all. It can be an easy way to see connections that otherwise might not be apparent."

Visualization tools can easily become reflections of the creators' assumptions. Kaufman believes, "Any type of display you use comes with underlying assumptions that can lead you astray. I saw one really cool visualization, but instead of just taking that for an answer, I asked if there were any other assumptions that might have been made and could the data be visualized in another way? When we ran this visualization with different patterns, we saw no pattern whatsoever." The question becomes: am I seeing an actual pattern or am I making it up? In theory, one way to address the problem of introducing biases is to run "Monte Carlo simulations" (a statistical method that uses random variables and multiple trials to estimate solutions—somewhat reminiscent of games of chance at a casino). The problem with that approach, Kaufman notes, "is that you can end up with so many variations of what was in the data that the cost of filtering through the results is higher than the returns of what you get back." The reason certain kinds of simulations work well in fields like neuroscience and cosmology, Kaufman says, is that there are phenomena that you can observe. In the computer-science world, nothing exists until you create it. "In the absence of factual ground truth, what you often have to rely on is human intuition. If you allow me to quickly and easily look at data and move it around, I can begin to apply my intuition."

In games, people's skills are typically benchmarked by the performance of competitors. In both neuroscience and cosmology, the ultimate competition comes from reality itself. How well can human reasoning and intuition, augmented and simulated with computer support, measure up against the complexities confronting us? As Kaufman notes, the strongest teams to meet these challenges will be comprised of humans *and* machines, rather than either humans or machines alone.

Conclusion

People love puzzles and there are none greater than those presented by considering our own brains—or by looking up at a clear night sky. Arriving at solutions requires the tools and techniques that can maximize our perceptual capacities and lift our cognitive capacities to new levels. Like any good tools, the approaches described in this chapter can help us exceed our limitations and take advantage of our strengths. By considering the range of visual options, conceptual frameworks, and computational capacities, we can take design to new dimensions that reveal the answers we seek.

Just as emerging technologies open up new ways for scientists to collect and work with data, they also present designers with new options for how to construct visualizations. As we've seen, new forms of visualization can arise from the integration of ideas from disparate disciplines. A company such as Inscopix does work that is made possible by such a combination of techniques drawn from many areas. Although neuroscience and cosmology provide interesting illustrations of technology convergence and cross-disciplinary collaboration, many other areas are going through similar transformations. To adapt and evolve visualizations, designers of various stripes might consider the themes highlighted in this chapter including:

- As the technologies behind multimodal interfaces and interactive 3D displays continue to improve, the toolkit of practical visualization options will keep growing. Along with the new capabilities to use, there will be interesting new design decisions to make.

- Conceptual models are essential tools in science and, of course, many other disciplines. There's an art to visually representing these models so that their limitations are clear and their utility is maximized. Highly specialized terminology and semantics can sometimes interfere with sharing the key point of a model. Well-designed visualizations can play a pivotal role in providing a common visual vocabulary for communication of ideas, which in turn can enable better collaborations.

- Many of the complex problems people need to solve require close collaborations between people with widely different skill sets as well as partnerships of people and machines. Design itself is not a monolithic field. Designers with various backgrounds, from UX to games to sound, can learn from one another. Whether it's exploring the interior of the brain or the deepest reaches of space, an open-minded approach to design can help us get there.

[8]

Embeddables: The Next Evolution of Wearable Tech

ANDY GOODMAN

Technology That Gets Under Your Skin

Wearables are getting all the headlines at the moment, but future headlines will be all about *embeddables*, tiny computing devices implanted inside your body that monitor your health, improve your functioning, and connect you to the digital world.

In addition to wearables, there is currently a lot of buzz in technology and design circles about living services, the Internet of Things, and smart materials. As designers working in these realms, we've begun to think about even more transformative things, envisioning a future in which evolved technology is embedded inside our digestive tracts, sensing organs, blood vessels, and even our cells. Everyday objects will become responsive and predictive, connecting us to the data sphere and reducing the distance between our skin and the surfaces of the technological world around us. As Figure 8-1 depicts, what we see further out, beyond the realm of wearables and implants, is the future symbiosis of the human body and the machine.

In his 2005 book *Radical Evolution: The Promise and Peril of Enhancing Our Minds, Our Bodies—And What It Means to be Human* (Broadway Books), Joel Garreau explores the progression toward a post-human future defined by four converging technologies that are going to radically transform our interaction with the world: genetics, robotics, information, and nanotechnology. He dubs these the GRIN technologies, and they will drive the development of embeddable devices. With a few exceptions such as pacemakers and artificial hips, technology has always been at one distance removed from our bodies and brains. Not for much longer. The interface between the manufactured world and humans is going to become almost invisible.

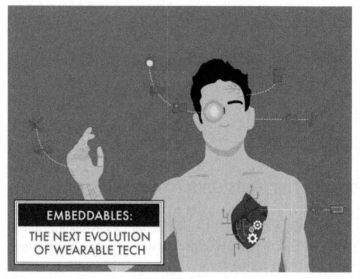

Figure 8-1. The future symbiosis of the human body and the machine

The monolithic device with a screen might be on the verge of disappearing. It is being enhanced with numerous smaller devices, which might soon replace it as the way to access information. We will arrive at a more ambient experience in which sensors capture information about us and feed that information into systems quietly working away in the background. Wearables will give way to embeddables, nano-scale machinery inside our bodies, which can monitor, modify, assist, and enhance us.

These systems will act as mental and sensory prosthetics, increasing exponentially our knowledge, perception, and manipulation of the world around us. The early uses we are seeing in domains such as healthcare and fitness will extend further to virtually any domain we can think of. Communications, entertainment, socializing, learning, work, even self-actualization—any human activity we can think of is going to be modified and amplified with an invisible mesh of data and processing that we will drift through, mostly obliviously.

Embeddables are not just going to be a revolution in functionality, but will dramatically alter how people fit into society, affect human psychology, and even propel us toward intellectual transcendence.

Just looking at visual experience and sensing, we can see how this could come about. Imagine being able to perceive different light frequencies, the world in microscopic detail, or far distant objects in the universe. This would have a profound effect on our understanding of reality and our place within it.

Before we can start dreaming about the evolutionary acceleration that might be granted by these technologies we have to come back down to Earth for a while. There are many practical barriers that need to be considered. Embeddables will be sitting so close to us that the right balance between unobtrusiveness and practicality will have to be found. Systems that can predict and even meet our needs without us having to intervene will be the ones that resonate and find an audience.

We can already see with the rather too rapid backlash against Google Glass that people are very particular about what they put onto their bodies and how "social deviance" could become a big barrier to adoption. Parodies of people wearing Google Glass on shows such as *Saturday Night Live* and the fact that the *New Yorker* has dubbed early adopters "Glassholes" shows exactly the problem with wearable tech. It can open us up to ridicule. The designs of future wearables will need to subtly integrate with our clothing and our bodies or become fashion statements in their own right if they aren't to become an evolutionary dead-end on the technology tree.

Likewise, the design paradigms that we invent for these ambient systems in which the entire body becomes an interactive canvas will need to steer clear of a different kind of social deviance. Maybe in the future we will become accustomed to the jerking, twitching, winking, nodding motions of the Glass wearer in the way that it has become socially acceptable to browse your phone while someone is talking to you ("phubbing"), but for now it looks deeply peculiar.

Although conversations on the subject are not mainstream yet, embed-dables are emerging as a new topic for debate. According to a recent panel at Venture Beat "'Wearable' computers will soon be inside us."[1] Embeddables are going to have significant consequences for the delivery of digital services as screen-based interaction becomes less prominent, and possibly even disappears.

This chapter discusses the scientific, social, and creative context of the embeddable revolution. It addresses what you, as a designer or engineer, will need to take on board to operate in this space. What was once a craft based on visual cognition will change dramatically into one that takes account of other senses and will need to be based on a much deeper understanding of human culture, rituals, psychology, physiology, and motivation.

Permeable Beings: The History of Body Modification

To see the future, first we must understand the past. Humans have been interfacing with technology for thousands of years. We seem to be intrinsically built to desire this communion with the manufactured world. This blending of the mechanical and biological has often been described as a "natural" evolutionary process by such great thinkers as Marshall McLuhan in the 1950s and more recently Kevin Kelly.[2] So, by looking at the long timeline of body modification we can see waves of change and future ripples.

For as far back as we have physical evidence, humans have been changing the appearance of their bodies deliberately both for art and seduction and as an unconsciously instinctive action. The purpose could always be distinguished as one of two categories: first, to modify states of social acceptance; second, to improve physical attributes and to repair or mask damaged or aging body parts. Far from the religious ideal of humans being born perfect, it is quite clear that we are painfully aware of our physical shortcomings and will do sometimes quite extreme things to present a more pristine, memorable, or powerful image.

---

1 Young Sohn, Samsung chief strategy officer at MobileBeat 2013, San Francisco (*http://bit. ly/1CJ3Lwf*)

2 *What Technology Wants!* by Kevin Kelly (Viking, 2010)

The resigned, almost welcoming capitulation to aging and death that shaped religious and philosophical narratives of early human cultures is certainly no longer a norm (if indeed it ever was).

Few people are totally content with the bodies they ended up occupying, but recently, we have developed the capability to change them in much more fundamental ways, from the gene up. The enhanced human will have improved attributes such as sensing and thinking (aided by computation), and better physical characteristics, such as endurance, resistance, and longevity. If you think this is a distant prospect, recent developments in artificial organ technology and robotics are bringing this sci-fi scenario closer than we might imagine. Although it is too early to agree with Aubrey De Grey's assertion that we will be the last generation to experience death,[3] it is safe to say that our children and grandchildren will certainly have a very different physical life experience that any humans who came before.

If we previously defined the two primary categories of body modification as "decoration" and "optimization and repair," there is now a third category of body modification brought about by the GRIN technologies. We can call this *extension*. Even though it is unlikely that we will be able to fundamentally change our physiology—we aren't likely ever to be able to fly for instance—there are myriad enhancements available to our standard functioning that will boost us in a dizzying range of ways.

Decoration, Meaning, and Communication

Before we plunge through into this future of the extended human, it is worth thinking a little about the past, to see from where the motivations and roots of this seemingly universal urge came. What is it that made people so yearn to change themselves, and what is it about this urge that in the end makes us human?

MARKING THE SKIN

Tattoos have been a part of human culture as far back as we can find evidence. The earliest records are from the Palaeolithic era, 35,000 years ago. We can only assume that we humans have been marking

---

3　"I think it's reasonable to suppose that one could oscillate between being biologically 20 and biologically 25 indefinitely." —Aubrey de Grey, 2005

our skin even further back in prehistory. The reasons have varied over time. Otzi the Iceman from 33,000 BC had what is known as acupuncture tattoos; these symbolic dotted and dashed lines were placed as a method to "heal" various parts of the body. Tattoos have often been used to supposedly confer magical powers.

Later, the Picts in Britain used Woad markings to scare their enemies. This theme continues in many other cultures where the tattoo is the mark of the outsider and the underclass. Japanese and Chinese bandits used tattoos to mark themselves as a member of a criminal fraternity, and still do to this day. The art receded in Western culture for a long period but was reintroduced in the nineteenth century by explorers returning from the Pacific and Southeast Asia. Tattoos then began the slow transition from a sign of someone outside of mainstream culture toward their present manifestation as a commonplace decorative lifestyle choice.

PUNCTURING THE FLESH

In parallel to skin coloration is the practice of piercing, puncturing, or putting objects inside the skin for ritualistic and decorative purposes or to communicate meaning. One of the most graphic and memorable is the Sioux Sun Dance during which young males enter manhood by twirling around a pole on ropes attached to their bodies with sticks pierced through their chests. Less dramatic but even more invasive are the stacked hoop necklaces worn by young Masai women in Kenya, the horrific practice of Japanese foot binding, and the extreme physical acts of the Indian sadhu or European monk scourging himself with whips and branches. It is a short distance from these practices to the extreme body modifiers, reshaping their form to ones they find more pleasing, even if it means having surgery to appear more like a tiger or a Vulcan (whether they live longer or prosper more has yet to be determined).

Self-injury and mutilation is deeply ingrained in culture and cannot be ignored in the continuum of embedding. These have strong historical precedents in Shamanic ritual and are in a way a distant beacon that anyone who desires to modify their body heads to in some sense. Body dismorphism and gender reassignment, female genital mutilation, and eunuchisation exist in many societies. Whether we see these acts as extreme behavior, oppressive cultural ritual, or as just a quirky part of the spectrum of human sexuality and self-image is not the discussion for today.

RESHAPING THE BODY

Changing the body, its shape, its color, even its gender is becoming acceptable in contemporary society; the roots of this inevitably go back further than we would imagine. Many cultures have long traditions of surgically changing the sex organs, for ritual or social purposes, or of performing dramatic reshaping of other body parts.

Although many of these examples can be shocking from our current perspective, we can think of extreme body modifiers as potential "early adopters," and in the same way that tattoos and piercing have become an everyday fashion statement today, perhaps these more extreme modifications will become normalized eventually. A *Terminator*-style robotic eye projecting scarily from your head might be just seen as a cool accessory 20 years from now, especially if it plugs you in constantly to the grid and means you never need to miss a tweet or a Facebook status update.

THE FUTURE OF BODY DECORATION

What would the embeddable version of Facebook be like? We can maybe see some premonition of it in a recent advertising stunt in Japan in which young women were paid to have advertising displayed on their skin; a few rather foolhardy individuals have even agreed to have brand logos tattooed on their bodies. No doubt some clever marketing company in the future will persuade people to plaster themselves with advanced OLED films and spray their hair with nanoparticles that can change color, the pixel becoming molecular.

In this perhaps quite unappealing future we lease our skin to advertisers who can display their latest products and services across the surfaces of our bodies. Animated soda jets shooting up your chest, and tropical holiday montages rippling across your back. Sponsored narcissism!

SCREENS AND INDICATORS ON SKIN

The ground breaking work done at MIT by Pattie Maes to turn the Internet into a sixth sense explores how micro projectors and gestural interaction can lead toward intangible interfaces that float around us and hover over the surface of our bodies. It is not a big leap to imagine a more advanced technology wherein the glowing pixels are actually under the surface. Emails could appear on the back of your hand, a fingertip could go blue when you are mentioned in a tweet, or an entire display with all your social messages could appear on the inside of your wrist or open palm. Bizarre, maybe, but our constant need to be connected could see this kind of scenario happen (Figure 8-2).

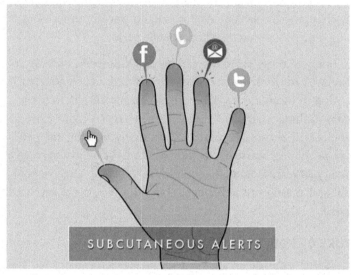

Figure 8-2. What would the embeddable version of Facebook be like?

We do like to have and hold shiny plastic and metal devices, but they are pretty annoying as well, getting stolen, running out of batteries, or being dropped and shattering on hard surfaces. Beyond the physical inconvenience of a device with a screen there is a deeper problem happening; this is the "connected but alone" alienation created by screen devices.

SCREENING OUT THE WORLD

Screen is an interesting word; it simultaneously means an object we look at and something behind which we hide. Even a small hand-sized device becomes a barrier in social situations, absorbing our gaze and taking us elsewhere, away from our present company. Soon, however, we might be able to discard the screen altogether. Voice-activated tech such as Siri, Tellme, Google Voice, Kinect, and Nokia Drive all lead toward *zero UI*.

Zero UI refers to systems by which our movements, voice, and glances can all cause systems to respond to us through our environment. At its extreme, it implies an invisible user interface (UI) without a screen where natural gestures trigger interactions, as if the user were communicating to another person. It would require many technologies to converge and become significantly more sophisticated, particularly voice recognition and motion sensing.

Advanced context-aware automation will take us to the brink of a truly connected world in which sensors and embedded intelligence help us glide through space, subtly enhancing us and adding layers of information to the world. Humans are, in the end, analog beings. Our digital tools should only be an aid to reality; they should not replace it.

So, a combination of pigment altering implants—some kind of evolution of OLED technology—voice control, and ambient sensing will actually allow us to ditch the device entirely, to achieve a kind of telepathy, and for the body to become a remarkable interface to the digital world. The hope would be that this would actually begin to break down the barriers of atomization and disconnection that we have blindly put up around us in the march to the future. The likely truth is probably that we would become even more distracted, self-absorbed, and disconnected from the physical world around us.

Optimization and Repair

The amazing thing about the body, and the mind likewise, is how malleable it is, how easy it is to change it though habitual activity (either toward refinement or toward degeneration). We are not just permeable beings, we are fluid beings.

The speculative futurists writing at the beginning of the twentieth century proposed a future human, thin, weak, and with poor eyesight, but always with a giant head and brain. I suspect they would be very surprised to see what we have become a century later. Even now we find this image compelling. Dr. Alan Kwan[4] has imagined what we will look like 100,000 years from now, with the need to have adapted to space travel, and he revives that familiar image of the large-skulled, saucer-eyed alien.

In contrast to supposed evolution to a big-brained weakling, the body is now hard and taut, we are taller, we live longer, and we run faster, jump higher, throw farther, and hit harder than those early futurists

---

4 Dr. Alan Kwan, M.Sc., Ph.D. Bioinformatics, Computational Biology, Washington University and MIT

could ever have imagined. Rather than diminishing the importance of the body, our techno-knowledge era has deified it, made it something to worship, strive toward, and attain, whether by hard graft or quick expensive shortcuts.

The science-fiction trope of the not-too-distant scenario in which we are plugged into some virtual reality simulation while our bodies waste away in nutrient pods would seem to be a complete misdirection. Rather than becoming immaterial and disconnected from the body, our contemporary self-image is becoming even more located in our physicality, our looks, our youthfulness, and our fitness.

STOPPING THE CLOCK

The counterpart to *optimization* of the body is *repair* of the body, with the aim of delaying the onset of aging. Until very recently, this has involved very crude types of body part replacement, with some of them of questionable benefit. As medical science and genetics has progressed, we are finding that there are some significant barriers that will limit our ability to stop the clock. Our cells have a definitive lifespan, known as the *Hayflick limit,* which determines how many times an organism's cells can recycle before they die. In humans, it is 50. Almost all animals share this property and it is for very sound evolutionary purposes. It seems like the battle against the onset of death is doomed to failure; the only way to stop the cell clock from counting down would be to introduce telomerase into the cell. The problem with this is that instead of dying slowly of aging, you will with almost 100 percent certainty die quickly from cancer.

The notable exception to the aging process was thought to be the species of lobsters found off the coast of the northwest United States. Theoretically immortal, these creatures simply did not age, and their cells did not grow older; they just keep growing bigger and bigger. Sadly it has been recently proven that they do succumb to old age, but not in the way we would consider normal. They become so big that eventually they don't have enough energy to molt and die inside their shells.

THE ARTIFICIAL BODY

Almost a million people in the United States have certain joints replaced every year. This is a relatively new science, with the first hip joint surgery being as recent as 1948. This type of surgery has of course much older and cruder antecedents with varying levels of effectiveness. Glass eyes are still in use and peg-legs seemed to work pretty well for pirates, but one wonders how useful a set of wooden teeth would be. It is actually apocryphal that George Washington had wooden teeth; in fact, he sported a rather fancy pair made from metal, ivory, and actual human teeth. Happily, the science of body part replacement has accelerated dramatically in recent decades.

Now, of course, we are progressing rapidly into two exciting areas: very advanced robotic prosthetics, and 3D printed body parts. These technologies seem destined to be immensely important to humanity as we struggle to repair the damage that we inflict upon ourselves through the simple act of living.

Great leaps forward in robot hands and prosthetic limbs are beginning to redefine the experience and definition of disablement. As Paralympic athletes are beginning to demonstrate, technology (allied to iron will) can eradicate the difference between someone with their body intact and those with parts missing or broken. What the technology is making possible is not just to repair or replace the body but to improve it. We will explore this in the third part of this chapter.

There is amazing progress being made in the field of artificial eyes and ears. Hearing aids are becoming increasingly sophisticated, and when combined with a Google Glass–like technology, the possibility of totally neutralizing the effects of deafness is almost upon us. Sensory augmentation provided by object-sensing canes for the blind and bionic eyes sending electronic images straight into the optical cortex might eventually eradicate blindness.

These advances, though, will seem archaic compared to the optimization and repair that will be possible when nanotechnology reaches maturity in the healthcare domain. It is easiest to imagine the technologies being applied here because in a sense they already are, particularly with the early exploration of gene therapy we have been seeing for the past 20 years. Gazing out a little way into the future, we can see treatments and products emerging that are not only tuned to our own individual genomes but specifically to the genome of the bacteria or DNA of the virus that is the causing the problem. When nanotech and genetic technologies merge, interventions would be performed in a much less invasive way, and we could change the way we cure diseases utterly.

Futurists gazing at healthcare describe a "medicine factory," a pill-sized capsule containing a miniaturized camera and other sensing apparatus designed to analyze gut flora for imbalances that could lead to diseases. Imagine that you swallow one of these factories (Figure 8-3), which then sits quietly in your intestine, monitoring the growth of different bacterial colonies. When something harmful is detected, this information is transmitted wirelessly to your doctor, who would instruct the medicine factory to start manufacturing the appropriate genetic treatment delivered through a "deactivated" virus vector. Over time this process could actually be automated and take out the presence of a human being altogether so that the factory goes about its business curing you of disease with little fuss. These sophisticated new treatment protocols would make a modern gastroscopic exam look positively medieval.

Figure 8-3. A pill-sized capsule containing sensing apparatus designed to find imbalances that could lead to diseases

The Extended Human

The subject of the extended human would not be complete without looking at our ongoing work to develop thinking machines. Although we have so far explored the physical and visual side of body modification, it is equally important to understand how we are going to enhance human cognition and sensing. There is a fantastic joke on the webcomic XKCD, which states, "Every time Wikipedia has a server outage my apparent IQ drops by 30 points." We are in a very real way already augmenting our minds with computational power, it's just that there is no direct connection into the brain, and we still need to use relatively crude interface tools to make use of the enhancement.

Of course, calling these relatively crude is only partially serious; they are in fact fabulously sophisticated compared to the way we have historically interfaced with machines. From the abacus and the Pascal adding machine, through to the nineteenth century Jacquard loom, and even the extraordinary Colossus and the punch card computers of the 1950s, during our first few millennia of machine cognition we were not able to make machines that were anything like us. To use these machines we had to become like them. We had to think like them and talk to them in their language. They were immobile, monolithic, mute devices, which demanded our sacrifice at the twin altars of engineering and math. Without deep knowledge, they were impenetrable and useless lumps of wood, metal, and plastic. What happened next (in a truly "ahead of its time" invention) was the first idea that began the slow shift in emphasis to a more human-centric way of interfacing with the machine.

THE MOTHER OF ALL DEMOS

Something in the zeitgeist demanded that the 60s would see a humanistic vision appearing in the rapidly expanding sphere of computer engineering. Right on cue, in 1968 an event occurred that would forever change the way we interacted with computers. In one epochal presentation, Douglas Englebert demonstrated a mouse, hypertext, and video conferencing for the first time to an astonished audience. This demonstration wasn't just remarkable because of the raft of totally transformational technologies that had emerged seemingly fully formed in a single instant, but the fact that they all pointed to a relationship with the machine that was now loaded in favor of the human. Anyone could use this technology; it was a true liberation of the secrets that had been locked up with the Engineer High Priests.

As is typical, for a long time after this game-changing moment, nothing much happened, except, that is, iteration after iteration of the same metaphors shown on that day in 1968, each a further refinement or regression, depending on the quality of design.

The next truly systemic change really came about 30 years later in the 1990s with the first experiments in virtual reality, touchscreens, and voice control. Again, a long period of refinement followed, and those technologies are now commonplace and are defining new forms of human-computer interaction, with the emphasis very firmly on the human.

So, when put in a timeline, it is clear that we have dramatically shifted the meeting point of man and machine, as depicted in Figure 8-4. It is now almost entirely weighted toward the human languages of symbols, words, and gestures. Nevertheless, that last inch seems to be a vast chasm that is very hard to breach. Think about all those interpretation errors that Siri makes (after all it is in some ways no smarter than an 80s text-based adventure), all those frustrating attempts to navigate virtual spaces and grab virtual objects, the clumsy approximation of body mapping of the Kinect, and the obvious flaws of the Leap Motion (trying to use it for applications in a desktop interface is inconsistent and very frustrating).

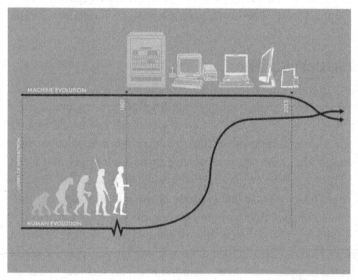

Figure 8-4. The meeting point of man and machine has dramatically shifted over time.

On top of that we have the amusingly titled *gorilla-arm syndrome* that plagues all gesture controlled systems; simply put, it is just too uncomfortable to hold your arm in the air for extended periods. It looks cool when Tom Cruise is flicking through swathes of digitized criminal records in the movie *Minority Report*, but it probably isn't as much fun using a gesture system to work on an Excel spreadsheet for five hours. Fret not! Help might be around the corner, from perhaps an unexpected direction—algorithms.

A PREDICTIVE WORLD, A WORLD OF SENSORS

We are yet to devise interfaces that can effortlessly give us what we want and need. We still must learn some kind of rules and deal with an interpretation layer that is never wholly natural.

Some early attempts at predictive interactions exist: the Japanese vending machine that recognizes the age and sex of the user and presents choices based on demographic breakdown, and the brilliant but scary ability of McDonald's to predict what you're going to order based on the car you drive with 80 percent accuracy. The latter was necessary so the fast-food chain could reduce the "unacceptable" 30-second wait while your drive-in order was prepared.

The sensor world that makes these kinds of predictive systems possible will only become richer and more precise. Big data will inform on-demand services, providing maximum efficiency and total customization. It will be a convincing illusion of perfect adaptation to need (Figure 8-5).

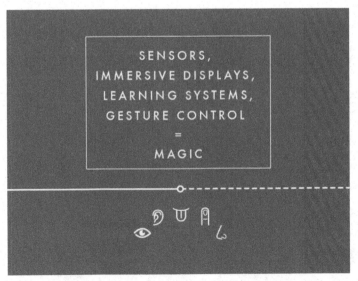

Figure 8-5. A convincing illusion of perfect adaptation to need

EMBEDDED TECH BRINGS A NEW LANGUAGE OF INTERACTION

The new language will be ultrasubtle and totally intuitive, building not on crude body movements but on subtle expressions and micro-gestures. This is akin to the computer mouse and the screen. Apple's Macintosh interface would never have worked if you needed to move the mouse the same distance as it moved on the screen. It would have been annoying and deeply un-ergonomic. This is the same for the gestural interface. Why swipe your arm when you can just rub your fingers together. What could be more natural than staring at something to select it or nodding to approve something? This is the world that will be possible when we have hundreds of tiny sensors mapping every movement, outside and within our bodies. For privacy, you'll be able to use imperceptible movements, or even hidden ones such as flicking your tongue across your teeth.

Figure 8-6 presents an interesting scenario for you to ponder: you see someone at a party you like; his social profile is immediately projected onto your retina—great, a 92 percent match. By staring at him for two seconds, you trigger a pairing protocol. He knows you want to pair, because you are now glowing slightly red in his retina screen. Then, you slide your tongue over your left incisor and press gently. This makes his left incisor tingle slightly. He responds by touching it. The pairing protocol is completed.

Figure 8-6. A new language of interaction

What is nice about these microgestures and expressions is that they are totally intuitive. Who doesn't stare at someone a second too long when they fancy them, and licking your lips is a spontaneously flirtatious gesture. The possible interactions are almost limitless and move us closer and closer to a natural human-computer interface. At this point, the really intriguing thing is that the interface has virtually disappeared; the screens are gone, and the input devices are dispersed around the body.

Is this scenario really that outlandish? Let's look at the technologies being developed currently that might make it possible.

Immersive displays

Samsung and other technology companies are currently working on contact lens screens; these are experimental right now and suffer the problem of how they are powered. The answer to that might be very close at hand, though, as other research is being conducted into using the body's energy (both kinetic and heat) to power embedded devices.

Skin-top computer

The skin-top computer would use some kind of distributed circuitry on and in the body that can map movement and capture all kind of body data such as blood flow, temperature, sweating, hormone levels, and so on. The first tattoo-like printed circuits are already available; it might not be too long before a Skin-Top Arduino community emerges.[5, 6, 7]

Thought control

Finally, there are the developments happening in thought control. We have already seen early experiments in creating visual maps of the thoughts of dreaming people, and though this is probably some distance from enabling telepathy it is certainly intriguing. Crude mind control of computers has been around for some time and in a rather alarming experiment conducted in 2013, one scientist could make a subject move his arm to push a button just by thinking about it. Both participants had nothing more than an electrode cap on and some

---

5   Paintable circuits on the skin, developed by Bare Conductive, UK.

6   "Epidermal Electronics" Paste Peelable Circuitry On Your Skin, Just Like A Temporary Tattoo, Popular Science Magazine, Nov 2011.

7   Stamp-On Circuits Could Put Your Phone On Your Finger, FastCo Design, Nov 2013.

clever code connecting them. Apparently, the subject could resist if he wanted, which provides some reassurance that we won't soon all become remote-controlled zombies.

WHAT WILL IT BE LIKE TO LIVE IN THE EMBEDDED WORLD?

Technology often outpaces our ability to understand and accept it, especially if you are over a certain age threshold. Eventually, though, we normalize everything; carrying a computer in your purse that is more powerful by a magnitude than those that ran twentieth century corporations and launched man into space is no big deal, we just use it to play Candy Crush mainly anyway. But, it would have seemed inconceivable to previous generations.

However, we can assume with some assurance that embeddable technology will have a more profound effect on us than we can imagine. A famous experiment, the Libet test, attempted to measure how quickly the conscious mind can send a simple somatic control (for example, press the red button). The extraordinary discovery was that the conscious mind triggers after the order is sent to the finger to push the button by a few microseconds. What does this mean? Essentially an unconscious part of the mind is deciding to push the button and the conscious mind is just agreeing with it. Imagine if we have systems operated in this way running around us in all scenarios. We would constantly have this disconcerting feeling that we were not operating under free will, but that some unknown force was driving us. There actually is: our genes, as Richard Dawkins points out.

So, how can we devise systems that don't force us down into the *uncanny valley* (which you can read about in more detail in Chapter 6). We need to make magical systems, where sensors, immersive displays, learning systems, and mind and gesture controls harmonize to give us exactly what we always wanted.

Consider one final scenario, presented in Figure 8-7 and Figure 8-8: you are sitting at home drinking coffee from your embedded-connected Nespresso service. The sensor in your tongue captures the response of your taste buds and the little nanobot that has made its home in your veins monitors the release of endorphins into your bloodstream. The data gathered are sent to the Nespresso factory, which analyses the readings and discovers that the flavor and caffeine level are not creating an optimal response in your body. Later that day you are standing at a bus stop; the Nespresso factory has custom-made a coffee that is perfectly suited to your tastes. It sends the aroma profile to an interactive poster next to you, which releases the delicious smell and tells you that the new flavor is available for delivery to your home, and that you will get an introductory 15 percent discount if you purchase it right away.

Now, that's not creepy in the slightest, is it?

Figure 8-7. The sensor in your tongue captures the response of your taste buds

Figure 8-8. The factory has custom-made a coffee that is perfectly suited to your tastes

Just Science Fiction, Right?

If the emerging technology curve approaches anything like the kind of acceleration predicted by such futurists as Kurzweil, Watson, and Kelly, the issues discussed in this chapter will become central to designing new digital services over the next few years. As designers and technologists we must ensure that we are prepared for the next wave or we might find ourselves left behind. The revolution is only just beginning.

Key Questions to Consider

1. What kind of learning systems will be needed to take complexity and strangeness away from the users of these services?

2. What kind of services that predict and even meet our needs without us having to intervene will be the ones that resonate and find an audience?

3. How will embeddables be designed so that they blend invisibly with the body? How will we avoid looking like the Borg in *Star Trek*, or becoming socially inept when we begin putting technology onto the surface and inside our bodies?

4. What is the timeline for the embeddable revolution, and what do tech companies need to do to prepare for this future?

5. What are the new types of control mechanisms and interaction metaphors that we are collectively going to have to consider for these types of intangible interfaces?

6. What skills will designers need to learn as we move away from a visual craft to one that takes into account the other senses, the body, and the mind?

Prototyping Interactive Objects

SCOTT SULLIVAN

There's an enormous opportunity in design right now, and it's upon us for two reasons. First, consumer expectations have evolved to a point at which they are not only open to but are expecting advanced digital functionality in their off-screen lives. Digital natives don't even remember a time when Internet-based tools did not exist, and those tools shifting into their physical space seems completely natural. The second reason is the increased accessibility of technology. When I say accessibility, I mean not only the incredibly low—and still plummeting—monetary cost of computing, but also the democratization of the production of technology. Thanks largely to the *Maker* movement and the open source movement, people who do not have an engineering background can create their own tools that are customized to their individual needs.

As digital product designers, we are positioned perfectly to enter the field of emerging technology. Our jobs as designers have always been to take in many inputs and synthesize a solution. Many times, these inputs are business goals, the needs of users, and knowledge of the platform in which the design will be constructed. What changes in the case of designing for emerging technology is the platform of the product. The platform that we are designing to currently is people's physical lives, and that platform is mediated through the input and output of data. New tools and resources open up new areas of design, such as connected devices, wearable smart objects, and contextually aware communication. These are all things that need to go through the same types of prototyping feedback cycles that have been around for screen-based product design for decades. Using Arduino microprocessors, XBee and Bluetooth radio communication, and Processing, designers can make their own tools to get the feedback that we need to create well-crafted and meaningful digital products that exist in our physical space.

I've had Internet access since I was 10 years old, and growing up with the control and awareness of data at my fingertips has opened my mind to believe that this control and awareness can, and should be, available to me in my physical environment. For example, earlier this year I bought a puppy. When I was crate-training him, I wanted to be able to check on him when I wasn't home. I installed a few web cameras in my house so that I could see what he was doing, and in the process, I realized how absolutely natural it felt to be able to access the data (visual data in this case) of my physical space on demand. Even after my dog was a little more independent, I still keep web cameras in the common areas of my house because I grew accustomed to having access to the data of my physical environment, and I didn't want to lose that, not to mention that it costs less than $100 and my dog could set it up.

Misconceptions Surrounding Designers Learning to Code

Screen-based digital products have very clearly defined limitations and established platforms. Designing for a two-dimensional screen with a cursor and keyboard is relatively simple. With little knowledge of the underlying technology you can sketch out solutions that very closely resemble the final product. With your two-dimensional sketches, you can get feedback and interaction from users and iterate toward a design solution that exists within a framework with which users already have an established association. In emerging technology, that established platform does not exist, and the few limitations that do exist are far less defined.

SKETCHING WITH CODE

Designers need to learn to code. They do not need to learn how to write production-level .NET web applications that are going to be pushed out to servers and used by millions of people. The type of coding that I'm referring to is a sketching medium that comes from a place of exploration, and it has very little to do with final implementation. This type of design coding is quick and dirty, relies heavily on frameworks, and is more about proof of concept than actually building a product that can scale up and be extended when needed.

Related to the conflation of code and implementation is the idea that when a designer learns to code she's making a career change, that knowing how to code makes you a developer. A lot of these misconceptions come from our compartmentalized ideas of what it means to be a designer and what it means to be a developer. The current pervasive relationship between a designer and a developer is that the designer will make nontechnical decisions around the structure, functionality, and appearance of a product, and the developer will implement those decisions the best he can. How this relationship changes in designing for emerging technologies is that the materiality in which the designer is designing with the technology and data itself. For designers to have the command that they're used to having in more established platforms, they must be able to create prototypes and interpret the data that our prototypes produce.

In terms of technical skills or traits that are needed for design in emerging technology, the most important among them by far are curiosity and the willingness to learn new skills to make things. The boundaries of what you're designing are practically nonexistent, so there's not a single set of skills that you must learn. For example, to prototype a sensor network within a physical space to a similar level of fidelity of a static pixel-based wireframe, an emerging technology designer would need to have a very basic level of knowledge of computer programming, microcontrollers, sensor technology, wireless networking, three-dimensional modeling/printing, data collection, data structure, and data visualization. I am in no way saying that you need to understand any of these things before beginning a project; you just have to learn them as you go and slowly build your skill set as you encounter those problems.

PROCESSING AND ARDUINO

The two primary tools that I use are Processing and Arduino. They are both open source and there are plenty of great online resources to help with the learning process including extremely helpful online communities. You can see the results of one my projects in Figure 9-1.

Initially created to serve as a software sketchbook and to teach computer programming fundamentals within a visual context, Processing evolved into a development tool for professionals. That was great for me as a visual learner: using Processing let me see exactly what was going on with the code as I was being introduced to more abstract concepts.

Figure 9-1. One of my hardware-controlled augmented reality projects using Arduino and Processing

Arduino is both a hardware platform as well as a programming language built on C/C++ with which you can take simple electrical signals from sensors and output them to physical actuators or your computer. For example, you can take a simple motion sensor and configure it so that a light turns on whenever it is triggered, such as is shown in Figure 9-2. You could also plug the Arduino into your computer and count the number of times the motion sensor has been triggered in a simple program.

Figure 9-2. An Arduino R3 plugged into a PIR sensor

CASE STUDY: CAPYBARA

Capybara is a project of mine that uses a wireless network of Arduinos to collect anonymous movement data from patrons visiting a small retail store. The data was collected and visualized in Processing and used to inform decisions such as store layout and product placement as well as to measure which days of the week and times experienced the highest number of visits.

Capybara started out with a simple goal: I had wanted to learn about microcontrollers and sensor technology. I had been interested in both of these for a while and had done some very basic projects with Arduino and Processing, but I needed an interesting, real-world project to really get me moving into more advanced areas. I could have begun tracking activity in my home, but that seemed boring. I wanted to physically sense the activity of people in a public space, but this presented some difficult challenges: if I located the sensor outside in actual public space, it could be stolen or destroyed by weather. I also didn't know how to power a sensor without access to power outlets. Another concern was the legality of collecting data in a public space. And finally, there was the issue of how to communicate and store all that data without WiFi.

I began to look around my neighborhood for a place that I could install my sensor, and I ended up walking into a small boutique clothing store named Tigertree (Figure 9-3), just a few blocks away from home, which happens to be owned by two close friends. I asked their permission to put a sensor in their store, and they agreed. I probably would have put the entire project off for another year, but the next day one of the store owners called me and asked, "Why don't you put a whole bunch of sensors in the store and give me some data that's actually useful?" That's when the project became very real and very exciting.

I began by searching online electronics hobby shops for sensors that could detect physical activity. I found the passive infrared (PIR) sensor at a local RadioShack store and began plugging away. Most of these sensors have plenty of example Arduino code to get you started and after about an hour of figuring out how to wire up everything, I was looking at a terminal output that printed a "1" every time I waved my hand in front of the sensor. I cannot explain in words how this felt. Even though I was using example code, an example wiring schematic, and the most basic of all sensors, I had created something dynamic that responds to real-world physical movement! I spent the next hour speaking in rapid incomprehensible bursts while waving my arms around frantically, trying to convince my girlfriend that this was the most amazing technological breakthrough since the microprocessor, because that's what it felt like. (She demurred, but patiently let me go on.)

Figure 9-3. The test bed for my sensor project: Tigertree

The next step was to get this sensor to communicate with Processing. I had a bit of previous experience with Processing, and I knew it was possible to hook up an Arduino to a Processing sketch. I found Firmata, a Processing library that reads serial data from an Arduino, and after a couple of hours of installing libraries and looking up error messages in Google, I had those ones and zeros flashing in bright orange in a 300 x 300 pixel Processing sketch.

This was the second major technological breakthrough of my life, and once again I spent another hour waving my arms around and marveling in my futuristic achievements. (My girlfriend sighed and moved on to another room.) After the excitement ebbed a bit, I set out to learn how to increment the number on the screen. I needed to keep track of this data, so after searching for more example code, I found something that I thought might work. I was able to piece enough of it together with the example code I already had that I was able to get it counting, even though I didn't really understand how it was doing it.

This is my first real exposure to code. When I attempted Processing tutorials in the past, I would always lose interest because the tutorials lacked a tangible goal. Now, I had a practical need to understand and absorb how these things were working. I spent the next week asking developers with whom I work to explain every line of code to me while I simultaneously annotated comments within the example code. When I had a tangible and meaningful example of what the code was doing, suddenly the more abstract concepts such as variables and for-loops became much more accessible. I used my body movements for an input and tracked this movement through the lines of code to see exactly what was going on to that caused the pixels to move on the screen; the excitement of this new knowledge combined with creating something dynamic and physical was addictive.

LOSING THE WIRES

By that point, I had a pretty solid foundation; I had a people sensor reading in to a program that was counting. My design studio partner became involved with the project, and we converted it to a studio-funded effort. Now, I needed to think about getting the sensors into the store. It was impractical to have six or seven sensors all physically wired to a central laptop in the store, so I needed something wireless and battery powered. Luckily, I discovered the Arduino Fio, an Arduino that has a plug-in for an XBee radio for wireless communication. I also came across a JST plug that made it possible for me to power everything using lithium-ion batteries.

Learning to use the XBee radios started off simply; after a few hours of reading and configuring everything, I was able to get a basic one-way communication between two radios (another one of those life-altering technological breakthroughs; my girlfriend gave up and went shopping), and now all that remained was to do it with a handful of radios. This required the XBees to be placed in what's called API mode. It also marked the beginning of a very dark couple months for me, being very much over my head in terms of technological ability. The project nearly derailed, but thanks to a little help from some of my more technically savvy friends, I was able to get the radios working.

After swapping out the PIR sensor for the more granular ultrasonic range finders, we were ready to install the hardware. The only obstacle to overcome was recording the data itself. I had solved the problem of acquiring the necessary data and displaying it on the screen, but I had no way of saving it in a useful form. I needed two things for every piece of data: I needed to know what sensor was triggered, and I needed to know the exact time of the movement. This was its own little coding rabbit hole. I had to learn how computers understood time. Fortunately, Processing is built on Java, and Java has a date format that represents time in the milliseconds since January 1, 1970, 00:00:00 GMT (otherwise known as epoch time or Unix time), thus turning time into a number that you can use and calculate in a linear fashion. With the time and sensor identification all figured out, I was able to create a comma-separated value (CSV) spreadsheet output that had a line for every time the sensor was triggered, in which the first column was the sensor and the second column was the exact time.

GOING TO BETA TESTING

To be certain, nothing that I had crafted could be considered the most elegant or safest solution, but it did complete the prototype setup, enough that we could install the sensors in the store. You can see it deployed in Figure 9-4.

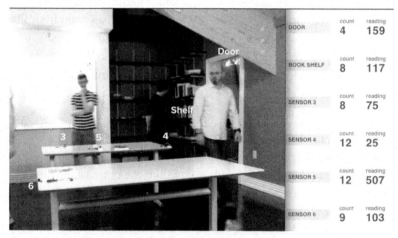

Figure 9-4. Testing the sensor network in the studio

The initial beta installation went smoothly; we had the sensors up and running and they began to immediately collect data. Over the first week, we made no effort to visualize the data, but I recieved a call from the store owners saying that just looking at the raw totals they had already identified a bad flaw in the layout of the store. When the store became slightly busy, there was a bottleneck that formed in the middle of the floor that then caused one-third of the store to be essentially cut off. The owners are there six days a week, and the store had been open for years, yet they had never noticed this behavior until they actually saw the data. They immediately set about rearranging the store layout to correct it. Something else happened the first week: people in the store began to notice the sensors. At that stage in the project, the sensors were bare PCB boards with wires and a battery sticking out of them with a small red LED power indicator light. This was right after the horrific bombing of the Boston Marathon, and people were genuinely alarmed by these crude-looking little devices they were discovering all about the store. I received a call one weekend from the store owners asking me to do something after three people approached them to let them know that they found a bomb under one of their display tables (see Figure 9-5) and were getting as far away from the store as possible. We learned the first big lesson from beta testing: the sensors must look like they belong in the space. We immediately obtained a Makerbot and very quickly designed and printed cases for the sensors.

Figure 9-5. A bare sensor taped under a display table in Tigertree

We had the first beta round up for a couple weeks. We gathered a good amount of data and began working on creating meaningful tools out of this new information source. We had originally called the sensors "people counters" because, well… that's exactly what they do; they count people as they walk by, but when you looked at the raw data and saw the clumps of activity, something didn't seem to line up. We ended up sitting in the store for long periods of time and observing what was happening and comparing it to our data. People didn't just linearly walk around the store; they would go to one part of it and meander back and forth multiple times or stay in front of one display for a while and move back and forth, each time setting off the sensors. Our sensors weren't people sensors, they were activity sensors. Fifty different people didn't walk by one sensor in five minutes; one person was concentrated in that single area for those five minutes and triggered the same sensor fifty times. We realized that we needed to recontextualize the sensor data, and to more accurately convey what was actually happening in the store, we needed to know exactly how many people were in the store at the time of the activity.

TRACKING PIXELS

We started searching for a new type of sensor. We did have one sensor on the door that would tell us how many people came into the store, but it couldn't tell us if they were going in or out. None of the microcontroller-based sensors that we could find seemed like they were going to work. We continued looking around and eventually came to the conclusion that we needed to use a video camera and *blob tracking*. After learning so much about Processing, at this point it wasn't completely out of the question to create a simple computer vision system. There were a couple Processing libraries that I was aware of and I was excited to learn something new and potentially very powerful. Again, I had to source a wireless solution for my new camera sensor. I found some simple, inexpensive web cameras that connected to a wireless network and which I could access over the Internet. I also found a Processing library to get that video feed into a sketch. It took a couple months to write the code, and I was forced to learn all kinds of interesting things about exactly how digital images work and yet more advanced programming concepts such as array lists, but it all worked. Well, it worked in the very controlled environment of our studio, where I would have our summer intern walk in and out of the kitchen countless times (see Figure 9-6).

Figure 9-6. Camera sensor output

When we started testing the camera sensor in the store it was a different story. There were a lot of unforeseen issues. For instance, rapidly fluctuating light levels coming in through the windows would register as noise. Also, the store's wireless Internet couldn't handle the amount of data that was needed to support the camera. At the same time, we began having conversations within the studio around the invasiveness of using a camera and privacy issues. A lot of the more established retail analytic solutions that are very expensive and primarily used by larger retail chains use computer vision systems to track the exact path of individuals through their entire visit to the store, and even identify their gender and approximate age (and more). We specifically did not want to create a product like this, and even the idea of using a camera in a noninvasive way began to make us feel uneasy; thus, we decided to scrap the entire camera effort and work on a less invasive solution.

We reinstalled the sensor network almost exactly as the first beta was installed, and are using the less granular door data to get a rough idea of the current occupancy to contextualize the internal activity. Our second beta installation has a goal of acquiring six months of uninterrupted sensor data from within the store, which is presenting its own unique challenges.

IT'S NOT EASY, BUT YOU CAN DO IT

All of this can be extremely intimidating. I spent years wanting to get into Processing and Arduino before I actually made the leap because I was apprehensive. I had never really made anything dynamic before, and writing code seemed incredibly foreign to me. I've likened this process to being punched in the face: if you've never been punched in the face, it seems like just about the worst thing that could happen to you, but when it happens you think "oh that wasn't so bad, I survived and it doesn't hurt too much," and from that point forward you're not so scared of that punch anymore! Learning technical skills is very similar: before you start it's terrifying, but after you get "punched," learning to code is actually quite fun! Every time you do something new, you feel like you've just climbed Mt. Everest, and that feeling pushes you through the next challenge until it happens again.

After you become familiar with physical prototyping techniques, a whole new dimension of product design is available to you. You can create vetted products that extend into people's worlds and provide us with knowledge and capabilities that have only been available in conventional digital products. With cheap and accessible microcontrollers such as the Arduino, we can track physical movement in a store at the same level that we can track clicks through e-commerce platforms; we can place them on our bodies to passively collect information about our behavior that used to be nearly impossible to track; and we can enable new experiences that rely on our devices being aware of one another. These products are entering our lives and we're going to be certain that when they do, we ensure that they're the right thing to enter our lives and they're doing it in the least disruptive way possible.

Emerging Technology and Toy Design

BARRY KUDROWITZ, PHD

There is an important distinction between a toy and a toy product. A toy is an object that is used for play. A spoon can be used as a toy. A box can be used as a toy. A 3D printer can be used as toy. But none of these items are *toy products*. A toy product is an item that is intentionally designed, manufactured, and sold for the primary purpose of play. A tinkerer can make a toy in his basement with an Arduino or a similar device. There are many resources available for tinkering, such as *instructables. com* or *Make* magazine, which show people how to "hack" or prototype some exciting toy concepts. These, however, are not *toy products*, because they are not intended for manufacture and sale. This chapter targets designers who want to work in the toy product domain, not the toy hacking domain. Toy hacking has no restrictions and thus one can almost use any emerging technology imaginable when the intent is not mass production. I am also distinguishing toy products from video games; these are separate markets. For those who want to bring toy products to market, there are several barriers of which you need to be aware. Let's dig in and begin investigating.

The Challenge of Toy Design

Designing in the toy industry is more difficult than one might expect given its playful nature. There are several reasons for this:

- In addition to the form, function, and manufacturability concerns that are inherent in all product design, toy designers have two customers: the adult caregiver/purchaser and the child/end user. These two customers tend to have very different needs and preferences.

- Toys are required to pass a variety of international safety standard tests related to choking hazard, sharpness, magnets, chemicals, moving parts, strangulation hazard, projectiles, drowning hazard, and so on. Often, every piece of a toy must undergo a series of these tests to prove that the product does not represent a threat to a child's safety in any of these areas.

- The toy industry is seasonal and experiences the largest amount of sales during the holidays. Most revenue is generated in Q4. Popular trends/brands/properties/characters are constantly changing, so the timeline from concept to shelf is very tight if you want to have a new product ready for the holiday season. This seasonality also makes it difficult to plan inventory and get realistic feedback during the year.

- Toys are inexpensive. Very few toys are at a price point comparable to a consumer electronics item. As children grow older, they become interested in different things. Their skills and abilities change and therefore they regularly desire new and different toys. The purchasers are aware of this, so the price they expect to pay for toys is typically lower than that of other consumer goods. The relatively expensive toys that are marketable tend to be large (for example, ride-on vehicles) or electronic gaming systems that are not typically considered toy products.

- Currently, there are not many toy company options for licensing ideas. In the 1970s there were many medium-sized licensing manufacturers, but the large toy companies (Hasbro and Mattel) purchased them. Similarly there are fewer small-sized toy retailers today than there were in the 1970s. This makes it more difficult for an independent toy inventor to get their product onto store shelves.

To overcome these challenges, toy designers must innovate robust, low-cost products that appeal to both children and adults in a short amount of time to keep up with a rapidly changing market.

How does emerging technology fit into this design challenge? Often, it does not. This is an artifact of two of the aforementioned issues: time and money. Although there are a variety of exceptions, which we will cover in this chapter, toys are generally not using what would be called emerging technology. The toy industry might be utilizing new manufacturing practices or materials, but it is not common to walk into a toy store to find an emerging technology that was recently highlighted in a scientific journal or magazine.

Toys and the S-Curve

The *S-Curve* refers to the general shape formed by plotting a technology's performance over its lifetime. There are typically four main phases of a technology life cycle (see Figure 10-1). The first phase is when the technology is emerging through research and development. In the second phase, the use of the technology is growing in the marketplace and it is becoming widely accepted. The third phase is maturity, in which growth slows down, the technology is widely understood, and few new players join the market. The final phase is the decline of the technology, which is typically the result of a newer technology replacing the utility of the original technology. These stages are sometimes referred to by different names, but the general concept remains the same.

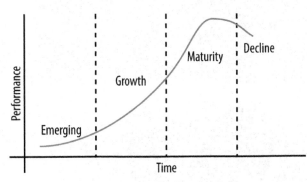

Figure 10-1. A technology's life cycle: the S-Curve

In the Toy Product Design class I created and taught at both the Massachusetts Institute of Technology (MIT) and the University of Minnesota (UMN), the students take their own toy ideas from concept to functional prototype with the help of children and industry. In these classes the students often try to incorporate technology during the growth stage, such as specialized sensors and actuators that can cost $20 to $30 online. A toy concept might be fun and feasible, but a special part that costs $10 to manufacture might contribute at least $40 to the retail cost of the toy. Will parents want to purchase a toy that costs $100 to $200, particularly if it offers only one type of play pattern? The likely answer is no.

In most cases, toys begin using a technology years after that technology has been moving up the S-Curve of its life cycle. A technology is used when the cost of the manufacture of that component has reached a price point at which it can be profitably incorporated into a toy. Figure 10-2 presents two examples of this dynamic. Of course, this is the case for most consumer products; however, toys are typically on even tighter budgets.

Figure 10-2. Toy prototype examples using mature, inexpensive electronics

As an example, BEAM (Biology, Electronics, Aesthetics, and Mechanics) robotics uses simple parts to produce robots that mimic life. Scientists, engineers, and hobbyists have created human-like robots for years, but it wasn't until 2004 when it became affordable enough to mass produce a personal anthropomorphic IR-controlled robot toy such as Mark Tilden's RoboSapien. Similarly, small motors and microphones existed for a long time before Innovation First released Hexbugs in 2007. The technology was just affordable enough to be profitable when sold inside a $10 toy bug.

This is not to deter designers from experimenting with new technology in toy concepts. It is meant solely as a cautionary note that it might take several years before the technology is inexpensive enough to make a profitable toy product. Toy designers need to imagine how technology that's emerging today might be incorporated into future playthings when the technology becomes affordable for mass production.

Toys and Intellectual Property

The toy industry is a bit like the fashion industry: tastes change rapidly and products have a short life cycle of one to three years. This makes it difficult to protect intellectual property. It might not make economic sense to file a patent to provide a 20-year monopoly especially if it takes 2 to 3 years to prosecute. For example, guitar toys were trendy from 2005 to 2010 with Guitar Hero and Paper Jamz driving sales. If someone had a great guitar-toy concept toward the end of this trend, there would have been no sustainable market by the time she filed a patent. A major exception would be technology that could be used in multiple products or for creating a new product platform.

The overarching point here is that toy ideas from independent inventors do not necessarily need to be patented before licensing to a toy company. Sometimes, this deal between the inventor and licensing company is based more on trust than on concerns over protecting intellectual property.

It is for these reasons that intellectual property in the toy industry tends to take the form of a copyright, trademark, or *design patent* rather than a *utility patent*. A design patent is less expensive and takes less time to file than a utility patent. A design patent protects the ornamental features of the invention, whereas a utility patent protects the functionality of the invention.

A large toy company has the resources and capital to protect all of its new technology; however, a smaller toy company or independent inventor might not have the ability to invest in protecting an idea if the market is erratic and if the patent is not required for licensing. In the past 10 years, Japan is the only country that has filed more toy-related patents than the United States (112,457 versus 52,774) from USPTO. Historically, Mattel holds the most United States toy patents with 4,185; Hasbro has filed 601. Putting this in perspective, these numbers are almost on par with some famous individual inventors—Thomas Edison filed 2,332 patents, and Jerome Lemelson filed 605. Relative to other industries, technology in toys tends to be less protected and the industry puts less emphasis on research and development. Protecting intellectual property usually makes sense in the toy industry only when the toy idea is timeless and one can write broad claims to describe the concept.

Emerging Technologies in Toy Design

Even though the toy industry tends to adapt technologies later in their life cycle, there are plenty of examples of emerging technology being incorporated in toys:

- The emerging technology is an accessory to the toy (for example, using a smartphone to control a toy car).

- The emerging technology is affordable enough to be immediately implemented. This includes things we tend to not think of as technology such as a new type of mechanical connector for building blocks.

- The technology might not serve more practical purposes, but is interesting enough to be desired for its playfulness. A great example of this is Silly Putty.

- Novel sensors and electronics are used and the cost reflects the investment. Consider the electronic toys you might find at Brookstone.

- The emerging technology is in the production/manufacturing of the toy (for example, 3D printing).

EMERGING TECHNOLOGY ACCESSORIES

One way toys are using emerging technology is by being an accessory to an established product. Many toy companies do not have the means to move into an entirely new domain, so they adapt their strengths and manufacturing resources to produce a complementary product.

Several companies have developed products that wrap around a smartphone or tablet, turning it into a creature with a screen. The hardware typically comes with a software app that one would download to utilize the previously owned technology product in a new way. Figure 10-3 shows examples of Totoya Creatures "plush toy" accessories that turn a tablet or smartphone into an interactive stuffed animal. (Ubooly is another prominent name in this sector.) The tablet or smartphone becomes the face and brains. This makes it possible for a toy company that once made stuffed animals to now have a product in the consumer electronic aisle.

Figure 10-3. Totoya Creatures are plush monsters that utilize a smart device with a special app

The Disney AppMATes and Mattel Apptivity line of products consist of toys that interface with tablet devices. Users can control the app with a physical action figure as a playful stylus. With these products, users can race a physical car directly on the screen or battle with physical action figures. In the past, video games have utilized physical interfaces outside of a controller (Nintendo Power Glove, Power Pad, and Zapper); however, in these examples, the physical item is not a toy on its own. Skylanders: Spyro's Adventure and Disney Infinity have blurred the lines between the video game and toy industries. In the Skylanders and Infinity gaming platforms, the video game has a physical toy component. The user purchases and plays with action figures that are "transported" into the video game world, bridging the gap between real and virtual play. The toy component contains very minimal technology (an RFID chip); the real innovation is in the interaction with the video game.

In these prior examples, the existing smart device is controlled with a physical toy. Conversely, there are examples in which the physical toy is controlled with the existing smart device. There are a number of wireless vehicles such as cars, planes, and helicopters that a user can control with a smartphone (the Parrot AR.Drone, iRemoco, Griffin helicopter, and Rover Spy Tank are all examples). A recent innovation by Orbotix is the Sphero Ball, which is a simple looking sphere that contains internal motors that roll the ball wirelessly with a smart device interface. The physical toys in these examples are a bit more advanced than the RFID or stylus action figures because they both receive and transmit information.

In all of these examples, a smartphone or tablet is the host technology. Smartphones and tablets are likely the most advanced technology that modern families own and entrust to children. However, as technology begins to incorporate into the home and community in new ways, there will likely be other hosts for physical toy accessories.

One concern when designing a toy as an accessory is that the toy's success is dependent on another company's platform. The designer has less control over the future iterations. One might release a product to find that it no longer works with the newest platform.

SIMPLE AND AFFORDABLE EMERGING "TECHNOLOGY"

Emerging technology in the toy industry might not look the same as emerging technology in medicine or personal electronics.

In 2010, if you were to do a survey of the top 100 best-selling toys on Amazon.com, you would find less than 10 items that contained any electronics. A survey in 2013 revealed that not one of the Amazon .com top 10 best-selling toys contained electronics or even any significantly advanced technology—the top sellers included card games, rubber bands, and injection molded blocks. Popular toys (excluding video games) tend to be simple, low-tech products such as Silly Bandz or Squinkies. In a culture of video games and smartphones, there is still a market for simple physical play. Even with the popularity of the virtual building block game, Minecraft, sales for low-tech stalwart Lego were up 20 percent in 2013 over 2012. Digital play currently lacks the face-to-face social element and the tangible interaction.

In society today, one can almost view digital toys as a separate market. There is a toy box and there is a smart device. These realms are beginning to collide. What is called a *toy* today might not what you typically find at a big box retailer such as Toys R Us. Children are playing with tablets, smartphones, and laptops. A smartphone can hold thousands of games (an infinite number, if web based) and many are free. How can the board game industry compete with unlimited and free? One answer is that the physical and social bonding element cannot be replaced with the digital equivalent. Designers are still inventing new types of blocks and sticks and children still want to play with them.

YOXO is a Minneapolis-based company that inspires children to create their own play. There is an old adage that the best child's toy is a cardboard box. That is exactly what YOXO sells: connectors for toilet paper rolls, boxes of boxes, tubes of tubes, a giant empty refrigerator box, and so on. Sometimes, less technology is less restrictive.

Innovation can be incremental and it can be radical. Incremental innovation is about doing something better, whereas radical innovation is about doing something different. The toy industry tends to be more incremental. Often incremental innovation is more easily assimilated into culture as people can quickly understand and relate to it. From experience talking with toy agents and toy companies, if the idea cannot be explained by looking at a box image for a few seconds or with a 20-second video demonstration, the concept will be more difficult to sell.

As a personal example, in my Master's thesis at MIT, I designed a bi-stable spring mechanism that can be used to launch foam balls. This technology was used in the Nerf Atom Blaster, but it is not highly visible in the product. The mechanism allows for a slightly different interaction with the toy and a reduction in part count.

Recently, YOXO filed for a patent on a connector design for assembling toilet paper tubes. This technology is the basis for their product line, with which children can construct their own toys with cardboard and other recyclables, as illustrated in Figure 10-4.

Figure 10-4. YOXO is a construction toy developed by Jeff Freeland Nelson

In these two toys, there are no cutting-edge sensors or algorithms, but they are both examples of patent-worthy technology that are valuable and innovative in the toy industry. The technology is simple, subtle, and inexpensive. If you visit a toy fair at which industry and inventors are demonstrating and selling new products, the response to emerging technology there is more like, "Why didn't I think of that?" as opposed to "How did they do that?"

Inherently Playful Technology

Einstein said, "If at first the idea is not absurd, then there is no hope for it." When one first discovers or invents a new technology the first reaction is likely surprise. It can be confusing at first, and if there is an "Aha!" moment of insight, the surprise could lead to laughter or joy. This is how the novelty of a raw technology itself can be converted into a toy.

In 1943, James Wright combined silicone oil and boric acid to invent a material that behaved as a solid over short periods of time and a liquid over a long period of time. He could not find a market for these unique material properties. In 1950, the search for practical uses ended and it was sold for its playful properties under the name Silly Putty.

More recently, in 2009, Mattel released Mindflex. This is a game that utilizes an EEG (electroencephalography) headset with which a user can control a fan by using brain waves to manipulate a ball in the air. In a sense, the user is controlling a ball with their mind. The toy retailed between $60 and $120 and was successful on its first release in the market. A company called NeuroSky founded in 2004 developed the technology used in this game. Since 2009, the company has applied its technology to applications outside the realm of toys. Mindflex is also used as a platform in the hacker community as a low-cost means of making tools and toys controlled through EEG.

The POPmatrix tongue display unit developed by Aisen Chacin is a grid of electrodes that can be placed on the tongue that allows users to "see" through touch. This is a prototype toy version of a serious invention published by Dr. Paul Bach-y-Rita in 1998 called the BrainPort with which users can see via their tongue by substituting optical nerve input with tongue nerve input. This device when connected with a camera makes it possible for sight-impaired users to visualize a real-time pixilated version of the world in front of them. In this case, a technology that was specifically developed for users with visual impairments had a strong curiosity or "wow" factor that broadened its potential user population.

A designer does not simply sit down and create this type of "tech-wow" toy. These concepts typically start in a research lab in the process of trying to develop something else and the toy product results from serendipity. A designer who does not have a science or engineering background will likely not have the resources to invent new technology;

however, she can always be observant of interesting phenomena in the world. Any naturally occurring phenomena that are surprising or intriguing might be worthy of further exploration.

The downside to "tech-wow" toys is that the wow factor can fade. If the fun is solely in the newness of the technology, eventually it will be less interesting. For example, when Glo Worm (1982) and Teddy Ruxpin (1985) were released they had tremendous a "wow factor" because few stuffed animals could illuminate and talk, but today this technology is commonplace.

Sensors and Toy Design

Electronic sensors tend to be what people associate with technology. Sensors are often used to enhance the interaction potential of the toy. If the toy can understand what you are doing, it can respond appropriately and perhaps even learn. This could lead to a more playful experience as the toy can adapt to the user's abilities to maintain an optimal level of challenge. An optimal challenge is critical for play because it keeps the user engaged.

Sensors can also add functionality, and functionality adds affordances. A toy with more affordances might have more play value because it could allow for more types of play. One can also argue that sensors take away from the user's ability to design their own play patterns. In any case, as the cost of sensors decrease, we will see more of them in toys. In the future, we might see low-cost (or even free) smart toys for which the cost of the technology is offset by the related digital revenue, similar to how smartphone costs are subsidized by purchasing service subscriptions.

Sifteo is a company founded in 2009 by Dr. David Merrill and Jeevan Kalanithi after leaving the MIT Media Lab. Their product, also named Sifteo, is a gaming platform comprising a set of small blocks with screens (see Figure 10-5), sensors, and wireless communication that gives them the capability to interact with other blocks. There are a number of games one can play on the Sifteo platform with images, words, and video.

Figure 10-5. Sifteo is a gaming platform developed by Dr. David Merrill and Jeevan Kalanithi

In 2011, when the product was finally released, the starter set of three cubes was priced at $149; the following year it dropped to $129. Both the price point and play potential of Sifteo is comparable to electronic gaming systems such as the Nintendo DS, which makes it a more serious and considered purchase than most toy products. In 2010—between the time when Sifteo was introduced at TED in 2009 and its commercial release in 2011—Hasbro released a competing low-cost version of the concept that greatly simplified the play by eliminating some technology, which allowed it to enter the market at a $30 price point.

And yet, Sifteo not only survived this competitive onslaught, it thrived. Why?

One can have a great idea for a new tech-toy, but the price needs to be comparable to the other products that have similar functionality. As a designer, you can try to guide the product to be anchored with a specific category of products, but this is not always in your control. In the case of Sifteo, its toy product was successful at that price point against lower-cost alternatives because it could be anchored with consumer electronics instead of the inexpensive board games.

Kurt Roots and Dr. Monika Heller founded CogCubed shortly after the release of Sifteo in 2011. They realized that sensors in toys might have the ability to understand user behavior. Specifically in the health domain, these sensors can be used to assess and improve cognitive deficits. CogCubed captures data as players manipulate objects, which can be used to create a behavior profile. These profiles can then be used to distinguish abnormalities, but they also can be used to customize challenges for the specific player. As sensors become more prevalent and interconnected, toys and products in general are going to create more engaging, personalized experiences that have the potential to positively impact cognition and behavior.

There are some open source platforms such as Arduino and LittleBits (Figure 10-6) that make it easy for designers, artists, and tinkerers to create functional electronic toys with sensors and animation. A relatively new sensor that is sold through *sparkfun.com* is the XBee, which allows your prototype to communicate with the cloud. Imagine designing toys with this technology. Your doll could know more about the world than you do. Websites like *inventables.com*, *sparkfun.com*, and *instructables.com* are great inspiration sources for all designers.

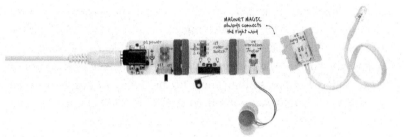

Figure 10-6. LittleBits are sets of easy-to-use electronic building blocks developed by Ayah Bdeir

Emerging Technology in Production and Manufacturing

The technology in toys can be showcased (like in Sifteo), hidden (such as my spring mechanism of the Atom Blaster), or it can be the toy itself (such as Silly Putty). Another area in which the technology fits into to the toy industry is in the process of its manufacture.

The laser cutter has recently emerged as an integral manufacturing tool in the toy industry. It is a fast, inexpensive, and exact means of cutting thin materials including plastic, wood, fabric, and metal. With advances in technology, smaller toy companies, such as YOXO, and individual toy designers can now afford to own a laser cutter. Consumers are seeing more flat-packed, thin wood toys in gift stores and at toy shows. With this tool, graphic designers who are not trained in 3D-CAD (computer-aided design) modeling software can now produce physical product with their knowledge of vector-based 2D software such as Adobe Illustrator.

3D printers are also becoming more affordable and faster. In the near future, people will purchase 3D printers similar to the way they currently purchase 2D printers (the cost of the print cartridges will likely be expensive to mitigate the cost of the device). Children and parents can download and print CAD models of physical toys for their children just as they would download a new game onto a smartphone. This is already happening on a small scale with the Maker Bot Digital Store, where children can choose from a set of predesigned action figures to download and print (*https://digitalstore.makerbot.com/browse*), as shown in Figure 10-7.

Figure 10-7. At the Maker Bot Digital Store, children and parents can purchase toys to print at home

In the future, parents and children might play the role of designer by creating new toys and printing them at home. This poses problems. Parents are not exposed to the many quality assurance checks that the toy industry is required to perform on each piece of every toy. One can imagine parents creating toys that are choking hazards or parts that can shear into small sharp points. Parents might embed magnets in ways that allow them to release or create customized projectiles. How can we better prepare ourselves for the future when anyone can be a toy designer with the purchase of an inexpensive rapid prototyping machine?

This future is almost here. Companies such as Ponoko provide the rapid prototyping and 3D printing services. Users can upload their own CAD models for others to purchase. The company prints and ships the model. This is only one step away from a future of home toy production.

SUGGESTIONS FOR DESIGNING TOYS WITH EMERGING TECHNOLOGY

1. Imagine the possibilities of current technology when it becomes affordable enough to be applied to a toy. For example, smartwatches that interface with your smartphone have recently entered on the market. Imagine if that technology becomes even more affordable and one can place small sensors with screens around the house that can communicate with one another from a distance. This opens up a realm of toy and game possibilities.

2. If you are developing new technology, keep in mind cost and time. Often incremental innovation is easier to bring to market. The toy industry is like the fashion industry and style changes regularly and rapidly.

3. Make the toy about the play not about the technology. The play that the toy affords should be timeless. The activity should be fun and enjoyable in and of itself. As a designer, use the technology to achieve, enable, or enhance the desired play, not simply provide a "wow" factor. Ask yourself if future generations will still find the toy engaging after the technology is commonplace.

4. Stay informed about new manufacturing processes and rapid prototyping tools. Understanding how toys and products are manufactured will not only make you a better designer, it might also inspire creative ideas.

5. Attend a toy fair. There are a number of toy fairs around the world and they often showcase different vendors. Toy fairs are the conferences of the toy industry where the newest toy products are introduced and presented.

Summary

The role of the toy designer is changing. In the past, toy designers were likely to come from Industrial Design Bachelor of Arts programs, trained to make drawings and foam models. These are still valuable skills, but in today's society, the industrial designer is also expected to know how things work, how things are manufactured, and how to incorporate electronics, sensors, and new technology. The industrial design discipline is slowly blending with the discipline of engineering design. In academia, this fusion has already begun: there are industrial design degrees that are based in schools of science; there are schools offering interdisciplinary product design degrees; there are graduate programs in industrial design; and there are engineering programs that have product design tracks. In industry, large toy design companies have entire engineering divisions dedicated to research and development. I am hopeful that in the near future, most academic design programs will require a class in computer programming to prepare students for the digital future they will be designing. Although the toy design industry is slow to implement emerging technology, we are always advancing and innovating.

[11]

Musical Instrument Design

CAMILLE GOUDESEUNE

Experience Design and Musical Instruments

Experience Design (XD) extends the field of user experience (UX), just as UX extended the older concept of usability. Usability appeared in the 1980s, applying ergonomic principles to that era's emerging technologies: word processors, spreadsheets, and others. In turn, the emerging technology of the 1990s—online shopping, SMS (texting), early camera phones, pre-smartphone PDAs—brought forth UX.

Again, today's emerging technology demands broader design, as previously separate elements combine to form new experiences, such as our society where almost everyone, from awaking to falling asleep, carries a smartphone for browsing and posting to websites for social media. Hence, the need for XD: as the experience is broader than one person using one device, so the designers of the phone's components (camera, operating system, apps, network infrastructure, even its fee schedule) must look beyond their individual specialties to construct the overall experience of the individual and the society. For example, the public was unprepared for the calamity of texting while driving. Only recently has this danger prompted one telecom company to commission a famous movie director to make a documentary about it, distributed for free; but as long as the always-online lifestyle is promoted in advertisements that are also distributed for free, such films will be taken just as seriously as the brewery billboard footnotes that advise consumers to "drink in moderation."

The point of this admittedly sensational example is that texting while driving is not a Designed eXperience. There is a need for XD. To that end, I offer an example from which XD can learn: the field of musical instruments. It clearly connects to human-device interaction. Its social roles are well studied. Less obvious is its long history of disruptive high technology. Already three centuries ago, the interface for the pipe organ had grown to several keyboards, a pedalboard, and a dizzying array of other buttons, drawknobs, and levers, as depicted in Figure 11-1. So complex were these controls that page-turning assistants were needed to operate them. Organists were the space shuttle pilots of the day, and much effort was spent to help them get the best possible sound out of something that had been built at proportional space shuttle expense.

The design of musical instruments illuminates XD, because these devices present interfaces that are sophisticated, elaborate, refined over centuries, beautiful, and exquisitely adapted to the shape, capabilities, and senses of the human body. (To prepare for rapid change in the future, it helps to take a long view of history.) The interfaces of musical instruments also demand—and reward—tens of thousands of hours of continued use and study. One cannot say the same of handheld electronic doodads. Even if these facts alone warrant the study of musical instruments, the parallels to XD go deeper still. Let's begin with the organ.

Figure 11-1. Console of the pipe organ at St. John's Catholic Chapel, Champaign, Illinois

The organ's primary feedback mechanism is not acoustic, but haptic. (The pipes can be so far from the console that organists joke about playing a fugue and then sitting back to listen to it.) Precise standards are set for the keys and pedals: required force, traveling distance, travel point where air gets admitted to the pipes, surface friction. Physically, keyboards have not grown in width like the piano has, because the lowest and highest notes are attained through other means than mere reach. On large theatre organs, the upper keyboards tilt down, sometimes almost vertically. Cognitive issues relate to which pipes are sounded by a particular keyboard. (To the newcomer, the organ's profusion of modes may be its most terrifying aspect.) Individual drawknobs enable particular timbres, such as clarinets, flutes, or trumpets. "Mixture" drawknobs enable several timbres (ranks of pipes) simultaneously. Combination pistons set an entire collection of drawknobs with a single push, from a thumb or a toe, whichever is free at that moment during a performance. Couplers connect one keyboard's pipes to another keyboard, or sound pipes an octave higher or lower than usual. A bass coupler connects the pedalboard's pipes to the lowest note currently held on a keyboard. Most revealingly, even with recent computerization and touchscreens, organs don't try to helpfully draw a diagram of active connections. That would only be a cluttersome distraction; instead, visual feedback is limited to indicating which couplers are active. The organist memorizes how these are wired together, a task not much more complicated than memorizing the layout of a car's stick shift.

Speaking of computers, the parallels to XD grow stronger for newer musical instruments that incorporate software.

[NOTE]

Later in the chapter, we'll see how adding a tilt sensor to a pitch-tracked electric guitar can make it either easier to play or impossibly harder, depending only on the software. We'll also see the many ways that dancers can affect the music to which they're dancing by using software to interpret their movements sensed by a motion capture rig.

Even if a software-based instrument lacks the organ's combinatorial explosion of mapping keyboards to ranks of pipes, software's sheer flexibility seduces the designer into making the instrument so reconfigurable that the player has little attention left for actual playing. (In the limit, live coding replaces all traditional performance with writing software. But this chapter deals only with instruments that still respond to real-time physical gestures.) The player's cognitive limits must be respected but also challenged: the kazoo has spawned no Mephistophelean virtuosos, no grand concertos. A reasonable challenge rewards the player with repeated levels of mastery, like a well-paced video game.

Software lets us arbitrarily connect the player's physical gestures to the resulting sounds. Properly exploiting such richness requires guidance from XD. Only then can that realm of infinite possibility be concentrated into one instrument, one that is not merely enjoyable to listen to, but also worth playing and worth mastering.

The Evolution of the Musician

Constant change, despite its related pains, has been celebrated in music for centuries. Musicians have been quick to embrace emerging technology from the printing press to assembly-line instrument manufacturing. In our own day, we have seen not musicians but rather lawyers feebly oppose technological changes in how music is recorded, distributed, and sold.

In Mozart's era, musicians specialized. Composers wrote, cellists performed, craftsmen chiseled, princes commissioned, aristocrats in overstuffed armchairs listened. Certainly there was crossover: in his time Bach's only fame was as an improvising organist; Mahler's compositional skill came from many years of orchestral conducting; and even Frederick the Great was respected as both a composer and a flutist. But within a particular evening's entertainment, these roles were clear and distinct.

But, we no longer live in this "common practice period." Since then, musical language has fragmented into thousands of genres. Musical technology, too, has fragmented into a market of software and hardware designed for narrow niches. This would appear to demand even more specialization than what musicians accepted 250 years ago, but in fact the opposite is true. One can no longer be just a composer, just a performer, just an instrument designer. Mozart could simply complain about how a tanner had improperly cured the leather on the hammers of his fortepiano. But these days, he himself would have to dig through submenus to tweak the hammers' oil and tannin content. The common practice period's model of the social interactions of music-making no longer fits. By now, the word musician has grown to encompass many more activities:

- Designing a musical instrument, learning to play it, and then learning to compose for it (or the reverse, or back and forth)

- Repackaging recordings, from humble playlists and mix-tape compilations to elaborately crafted seamless multihour DJ shows

- Moving living room furniture and tweaking tone controls to adjust reverberation and find the sweet spot

These days, it has become difficult to reconstruct who made what decisions that led to the final acoustic result. In short, today's musician does many things, not just one thing. We see this in how popular music has adopted technology. Two early examples are the prog-rock guitarist and stompbox wizard, Adrian Belew, and his inspiration Jimi Hendrix; since then, the vocoder/synthesizer duo Daft Punk has hardly restored the eighteenth-century demarcations.

Specialization now moves in a different direction. Instead of improving one instrument, say, a violin that can play anything from polkas to Pachelbel, the musician explores one subgenre, perhaps as narrow as Electro House Moombahcore. This exploration includes all aspects, from instrument design to performance. Having all aspects in a single person or a small group happily compresses the feedback loops that optimize the instrument for that genre. On the other hand, this rapid optimization might explain why genres come and go as quickly as Lower East Side restaurants.

Nowhere is this constant change and recasting of specialization more evident than in instrument design.

THE NEW INSTRUMENT

In our era of ubiquitous music, why are musical instruments still intriguing? Hikers and kayakers lug them along. Airlines make special exceptions for these fragile devices. Even NASA spent almost six figures to include an otherwise unremarkable guitar in a cargo shipment to the International Space Station.

The difference between an iPod and an instrument is not output—sound—but rather input. If playing an instrument is like driving a race car, then using an iPod is like being chief of a pit crew. The crew chief makes decisions at most every few minutes, radioing commands to drive more aggressively or to stop for fresh tires. The driver, on the other hand, continuously makes precise muscular movements, notes their effect, corrects for subtle misjudgments, and makes snap decisions based on thousands of hours of direct experience. That kind of enjoyable activity is why people schlep musical instruments to campsites and space stations—and perhaps why few five-year-olds dream about growing up to become a crew chief.

So a musical instrument is something that turns your physical gestures (more than just occasional button-pushing) into sounds. How much you enjoy the act of playing, in the moment, is tied to how intimately and immediately those gestures are connected to the sounds— consider a toddler with a wooden spoon and a few pots and pans. How much you enjoy *mastering* the act of playing, over thousands of hours, is tied to how sensitive that connection is, how much expressive variety of sound you can get. Kitchen percussion quickly reaches its limit; but as a jazz set moves from ballads to bebop, a graybeard saxophonist can coax whispers, groans, flurries, or howls from his horn. It's hard to say who enjoys this more, the jazzman or the audience. Still, the audience clearly enjoys not just the acoustic result, but also the fantasy of being so expressive themselves. This vicarious thrill is found in motorsport, too, where pit overviews are broadcast less often than onboard views.

But since the days of Adolphe Sax, technology has hardly stood still. The critical connection from gesture to sound can now be mediated by something even more byzantine than valvework: the hyper-flexible material called software. The number of ways to connect inputs to outputs now dwarfs even the billions of combinations in Rubik's Cube advertisements. The question becomes how many of these mappings are worthwhile? (As a mathematical analogy, consider how few images are interesting to humans, of all the possible collections of pixels that could be displayed on a computer screen.)

As an example of this input-to-output flexibility, consider a simple drum. It's louder when you hit it harder, and sounds slightly different when you hit it in different places or with a different kind of stick. But what about an electronic drum, a pressure-sensitive pad connected to software connected to a loudspeaker? That could play louder when you hit it softer; or, different parts of the drum head could sound quite different, like a set of pitched tom-toms; or, softer sticks (mallets or brushes) could delay the sound's onset; or, continued pressure after impact could sustain and modulate the sound, turning a percussion instrument into a melodic one—or, all of the above at once. In a few sentences, software has just let us design a rich instrument using a Stone Age interface. Later on, we'll see some more intricate examples.

THE CURSE OF FLEXIBILITY

The flexibility introduced to musical instruments by software has a dark side. When the pace of high technology meant better varnish than 20 years earlier, a lutenist could reasonably expect that his skills would transfer from one lute to another; that his investment of hours of practice was secure; that, no matter how skilled he became, he could find good teachers; and that he could find a steady supply of freshly composed music to play.

Every one of those expectations is destroyed by software.

- A software-based instrument is often a unique device. Even worse, as obsolete technologies in it are upgraded, it can change irreversibly.

- Developing playing skill on an instrument with an installed customer base of one, and with an expected lifetime of a few months, is a poor investment.

- Performers must be their own teachers.

- Of the few composers who even hear of the instrument (before it changes yet again), even fewer will be motivated to write for an instrument with so few performers and so little chance to develop their own compositional craft. The story is told that Haydn, at the time having completed almost a hundred symphonies, confessed that he was finally getting the hang of writing for woodwinds.

These problems are milder, but not absent, outside music. The faster the pace of technology, the less patience its consumers have for reading instructions. Why master every aspect of your mobile phone, when you expect to replace it within a year? Worse yet, how can you master it when everyone around you also quickly discards it, preventing good teachers from appearing?

Imagine reprogramming your car to make the brake pedal adjust windshield wiper delay, and brake when you blinked your left eyelid in Morse code. Your friends wouldn't dare to drive it. You yourself *could* learn to drive it, but mastering that skill would be expensive.

EMERGING TECHNOLOGY: COMPUTATION, SENSORS, AND AUDIO SYNTHESIS

Recall the music technology of 50 years ago, during the British Invasion of 1964. The Beatles, the Who, and the Rolling Stones began to use feedback from electric guitar amplifiers. In academia, mainframes took hours to compute one minute of acoustic signal, to be performed by a tape recorder. Going beyond tape to so-called live electronics, Karlheinz Stockhausen had just begun to experiment with microphones, sine wave generators, and ring modulators.

But nowadays, laptop orchestras are everywhere. If you extend Moore's Law from Stockhausen's four-diode ring modulator through today's billion-transistor laptops, 50 years from now an everyday musical instrument should have more transistors than the entire planet had 5 years ago. An instrument more powerful than all Big Four music labels combined could create an entire genre of music as easily as a Casiotone creates a bleep. (Granted, this overlooks implementation details such as power consumption and heat dissipation. But it will be several decades before such hardware is even invented. These technicalities will be solved.)

What about sensors? They have not advanced as startlingly as the microprocessor. Indeed, *what* they sense—position, pressure, light, EEGs—has hardly grown in half a century. But *how* they sense has advanced, in size, cost, power consumption, and speed. Smartphones, where every milliwatt and every cubic millimeter counts, include sensors for temperature, barometric pressure, humidity, tilt, and of course GPS position. Compare that to the 1964 predecessor of GPS, TRANSIT, which was too heavy for a man to lift, took thousands of times longer to report your location, and was 40 times less accurate.

The sophistication of sensors has also advanced. For example, some image sensor chips in mobile phones report when they detect a smile. (This is not merely software: this is in the chip itself.) Also, combining colocated measurements, called sensor fusion, yields what Stockhausen would have called magic but what we call commonplace: a photograph that is not merely geotagged but also tagged by content such as email addresses of human faces, or websites of storefronts and visible landmarks. Wilder magic happens when the sensors are online, such as pointing a smartphone's image sensor at a barcode on a supermarket shelf to learn the item's price in nearby stores.

Sensor fusion can also increase noise immunity and decrease latency. For instance, when measuring the pitch of a plucked string, we can fuse conventional pitch-tracking software with a sensor that measures where the string contacts the fingerboard. At low pitches, the software by itself is too slow as it waits for an entire waveform or two. But that's exactly when the contact sensor is fast and precise.

Sensor fusion can also increase sensitivity. Eulerian video magnification amplifies a video signal's otherwise invisible variations of color or motion, such as respiratory motion, the reddening of skin with each heartbeat, or even (as before) the vibration of a guitar string. Fusing a dozen video cameras yields a motion-capture system that tracks the positions of hundreds of points with submillimeter accuracy throughout a large room, thousands of times per second. Fusing several microphones or radiotelescopes into a beamforming array gives them instant, precise aiming. Finally, combining a microphone with clever software yields a sensor for speech—what we usually call speech recognition.

Fifty years hence, we can imagine sensors that are ubiquitous and practically uncountable; cognoscenti call this utility fog. In today's language, a safe generalization is that you will measure anything you can name, as accurately as you want, as fast as you want, under any conditions.

As far as audio synthesis algorithms go, much of the history of computer music consists of clever tricks to extract ever more interesting sounds from only a few—or a few million—transistors: tricks such as filtered broadband noise, frequency modulation, or plucked-string simulation. But such optimizations are pointless when you have a brain the size of a planet. Brute-force additive synthesis of individual sine waves is easy. So is brute-force simulation of a plucked string, all the way down to the molecular bonds that determine the plectrum's stiffness and the string's inertia.

When we summarize all this, the language becomes theological. We get a musical instrument that (within its domain) is omniscient, omni-cognizant, and omnipotent. It observes all that can be observed, ana-lyzes these observations completely, and from those conclusions then produces whatever sound is optimal for a particular purpose.

What this means for musical instruments is hard enough to assimilate and ponder. But what such prodigious sensing and computation means for human culture, no one can predict in detail: uploaded minds, com-putronium (converting all matter into computers), the blurring of human and machine (palely foreshadowed by mobile social media), and immortality. These are aspects of what some call the *Singularity*, the point in history when change becomes so rapid that language before then cannot even describe it. How we then shall make, share, understand, and enjoy music must remain a mystery.

Still, this undoubtedly highfalutin' talk informs the XD of today. Occasionally taking the long view, either the half century since the British Invasion or the eons of the pipe organ, escapes the rut of the past week's RSS feeds, the past year's product launches. When con-fronted with the Accordion of Armageddon, even the most far-out cre-atives must concede that their imaginations could be wilder.

Now, let's rewind those 50 years, to consider nuts-and-bolts details of some unobtanium-free designs that require only a few billion transistors.

DESIGNING FOR SOFTWARE INSTRUMENTS: FROM GESTURES, THROUGH MAPPING, TO SOUND

When designing a software-based musical instrument, either from scratch or by extending a familiar instrument, choosing its inputs and outputs is relatively easy. The instrument's inputs are buttons, knobs, tilt sensors, cameras, or even whichever of these is found in a smart-phone. Its outputs might just be dictated by what commands can be sent to the instument's audio synthesizer, be that a chip or software. Common outputs are pitch (how high a sound is) and loudness. Other aspects of timbre can come from a set of discrete presets, such as the trumpet and harpsichord buttons on a department store keyboard.

At this point, after choosing inputs and outputs, the real work of XD begins. To see what a difference is made by the input-to-output mapping, let's consider three real-world examples that use the same gesture-inputs and sound-outputs, varying only the mapping.

1. Conventional pickup-and-amplifier instrument, such as an electric guitar or electric violin, plus a tilt sensor. (Duct-tape a smartphone to the instrument.) Feed the pickup and the tilt sensor into a computer (perhaps that same smartphone), which computes sound to send to the amplifier.

   Inputs: tilt, pitch, and loudness.

   Outputs: pitch and loudness.

   Unless otherwise specified, pitch maps to pitch, and loudness to loudness.

Rock star

High notes are dramatic in everything from Van Halen to Wagner. To make them easier to play while maintaining drama, when the instrument points up, raise the output pitch by an octave or two.

Controllable Auto-Tune

More tilt applies stronger pitch correction, so you can rely on this crutch only in difficult passages.

Brain melt

Ignore tilt, but map pitch to loudness, and loudness to pitch. (Think about that for a moment.) The language that experienced players use to describe this is unprintable.

Brain evaporate

Tilt crossfades between brain melt and conventional pitch-to-pitch, loudness-to-loudness. (Don't even try to think about this one.)

The first two mappings make the instrument easier to play. The last two make it disastrously difficult, but not artistically pointless: the equally obstreperous programming language Brainfuck has inspired surprisingly many publications, by art theorists as well as computer scientists. So, mapping affects at least ease of use. Let's see what else it can affect.

2. Pressure-sensitive tablet computer, scrubbing through an audio recording.

    Inputs: pressure and x-y position of the fingertip on the tablet's surface.

    Secondary inputs, computed from the primary inputs: speed of fingertip, and duration (so far) of the current stroke.

    Outputs: index into recording (position along the audiotape segment); filter parameters (wah-wah); other effects processing.

Scrub

    Map x to index, pressure to loudness, and y to a filter sweep. The x-mapping works like Laurie Anderson's tape-bow violin.

Quiet scrub

    Also map tip speed to reciprocal loudness, so faster scrubs are quieter. This emulates how, in a movie, we see a whip pan as being out of focus.

Wah-wah pedal

    Also map stroke duration to filter sweep, so each stroke sounds like a "wah."

Holding pattern

    Map tip speed to index, and ignore all other inputs. Thus, when the tip circles steadily, you hear one fragment of the recording. When the tip speeds up, scrubbing moves forwards in the recording. When it slows down, scrubbing rewinds.

    These last two mappings use secondary inputs. They demonstrate the antics that become possible when you use not just an input's raw value, but also that value's history and how fast that value is changing. The formal name for this value-history-change triplet is proportional, integral, and derivative (PID) control. (This is a fundamental mathematical way of connecting inputs to outputs, such as sensors adjusting a car engine to keep it running smoothly, or accelerometers in a quadcopter adjusting rotor speeds to compensate for wind gusts.) The point here is that a mapping need not be moment to moment, where this input value always yields that output value. Instead, the mapping might determine the output from the *trajectory* of input values. A similar trajectory-based mapping tool is hysteresis, which behaves like gearwheel backlash or the slop in the middle of a joystick's range of motion.

Now that we've seen both playability and input-value trajectories, let's consider how literal a mapping should be.

3. Room-size optical motion capture, playing only the black keys of five stops of a pipe organ. (Although this looks like a connected environment or smart room, it still behaves like a musical instrument.)

Inputs: x-y-z positions of a few dozen markers on the costumes of dancers (see Figure 11-2).

Secondary inputs: average and spread (mean and standard deviation) of x, y, and z individually.

Outputs: pitch average, pitch spread, loudness of each organ stop.

Crossfade

Map average z (height) to overall loudness. Map x to pitch, in both average and spread. Map average y to a crossfade through the organ stops in a fixed sequence. The audience immediately notices that when everyone is near the floor, it gets quiet; many raised arms make it loud. Next, they see that walking from left to right (x) is like moving up the organ's keyboard. Finally, they notice the upstage to downstage crossfade.

Zones

Within the danceable x-y-z volume, define five subvolumes, possibly overlapping. Map the number of markers in each zone to the loudness of the corresponding organ stop. Map x to pitch as before.

Spread-average swap

Map spread of y to organ-stop crossfade. Map average x to spread of pitch, and spread of x to average pitch. Map z to loudness as before. (Ignore average y, to use as pure dance with no musical consequences.) Now the audience still detects a strong cause-and-effect, still feels that the dancers directly affect the music. But the audience isn't quite sure how. Not many could verbalize what happens on stage: low pitches when everyone's tightly clumped left-right, high when they're spread out; different stops depending on upstage-downstage clumping; single pitches at stage left, broad clusters at stage right.

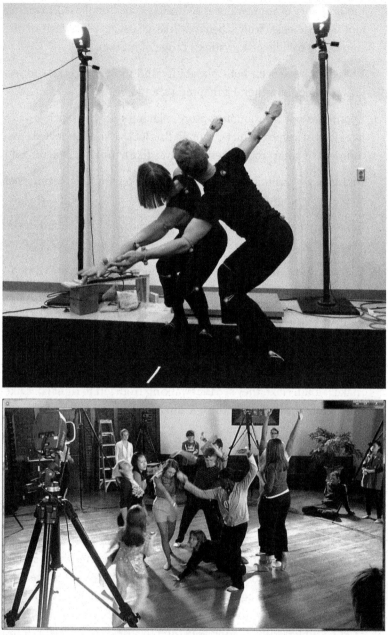

Figure 11-2. Motion-tracked retroreflective balls, worn by a few dancers or many dancers, can be the input gestures for a musical instrument (top: University of Illinois dance faculty Kirstie Simson and Philip Johnston experimenting in the laboratory; bottom: students improvising during a public performance)

In an evening's performance of several dances, a simple mapping such as crossfade works well early in the program, to ensure that everyone in the audience comprehends that the dancers directly control the music. But mickey-mousing won't stay captivating all night, so it's good to finish with less literal mappings. Such a development of mappings, a progression from what is instantly comprehensible to what can be savored longer, also applies outside music and dance. Right after a hard day's work a pilsner quickly slakes your thirst, but later in the evening it's nicer to tarry over an aged port. The holy grail of an intuitive interface is better for a 20-second experience (reclining the driver's seat) than for a 20-hour one (repainting the car). The nonintuitive stick shift may soon be preferred more by videogamers than by commuters. When designing an experience for a specialist, be they seasoned concertgoer, gourmet, car restorer, or videogamer, the experience's very duration justifies some up-front training cost, that is, conscious reasoning (the antonym of intuition).

ASPECTS OF MAPPINGS

Designing a mapping that ends with pitch and loudness is, however, incomplete. That's like designing a cruise control that presses the gas pedal so many inches and leaves it at that. A better mapping goes beyond the convenient abstractions of pitch and loudness, all the way to what enters the ears of the musician (and the audience).

How, then, do we measure sound? A cruise control measures only one number, miles per hour; but describing the full gamut of an instrument's sounds can require many more dimensions. However, we can take a shortcut. Because we finish designing the mapping before the instrument is deployed in performance, we need not actually measure billions of individual sounds; it suffices to measure the *difference* between two sounds. A quick and dirty way to do this is, for both sounds, to measure the loudness in each psychoacoustic critical band, then build a vector of those loudnesses, and then apply to those two vectors a $p = 5$ Minkowski distance metric. (Don't worry about those details. The point is that acousticians really do consider this to be quick and dirty, rather than rocket science. Meaningfully measuring the difference between two arbitrary sounds is indeed possible.)

Then, from a large set of sounds, we know which ones are near each other and which are far apart; that really helps to design a mapping that makes the instrument feel perceptually uniform. The variation of sound is spread smoothly over the range of input values, without any startling areas where the sound suddenly jumps. By analogy, say you want to place expensive gas stations, not too far apart, but without wasting several stations close together. Given a collection of candidate sites, you don't need a map; you need only a table of distances between sites. This table is just what acoustic difference measurements give you, for a map that is undrawable because it has far more dimensions than the two of latitude and longitude.

Even with a mapping that goes all the way to perceived sound, still more designing is needed to complete a musical instrument. After all, its design considers not just the listener's experience but also that of the performer. Performers desire three things in particular:

- Consistency. The same input gesture should produce the same output sound.

- Continuity. Changing a gesture slightly should change the sound slightly.

- Coherence. The direction that the sound changes should not be astonishing.

Consistency

This is essential for learning and mastery. Elaborations like PID control violate consistency, but only in spirit: there, the same result comes from the same input trajectory. For example, on a racetrack, the same timing of braking and steering commands results in the same lap time. The driver can master the car, even though yanking the wheel hard has a different effect when he's been doing 20 mph than when he's been doing 90.

Continuity

Another essential for mastery, but this one is on a time scale of milliseconds rather than months. Even the best singers overshoot or undershoot the change of pitch from one note to the next, and then lock into their target after a few moments by modulating vocal cord tension, diaphragm pressure, and many minor muscles. Without continuity, that lock-in would suffer glitches and hiccups that would sound like a new driver missing a shift from first gear into second. (Early singing-voice synthesizers, which understandably omitted deliberate overshoot, sounded like spooky robots.) The discontinuity in vocal range called the passaggio takes singers years of study to master. Back in the car, the transitions between dirt and asphalt in rallycross racing are particularly challenging, as the tires' grip suddenly changes, affecting all of the driver's commands.

Coherence

Just like consistency is refined by continuity, continuity is further refined by coherence. Drummers protest when a harder whack makes a quieter sound. This example generalizes: more physical energy in means more energy out, of either the acoustic or the aesthetic kind. It's often obvious which direction of change is proper, but what may be unnoticed is that there is a choice of direction to be made.

Stepping away from mapping for a moment, let's look at just how the sound can change. More than just two or three aspects should change. For example, when pitch changes all by itself, you get the cheesy pitch-bend sound of early 1980s synth pop (Spyro Gyra). When other things change with pitch but in only one way, along only one continuum, you get the milder tasting but still eventually tiresome sampler sound of early 1990s synth pop (Pet Shop Boys). So-called one-to-many mappings are prone to producing such fatigue. Those can't compete with a real violin, whose bow can, from moment to moment, move fast or slow (loud or soft), press firmly or lightly (crunchy or breathy), and be near or far from the bridge (glassy or deep).

Changing many things independently suggests a design that uses many inputs, but this has limits. When performers can no longer attend to all the instrument's inputs, they risk falling back into thinking about what to operate, rather than what sound to produce. The graybeard jazzman's state of flow then collapses into stumbling beginner-think. No general design rule can say where the happy medium is. Instead of a strict rule for all possible designs, we follow a guide: try two designs, one deliberately cheesy, one deliberately overwhelming. If users confirm that of these two, one really is too cheesy and one too hard, then split the difference and repeat. I'm tempted to call this the Goldilocks Guide, but decades ago programmers dubbed it Binary Search and proved that very few iterations are needed before it reaches the happy medium.

Conclusion

Musical instruments are hardly the only things that now use software. Toothbrushes, toasters, and toilets can now sprout a dozen buttons and blinking lights. It's no surprise that the designer, daily immersed in state diagrams, flowcharts, and circuit layouts, might eventually surmise that what needs its teeth cleaned is just another computer. The same point is made by the story told of John XXIII, who rejected an architect's blueprint for the papal apartments with a scribbled *Non sunt angeli* (we're not angels): there were no bathrooms.

However, unlike most consumer appliances, musical instruments *demand* quality XD. An instrument with poor XD is simply abandoned: it's socially more acceptable to not play the oboe than to not brush your teeth. Because of this, instruments make good models for XD. Here are some examples of these musical concepts in extramusical contexts.

- Videogames from the 8-bit era imitated a pressure-sensitive gas pedal by augmenting a simple on-off switch with PID control. The longer you held the button, the faster you went; and when you let go, you slowed only gradually.

- Handheld devices repurpose four on-off switches as a scrollwheel, a secondary input. Tokyoflash's wristwatches have raised to an art form both these scrollwheels and riotously nonintuitive mappings from hh:mm:ss to pixels.

- When analyzing mouse behavior in a viewer of 3D worlds, an end-to-end mapping considers how mouse-pawing and scrollwheel-flicking might unnaturally stutter a rotating gaze or a highlight moving down a menu.

- Consistency, continuity, coherence. Online games that charge monthly fees have excelled for a decade at giving users a sense of mastery with little sense of astonishment, at time scales from milliseconds to months.

Of course, trying to enumerate every application of these principles would produce a list that was obsolete before it was finished. The best summary for what musical instruments have to offer your own XD is pure metaphor. Imagine someone brushing their teeth or toasting bread as emotionally and expressively as rocking out with a guitar.

Happy designing!

[12]

Design for Life

JUHAN SONIN

Bloodletting to Bloodless

Technological and societal trends are converging and pushing design to the forefront of health.

Health, as an experience and idea, is undergoing an epic shift. For millennia, humans have treated health as the rare spike that requires intervention. At a very basic level, when it comes to health, we humans experience our physical condition today much as our more furry ancestors did. We roam around. We eat mostly green stuff with the occasional indulgence in a tasty snack of fresh-killed meat. We drink water—well, some of us "hydrate"—and have sex and procreate. We stick with our tribe and try to steer clear of hostile marauders. And as long as we're feeling OK, we think we're OK.

Generally, that's true.

Then, health happens, usually when we least want or expect it. We stumble on the trail or travel far from home and come back with dysentery. One of these health events prompts a visit, so you go to a tribal elder who sets bones, or you seek out the town doc to ease your intestinal disturbance, or, after catching your son flying off the living room couch, you get an MRI to reveal a bicep tendon rupture.

What we call health is made up of these episodic issues and interventions. Even periodic exams are events that we bathe and dress up for. In fact, we are most conscious of our health during these moments. For the average person—one without chronic pain or illness—health is conceived of and managed as an exception.

Few would deny that health is the single most important factor for any human, at any age, living anywhere on Spaceship Earth. The potential impact of a health setback on our lives can reach into all other areas of our lives—work, finances, love, and hobbies—and even affect the community. The stakes of dealing with health are significantly high. For example, a high school math teacher with a kidney stone calls in sick, the principal hires a per diem substitute teacher, and the learning of 20 high school kids dwindles. In our era, the complexity of health has surged dramatically. Remarkable things have transpired over the past 100 years, the past 40 years, and the past 5. In 1909, for example, hospitals treated third-degree burn patients with opiates, frequent application of moist antiseptic dressings, and sometimes baths;[1] today, clinics spray-paint on new skin, based on the burn victim's cells.[2] The jump in technology and our understanding of biology and the health sciences is startling, which has ratcheted up both the system complexity and awareness of it. What's good for one patient might not be quite right for the patient in the next bed over.

Yet, same as 1,000 years ago, humans don't want to think about health until health happens—or more accurately, a health event happens. This state of denial is evidenced by the declining health rankings of the United States compared to 33 other wealthy nations. From 1990 to 2010, although Americans' life expectancy increased, our health rank decreased notably across six key measures.[3] Although there might be social and cultural forces at play in these disheartening statistics, the continued decline of the health of the population in the United States suggests that we're still stuck in the land of episodic medical care, not only with respect to treatment, but also thinking, engineering, and designing for health.

There is a way out of this, and the remedy is not just a pill, diet, or implant. To illustrate the possibilities available to us right now, take a moment to consider the following thought experiment.

---

1 *http://bit.ly/1sShQpX*—also follow the link to the book *A Text-Book of Minor Surgery* by Dr. Edward Milton Foote (1909) on Google

2 *http://news.discovery.com/tech/spray-on-skin-cells-for-burn-victims.htm*

3 JAMA study, *http://bit.ly/1nTACLO*; and *http://www.healthypeople.gov/2020/about/genhealthabout.aspx*

Suppose that all of your data is simply and automatically collected—every number related to your existence, from the financial (which we're nearly doing today), to travel (again, captured today), to habits, to eating, to exercise, to examining your daily biome. It's captured. It just happens, unobtrusively in the background.

Now suppose that your captured data is visible: you can see the data points, see the trends, and even see the data of your close friends and family, such as is depicted in Figure 12-1 and Figure 12-2. This visualization would effectively convey important data at sizes both large and small, and enable you to recognize patterns in yourself and others so that you can make positive decisions and affect beneficial change (see also Figure 12-3).

Figure 12-1. The hGraph: your health in one picture—an open source, standardized visual representation of a patient's health status

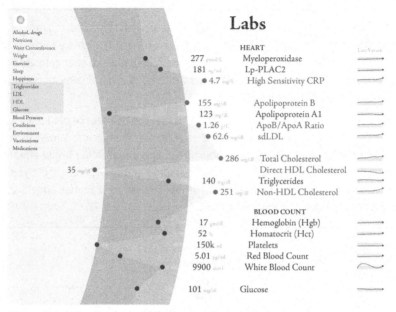

Labs

	HEART	
277	Myeloperoxidase	
181	Lp-PLAC2	
4.7	High Sensitivity CRP	
155	Apolipoprotein B	
123	Apolipoprotein A1	
1.26	ApoB/ApoA Ratio	
62.6	sdLDL	
286	Total Cholesterol	
	Direct HDL Cholesterol	
140	Triglycerides	
251	Non-HDL Cholesterol	

	BLOOD COUNT	
17	Hemoglobin (Hgb)	
52	Homatocrit (Hct)	
150k	Platelets	
5.01	Red Blood Count	
9900	White Blood Count	

101	Glucose	

Alcohol, drugs
Nutrition
Waist Circumference
Weight
Exercise
Sleep
Happiness
Triglycerides
LDL
HDL
Glucose
Blood Pressure
Conditions
Environment
Vaccinations
Medications

35

Figure 12-2. hGraph users can easily identify which metrics exist in a normal range versus those that might be too high or low

The foundations of this new paradigm are in place. The structure is ours to make.

Our thought experiment provides a stark contrast to the current state of design thinking on life, on health, and on data. We have minimal transparency into key health metrics. For the data we do have, the overhead required to collect it is enormous. People have a hard enough time changing their Facebook privacy settings or figuring out mortgage refinancing. The systems we deal with are increasingly complex, and the user interfaces are more like puzzles than designs. As decision makers, we are swamped with conflicting data.

As designers and engineers, our work is increasingly multidimensional (not a flat-decision space), and linear-thinking human beings are not good at nonlinear thinking. Seeing every variable and doing the mental calculus to orchestrate better decision making is not our species' forte. We fly by the seat of our pants until we get tired and land—thump—not always in the right or best place. One major variable in the everyday behavior change game is sensors. Invisible sensors.

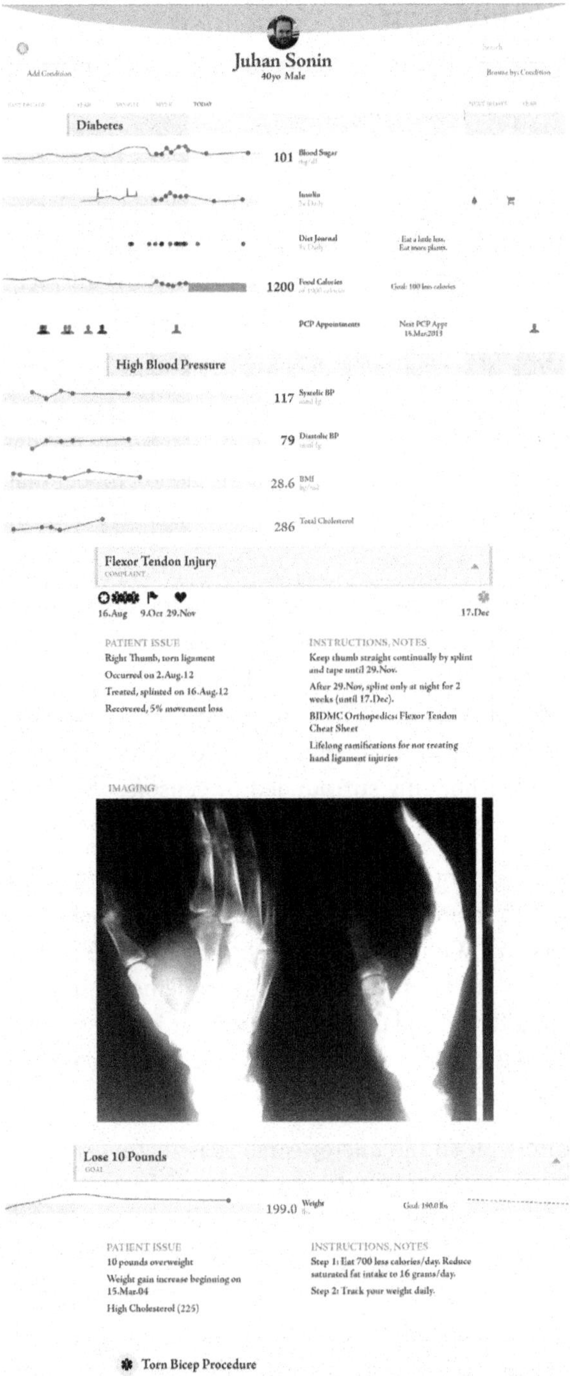

Juhan Sonin
40yo Male

Add Condition

Browse by Condition

Diabetes

101 Blood Sugar

Insulin

Diet Journal
Eat a little less.
Eat more plants.

1200 Food Calories
Goal: 100 less calories

PCP Appointments
Next PCP Appt
14.Mar.2013

High Blood Pressure

117 Systolic BP

79 Diastolic BP

28.6 BMI

286 Total Cholesterol

Flexor Tendon Injury
COMPLAINT

16.Aug   9.Oct 29.Nov   17.Dec

PATIENT ISSUE
Right Thumb, torn ligament
Occurred on 2.Aug.12
Treated, splinted on 16.Aug.12
Recovered, 5% movement loss

INSTRUCTIONS, NOTES
Keep thumb straight continually by splint
and tape until 29.Nov.
After 29.Nov, splint only at night for 2
weeks (until 17.Dec).
BIDMC Orthopedics Flexor Tendon
Cheat Sheet
Lifelong ramifications for not treating
hand ligament injuries

IMAGING

Lose 10 Pounds
GOAL

199.0 Weight   Goal: 190.0 lbs

PATIENT ISSUE
10 pounds overweight
Weight gain increase beginning on
15.Mar.04
High Cholesterol (225)

INSTRUCTIONS, NOTES
Step 1: Eat 700 less calories/day. Reduce
saturated fat intake to 16 grams/day.
Step 2: Track your weight daily.

✱ Torn Bicep Procedure

Figure 12-3. Learn more about hGraph at *http://www.hgraph.org*

The Surveillance Invasion

Wearable sensors impressively track personal health metrics, but the bands are still as easy to take off as they are to put on.

These days, my thoughts turn frequently to the image of the Voight-Kampff interrogation machine in the science-fiction movie classic *Blade Runner.* It was a tabletop apparatus with a mechanical eye that peered into a human (or robot) eye to noninvasively determine his/her/its "health" status. It's either really creepy or really practical.

The current confluence of sensor tech, data analytics maturity, hardware durability, miniaturization, and industrial evolution has created a perfect storm for capturing biologic metrics and determining trends. In a year, we'll have a good first cut at a human prediction model that is personally meaningful and changes behavior (and is only 5 percent wrong).

As I look around in the Involution Studios design studio (*http://www. goinvo.com*), I count a half-dozen different wearable health devices on the limbs of our staff, from a Basis watch, to Fitbit pedometer, to a BodyMedia band, to a Jawbone UP, to a Philips pedometer. Digital scales, AliveCor EKG iPhone cases, cameras that detect blood pressure through your face—we're not only surrounded by sensors, we adorn ourselves with them.

One problem with the current batch of wearables is just that: they're wearable. Engaging with them requires a ton of mental overhead. For example, take the very cool Withings Pulse, as shown in Figure 12-4: it tracks steps, general activity, sleep, and heart rate on demand. It has a touchscreen, solid form factor, and decent contrast user interface (UI)/screen. Yet, I forget to put it in my running shorts pocket only to realize later that I'm device-less and data-less.

The biggest complaint with all the microwearables is that most users are not wearing their sensors 24/7. Sticking them in your pocket is easy, but it requires pants; when I'm at home, I'm often wearing pocket-less garments such as sweatpants and workout shorts. Furthermore, I don't wear it at night. The switch to turn it to "night" mode, which then requires a flip back to daytime usage, is one switch too many for me. Even my BodyMedia armband isn't set-it-and-forget-it (you can see my dashboard in Figure 12-5). I have to take it off when I shower and when the device needs charging. So, even slick new devices such as the Misfit Shine—a wireless, wearable activity tracker—all suffer from the same issue: they're a branch of devices called the "nonforgettables."

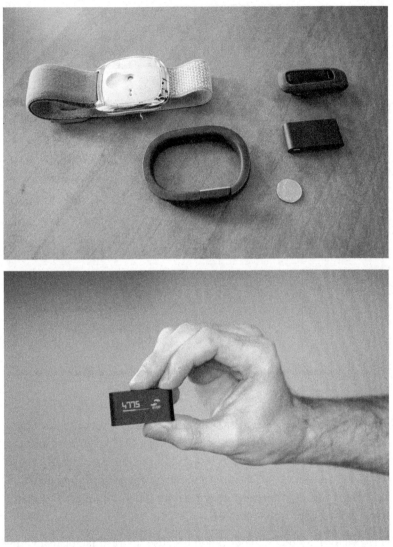

Figure 12-4. The BodyMedia armband, Jawbone UP, Fitbit, and Withings Pulse (on the bottom)

Now for the flip argument: from a wellness point of view, do "off times" really matter?

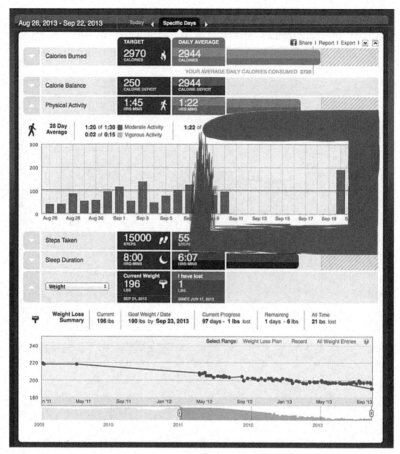

Figure 12-5. A BodyMedia dashboard with missing data

I often forget to wear devices. During the first few months wearing a new health monitor, I'm exposed to new data. After I understand the patterns, the hardware becomes less and less useful (other than to have a bead on those metrics). I want the little health plug to strap on when sickness is coming that reduces symptoms and duration by 70 percent. Now that's a helpful microdevice.

Form factor isn't really the question because no form factor really hits it on the head. Maybe it's the implant; or, the invisible.

Hardware is the gateway drug to services and data. (If you're planning to get into health hardware, you're too late.) The current device lineup has little to do with the commodity of hardware—it's all about your information and decision making.

Life First—Health a Distant Second

The next challenges for designers and engineers in healthcare involve data... collected invisibly.

Designers and engineers have demonstrated that they can make cool sensors. Next, we are going to redesign those products and create new ones that capture data beautifully, and usually that means invisibly. As shown in Figure 12-6, sensor proliferation is exploding—the DARPA line from the 1980s is catching up: smart dust is all around us. Picture this: as I walk around my house, stand at my desk at work, have a cup of coffee, and go to relieve myself, all of that physiological data will be captured to perform DSP analysis that signals "getting worse" or "getting better" on a defined timeline (based on known prior results). This is where machine learning (ML), Big Data, and design crash together.

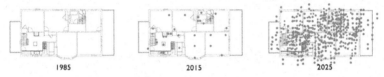

1985   2015   2025

Figure 12-6. Sensor proliferation is exploding—the DARPA line from the 1980s is catching up: smart dust is all around us

What we learn from the design of personal wearable sensors will ultimately be applied to in-hospital devices.

There are still massive amounts of pain and mistakes in institutional and corporate healthcare:

- Patient safety is a tremendously important issue. There are 180,000 deaths by accident per year in hospitals in the United States. That's 500 deaths per day.

- There are scores of classic examples such as anesthesia gone wrong during surgery and known allergies overlooked. Go to the ECRI Institute website if you want to take a detailed look into improving patient safety and quality.

- Cullen Care was sued over a claim that the pharmacy made a dosing error, dispensing 10 times the required amount of morphine to a child. The mistake was attributed to human error.

More people die annually from overdosing by prescription drugs such as oxycontin than car accidents. Humans and machines need to be points in the same loop, checking and amplifying each other's work and output, because both, especially humans, make mistakes. One way to audit and be exposed to near-real-time care data analysis is a natural extension of HAL 9000: the recording of all procedures within the walls of hospitals. Every injection, every surgery, every patient-clinician encounter will be on camera, microphoned, and recorded. Clinicians wearing Google Glass–esque monitors that automagically capture the patient's mood, tiny facial triggers pointing to emotional state and potential conditions, and other metrics, will be whispered hints and diagnosis by the cloud-based Dr. Watson. Longer-term hospital visits will require patients to wear individual trackers. Then, when conflicts occur, or right before a tragic maneuver, the hospital and patient trackers will run "interference."

Machines and humans are about to synchronize in an entirely new way at home. Let's begin exploring how, starting in the bathroom.

Your bathroom will be an invisible sensor haven.

Figure 12-7 illustrates the wealth of information that room collects and how it could be assessed, sooner rather than later. Hair follicles collected in the shower drain. Gastrointestinal samples and urinalysis from the toilet; your biome sloughing off into the sink; weight, heart rate, blood flow, and facial expressions recorded automatically. It just happens, with regular feedback loops but no mental or physical overhead. It isn't the bathroom anymore; it's the health room.

Hospitals are rolling out patient portals and insurance companies are experimenting with electronic health records, but the usefulness of those repositories is limited to patients. More critical are teachable moments in data that signal potential outcomes and prompt micro behavior shifts that in turn will offer feedback and affirm new behaviors or nudge new ones.

In the bathroom and, eventually, in other environments like the hospital room, the majority of your physiologic signs will be snagged noninvasively, through sensors that passively sniff you. No blood draws; no awkward stool sample cards; just whiffs and sniffs and the occasional photograph. All of this must be designed to feel wonderful, so that you think more about life and less about "health" and "security."

Background, automatic health sensing will let us focus our consciousness on the dream life we want to live. Healthrooms will proliferate and scale, as illustrated in Figure 12-8.

Figure 12-7. Your bathroom, turned into a health room (illustration by Quentin Stipp)

Figure 12-8. Healthrooms will proliferate and scale as they turn into ready-made, all-in-one, drop-in units (illustration by Quentin Stipp)

Talking about passive sensors, I always picture the orgasmatron from Woody Allen's 1973 movie, *Sleeper*, which was set in the year 2173. This fictional device, a cylinder large enough to contain one or two people, rapidly induced orgasms. A character would walk in, have a blast, and walk out mere seconds later. That's how I want healthcare delivered. That's where engineering and design can really have impact.

Sign me up.

Stage Zero Detection

Continuous assessments make real-time adjustments not only possible but desirable and doable.

We get biome analysis, emotional analysis, breath evaluation, and voice analysis. Bots (some with cameras) are in our stomachs and blood streams, churning through our bodies and molecules, gathering intelligence. We are able to detect disease and conditions as they erupt at the cellular level, and not have to wait until they physically manifest such that our eyes and bodies can "see" them. (By the time we can see it with our own eyes, it's too late.)

That's the future, and it is near. If health is beautifully integrated into our daily life so that we're getting continuous assessments, we'll be able to adjust in near real time.

Next, here's what's on the horizon:

- Scanadu, a hockey-puck-sized, 10-major-metric, noninvasive data collector.

- Make-my-pill (based on my dynamic careplan, biology, conditions, geo, and so on) vending machine by Walgreens.

- Adamant, a breath sensor out of Penn State that detects differing signatures in 25 variables of your breath.

- One-nanometer resolution spectrometers, priced at $20, for instant food analysis at the molecular level. "Does this food have any peanuts in it?" Check it with a smartphone.

These are neat. But, as designers and engineers, we can do more, and we should. It won't be until our digital health "guards"—the digital services that pound on those massive data sets and prior patterns to keep us healthier—can identify trends and thereby exponentially reduce our sickness rates that we'll reach Phase Two. My health and my family's health will be actively guarded. The technology is already widely used. For instance, for $10 per month, I subscribe to CitiBank's so-called fraud security net, which monitors any transaction that didn't appear to come from me or my family, anywhere across the planet. If there is any suspicious action, the bot notifies me immediately, and together we investigate the issue in near real time. An analogous (and currently fictitious) product service is LoveLife, a Netflix-type model by which I pay $10, $20, or $30 per month for the service to look over and protect my data, know who is touching it, predict behaviors, and tease me to change my behaviors. This cloud guard will autodetect and alert me to the make-my-pill vending machine getting hacked—protecting all the trains of trust.

In the future, we'll eat our medicine and lookout bots. They will monitor and command seek-and-destroy missions at the cellular level in conjunction with external readings and decision-support tools. We won't feel or notice a thing.

I'll be notified that my biome composition has shifted and that a cold is coming on in a day. My day-treat—concocted specifically for me based on my genomic and personal data set—can be ready in 60 minutes at my local pharmacy. I take the Skittle-sized gel tab orally. The tab is a living set of custom organisms ready to swim into my blood stream where it melts away immediately, and within several dozen minutes I am back to my unique, diverse, healthy biome. No stuffy head, no aching muscles, no fever, no sign of "health," good or bad. I simply am.

This design space needs to chew on the massive volume of data and massive volume of human factors and their interrelationships. I mean taking every connecting piece of information from what we're eating, how we're moving (or not), how we work, and what makes up our genome, and expanding that out to the entire system-picture of a human living on Planet Earth. All of that interconnecting and interlocked information tissue needs to be condensed into a single decision space that's not a data dump but a highly personalized, insight crystal ball.

That insight service is getting close on the research and science side.

Sound scary? It is... a little.

From Protein to Pixel to Policy

Design-for-health possibilities and responsibilities are immense.

Our medical records—our life records—will be available for computational use, as we currently have with social data on Facebook and Google. ML and prediction will vastly improve our ability to live life, to see conditions at their earliest manifestation as we get fabulous, personalized, medical diagnostics and advice.

This sensor cloud will monitor my physical activity and my online activity, too. It will observe, for example, that 90 percent of my bandwidth is porn and propose that the erectile dysfunction I experience when faced with a live boyfriend is correlated with online activity. (Data is starting to trickle in on this, even though the researchers are having a hard time finding a control group.)

The power of the data and tools is impressive. The implications are daunting to the same degree. Designers and engineers will need to deliver products that are functional and invisible, but also make designs that are inviting not intimidating, reassuring, and not anxiety-producing. We want to improve humanity, not put it under house arrest.

What Orbitz did to travel agents, medical technology, design, and culture shifts will do to doctors and the traditional practice of episodic medicine.

As a designer, I want my fingers, hands, and eyes on all the moving parts of a product, no matter how small or big. I want to influence the world from protein, to policy, to pixels. That means expanding our skills and knowledge to have impact at levels of science and society as well as design and engineering. That degree of immersion into problem solving and the holistic context of my clients enable our design studio to make extraordinary impact, at a level that transcends the important issues of our clients but get into issues of meaning and the longer future.

And at some point in our careers, designers and engineers need to be involved in policy—in the crafting, in the designing or development of guidelines or law that drive how we as a people operate together (or not). Some efforts are grassroots, like the open source Inspired EHRs guide (*http://inspiredehrs.org/*), which starts with just a few people. This is attacking at the fringe, from the outside in. Data standards and policy making (such as HL7 or HIMSS) need good engineers and designers to participate. This is not super-sexy work. Although the pace of sculpting governance is enormously slow (these kinds of efforts take years and are often frustrating experiences), the ultimate outcome and impact can be long-lasting. And making this kind of change is why I'm in business.

Final Thoughts

Figure 12-9. No human in the metrics-collection loop—it just happens (illustration by Sarah Kaiser)

Data let us live aware of our health. For example, when we are told that ice cream is high in fat, high in sugar, and high in cow's milk, we process that as "OK, that's bad, but so what?" As soon as that message becomes quantified, and not by keeping annoying food diaries and looking up the nutrition content of every bite or sip, we get religion. Data takes us by the shoulders and shakes. We notice that eating this way, and continuing to do so, has taken days or even a few years off our precious life expectancy. That is when the entire world changes—but not before.

It's up to us.

[13]

Architecture as Interface: Advocating a Hybrid Design Approach for Interconnected Environments

ERIN RAE HOFFER

The Blur of Interconnected Environments

We spend 90 percent of our lives indoors.[1] The built environment has a huge impact on human health, social interaction, and our potential for innovation. In return, human innovation pushes our buildings continually in new directions as occupants demand the highest levels of comfort and functionality.

Our demand for pervasive connectivity has led us to weave the Internet throughout our lives, to insist that all spaces link us together along with our handheld devices, that all environments be interconnected. Internet-enabled devices creep into the spaces we inhabit, and these devices report back on spatial conditions such as light, radiation, air quality and temperature, count the number of people stopping at retail displays minute by minute, detect intruders and security breaches, monitor locations and track characteristics of equipment and supply chain elements, enable us to open locked doors remotely using our mobile devices, and pass terabytes of data to backend systems that analyze, report, and modify the environments we occupy.

---

1 *http://www.arb.ca.gov/research/resnotes/notes/94-6.htm*

The space that surrounds us is transforming to a series of interconnected environments, forcing designers of space to rethink the role of architecture and the rules for its formulation. Similarly, designers of emerging technologies are rethinking the role of interfaces and the rules for their creation. During this period of experimentation and convergence, practical construction, and problem solving, architects must reinvent their roles and become hybrid designers, creating meaningful architecture with an awareness of the human implications of emerging technologies.

DESIGN TRADITIONS FROM ARCHITECTURE

Architects begin with a human need and develop solutions through inspiration and information—human, social, natural, economic and technological. The architect is charged to envision a new reality that addresses explicit and tacit needs, to create an expansive solution set that suits this vision. For millennia, architects have been given the task of imagining spaces to support people and human interaction, describing design intent, and producing concrete instructions for realizing designs as objects in the physical environment. Admittedly, many spaces are designed by builders or lay people, not by licensed architects. Whatever the professional and academic background of the creator, a building design stems from centuries of traditional practice and refined interaction models.

Upon encountering a device for the first time a user or occupant builds a conceptual model about it. The same approach plays out when humans encounter new environments. To design a space, an architect makes assumptions about the building's future occupants. As cognitive scientist and design critic, Donald A. Norman points out, "Good design is a communication between the designer and the user." This manifests through the appearance of the device (object or space) itself.[2] In terms of the built environment, Japanese philosopher Kojin Karatani observes that the dialogue between an architect and an occupant of a space occurs through a system of communication without commonly understood rules.[3]

---

2 Norman (2002)

3 Karatani and Speaks (1995)

Over time, architectural problems have become increasingly complex, driven by economics, technological innovation, and changing societal needs for buildings to support new functions and offer innovative features to improve efficiency and safety. Practitioners rely on a body of design theory that influences the products of architectural design, and highlights the duality of a profession whose aspirations are to create artifacts that serve practical needs at the same time that they encode meaning for individuals and communities.

The pervasion of Internet-enabled elements into the physical space of everyday life and work forces us to rethink both the requirements of our world and the way we design it. Today's consumers can connect a smartphone-enabled door to a system of security; comfort-focused devices that transmit video sense and adjust temperature and lighting. As interactive environments proliferate and these choices expand in the future, designers must expand theory to apply these new modes of interaction and meaning to our most pressing objectives.

ARCHITECTURAL DESIGN THEORY: MODELS OF INTERACTION AND MEANING

Architectural theory analyzes and describes architectural design in terms of appropriate elements, their relationships to cultural understanding, and the process of devising them. In this context, *theory* is an explanation that does not proscribe a specific end result. It is a structure of concepts, categories, and relationships intended to explain things or to advocate, not a defined roadmap or a step-by-step methodology.

No single comprehensive structure of ideas can be applied in the same rigorous way to resolve all design problems in architecture. It is unlikely that a formal set of rules lie behind all of the many complex decisions that produce an existing building. However, practitioners have long valued theory in making decisions on complex projects or to retrospectively clarify a body of work.

Architectural theory can be traced back to the first century BC. The Roman writer and architect Vitruvius[4] wrote a treatise that laid out the salient aspects of Roman architecture in a series of volumes. The *Ten Books of Vitruvius* illustrated the principles of design and construc-

---

4 Vitruvius (1999)

tion and emphasized the three "laws" placing architecture above mere building, namely that a work of architecture must possess the qualities of Firmness, Commodity, and Delight.[5] These three laws clarified that a work of good design must be physically and structurally sound, must support the functional and practical needs of its occupants, and must be aesthetically pleasing to the viewer.

By comparison, Hewlett-Packard User Experience Lead Jim Nieters's blog on Interaction Design lists the goals of an interaction model as being Discoverability, Learnability, Efficiency, Productivity, Responsiveness, and, not coincidentally, Delight.[6] Although these two thinkers lived in different times, these somewhat analogous sets of "laws" underscore the relevance of aligning UX design with the design of interaction and experience in physical space.

Since the time of Vitruvius, architectural theory has relied on classifications and definitions—grouping buildings into types, defining accepted applications of morphology, focusing on uses, appearances, and the appropriateness of combining elements from different periods, styles, or construction types. Theory has even suggested that the components of architecture exist as elements of a language that has a particular grammar, as elaborated in *A Pattern Language: Towns, Buildings, Construction* by Christopher Alexander et al. Alexander laid out the idea of pattern and usage as a way of building what he called "timeless." He states, "Towns and buildings will not be able to come alive, unless they are made by all the people in society, and unless these people share a common pattern language, within which to make these buildings, and unless this common pattern language is alive itself."[7]

Theorizing Digital Culture: New Models of Convergence

In more recent times, computers became prevalent in society and architects theorized about the impacts of digital culture. Observers of the design professions considered the implications of digital technology, both for the environments we would occupy alongside these new

---

5 As translated by Sir Henry Wotton in the 17th Century

6 Nieters, Jim, "Defining an Interaction Model: The Cornerstone of Application Design" blog post, *http://bit.ly/1nTB1h5*.

7 Alexander et al. (1977) and Alexander (1979)

devices, and for the process of design itself. Theorists in the 1960s and 1970s discussed cybernetics,[8] digital approaches to systems of work and habitation, and explored through programming Negroponte's concept of "the architecture machine,"[9] a theory about the ability of machines to learn about architecture as opposed to being programmed to complete architectural tasks.

More recent investigations of the merger of digital and architectural realms have been undertaken since the 1990s, with research considering the concept of adaptive feedback loops,[10] of environments such as Rodney Brooks' Intelligent Room Project,[11] or environments such as the Adaptive House.[12] These experiments explored the principles of combining digital with architectural environments and processes. Malcolm McCullough observed an impending future of opportunity when computing pervades architecture and activities are mediated in new ways. He commented that, "The rise of pervasive computing restores an emphasis on geometry.... In locally intensified islands of smarter space, interactivity becomes a richer experience."[13]

Theories and manifestos proliferated with a focus on the cultural and societal imperatives that should guide practitioners in navigating the choppy waters between meaningful and merely practical arrangements of space. As Michael Speaks described in his introduction to Kojin Karatani's *Architecture as Metaphor*, a tug of war ensues between two metaphors, "Architecture as Art" versus "Architecture as Construction."[14] If we are to believe Vitruvius, the aspiration of architecture has always gone beyond function and effectiveness to incorporate the difficult-to-define idea of "delight," a notion beyond aesthetics. In today's post-modern age, we expect a work of architecture to mean something to inhabitants and observers. Architecture has always con-

8 Frazer (1993)

9 Negroponte (1970)

10 Eastman, in Cross (1972)

11 R. A. Brooks. 1997. The Intelligent Room project. In Proceedings of the 2nd International Conference on Cognitive Technology (CT '97). IEEE Computer Society, Washington, DC, USA, 271-. *http://people.csail.mit.edu/brooks/papers/aizu.pdf.*

12 *http://bit.ly/1nTB2BH*

13 McCullough (2004)

14 Karatani and Speaks (1995)

veyed meaning, or "spoken to us" through form, since the time when illiterate occupants needed the cathedral to convey the meaning of religious texts. Alain de Botton stated that, "Belief in the significance of architecture is premised on the notion that we are, for better or worse, different people in different places—and on the conviction that it is architecture's task to render vivid to us who we might ideally be."[15]

ENTER INTERCONNECTED ENVIRONMENTS

Our intention as architects to design meaning into space broadens when we conceive of spaces as interconnected environments, linking devices to devices, and thereby connecting occupants with remote individuals, communities, and information sources. Although we have long incorporated the practical opportunities of automation—environmental control systems that manipulate building heat and cooling, raise and lower window shades, and control other architectural elements and systems with little or no human intervention—emerging technology can move us beyond digital integration with architecture as "practical construction" to digital integration with architecture as "art."

We are surrounded by smart homes, schools, workplaces, shopping malls, and even the city itself with its smart grid. These anticipatory models purport to make all decisions and do all the work for us. But, our models for digital interaction have evolved, and the conceptual models for user interaction now stretch to accommodate decentralized structures that include mobile "anywhere" access, feedback and input from "the crowd," increased transparency, simulation, and analysis. We are moving from anticipatory centralized models such as the Encyclopaedia Brittanica[16] to adaptive decentralized ones along the lines of Wikipedia.[17]

Christian Norberg-Schulz said that the job of the architect was to visualize the spirit of the place and to create meaningful places for people to inhabit.[18] Perhaps the modern person is less able to understand the meaning of architecture because our education and training no longer emphasizes this appreciation. Nevertheless, architects still

---

15 De Botton (2006)

16 http://www.britannica.com/

17 http://www.wikipedia.org/

18 Norberg-Schulz (1980)

aspire to produce buildings and spaces that go beyond function and effectiveness, which can become meaningful to people who occupy or encounter them. With the advent of digitally connected architecture, we have an opportunity to reinvent architecture as a source of meaning. Pervasive computing will provide feedback about perceptions and physical experiences as our bodies interact with our spaces. Documentation and analysis of feedback will increase our awareness of what it means to embody and occupy space. To move to this next stage, digital experience designers and architects must enlighten one another and collaborate to inspire hybrid models of design practice (Figure 13-1).

Figure 13-1. Hybrid design will emerge when the patterns of digital experience designers and architects converge (courtesy of the author)

Hybrid Design Practice

Traditionally, architects are trained to think about interaction in terms of form and physical occupation, activity, and movement bounded by space—walls, floors, and ceilings, illuminated by sun or artificial light, defined by materiality. There is no dominant theory that governs the work of all architects. Rather, practitioners follow a range of methods and apply design theories based on their academic training and compliance with firm methods in keeping with their own personal approaches. After spending time gathering information about the context and deepening their understanding of the problem, some architects aggregate programmatic elements into systems. Others might begin with a metaphor and work to fit client requirements into physical forms that represent their vision. Tomorrow's spaces will be formed from interconnected and intelligent components that are aware of the human presence, able to communicate, assess, and act. The role of the designer must evolve to incorporate both sets of skills—architect and interaction designer—so that we can create meaningful places that support systems of linked intelligent devices. This mix of methods and sensibilities can be termed *hybrid design practice*.

Hybrid design practice will augment metaphor or context awareness with maps of information and communication from digital sources and delivery systems. The work of hybrid design calls for new theories to help us create meaning from electronic communications and digital resources as well as physical ones. As McCullough observed, "The more that principles of locality, embodiment, and environmental perception underlie pervasive computing, the more it all seems like architecture."[19]

TRAPELO ROAD CASE STUDY

Figure 13-2 shows a rendering of Autodesk, Inc.'s Trapelo Road[20] office just outside Boston. This fit-out is an example of a project that aspires to integrate Internet monitoring and control systems in the architectural design of a commercial office interior. Sensors that collect data about comfort and energy utilization are linked to the building automation system, which taps into weather data from an external system. Data provided by the sensors helps facility managers realize energy efficiency improvements by refining the sequence of operation for building HVAC equipment while continuing to meet temperature requirements at business start time each day. Experimental projects applying sensor data at Trapelo illustrate how designers can become smarter about the way space and systems need to be laid out to enable sophisticated measurement and increased efficiency. Better data gained from interconnected devices embedded in architecture enables continuous diagnostics and automated commissioning so that anomalies in the system can be flagged more quickly and addressed sooner. The

19 McCullough (2004)

20 "Autodesk's East Coast Headquarters Draws Accolades for its Sustainable Design and Collaborative Building Process," EDC Magazine, August 2010, *http://bit.ly/1nTBik8*.

insight gained from sensors is now displayed to employees and visitors through a prominently placed plasma screen, potentially shifting occupant behavior as individuals "see" the impacts of their actions.

Figure 13-2. A Building Information Model of the Autodesk HQ provides a framework for information about usage and resources (courtesy of KlingStubbins)

Ultimately, this experiment suggests the way that the entire space could be reconfigured to put both information and means of control at the fingertips of all occupants at all times. But beyond the practicality of an application designed to drive energy efficiency, how will occupants of the space interpret the meaning inherent in the display—both in terms of the practicality of efficient use of energy and of the significance of the initiative in the context of the social community and issues of climate change?

HUMAN TO MACHINE, MACHINE TO MACHINE

The explosion of Internet and web creates new interaction models that lead to dynamic configurations of people, networks and machines. The hybrid design practice will accommodate these new interaction models. To our traditional human to human (H2H) and human to architecture (H2A) interactions, we've added human to machine (H2M) and machine to machine (M2M).

H2M interaction models connect humans to machines in "everywhere" mode—from any device, at any time and place. Manufacturers of building elements—garage doors,[21] ceiling fans,[22] appliances,[23] and many other automation systems—are smartphone-enabling spatial elements so that people can control devices and receive messages and images. Our machines are speaking to us. "The garage door was left open." "Your dog Ella's heart rate is elevated. She has found the stash of chocolate hidden inside the upstairs closet."

With M2M, a sensor or monitor device can capture an "event" (such as the state of temperature of light, or other environmental or asset conditions). The state can be transmitted over the Internet or a local network to a cloud-, desktop-, or server-based software application that analyzes, stores, or processes the information, or applies it to a downstream action. Apple Computer's iBeacons, based on Bluetooth Low Energy (BLE) technology, enable place-aware applications to light up when you enter a room (or at least when your smartphone does).[24] Beacons embedded in architecture can sense when you approach and reach out to you in location-specific ways.

EMERGING MODELS OF CONVERGENT DESIGN

Beyond machines, spaces themselves can speak to us. Alex Hawkinson of SmartThings[25] connected the architectural elements—floors, walls, ceilings, windows, and doors—of his home based on low-power sensor network standards such as Zigbee.[26] Wired editor Bill Wasik described this house as he predicted three phases of evolution on the path of ubiquitous and full integration of devices and digital intelligence into the physical world—proliferation (more devices, more sensors), interdependence (devices learn to rely on one another to take action), and integration (sets of devices organized into programmable systems).[27] Wasik's vision of the third stage of fully integrated devices suggests that hybrid design practitioners will be called upon to map space in terms of the

---

21 http://www.liftmaster.com/lmcv2/pages/productfamily.aspx?famid=213

22 http://bit.ly/1nTBiAL

23 http://www.whirlpool.com/smart-appliances/

24 http://bit.ly/1nTBm3q

25 http://www.smartthings.com/

26 http://www.zigbee.org/Standards/Overview.aspx

27 http://www.wired.com/gadgetlab/2013/05/internet-of-things/

system of data and decision flows as well as the flow of people and human activity, to work simultaneously as interaction designers as well as designers of physical space.

The age of space populated by integrated and interconnected devices will require an important skillset, which can be labeled *network understanding*. Albert-László Barabási of Northeastern University observed, "Today, we increasingly recognize that nothing happens in isolation. Most events and phenomena are connected, caused by, and interacting with a huge number of other pieces of a complex universal puzzle. We have come to see that we live in a small world, where everything is linked to everything else."[28] Barabási applies tools of network science to increase understanding of the way the information network of the Web is structured and how it develops. The complex linkages of the individual to a community, society, and a world are becoming manifest through architecture. Beyond providing opportunities for efficient communication and problem solving, this manifestation will change the nature of our relationship to architecture. Network understanding, or insight about the way elements exist in dynamic patterns of cause and effect, will be needed alongside traditional architectural skills. The hybrid design practice will incorporate network understanding alongside knowledge of technical requirements for particular spaces for human occupation.

Interconnectedness in the design process opens up opportunities to invite stakeholders or "the crowd" into decision making. Hybrid design practitioners will understand how to tap the wisdom of communities through a connected design process. Design influence by consensus is not new. It is often applied when projects require community support to thrive. Christopher Day, in his book *Consensus Design*,[29] discussed the benefits and pain of socially inclusive processes. A design professional gives up control over project decisions, faces the challenge of getting a group to align around the needs of a situation, and reaps the value of the contribution of many voices to strengthen a project. This practice requires leadership, social skills, and conviction in the outcome. Yet,

---

28 Barabasi (2003), *http://www.barabasilab.com/*
29 Day (2003)

how these skills will be translated into situations in which the crowd is geographically distributed and linked by the Internet remains to be seen.

Changing Definitions of Space

As interconnected environments become commonplace and our interfaces move from H2A to H2M to M2M and beyond to aggregations that link people and machines and architecture into emerging systems—H2M2M2A2H—we need to consider the meaning inherent in design decisions. Successful hybrid design demands insight about how people interact with space as much as knowledge about digital interfaces. The connectedness represented by these new models compels designers to understand the simultaneous effects of digital and spatial experience, to anticipate the effects of design on human, machine, and architectural contexts. And beyond successful problem solving to achieve functionality, the designer must consider what conceptual model of the future community is encoded in the solution.

Hybrid designers will embed architecture with programmable interconnected devices and apply knowledge, content, and interpretation that make interconnectedness meaningful in a social context as well as practical in a physical context. As increasingly sophisticated systems of information inherent in social networks are integrated into physical spaces, interconnected environments will do more than sense the need for change in environmental controls. Layers of information—virtual geometry and relevant data—will be interpreted and presented to us as we scan space with augmented reality devices. When we encounter architectural elements, we will have the opportunity to unpack history and connect to counterparts elsewhere in space or time. Upon arriving at my hotel room for the first time, I look out the window and have access to digital messages and artifacts left by decades of past occupants, pointing out noteworthy features of the city outside. The window can inform me of the best approaches to reducing the energy footprint during my stay by manipulating the window position, shading, or reflectivity. But the way this information is positioned relative to the room will make important statements about the relationship between these individuals and my occupation of this particular space at this specific time.

Space itself will become malleable, capable of reconfiguring to suit our profiles—presenting differences in lighting, materiality, even form as we move from place to place. The design of interaction between architecture and machine—A2M—incorporates the technology of smart buildings, structures whose systems are automated in order to improve their efficiency. In fact, the earliest building automation systems and "smart building" examples provide an important foundation for hybrid design. But emerging technologies—pervasive and mobile access, social community, and augmented reality, among others—will highlight new opportunities for innovation and development of A2M models.

Lorraine Daston noted the importance of objects in the environment and the deep connection of things to human communication. Daston states, "Imagine a world without things... without things, we would stop talking. We would become as mute as things are alleged to be. If things are "speechless," perhaps it is because they are drowned out by all the talk about them."[30] As we move toward a world filled with articulate things, a categorization of these new environmental elements positioned by their sphere of application will help us gauge the progress we've made, give us ideas for innovation, and start us on a path toward a hybrid design theory for interconnected environments.

A Framework for Interconnected Environments

To categorize the contribution of interconnected sensors and devices, observe that the modes of H2M interaction are already a primary differentiator for the applications that have emerged in the marketplace. A framework can help clarify opportunities that might exist at the intersection between modes of interaction—the different ways that humans engage with machine-enabled architecture—and spheres of inquiry— the different objectives that we have, or the purpose for engagement. By interrogating each cell of this framework, shown in Figure 13-3, a range of directions for hybrid design practice will emerge.

---

30 Daston (2004)

MODES OF INTERACTION

There are a number of modes of interaction, spanning information gathering, understanding, transmission, manipulation, and storage. Different interaction modes suggest the types of information to be stored, processed, and exchanged. Each mode addresses a specific question, and as a collection they offer the potential to build sequences of interactions, eventually linked to form increasingly sophisticated collections of tools, or systems.

1. Awareness: what can we measure, what can we learn?

   At a fundamental level, sensors track a condition in the environment. Sensors can report on the presence or movement of individuals or objects in a space. They can determine temperature, light levels, or detect moisture. Awareness of a condition is a fundamental step required for reporting and decision making.

2. Analysis: what useful knowledge can we glean from data?

   When an environmental condition is detected, the interconnected environment can make this information useful by using it in a predefined algorithm that layers data about the condition with a judgment about the implications of that condition. If the sensor reports light, the algorithm might compare the illuminated condition with data about current weather conditions, time, or solar positions. If it is nighttime, the office is closed, and the room is suddenly illuminated, this might mean that someone has entered a space unexpectedly. The Analysis interaction mode might include more sophisticated algorithms, for example to calculate the amount of energy used by the light, or heat that the light could predictably generate.

3. Communication: how should insight be reported?

   The judgment call stemming from the Analysis mode of interaction would activate the next mode in the sequence: Communication. If illumination is not anticipated, the next interaction is to send a message or flag an alert in a system that is monitoring the status of the environment. Messages would be directed to people or other machines. A system of integrated sensors, assessment, and communications could be designed to produce a complex set of effects based on situations and reactions.

4. Action: what action can a system initiate based on insight?

In addition to Communication, a myriad of Actions could be integrated into a system of cause and effect. Such actions might impact the space in which a condition is being observed. For example, an unexpected light might be analyzed and found to produce excess heat in a space, which would call for draperies to be repositioned, or for a cooling system to be engaged.

5. Feedback: how can we assess the impact and learn from action?

Ultimately, the detection, analysis, and action loop reaches a point where Feedback at a systemic scale becomes useful. After prolonged observation and analysis, assessment might determine a pattern of lights going on and off during certain periods. Appropriate judgments could be made and actions taken, based on this more holistic assessment. Ongoing assessment and prolonged interaction would improve decision making and suggest the most appropriate actions so that the space could reach an ideal environmental state.

6. Recollection: how can we retain knowledge for later access?

As the system proceeds through cycles of interaction, there will be value in maintaining a record of observations and changes. Storing the details and organizing the data into patterns provides a resource that can be tapped to improve the intelligence and performance of the overall system as it evolves.

Spheres of Inquiry

Across all modes of interaction, three spheres of inquiry describe the different objectives that we have for understanding or transforming the world through physical or human systems. As developers and designers of tools, inspecting the opportunities through the lens of objectives helps to suggest the prominent marketplace for tools based on interconnected environments (see Figure 13-3).

1. Environmental: how can we optimize and minimize use of resources to produce ideal conditions by combining data gathered through monitoring with external data sources?

Interconnected applications naturally gravitate toward tracking and improving the environmental conditions they are ideally suited to monitor. Applications can alert individuals to dangerous conditions in a surrounding space, for example if toxins are building up in a confined room,[31] if noise levels have increased,[32] if a space is threatened by flooding when water is detected on the floor. Environmental alerts can range in scale from a single room, to a building, complex, or community scale. Environmental conditions for a specific building or campus can alert individuals or systems to take action to control energy usage, for example.

Interaction Inquiry	Sensing/ Awareness	Insight/ Analysis	Communication/ Reporting	Action	Feedback	Memories/ Recollect
Environmental	Sense noise levels, spatial changes, temperature	Analyze environmental performance	Reports, dashboards of sustainable factors	Modify systems and spaces with mobile devices or interfaces	Provide feedback on performance impacts	Store environment patterns
Behavioral	Sense behaviors, movement	Analyze behaviors	Report on actions and impacts	Drive preferred behavior	Provide feedback on behavioral impacts	Stored space interaction patterns
Social	Sense social interactions	Analyze the impact of social interactions	Report on social network interactions and impacts	Drive preferred social interactions	Provide feedback on social interaction impacts	Store social interaction patterns

Figure 13-3. A framework for connected environments with examples of potential tools at the intersection of each interaction mode and sphere of inquiry

2. Behavioral: can we incent preferred behaviors? Can we monitor human interactions, and assess and modify conditions based on knowledge of preferences?

Environments are capable of exerting pressure on individuals and shaping behavior. Data about behavior or environmental conditions force individuals to confront situations and these confrontations can drive change. The proliferation of interconnected devices to drive improved health behaviors (such as WiFi-connected

---

31 *https://www.alertme.com/*

32 *http://www.widetag.com/widenoise/*

pedometers and scales)[33] and other monitoring systems enable people to track themselves, fostering improvement in behavior from diet and nutrition health[34] to greener environmentally friendly living.[35]

3. Social: how can we produce network-based discussion and action through social connection? Can we modify settings to be conducive to human interaction?

Architectural history teaches us that environments have tremendous power over the actions of communities and groups. They can be designed with the power to divide us, or to unite us. Interconnected environments will be capable of monitoring and impacting social patterns of interaction. Ranging from observation to assessment and action, the social sphere of application raises questions about how systems should be designed to provide the information and actions to the group and its constituents in a useful manner.

An Exercise in Hybrid Design Practice

Apply the Interconnected Environments Framework to design a space and an experience (see Table 13-1). You can use this sample narrative as a model:

Begin by considering an indoor place that has been meaningful for you. This might be a room from your childhood or a space you recently visited where a significant event occurred.

1. Write a brief narrative describing how this meaning is connected to your relationships and to clusters of knowledge that you possess or seek to tap.

2. Launch your design process with key questions. How do the answers contribute to the engagement of the visitor with the meaning of the space—in the past, and in the future?

---

33 *http://www.fitbit.com/*

34 *http://quantifiedself.com/about/*

35 *http://www.makemesustainable.com/*

3. Design the space and outfit it with a series of Internet-enabled devices. Be specific about the devices; specify the data they gather. What does each device do to process, store, analyze, or transmit information?

4. Next, design an interaction for a visitor to this space that takes advantage of emerging technology to convey meaning and engage visitors through experience. Script or storyboard this interaction.

TABLE 13-1. Sample

	ENV	BEH	SOC
SENSING	What light, sound, smells, and temperature should the visitor experience? How can sensors augment what the visitor should be aware of while occupying the space?	Who is the visitor? What is the purpose of the visit?	What interactions should occur between multiple visitors arriving at the same time, or one after another?
ANALYSIS	What analysis should be done on the environment—changes in light, accumulation of heat?	What insights should the space produce about the visitor's behavior?	What actions of others outside the space should be considered? How should they be analyzed?
COMMUNICATION	How should spatial conditions be communicated and conveyed? How should the space be organized to present these reports?	How should behaviors be reported?	Which social interactions should be reported? How can they be useful to visitors to the space?

	ENV	BEH	SOC
ACTION	What actions should the space take when certain environmental conditions occur?	How can the space drive the visitor to take a specific action? Should it?	How will the visitor be connected to others? How will others shape the visitor's experience in the space?
FEEDBACK	What response should the space provide based on the visitor's physical movement, gestures, directional gaze, facial expressions, or vocalizations?	Can the space provide feedback on the effectiveness of the configuration to support desired outcomes?	Can feedback be collected on the impact of the space on driving desired social interactions?
RECOLLECT	Would it be useful to record the environmental changes in the space over time?	How can the space record, document, and recall the actions of visitors?	Should visitor responses be collected and presented over time?

Architecture as Interface

The process of spatial design evolves continually and emerging technology opens up new modes of inquiry in design on a regular basis. Today, rapid prototyping of physical components is possible with cost-effective 3D printing of a wide range of materials.[36] Some designers adopt a fabrication-based design process by aggregating manufactured or 3D printed components. Form-generating experimentation driven by algorithms[37] is as valid as by heuristics. The existing world can be captured, rendered digital, and used as a backdrop for design and experimentation in virtual environments.[38]

---

36 "California duo create 'world's first 3D printed architecture,'" dezeen Magazine, *http://bit.ly/1nTBYpN.*

37 *http://bit.ly/1nTBXly*

38 *http://autode.sk/1sSidAJ*

The adoption of a model-driven design process enables architects to consider issues of geometry and issues of information simultaneously through building information modeling (BIM).[39] With BIM, the designers employ digital elements conceived as architecture—with parametric geometry that parallels each spatial entity, attached to data that describes the entity in terms of costs, manufacture, and physical properties. A new breed of BIM tools will be needed so that designers can assess the impact of spatial and user interaction decisions across different modes of inquiry.

Augmented reality, which layers digital visualizations with real space, as shown in Figure 13-4, must next incorporate an information visualization aspect so that environments and interfaces can be experienced virtually before they are actually constructed and programmed.[40]

Figure 13-4. Layering of digital and information visualization (courtesy of the author)

39 Eastman, Charles and Sanguinetti, Paola "BIM Technologies That Inform Concept Design," AIA Conference 2009, *http://bit.ly/1nTC28Z*.
40 Sanchez (2013)

Perhaps it is time to revisit Alexander's notion of patterns in the environment and to develop a pattern language for the age of interconnected environments. In this new pattern language, each pattern would be a formal response to a design problem linking interactive systems with spatial environments. As a starting point, the framework suggests a range of patterns that can be developed to link modes of interaction with spheres of inquiry.

Consider the bevy of building types that we inhabit and reimagine them in new ways—whether homes, workplaces, or industrial, ceremonial, or social settings. A museum that responds to your background and interests by highlighting key exhibits modifies the text that accompanies the artifacts to suit your knowledge of history. An exhibit might connect you to others with similar responses or comments, spawning a network of virtual relationships. Consider a nightclub that reconfigures to accommodate an impromptu gathering and points you to a room filled with graduates of your college when the club's "operating system" assesses the profiles of all visitors and finds commonalities. As you enter, the walls of the room have already shifted to reflect your group's publically posted images of your time together, along with music of the time period. Surgical rooms maintain awareness of the presence and movement of particles linked to infectious diseases, which leads to movement of equipment and lighting and modification of airflow to protect the patient from harmful conditions and inform clinical professionals of medical history and environmental changes.

Conclusion

Tomorrow's spaces will be formed from interconnected and intelligent components that are aware of the human presence, and are able to communicate, assess, and act. The role of the hybrid designer must evolve to incorporate both sets of skills—architect and interaction designer— so that we can create meaningful places that support systems of interconnected intelligent devices.

The hybrid designer will not be responsible solely for "concretization" of the building as an object, as described by Christian Norberg-Schulz, but rather for orchestrating a new context—a dynamic system of elements that flex and adapt to support our needs for environmental, behavioral, and social settings. Its choreography will be influenced by an evolving set of actors. As Nishat Awan states, "The dynamic, and hence temporal, nature of space means that spatial production must be understood as part of an evolving sequence, with no fixed start or finish, and that multiple actors contribute at various stages."[41]

The hybrid designer will go beyond problem solving and practicality, to write the manifesto and express what it means to live in an interconnected society through architecture. To articulate how our buildings have become gateways to communities of connection and alternative experience. Or, to personify each building as a character in the story of a life, responding to you, shaping your environment to suit your needs, analyzing situations, providing feedback, and recalling past experience. In fact, by giving voice to architecture through interconnectedness, we may re-create a time when humans had a closer relationship to space and its meaning. If nothing else, at least we can become better listeners.

References

Alexander C, et al. *A Pattern Language: Towns, Buildings, Construction*. New York, Oxford University Press, 1977.

Alexander C. *The Timeless Way of Building*. New York, Oxford University Press, 1979.

Awan N, et al. *Spatial Agency: Other Ways of Doing Architecture*. Abingdon, Oxon, England; New York, Routledge, 2011.

Barabási A-Ls. *Linked: How Everything Is Connected to Everything Else and What It Means for Business, Science, and Everyday Life*. New York, Plume, 2003.

Brand S. *How Buildings Learn: What Happens After They're Built*. New York, Viking, 1994.

Brawne M. *Architectural Thought: The Design Process and the Expectant Eye*. Amsterdam; Boston, Elsevier: Architectural Press, 2005.

Carpo M. *The Alphabet and the Algorithm*. Cambridge, Mass., MIT Press, 2011.

---

41 Awan (2011).

Conklin, E. J. *Dialogue Mapping: Building Shared Understanding of Wicked Problems*. Chichester, England; Hoboken, NJ, Wiley, 2006.

Conrads U. *Programmes and Manifestoes on 20th-Century Architecture*. London, Lund Humphries, 1970.

Daston L. *Things That Talk: Object Lessons from Art and Science*. New York; Cambridge, Mass., Zone Books; MIT Press distributor, 2004.

Day C, Parnell R. *Consensus Design: Socially Inclusive Process*. Oxford, Architectural, 2003.

De Botton A. *The Architecture of Happiness*. London; New York, Hamish Hamilton, an imprint of Penguin Books, 2006.

Frazer JH. "The architectural relevance of cybernetics." [Univ of U., Belfast (United Kingdom)]. *Systems Research*. Retrieved from *http://www.osti.gov/scitech/servlets/purl/457730*, 1993.

Eastman CM. *Adaptive-Conditional Architecture in Design Participation*, edited by Nigel Cross. London. Academic Editions. 1992;51-7.

Fox M, Kemp M. *Interactive Architecture*. New York, Princeton Architectural Press, 2009.

Hays KM. *Architecture Theory since 1968*. Cambridge, Mass., The MIT Press, 1998.

Jencks C, Kropf K. *Theories and Manifestoes of Contemporary Architecture*. Chichester, England; Hoboken, NJ, Wiley-Academy, 2006.

Jones JC. *Design Methods*. New York, Van Nostrand Reinhold, 1992.

Karatani KJ, Speaks M. *Architecture as Metaphor: Language, Number, Money*. Cambridge, Mass.; London, MIT Press, 1995.

Lawson B. *How Designers Think*. London; Boston, Butterworth Architecture, 1990.

LaVine L. *Mechanics and Meaning in Architecture*. Minneapolis, University of Minnesota Press, 2001.

McCullough M. *Digital Ground: Architecture, Pervasive Computing, and Environmental Knowing*. Cambridge, Mass., MIT Press, 2004.

Mayerovitch H. *How Architecture Speaks and Fashions Our Lives*. Montreal, Robert Davies, 1996.

Mückenheim MA., Demel JA. *Inspiration: Contemporary Design Methods in Architecture.* Amsterdam, BIS; Enfield: Publishers Group UK [distributor].

Negroponte N. *The Architecture Machine.* Cambridge, Mass., MIT Press, 1970.

Nesbitt K. *Theorizing a New Agenda for Architecture: An Anthology of Architectural Theory, 1965–1995.* New York, Princeton Architectural Press, 1996.

Norberg-Schulz C. *Genius Loci: Towards a Phenomenology of Architecture.* New York, Rizzoli, 1980.

Norman DA. *The Design of Everyday Things.* New York, Basic Books, 2002.

Rowe PG. *Design Thinking.* Cambridge, Mass., MIT Press, 1987.

Sánchez RA, et al. "Construction processes using mobile augmented reality: a study case in building engineering degree." In *Advances in Information Systems and Technologies,* Rocha Á, Correia AM, Wilson T, Stroetmann KA (Eds.). Springer Berlin-Heidelberg. 2013;206:1053-62.

Vitruvius P, et al. *Vitruvius: Ten Books on Architecture.* New York, Cambridge University Press, 1999.

[14]

Design for the Networked World: A Practice for the Twenty-First Century

MATT NISH-LAPIDUS

The Future of Design

Bruce Sterling wrote in *Shaping Things* (MIT Press) that the world is becoming increasingly connected, and the devices by which we are connecting are becoming smarter and more self-aware. When every object in our environment contains data collection, communication, and interactive technology, how do we as human beings learn how to navigate all of this new information? We need new tools as both designers, and humans, to work with all of this information and the new devices that create, consume, and store it.

Today, there's a good chance that your car can park itself. Your phone likely knows where you are. You can walk through the interiors of famous buildings on the Web. Everything around us is constantly collecting data, running algorithms, calculating outcomes, and accumulating more raw data than we can handle.

We all carry minicomputers in our pockets, often more than one; public and private infrastructure collects terabytes of data every minute; and personal analytics has become so commonplace that it's more conspicuous to not collect data about yourself than to record every waking moment. In many ways we've moved beyond Malcolm McCullough's ideas of ubiquitous computing put forth in *Digital Ground* (MIT Press) and into a world in which computing isn't only ubiquitous and invisible, but pervasive, constant, and deeply embedded in our everyday lives.

Augmented reality (AR) is here, already deeply engrained in our understanding of the world. The screen-based AR espoused by apps such as Layar is primitive compared to the augmentations that we all use on a daily basis. Google Maps, Twitter, Facebook, Nike FuelBand, and more are prime examples of how we are already augmenting our reality in fundamental ways that are less obvious and intrusive than digital overlays (which will see their day eventually, I'm sure). We have been augmenting our reality since the invention of clothing allowed us to live in harsher climates, and now we are augmenting it with networked technology giving us not just a sixth sense, but a seventh, eighth, and ninth, as well.

As augmentation and networks change our understanding of reality, we begin to understand old technology through our lens of new media. A chair is no longer solely a physical object that exists in our environment, it is now an interactive object by which specific behavior and person-to-person relationships can emerge from its use (Buchanan, 2011). A building is no longer only a collection of materials that defines a place, it is also understood through its interactions with people, the interactions it facilitates, and how it interacts or interferes with our networked augmentations. We are McLuhan-esque cyborgs, with media devices that extend our body and mind from the outside. Objects that exist as part of this network become more than their discrete pieces; we internalize their behavior and it changes the way we understand our world and ourselves.

We can see shifts in common language that allude to these changes. We talk about "downloading" knowledge from one person to another and "interfacing" with organizations. Words like "interface," "download," and "stream," once not commonly used outside of technological circles, are now part of our daily lexicon, used in reference to their technological meaning as well as applied to much older concepts in the physical world.

A 2007 study on mobile phone usage conducted by Nokia concluded that the mobile phone is now one of the most essential items for daily use around the world, putting it in the same social category as wallets and keys.[1] They identified that it wasn't only the object itself that is important to people, it is the social identity it provides that people value. The phone is more than an object—it is a lifeline, a gateway through which people connect with their family, friends, livelihood, and community. This is even truer now with the prevalence of smartphones with always-on Internet access. The smartphone has become one of the current embodiments of the networked world; more than its function, more than its form, it is a social safety net that allows people to travel or live further away from their home and still feel connected.

The smartphone is still a tangible object, one that we can understand through our hands and eyes, and it has connections to the network that we can see and feel. A greater shift is occurring now through objects that connect in less visible ways—objects that act on our behalf, or against us, without our explicit knowledge. The ethical implications and choices made by algorithms that determine the flow of traffic, our food supply chain, market pricing, and how you measure your fitness are present in our lives but are largely below the surface. As connected systems spring up around the world, often bypassing the more outdated infrastructure we are dealing with here in North America, we need to begin considering the biases and implications of our choices when designing these systems, objects, and networks. For example, the current sensors used to trigger traffic lights often rely on induction pads embedded in the road. These sensors only detect cars and other large vehicles, and are unable to sense bicycles and pedestrians. There's an implicit decision made about the relative importance of different modes of transportation. A traffic system built on an inductive sensor network will always prioritize car and truck traffic over cyclists, for example, making the city a less hospitable place to ride a bike. This can in turn impact population density, pollution, congestion, parking, employment, injury rates, and more.

As we move even further into a networked world, we as designers of these new devices and services need to understand all aspects of our new environment. The complexity of design and architecture will only continue to grow and require a new definition of design foundations, practice, and theory.

---

1 Cui, Yanqing, Jan Chipchase, and Fumiko Ichikawa. 2007. "A Cross Culture Study on Phone Carrying and Physical Personalization." Nokia Research, https://research.nokia. com/files/45590483.pdf.

This might seem daunting, but no more so than the nature of mass manufacturing and new materials seemed to the early industrial designers and architects of the twentieth century. We must look to new media art practice, design history, and new research in order to apply our craft to our current context. Designers make things that reflect their environment, but also shape that same environment through the objects that they create, laying the foundation for the future.

We have strong foundations stretching back over a century of art, architecture, and industrial design. We don't need to begin again, but we do need to continue to evolve our practice to incorporate new techniques, tools, and capabilities that help us understand the potential of today's technology.

What are the aesthetics of feedback, immersion, and communication? How can we apply foundations of interaction, such as time and metaphor, to the exchange of data between machines that facilitates an athlete learning how to perform better? What is a beautiful network and how do we recognize and critique it? These are the questions we now face, ones that we will continue to explore through our work and try to answer with objects, systems, places, and conversations.

New Environment, New Materials

[W]e have witnessed a paradigm shift from cyberspace to pervasive computing. Instead of pulling us through the looking glass into some sterile, luminous world, digital technology now pours out beyond the screen, into our messy places, under our laws of physics; it is built into our rooms, embedded in our props and devices—everywhere.
—MALCOLM MCCOLLOUGH, *DIGITAL GROUND* (MIT PRESS), P 9

Over the past couple of decades, our environment has changed significantly.

Screens are everywhere all the time. This means that the complex interactions afforded by screens are even more important to understand and design properly.

Physical objects are now imbued with "smart" features using sensors, networks, and physical interactions that are often invisible, having no screen whatsoever. This makes physical object design more and more important for designing modern products, shifting focus back toward industrial design and architecture and away from the myopic attention to screens that interaction design has had recently.

Machine to machine communication is at the heart of many interactions and systems that we can't live without. This means that designers need to think about not just the human actors in a system, but also the objects, networks, and algorithms that run our environments.

This puts the modern designer in a bit of a sticky situation. As an example, a project on which we recently embarked at Normative includes a mobile app that communicates with a physical box of electronics affixed to the back of a ski that is laced with embedded sensors, as shown in Figure 14-1. That box also needs to be aesthetically pleasing and fit the skier's understanding of how a ski accessory should look and feel. The skier needs to enjoy working with the companion mobile app in a way that enhances the skiing experience. The box of electronics that reads the data from the sensors embedded in the ski needs to communicate that data to the mobile device, and has to communicate that it is doing something to the person on the skis through a simple display of LEDs and recessed buttons. All of this needs to happen in a way that makes sense to the skier, doesn't detract from skiing, and withstands the environment of the slopes.

Figure 14-1. An early ski prototype[2]

---

2 Copyright Normative, 2013

In this example there are many types of design at work—industrial design for the skis and the electronics box; graphic design for the labels, ski graphics, packaging, and mobile app interface; interaction design for the mobile app; system integration; and coordinated communication between the app and the box. This is in addition to all the engineering involved in the hardware and software to make this all work.

What we witness in projects such as this one is a shift in the way we're working from the industrial model of design → build → sell to a post-industrial model wherein all those things happen simultaneously in an integrated and iterative way within a small team. The initial prototype of the circuit was created by an interaction designer using an Arduino, and then an engineer and the designer worked together to refine the circuit through iteration. An integrated team of designers from different practices, creative technologists, engineers, and fabricators is required to design, build, and iterate on a system this complex.

At the heart of this team is a design practice that coordinates all the moving pieces, keeps the overall system in mind, and is the arbiter of the aesthetic and functional coherence of the final product. The lead designer needs to have a refined sense of aesthetics as it relates to the appearance of the physical product, the software, and the system that makes them work together. Figure 14-2 demonstrates this team effort at work as the prototype begins to transition toward a more polished product.

The overall aesthetics and quality of the interactive system, product, and associated software is the purview of this new breed of designer, including the impact and implications of the product. The modern designer needs to have a foundation in traditional design disciplines and interaction foundations, which acts as a framework for thinking about the form of objects and interfaces, as well as good understanding of systems theory, cybernetics (the study of feedback, relationships, and communication within a system), and culture, including a basic grasp of ethnography and anthropology in order to understand different contexts and cultures.

Figure 14-2. A higher fidelity prototype of the electronics and enclosure for the skis[3]

HAPPENINGS, CONVERSATIONS, AND EXPLORATION

In late 1968 Jack Burnham, a writer and art history professor, wrote the following in his paper *System Esthetics*:

> The specific function of modern didactic art has been to show that art does not reside in material entities, but in relations between people and between people and the components of their environments.

He was looking at the emergence of large-scale interactive artworks and art events in the 1960s. Artists began to see their work as more than the object itself; they began to think about how the object interacts with the audience and environment to create a conversation.

Artist David Rokeby explored the emotion and aesthetics of environmental feedback systems in his early works Reflexions, Body Language, and Very Nervous System in the 1980s. Rokeby created one of the earliest examples of gestural interface by building his own 8 x 8 pixel digital camera and programming his own software to read the video input and

3 Copyright Normative, 2013

create feedback in the form of sound and video.[4] To fully understand the aspects of movement and feedback systems he was interested in, he had to learn new technologies, create innovative solutions to unknown problems, and build his own sensors and output devices. If this sounds familiar, it's because these are exactly the same types of activities and problems facing designers and artists today. Figure 14-3 presents a series of images illustrating the results of people interacting with the system.

Figure 14-3. Various people interacting with David Rokeby's Very Nervous System (1986 – 2004) at aceartinc., Winnipeg, Canada[5]

To explore new concepts, behaviors, and environments, artists and designers need to develop a new set of tools and skills. Architects and interior designers use physical models, known as a maquette, to experiment with form, materials, lighting, orientation, and other properties of their designs. Similarly, designers working with emerging technologies need tools to experiment, mold, and model the elements of networked devices, software, and complex systems.

---

4 Rokeby, David. 1982–1984. "Reflexions," *http://www.davidrokeby.com/reflex.html.*

5 Photos by William Eakin, Liz Garlicki and Risa Horowitz. Image arrray design Mike Carroll. 2003.

The success of new design tools to help work with somewhat intangible materials has to be measured based on how well it helps the designer understand the parameters of her design, and make choices based on experiencing aspects of the design in context. These tools should allow for different levels of generative and synthetic activities, varying fidelity, working with high-level abstract notions all the way down to the small functional and aesthetic details of the final product.

The current generation of digital design tools (CAD, Adobe Creative Suite) created new ways of working on traditional types of outputs. They gave us the ability to create many more variations of layouts, the safety of undo and file versions, and access to previously impossible or difficult processes for creating effects and working with new source material. However, they did not fundamentally change the component pieces of the designer's process, toolbox, or output.

These tools are coming up short as designers are beginning to work with complex communications between people and machines, interactions and movement that happens over long periods of time and many individual devices, and large data sets that can't easily be visualized using manual methods.

To add to this complexity, the entire notion of finality has changed. Designers traditionally create outputs that remain static, or have a small set of variations, once produced. Modality in traditional products was more a result of context, use, customization, or modification. In new types of products there is no "final version," rather the product itself is a system, reacting to its environment and interactions, continually changing and evolving with use.

TWENTY-FIRST CENTURY FOUNDATION

Designers in the twentieth century needed to internalize and deeply comprehend things like 2D and 3D form, physical environments, and typography (to name a few areas of practice). The twenty-first century designer needs to build on these foundations with a number of new elements. The traditional elements of design were well established by Rowena Reed-Kostellow and her colleagues in the 1930s: line, plane, color, volume, value, and texture. She used these as the basis for her groundbreaking design foundations pedagogy at Carnegie Tech.[6] Dave Malouf presented an initial set of interaction design foundations in an article for Boxes and Arrows in 2007,[7] and then expanded upon it in a presentation at Interaction'09. He includes elements of time, abstraction, metaphor, negativity, and motion in his set of expanded foundations.

The things we design now are beyond screens and objects and we are challenged to think of the next set of foundations for designing these systems. We can begin to draw inspiration and knowledge from cybernetics, soft systems theory, and urbanism along with more commonly referenced practices such as architecture and anthropology.

When working with invisible technology and systems that cannot be observed easily, visualizations become even more important. Often, the only way that a system and all of its interactions and decisions can be understood is through illustrations and narratives that look at the impact as well as the cause of each part of the interaction.

As we examine these systems we should pay special attention to the qualities, aesthetics, of the elements of the system. A set of aesthetics qualities of a system includes new foundational elements that build upon traditional design foundations and Malouf's interaction foundations.

Texture

What is the connectivity of the system? How do the pieces interact with one another, both human and nonhuman? The texture of the network is what we think about when we look at how easy it is to interface with its different parts. If the connections are obvious and accessible, we might describe the interface as smooth; if the connection points are difficult or confusing, that could be described as rough.

The notion of texture can be applied to graphical interfaces, gestural or spatial interfaces, hardware controls, and APIs alike, among other things. How might one describe the qualities of their bank's system?

6 Hannah, Gail Greet. 2002. *Elements of Design: Rowena Reed Kostellow and The Structure of Visual Relationships*, Princeton Architectural Press.

7 Malouf, Dave. 2007. *Foundations of Interaction Design*. Boxes and Arrows, *http:// boxesandarrows.com/foundations-of-interaction-design/*.

This could include their ATMs, customer service, transfer between institutions, and more. Often a designer (or critic) will only be concerned with a subset of a network system, but it's always good to pay attention to how that piece interacts with the whole and how the system responds to those inputs.

Agency

What is the component's capacity to act on the other parts of the network or the system as a whole? Can a person interfacing with the product influence the rules of the system? Or, are his potential actions constrained by other aspects of the system? How much freedom does each network component have within the system?

The agency of each actor within the system depends on its role. From a human perspective, agency can describe how much power a user can exert on other parts of the network, versus being limited to specific actions in specific contexts. Different actors will have different amounts of agency at different times.

Opacity

How clear is the network from the perspective of a participant or observer? Are the connections easily visible or are they hidden? The opacity of a network can influence how much agency each actor has and help to create the desired texture.

In our traffic-light example, we see a very opaque system, one where the means of interacting are often completely hidden. It would be easy to interact with the system and still not even know that it exists. In this example, the opacity has a direct impact on a person's agency, but if the system behaves properly, the texture might still be smooth. Roughness will become apparent if the system misbehaves and nobody can see what is happening.

Reflexivity

How do you know what is happening in the network? How does it inform the different actors, both human and nonhuman, what state it is in and if there are any problems? Feedback and communication is a vital piece of any system.

Reflexivity is the way in which the particular system provides feedback based on states, actions, and behaviors. This is an indication that the rules of the system are enforced. By providing feedback when a component attempts an action the system can let all of its parts know what is happening, if the action was completed, and what the new state looks like. The quality of this feedback is important to crafting the aesthetic of the system. Is it friendly? Verbose? Human readable? All of these things will change the overall feel of the products and services that are part of the network.

These are some possible aesthetic elements we can begin to use to discuss the qualities of a network system. None are inherently good or bad; they are the basis for a common language that lets us discuss the aspects of a network that affect its quality. An opaque network with little agency creates a certain type of interaction, one largely dictated by its owner. A low-opacity network with a lot of agency allows for more flexibility and potential wrangling by the person interfacing with the system.

The types of systems and products described by the above aesthetic language can be understood in two important ways (among others):

1. As a hard system: a system model that is concrete and constructed to achieve an objective. These types of systems are easy to analyze and model because they are generally made up of discrete pieces that each plays a set part, most often actual things that exist in the physical world.

2. As a soft system: a system model that is fuzzy and focuses on the understanding of the system from many perspectives. In this type of model each piece of the system is based on a subjective understanding of the whole, rather than specific objects that exist in the world.

For the type of design discussed in this chapter we are more concerned with soft systems, although both soft and hard must exist in order to fully understand and build a product or service in our networked world.

Soft systems methodology (SSM), a framework for thinking about epistemological systems, gives us tools to help understand an unstructured complex problem through modeling actions and subjective understanding of the situation. Unlike hard systems, soft systems models aren't about classification; instead the practice seeks to explain different relationships by describing them as they are seen, understood, and acted upon. A single set of objects and relationships could be described in many different ways, each one equally valid from a different perspective. Soft systems have always had a close tie to the way design-ers work. Peter Checkland, one of the SSM pioneers, said the following in his book *Systems Thinking, Systems Practice*:

> Its rationale lies in the fact that the complexity of human affairs is always a complexity of multiple interacting relationships; and pictures are a better medium than linear prose for expressing relationships. Pic-tures can be taken in as a whole and help to encourage holistic rather than reductionist thinking about a situation

Design's tradition of visualization and sketching fit very well with SSM's tendency toward visualization from the perspective of an actor within the system. In the networked world the designer's ability to understand, explore, and explain complex interactions between people and machines, and machines to machines, becomes even more import-ant. SSM gives us a starting point to understand how to reframe com-plex situations through a process that begins by embedding oneself into the situation, expressing what you observe and understand that situation to be, and then creating diagrams that express that under-standing. Once the system is visualized it can be compared to observed reality to understand which definition fits best in the given context and what actions one should take to affect the system, described in SSM as feasible and desirable changes. The use of visual tools helps the design-ers and stakeholders build the same mental model, rather than the ambiguity of individual conceptions.

Tools like this one become a primary piece of the twenty-first cen-tury designer's kit. Making sense of and expressing complex systems of relationships, communication, and feedback lay the foundation for good design decisions when dealing with complex networks, invisible interfaces, and nuanced interactions.

New Tools for a New Craft

Although much of the core design process is fundamentally the same as it was 30 years ago—beginning with exploratory methods includ-ing research and sketching, moving through models and prototypes of different fidelities toward a final product—the types of problems we're trying to solve and the tools we need to explore those solutions con-tinue to change and evolve. New types of products require new types of models and prototypes. Animation, electronics, 3D printing, and interactive programming are all necessary parts of the designer's repertoire when working with emerging technologies and twenty-first century products.

Tools traditionally thought of as the domain of engineers, data scientists, and hackers are now entering the designer's toolbox. For example, a designer working with emerging technologies such as sensor networks, data collection, and microcontrollers benefits greatly by learning some basic electronics. Being able to put together a quick prototype by using a platform such as Arduino means that the designer can experiment with the possibilities available to him based on the types of sensors and data at his disposal. Even if the final product will use a different engineering solution, this basic toolset gives designers the capability to model the interactions, data, and physical aspects of a new product at a high level, and with practice, at a detailed level.

Working with large and complex data sets is becoming the norm for designers working on new products. This data can come from custom collectors, such as sensors embedded in products, or from the tangle of information available through web services. When working with large data sets, there is no substitute for working with the data itself. Tools such as Processing or JavaScript and the browser canvas object provide an easy way to start creating rich interactive visualizations from any data.

Rapid fabrication starts to shift industrial design away from being industrial and back to a more artisanal craft. Designers can now imagine a new physical form, model it with traditional tools such as clay, do a digital CAD drawing, and have it fabricated in plastic or metal within a few hours. This facilitates a kind of rapid iteration and prototyping for complex objects that would have been difficult 10 years ago. It also allows for small run production; whereas purely artisan craftspeople could produce only a few objects, and industrial production could only produce high volumes of objects, these new methods make it possible for designers to produce dozens of objects, each the same or slightly different.

These methods can be thought of as a similar process to industrial designers making clay or paper models, or architects using foam-core to make scale models of a new building. None of these things is analogous to the final form, but they are hands-on ways of exploring integral aspects of the design in a fast, cheap, and easy way. Including this in the design process helps illuminate new possibilities and filter out ideas that don't translate. These are ways of sketching with interactivity, responsiveness, and movement, iterating to a model of the product or pieces of the product.

Along with new tools come new collaborations. The *Maker* community and local hack-labs, both groups of people who deeply experiment with new technology for creative purposes, are now home to many technologists and designers working together to make interesting and future focused things. These collaborations result in products such as Berg's Little Printer, the plug-and-play robotics kit, Moti, and DIY home automation tools like Twine. Bio-hack labs are also beginning to pop up, pushing into biology and chemistry, and experimenting with bioengineering in an accessible way. One such group in Toronto, DIYBio Toronto, hosts regular workshops. Companies such as Synbiota, an open source repository for bio-hacking, are forming to support the community.

These are just the beginning, as startups and large companies move into this new space. One of the most successful examples on the market today is the Nest thermostat, which combines innovative physical controls with small screens, microprocessors, and software to add a level of smart automation to the home. A product that started out as a better thermostat is poised to be the hub of a much larger home control system.

How do we begin to work with these new technologies, networks, and systems? There are a few ways to dive in that will help to understand the potential, constraints, and complexities involved.

Experiment

Arduino and similar platforms are easy to find at local stores or online, and they are cheap. Pick one up, find a tutorial, and dive in. Have an idea for a project you'd like to try? Just try it, don't worry if it seems complicated. Start with the simplest piece. These systems give you all the pieces you need to build network-connected objects.

Learn new skills

If you've never programmed before, pick up a JavaScript, Processing, or Ruby tutorial. If you've never designed a physical object, get some modeling clay and sculpting tools and try to make some interesting shapes. If you've never designed software before, try to map out a flow or design an interface; start with pencil and paper.

Be critical

When you've made your first new thing, take some time to think about its qualities using some of the frameworks discussed earlier in this chapter. Use what you learn from this reflection in your next experiments.

Always think about how your new device, software, or system fits into the larger connected world. What possibilities does it create? What potential does it remove? What does it give to people, and what does it take away?

You won't be satisfied with your first attempt, but design is all about iteration. These types of new skills open many possibilities for your practice as a designer, allowing you to incorporate new technology, processes, and techniques into your work.

MAKING THE FUTURE IN WHICH WE WANT TO LIVE

The active ingredient of the work is its interface. The interface is unusual because it is invisible and very diffuse, occupying a large volume of space, whereas most interfaces are focussed [sic] and definite. Though diffuse, the interface is vital and strongly textured through time and space. The interface becomes a zone of experience, of multi-dimensional encounter. The language of encounter is initially unclear, but evolves as one explores and experiences.
—DAVID ROKEBY ON VERY NERVOUS SYSTEM[8]

David Rokeby used the preceding statement to describe the nature of his Very Nervous System interactive installation. These same words now describe our relationship to an ever-increasing amount of invisible architecture acting around us. The metaphorical handles and buttons that we design into these largely invisible systems will determine

---

8 Rokeby, David. 2010. "Very Nervous System," *http://www.davidrokeby.com/vns.html.*

people's ability to comprehend, manage, and benefit from the things we design. Returning to our traffic sensor example, when a hidden sensor at a busy traffic intersection is designed to trigger the lights based on certain physical aspects of a vehicle, the designer of that system needs to decide what types of vehicles are allowed to trigger the lights. Will it work for cars, bicycles, or humans? That choice is a decision that will impact the shape of the urban environment in a way that most people using the intersection will never fully see. How do you indicate the system's texture, agency, opacity, and reflexivity? Do you add symbols to the road to indicate the existence of a sensor and what will activate it? Do you opt for a different solution entirely because of the needs of the city? These are design problems at a systems scale and are becoming more and more common in the work we do every day. We need to make sure we are arming designers with the tools they need to make these types of decisions intentionally.

Design is a special craft, one that allows us to imagine the future as we would like to see it, and then make the things that will help get us there. Pre-industrial products were the output of a single craftsperson, and expressed their understanding and view of the world. Industrial products represented a move to mass production and consumption, where a designer could envision a product and millions of people could receive an identical object. This was the expression of the collective— the design of objects shaped our environment and culture on a large scale.

As we move deeper into a post-industrial era new products are the expression of the network. Small groups can now cocreate and produce objects at industrial scales, or can create complex objects at minute scales for their own needs. Where pre-industrial objects represented a one-to-one relationship between creator and consumer and industrial objects were one-to-many, post-industrial moves into a many-to-many world. Everybody is enabled to create and consume. With this comes a great freedom, but also a great dilemma. Do all these new objects help us create a better future? Do they represent the world we want to live in? Each new creation warrants a consideration of these questions as we continue to redefine our environment using new technology, and to see the world through our new, networked lens.

This era of post-industrial design brings with it new opportunities and more complex challenges, and we should dive in headfirst.

[15]

New Responsibilities of the Design Discipline: A Critical Counterweight to the Coming Technologies?

MARTIN CHARLIER

Critiquing Emerging Technology

Whether it is 3D printing, wearable computing, or biotechnology and nanotechnology, the list of emerging technologies is long and exciting, the potential impact on our lives even more so.

Designers help make new technologies easy to use and find new applications for them. Increasingly, however, designers should be the ones questioning the promises and highlighting concerns about the side effects of what is on the horizon. Currently, this is not widely understood as *design*, so this chapter differentiates between *designers* and *design*, and argues why this new approach should indeed be considered part of design, especially when it comes to emerging technologies.

DESIGN IS ABOUT PEOPLE

In 1911, architect Walter Gropius was commissioned to design a new building for a factory in Germany. Gropius went on to not only design an aesthetically pleasing exterior for the building, but improved the industrial working conditions by also considering the interior of the building and the workers themselves. For example, his then revolutionary use of glass panels made the factory a bright and transparent working environment. To Gropius, design had a social and ethical responsibility as well as an aesthetic one. His belief was that design should bring social good.

The view that art should meet social needs became one of the central ideas of the influential Bauhaus school that Gropius went on to found. One of its aims was to apply design in a way that allowed a broad mass of people to be able to afford and own "good design," thus improving life for people of all classes.

Today, design has developed into a field with diverse focus areas, reaching from the creation of physical objects to the creation of more intangible aspects of daily life, such as the experience of engaging with software or services. In all of these areas, designers work across the fields of business, technology, and human factors to make their creations real.

This cross-disciplinary approach makes designers unique in our society. Designers are multiliterates, capable of speaking and understanding the languages of the different fields in which they engage. They are the translators and diplomats between the ever more specialized fields that make up our complex modern world.

One could say that designers, by and large, apply their cross-disciplinary way of thinking to help businesses make better products.

WHAT CONSTITUTES A BETTER PRODUCT?

What does it mean to "help businesses make better products"? It could mean making the operator of a system faster or more efficient at performing a task. It often means helping a business sell more of a product by making the product more attractive (aesthetically and through increased ease of use). When concerning itself with novel technology reaching market-readiness, design can mean helping a business to make this new technology understandable and user-friendly.

Design touches nearly every aspect of life and so the responsibilities designers hold in some ways are enormous. Designer Victor Papanek famously wrote, "There are professions more harmful than industrial design, but only a very few of them."[1] So, when a designer works on a product that will be mass-manufactured, using materials that are non-recyclable or even toxic, to solve a problem the designer didn't think needed solving, does that designer have an obligation to raise his concerns or moral and ethical standpoints?

---

1 Victor Papanek. *Design for the Real World: Human Ecology and Social Change.* (New York: Random House, 1972).

There are other designers voicing similar views on the role of their profession in society. In 2000, thirty-three designers renewed their support of a 1964 manifesto titled "First Things First," which calls for a change of priorities in the design profession away from a marketing-led application. Here is one the central tenets:

> There are pursuits more worthy of our problem-solving skills. Unprecedented environmental, social, and cultural crises demand our attention.[2]

The aspiration of some designers to address moral and ethical considerations in their work becomes ever more important in the context of emerging technologies.

Emerging Technologies

The personal computer, the Web, and the smartphone have had a deep impact on lifestyles and culture. It used to be that to carry out your banking you had to visit or call a branch and fill out paperwork; now you can access your accounts from wherever you happen to be and manage your finances at the push of a few virtual buttons. It used to be that to communicate with others around the world, you had to write a letter and send via multiple postal services or make expensive long-distance telephone calls; now we can talk to and see each other in real time, practically anywhere on the globe. Not long ago, to find our way around in an unfamiliar place, you had to ask locals or come prepared with a map and the skills to read it; now you simply press a button on your smartphone, and a small dot indicates your location and turn-by-turn directions are provided to guide you to your destination.

These are just a few examples of the ways in which technology has changed the way we live—in just the past 20 years. Nevertheless, it is important to see the full spectrum of each of these changes. Along with these new possibilities, we now also live in a world with the ever-present threat of online fraud, different behaviors around personal and intimate relationships (for better or worse), and the idea that data about

---

2 First Things First Manifesto, 2000. First published in Eye no. 33 vol. 9, Autumn, 1999.

where we've been at what times can be accessed and utilized by governments and others. These are just some examples of less-obvious side effects of technology that should be considered during development.

An extreme example for such considerations is the operating limit placed on commercially available GPS systems. To prevent the systems from being used in the operation of guided missiles, the chipsets switch themselves off if they are being operated in excess of a certain speed and above a specific altitude.

If you believe futurist and inventor Ray Kurzweil, the rate of technological progress is accelerating exponentially, meaning that the next 100 years of progress will actually be more like 20,000 years of progress when measured at today's rate.[3]

This idea is profound, and Kurzweil spends a lot of time explaining just how big the difference between an "intuitive linear" view is and such an exponential one. He argues that future technological feasibilities are often underestimated in predictions, because people intuitively assume the rate of progress would remain constant.

Given how lifestyles, societies, and business have changed in just the past 20 years alone as a result of the rise of computing technology, this outlook on technological progress begs the question about what the impact will be of what is yet to come. There are concerned voices about this, such as that of Bill Joy, a cofounder of Sun Microsystems. He believes that the technologies of the twenty-first century, such as robotics, genetic engineering, and nanotechnology, pose a new class of threat to the world.[4]

Joy is mostly concerned about the possibility of self-replication, and the small-scale nature of emerging technologies. This can become a threat because potentially harmful technologies are more easily accessible to individuals and small groups without attracting wider attention. Other points of discussion are the ethics of stem-cell research, what degree

3 "The Law of Accelerating Returns." last modified March 7, 2001, accessed November 27, 2013, http://www.kurzweilai.net/the-law-of-accelerating-returns.

4 Bill Joy, "Why the future doesn't need us," Wired Magazine, Issue 8.04 April 2000, accessed November 27, 2013, http://www.wired.com/wired/archive/8.04/joy.html.

of technologically enabled enhancement is fair in competition sports, and whether the advances in genetics will lead to a new kind of social divide.

THE DESIGNER AS TECHNOLOGY CRITIC

Even if not all of these concerns are justified, it is clear that the impact of today's emerging technologies, including genetic engineering, nanotechnology, artificial intelligence, and robotics, will be even more profound than that of the personal computer, the Web, and the smartphone.

The impact of computing technology on the field of design has led to an expansion of the area designers occupy. The methodical creation of man-made objects expanded to include digital technology, but the focus of design in digital technology is still largely the same: aesthetics and user-friendliness.

This focus needs to expand when it comes to the emerging technologies that are being discussed today. The post-digital designers need to engage with the promises and implications surrounding new technologies in a more critical way to act as a counterweight to a purely technology-driven form of progress.

John Thackara, the author of *In the Bubble: Designing in a Complex World* (MIT Press) summarizes the root to this critical sentiment:

> We've built a technology-focused society that is remarkable on means but hazy about ends. It's no longer clear to which question all this stuff—tech—is an answer, or what value it adds to our lives.[5]

This new role of designers is highly important and can be seen in different kinds of academic design projects and more experimental approaches design consultancies now take.

One example is the *Curious Rituals* project.[6] Designers Nicolas Nova, Katherine Miyake, Walton Chiu, and Nancy Kwon have analyzed and catalogued new kinds of habitual behaviors and gestures that can be observed in everyday life and that relate closely to widely adopted

---

5 John Thackara, *In the Bubble: Designing in a Complex World* (Cambridge, Mass., The MIT Press, 2005).

6 Curious Rituals project website, accessed November 27, 2013, http://curiousrituals. wordpress.com/.

digital technologies. For example, consider the peculiar new gestures people have adopted to calibrate smartphone location sensors, or to trigger motion sensors when timed lights go out. The designers take the role of observers and do not imply a particular opinion about these new behaviors. They simply uncover and show how digital technologies are adopted and used beyond initial intentions or expectations of their creators. Based on this research, the designers also explored potential new kinds of gestures for future technology applications, grounded in their observations.

In commercial design studios, this mindset can be seen in designers asking their clients "Why?" when faced with technology-lead project briefings where they are asked to shoehorn interactive screens or gestural interfaces into retail spaces or banking applications. It's not the businesses themselves, but the designers that drive the desire to first understand and analyze the real value of applying a technological solution, before going on to actually design it.

There are also altogether new kinds of design consultancies, such as "Superflux,"[7] that focus on emerging technologies in a variety of ways. Following a progressive design agenda, as Superflux founders Anab Jain and Jon Ardern describe it,[8] means that in addition to consulting businesses, Superflux runs self-initiated projects that allow them to explore and develop their understanding of emerging technologies.

These are signs of the right kind of development within the design community, but there needs to be a wider understanding along these lines. Designers need to boldly expand the area of authority of design, and embrace their unique ability to be the joiner of fragmented and specialized fields of thinking.

I want to propose three roles for design to engage with emerging technologies in a more critical way. By this, I mean an analytical way of working that is balanced in its prioritization of human and society-centric thinking in addition to strictly technological possibilities.

---

7 Superflux website, accessed November 27, 2013, *http://superflux.in*.

8 Anab Jain and Jon Ardern, interview with author, November 18, 2013.

1. Humanizing emerging technologies

British science-fiction author Arthur C. Clarke famously wrote, "Any sufficiently advanced technology is indistinguishable from magic." Magic can make people uneasy. Consider, for example, the scare related to mobile telephone use and what effects their radio waves might have on the human body.

"Humanizing emerging technologies" is about reducing the amount of mystery surrounding how a technology works and about helping people retain a sense of control over their changing environment. It is about understanding the mental models people use to make sense of technology and making technology fit people, not the other way round. It can even go so far as to question the need to use a particular technology to achieve a certain result in the first place.

This role of using design can be part of commercial work or of academic experimental projects dealing with market-ready or applied technologies.

An example of this way of applying technology is the Internet-connected pill bottle GlowCaps.[9] An often-cited example for what the emerging Internet of Things makes possible, the pill bottles use sensors and embedded computing to remind patients when their medication is due. They even use Internet connectivity to order refills and send adherence data to doctors. Looking at just the reminding function, the concept of a hitherto "dumb" pill bottle suddenly being able to communicate can be difficult to grasp and embed into daily routines and understanding, especially for less tech-savvy users. However, the system offers another channel to deliver a reminder: by automatically calling a phone. Although this is a decidedly low-tech experience, this way of reminding builds on an existing device with which even those who are not tech-adopters are already familiar, unlike glowing pill bottles. To these users, it is a more human way to engage with this system.

Another example for this is the *Touch* research project that took place at the Oslo School of Architecture and Design,[10] which investigates near-field communication (NFC) technology. Partly inspired by the fears and lack of understanding that exist around the electromagnetic fields

---

9 Vitality Glowcaps website, accessed November 27, 2013, *http://www.glowcaps.com/*.

10 Touch project website, accessed November 27, 2013, *http://www.nearfield.org/*.

of radio-frequency ID (RFID) and NFC technology, the project set out to make these invisible fields visible. The team used an LED to signal a probe's contact with the field and captured the probe's midair journey around the circuit using a combination of photography and stop motion animation techniques. The resulting photographs show the droplet-shaped spaces in which an NFC tag and a reader interact. This provides a graspable image for such fields, and the extent to which they reach into the world around the NFC reader.

Figure 15-1. Photo from the Touch research project (credit: Timo Arnall)

Although part of the outcome of the Touch project is a proposed icon to be used to signify NFC technology, the project relies on being seen and read about to have educational effect toward the public. However, a commercial project related to RFID and NFC could still be driven by the same human insight to achieve a more accessible and understandable experience.

Cofounder of design firm BERG Jack Schulze, who has been involved in the project, describes the role of design as "…empowering people to perceive opaque systems."[11] What he means is that radio communication (but also integrated circuits or the Web) is an example of a technol-

_____

11 Jack Schulze, interview with author, November 11, 2013.

ogy where it is impossible for humans to perceive what's going on. This means that without knowing how these technologies work through documentation or explanation, people simply won't understand them. Designers, however, can find ways of bridging that gap by offering metaphors or analogies that help people understand and feel in control.

The design studio Special Projects[12] even went so far as to question the need for additional technology in a project on which it was working. When Samsung approached it to design a phone for the elderly, Special Projects did not go down the well-trodden path of creating a device with bigger buttons, a bigger screen, or vastly simplified functionality. Instead, its solution revolved around a standard smartphone. Special Projects designed two hardcover bound books, with cutouts into which the device could be placed. By carefully creating the pages around the cutouts, they created a simple walkthrough guide that allows users to achieve tasks such as dialing a phone number by following printed step-by-step information with illustrations and arrows pointing at the relevant buttons on the positioned device. Special Projects humanized a piece of technology by actually removing technology from parts of its experience.

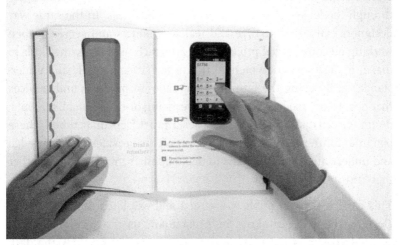

Figure 15-2. One of the hard-cover bound books with phone placed inside (credit: *http://www.special-projects-studio.com*)

12 Special Projects Studio website, accessed September 14, 2014, *http://www.special-projects-studio.com*.

2. Publicizing implications in understandable ways

Technology today is progressing faster than ever before, and the different fields of technology become ever more specialized. Technology is on a trajectory to reach deeper into everyday life, enabling car insurance companies to charge us based on how, where, and when we drive; making possible consumer products monitoring and scoring us on how much we exercise, or how healthy we eat; or letting advertisers understand what we like, dislike, or do in our spare time through the data we produce when using online services or social networks.

Often technology appears in the consumer market so fast and is integrated so quickly that users aren't given a choice or aren't truly aware of what technology is working in the background of their actions and experiences. For example, browser cookies have been used for years to track users across the Web and enable targeted advertising based on their behavior. However, many users are likely to only have learned about this recently, when the European Union passed legislation to force websites to declare their use of cookies up front.

Publicizing implications in understandable ways is about using the cross-disciplinary skills of designers to examine emerging technologies through the lenses of society, culture, and business. In the same way designers can conceptualize and realize products and services when working on commercial projects, this approach uses the same skills to make implications and potential future scenarios tangible and understandable. By using the familiar "language" of products and services that people are used to reading in advertising or retail establishments, designers can distill possible scenarios into artifacts that embody these potential futures in understandable ways. This provides the knowledge and understanding for citizens to make up their minds about whether these futures are desirable.

This can be seen in publicly awarded and exhibited academic work. Design student Bram Fritz in Amsterdam used a project briefing about designing an app using the city's open data to show the dark sides of this openly available information. He proposed the concept app "Makkie klauwe," which means "easy pickings." The app uses readily available public information about disposable incomes, crime levels, or reported problems of different districts to recommend streets and areas more suitable for theft and burglary. The student's audiences for this project were citizens and city employees. His aim was to provoke and raise awareness of the potential harmful ways of using open data. In this case, the smartphone application becomes the commonly understood language for achieving this provocation.

A designer who takes this even further in his work is Anthony Dunne. In his book *Hertzian Tales* (MIT Press), he builds on a previously suggested role for the designer by Ezio Manzini, who advises designers to, "...visualize alternative future scenarios in ways that can be presented to the public, thus enabling democratic choices between the futures people actually want."[13]

Dunne takes this a step further and puts forward an approach in which the designer "no longer knows anything for certain." This is a less didactic role than that proposed by Manzini, in which the designer has no moral stance but offers his skills as a resource to experiment with an unknown territory.

Projects with such an approach used to happen almost exclusively in academia. New kinds of design practices such as the aforementioned Superflux consider it part of their agenda and integrate this approach into their commercial offering. Nevertheless, funding often comes from public sources such as the European-wide initiative StudioLab, or galleries and museums.

However, this way of engaging with the uncertainty and unpredictability of the technological future needs to become more commonplace and inform long-term corporate strategy, as well. Design consultancy Superflux employs this approach to help businesses guide their strategic planning. The founders call this approach "Design for the new normal." Here's a synopsis:

> Design for the new normal works to cut through established narratives by engaging with two broad areas of interest: uncloaking the "strange now" [...] and extrapolating current trends to present the sheer breadth of, often unsettling, future possibilities that lie ahead of us.[14]

---

13 Anthony Dunne, *Hertzian Tales* (Cambridge, Mass., The MIT Press, 2008).

14 "Design For the New Normal," accessed November 27, 2013, *http://superflux.in/blog/newnormal-revisited.*

3. Influencing the scientific community

Today's scientific research builds on centuries of achievements and discoveries. This means that today's research efforts are highly specialized, fitting specific niches, and looking at problems in a very isolated way. This makes it more difficult for researchers to retain a higher-level view across different fields and to keep an eye on knock-on effects or sociocultural implications of their work.

Both the scientific community and designers themselves need to embrace what design has to offer. Designers are cross-disciplinary thinkers and makers who understand people, technology, and business. And although design traditionally comes in at the point of application of a technology, designers today need to enter at the point of research. Designers need to be the "buoy" that connects with highly specialized and deepened research efforts but stays in touch with the wider context of the world.

Influencing the scientific community is about collaboration between designers and scientists. It is about designers providing human insight and becoming the advocates of people and societies. That way, designers provide a counterweight against results-driven efforts, which ignore the potential for side effects or unanticipated outcomes.

A good example of this cooperation between designers and scientists was the European Union–funded Smarcos Project.[15] It set out to establish guidelines and best practices for "interconnected embedded systems" and was a collaboration between 17 research partners from both academic and commercial research centers. It also involved the commercial design consultancy Fjord, and I worked on the project as an interaction design researcher alongside my colleagues Claire Rowland and Helen Le Voi.

Even though the project was not aimed at the public or intended to create commercially available products, a team of designers was involved in it in a variety of ways. The Fjord team added user-experience considerations to the otherwise technical work, making guidelines and recommendations not just about technology, but also about the human experience of that technology. The team facilitated creative workshops

---

15 Smarcos Project website, accessed November 27, 2013, *http://smarcos-project.eu.*

with the researchers that drew out potential applications and real-world impacts of the research that was being done. Using design research methods such as ethnography, diary studies, and interviews, the team brought human insight to the discussions and opinions within the research project. Lastly, the team helped communicate the aims and outcomes of the project within the wider scientific community more effectively by making the work tangible and more accessible.

When it comes to emerging technologies that are further away from application, designers have to play an important role, too. Dr. Rachel Armstrong, a researcher in the field of synthetic biology, sees the established approaches to the funding and structuring of research projects as increasingly inappropriate for the complex and hard-to-predict nature of future technologies. She believes that a shift is required in the way future technologies are looked at, explored, and discussed, and that designers have a role to play in this new approach. Instead of the deterministic view that has been taken historically, the future needs to be seen in a probabilistic way.[16] This means that research into emerging technologies can no longer be directed and measured toward a particular desirable outcome. Instead, outcomes need to be considered as probabilities that can merely be influenced but not determined.

This requires a constant extrapolation of possible ultimate outcomes and their implications. This is where Dr. Armstrong sees the role of designers; they need to continually explore and experiment with these probabilistic futures. This goes beyond designers helping with public engagement or communication of research work. Instead, it is a direct collaboration with the scientist through which the designer speculates about the future and uses acquired skills to make these speculations tangible.

New Responsibilities of the Design Discipline

There is a tendency among businesses to think that technology can solve any problem, one way or another. Worse, there is a belief that economic success or innovative and desirable products are a result

---

16 Dr. Rachel Armstrong, interview with author, November 21, 2013.

of the application of latest technologies. This is only partly the case. Designers working with businesses are at risk of becoming mere executors of technology, further fueling the mindless application of it.

Especially when it comes to emerging technologies, a more considered approach is required and designers need to question implications, side effects, and sociocultural impacts much harder. This is not about rejecting technology; it is about fully understanding it. In the same way an industrial designer makes experiments with a new material to understand its limitations and possibilities, post-digital designers need to experiment with emerging technologies to understand their limitations, possibilities, and implications.

This builds onto the existing responsibility designers have toward people. In the past, designers primarily dealt with a product's user experience or its environmental impact. Now, designers need to expand their field of responsibility to include people's understanding of emerging technologies and their implications.

As mentioned at the beginning of this chapter, this approach might not be widely understood as design. However, practicing design requires a multiliterate and cross-disciplinary skillset. This skillset empowers designers to become the linchpin of the wide variety of stakeholders and parties involved with emerging technologies. With designer's skills to make and create this combines into the ability to manifest complex connections and narratives into tangible, understandable objects and artifacts.

It means that designers can provide an effective language that enables discussion among scientists as well as everybody who will be affected by emerging technologies. Science fiction, in some ways, has provided such a language. Designers can build on that and integrate their approach with the labs and scientists working on emerging technologies.

Although this role might not be what is traditionally understood as design, it needs to become part of the expertise of all emerging designers.

This has consequences for both the design and research communities. Design education needs to prepare and inspire designers to claim a post-digital area of expertise. Institutes and initiatives running research into emerging technologies need to be structured to facilitate deep collaboration with designers for the benefit of the research. The three approaches proposed in this chapter present steps toward this direction.

In some ways, this is no different to what design has always been about: empowering people, solving problems, making things easier to understand, and making products desirable. The accelerating progress and the increasingly disruptive impact of emerging technologies simply give this role of design a new, extended meaning.

Lastly, there is a risk of diluting this extended idea of design with moral philosophy, fine art, or "opinion pieces." Rather than judging, the outcome of this approach should be enabling others to judge for themselves.

Bibliography

Papanek V. *Design for the Real World: Human Ecology and Social Change*. New York, Random House, 1972.

Thackara J. *In the Bubble: Designing in a Complex World*. Cambridge, Mass., The MIT Press, 2005.

Kurzweil R. *The Law of Accelerating Returns*. Last modified March 7, 2001, accessed November 27, 2013, *http://www.kurzweilai.net/the-law-of-accelerating-returns*.

Joy B. *Why the future doesn't need us*. Wired Magazine, Issue 8.04, April 2000, accessed November 27, 2013, *http://www.wired.com/wired/archive/8.04/joy.html*.

Dunne A. *Hertzian Tales*, Cambridge, Mass., The MIT Press, 2008.

33 Signatories. *First Things First Manifesto 2000*. First published in Eye no. 33 vol. 9, Autumn 1999.

Smarcos Project. Project website, accessed November 27, 2013, *http://smarcos-project.eu*.

Special Projects Studio website, accessed September 14, 2014, *http://www.speical-projects-studio.com*.

Superflux website, accessed November 27, 2013, *http://superflux.in*.

Curious Rituals website, accessed November 27, 2013, *http://curious rituals.wordpress.com/*.

Touch project. *Immaterials: Ghost in the Field.* Timo Arnall, Jack Schulze and Einar Sneve Martinussen. Website, accessed November 27, 2013, *http://www.nearfield.org/*.

Vitality Glowcaps website, accessed November 27, 2013, *http://www. glowcaps.com/*.

[16]

Designing Human-
Robot Relationships

SCOTT STROPKAY AND BILL HARTMAN

You wake up in a rural hospital bed. You hear monitors sounding alarms, pumps clicking, and voices over an intercom. Confused, you look around and see a nurse, a young technician, and a third person, a doctor—or so she appears to be. But you see only her face on a screen, talking and moving toward you. She is interacting with you through a robot. The robot-doctor tells you not to worry; you were just involved in an accident requiring surgery and you are in recovery. Don't be startled by her robot body, she adds. She can't be there in person right now. As you begin to make sense of the situation, you understand that the robot is a telepresence interface between you and your doctor and that she is a surgeon who lives and works in another city.

As the robo-doc begins directing the other people in the room, you realize she's in control of your care. Although you begin to answer her questions, you learn that the distant doctor also performed your surgery in the surgical theater down the hall using another robot. A monitor in your room sounds an alarm. The remote doctor tells you what it is and she silences it somehow. Noticing your look of surprise, your surgeon explains that she's connected to all the hospital's systems and devices that are monitoring you right now. Soon, you find yourself forgetting that you're talking to a video doctor, and the robot begins to seem more like a person than a machine. That is until she says that she didn't like the way that one of your internal organs looked during the surgery. So, while you were under anesthesia, she released a few hundred nanorobots into your vascular system to scout around your body and report back on what they find.

If this sounds like a science-fiction scenario that you'll never experience, think again. Medical telepresence robots such as the RPVita from InTouch Health and iRobot are already in use across the country. Thousands of minimally invasive surgical robots such as Intuitive Surgical's da Vinci system are also being used around the globe. And although nanorobots seemed like the stuff of fantasy just 10 years ago, scientists and technologists are making huge strides in developing and testing these systems in leading universities around the world. We are probably only a few years away from the first nanorobot trials in medical procedures on humans.

Continuing a long tradition of pushing the boundaries of scientific knowledge with technology, doctors use state-of-the-art robots because these tools give them enhanced capabilities, improve healthcare outcomes, and contribute to the hospital's bottom line. Today, robo-tools, controlled by care teams, give patients access to the best physician for the situation and give that doctor enhanced surgical precision. Soon, these tools will report on and help your body's internal operating systems. As technologies advance and more healthcare professionals experience the benefits, medical robots will become increasingly common. And that's good—as long as the creators truly understand what the users of those robots expect from them.

Me Man, You Robot: Designers Creating Powerful Tools

Long before these tools were used on any patient, a product development team decided how the doctor, patient, and other care team members would experience the robots. In the introductory scenario, the doctor was given total control of the situation. You never had a choice between a local or remote doctor. You never chose to communicate through a telepresence robot. You didn't agree to surgery by a multiarmed robot that could deploy an array of instruments inside your body. You certainly didn't ask that the surgeon be in another city, state, or country. And when the conventional diagnostic tests indicated certain risks, you weren't consulted about the pros and cons or asked your philosophical or religious stand on the use of microscopic robots injected into your bloodstream. A person other than you, empowered by the control and feedback capabilities of these devices, chose a course of action for you.

Engineers, scientists, doctors, medical staff, hospital administrators, industrial designers, interaction designers, human factors specialists, and others all serve as user experience (UX) designers of medical robots. They decide which of the hospital's IT systems to connect to, what communication and control systems to create, which mobile phone and tablet computers to support, and how users will interface with these systems. They intentionally (or inadvertently) design the way robots interact with everyone and everything in our complex system of care. Everything that makes those sophisticated robotic tools useful in the first place is being envisioned and designed, including the human interactions that were mediated through the robot. UX designers are in the hot seat; not only must they design the way we experience the tool itself, they must design the way we experience each other through these tools.

The process of designing these experiences poses many questions. What experience should the various medical users have? What experience (and control) should you as the patient have? What does it mean to design a robotically mediated interaction between people? And, when do these tools start to carry out tasks that people do, perhaps autonomously; at what point does the tool become a being in and of itself? We will address these and other questions in this chapter, but first, let's back up to provide some context for thinking about the relationship between humans and robots.

THE ORIGINS OF ROBOTS

We commonly understand a robot as one or more sensors providing data to a processor. The processor compares the data to predefined rule sets or other data streams to observe certain conditions and then takes a physical action. Systems that do everything but move are generally described as artificially intelligent systems. Physical movement makes a robot a robot. Virtually all robots use artificial intelligence, but most artificially intelligent systems aren't robots. The motion of a robot can be controlled remotely by humans or other "drivers," or a robot can take actions autonomously based on information it perceives in its environment, sensing and reacting accordingly. Robots can be relatively simple machines: a pool cleaning robot that turns when it senses the water's surface is one example. Or, they can be robust, semi-intelligent machines that make subtle distinctions to adjust their actions, such as industrial robots that move materials along networks of painted lines, deciding which path is fastest. A robot can also be a wildly sophisticated *system of systems* that makes tactical decisions and performs complex actions without human intervention over long periods of time. The Mars rover is an excellent example of this kind of autonomy. Automatic machines in anthropometric forms have captured human imagination for thousands of years. According to a Chinese story from the third century BC, King Mu of the Zhou Dynasty was presented with a wooden machine that was so human-like and alarming that the king threatened the life of the inventor. Centuries later, the Greeks imagined Talos, a forged bronze giant that protected Crete day and night as described in Rhodius' *The Argonautica*. During the Renaissance, Leonardo da Vinci designed, and presumably built, a bronze mechanical knight for his patrons, the Sforzas.

But, it wasn't until around the turn of the twentieth century that the prevalence of industrial-age automatic machines, electricity, and remote control technologies (one of the first examples being Nicola Tesla's 1898 radio-controlled boat) ignited the imagination of the masses and gave birth to a new literary genre—science fiction. Channeling societal fear, or simply feeling uneasy about their rapidly changing worlds, many writers created Frankenstein-like plots in which things invariably went wrong and the robots rebelled against their creators.

In 1942 Isaac Asimov, a doctor of biochemistry who was disgusted with the ubiquity of that theme (or perhaps more accurately, who wished to argue against the idea that men pursuing knowledge through robotics would lead to dystopian futures) wrote *Runaround*. In this short story, Asimov introduced his "Three Laws of Robotics" that defined rules for a cooperative man/robot future:

1. A robot may not injure a human being or, through inaction, allow a human being to come to harm.

2. A robot must obey the orders given to it by human beings, except where such orders would conflict with the First Law.

3. A robot must protect its own existence as long as such protection does not conflict with the First or Second Law.

Asimov believed these ideas would be one of his most enduring contributions. Indeed, he did effectively clear the way for subsequent generations of technically capable kids (and science-minded adults) to imagine and pursue robotics for the good of mankind. With Asimov's help, and with the conclusion of World War II, creative minds began imagining possibilities and applying technologies in ways that would produce the sensor and processor building blocks of modern robots.

ROBOTIC SOCIAL CUES

Early robots were simple. They could only perform single tasks, but with amazing accuracy and repeatability. Almost immediately, robotic components found their way into industrial and assembly jobs, performing tasks that humans found dull, dirty, dangerous, or difficult (known as *the Four D's*, a kind of application criteria for considering robotic solutions). As sensors evolved, robots began to extend our capabilities—seeing better than the human eye, sniffing for traces of materials we can't smell, tasting and touching materials in environments where we can't go. Simultaneously, processors were getting smaller and faster, so when tied to sensors, machines began applying fuzzy logic to situations, making decisions about what they should do next: decisions such as "move this and move me."

But automated systems can only be so smart. As robots enter more varied aspects of our lives, robot designers are realizing that people need clues about the way robots interpret their environments so that we can understand their intentions, capabilities, and limitations.

Designing a robotic tool is less straightforward than one might think. Baxter, the robot created by Rethink Robotics, is an assembly line worker that is designed to work safely alongside human workers. Baxter is taught by his coworkers, so he learns what they want and expect. Although Baxter's sensors can help him avoid or minimize accidental human contact, those sensors can't always anticipate what his human coworkers might do. Baxter needed to help people stay out of his way and therefore harm's way, to aid customer adoption and increase coworker acceptance. Rethink Robotics gave Baxter a moving head and stylized human eyes for that very purpose. Baxter looks to his next target before he begins to move, giving coworkers a more human and humane clue about his intentions and a friendly warning, through body language, to get out of the way.

RPVita on the other hand, navigates its world autonomously. A remote doctor logs in to a robot and directs the robot to find a particular patient. The robot accesses the hospital's information systems, learns where the patient is, and goes to the patient on its own. This type of capability introduces new design problems that can be addressed by designed behaviors.

For instance, humans give clues (sometimes unknowingly) about their state of mind as they navigate a hospital hallway or any other setting. You know when you shouldn't interrupt. You know when someone is rushing to an emergency. You generally know which way someone is about to go as they enter a hallway intersection. Robots typically don't give people such clues because they haven't been designed for social situations. Using sensors, and processing the information they provide, RPVita is aware of its physical environment, avoiding not only stationary objects, but also anticipating which way a rushing nurse might be headed in order to take steps to avoid her. After all, technology stops adding value when it gets in our way. Here again, robots can be designed to give clues about their intentions so that we know how to get along with them. RPVita uses turning signals to indicate basic directional intent. It also has a color-coding system that indicates whether the robot is urgently rushing to a site on a doctor's behalf, if it's available only for quick chats, or if it's available for more lengthy conversations. These two intention-signaling systems replace or reinforce a third system—the doctor's face on the display—to give people the appropriate set of social clues for interacting with RPVita.

Designing ways for humans to read robot intentions is a challenge. Early work indicates that people read signals that imitate human behavior best because those are the signals we've evolved to detect. Yet the more human-like robot behaviors become, the more we expect from them. If robots misinterpret us or if we misinterpret them, a lot can go wrong. Communication errors in healthcare settings can be life threatening. How do we design the highest level of human control in these situations? When do we want to relinquish control and avoid certain obligations? And finally, whose responsibility do the actions of the robot become?

THE CONSEQUENCES OF INCREASING INTELLIGENCE

As new technology affords new capabilities, design questions and design problems multiply. The da Vinci system already gives a surgeon superhuman reach by changing the scale and freedom of motion she would otherwise have. As she becomes more comfortable with the robot, she and other surgeons will ask Intuitive Surgical, the company that makes the system, for refined features and more capabilities. It's easy to project capabilities on this sophisticated machine. It already senses more than a human can sense. Future generations of da Vinci systems could perform routine surgeries completely autonomously, applying machine learning to existing procedure data. The networked communication features accommodate multisurgeon input, but should a doctor be able to turn off these features like she turns off certain features on her phone? And as we stated earlier, the patient should have some level of control. Designers will have to decide if the patient will be able to review what was done. They might design in features that provide the option for sharing but leave that to the doctor's discretion. Then, designers must debate whether the theoretical benefit of sharing access is worth the risk to trial and adoption. Will robots with more autonomy create higher or lower degrees of anxiety in the doctor's mind with respect to malpractice?

The questions that must be addressed by designers of these systems don't stop here. Economic factors associated with caring for large populations are driving experience design innovation, too. What does a cost-effective medical robot look like? The "reverse innovation" idea (adopting less featured, lower-cost, "good-enough" technologies from developing worlds) is affecting the return-on-investment calculation of technology expenditures right now and suggests the need for new ways of accounting costs. Should specialist robo-surgeons be able to work from massive remote surgery centers, providing procedures to entire nations from a single location? That would make it easier to attain 24/7 technology utilization and drive down costs. But how would that change ideas about the doctor/patient relationship? How would local doctors need to be trained? How would this new model of distributed care affect continuity of care?

And, if we pursue a scenario that allows nanorobot-enabled diagnostics, experience designers should be designing the levels of privacy within the data visualization systems that doctors interpret. These nanobots will be sending data to handheld devices and various care providers. Will the privacy provisions in the Health Insurance Portability and Accountability Act of 1996 work for us? Designers and institutions will have to consider whether privacy should be based on the individual or based on the situation. One lost mobile phone could result in sensitive data being used improperly and that could have serious negative consequences for the individuals involved and for the institution. What levels of access should be given to different doctors (such as psychiatrists), family members, community service providers, insurers, or others? Mobile devices offer valuable convenience benefits that can aid recovery and rehabilitation, but they also introduce dangerous vulnerabilities we must consider. We could design the equivalent of resuscitation guidelines for health information privacy. Maybe we all should be offered a "robotic intervention preference guide" so that individuals can actively select the level of robot aid and privacy access allowed for every type of healthcare scenario—something akin to a living will.

Tools have instructions for use, and as robotic tools become more sophisticated, instructions and control will become more and more interactive. Designers must create simple protocols and clear clues about each robot's behavior so that we interact safely and effectively.

Me Man, You Robot? Developing Emotional Relationships with Robots

Let's return to the hypothetical story about you and your post-surgery experience. Just before being discharged from the hospital, you are given a friendly looking robot, about the size of a water bottle. The recovery-therapy specialist tells you that your robo-helper will monitor your recovery by asking you questions about your sleep, your pain, and other things your care team wants to track. The specialist also says that the helper robot will be a communication conduit: to the hospital in case anything goes really wrong, and to the staff in the health-coaching recovery unit so that they can help you with daily needs.

The first thing you notice is that the robot doesn't seem like a robot; it's more like a stuffed animal, but with moving parts. The next thing you notice is that it's aware of activity in the room. It looks in the direction of the last alarm, and it turns toward the person who just entered the room. Then, after the specialist introduces you to your helper robot, it addresses you by name and asks you how you feel. Your initial reaction is some combination of intrigue and suspicion. You think to yourself, "This thing is going to do *what*? You're going to track me *how*?" Knowing what's probably going through your mind, the specialist begins to address your first few questions, but then says, "Ask your robot. He can help you in lots of ways. In fact, when you're done getting acquainted, tell him you want to start your discharge interview and he'll do that at your own pace, no rush."

Author William Gibson's quote, "The future is already here—it's just not very evenly distributed," applies in the world of social robots. Today, universities and corporations around the globe are creating prototypes and testing them in healthcare contexts. MIT students are working with Boston's Children's Hospital on robot-enabled social experiments to understand the types and depths of emotional connections humans can experience in their relationships with robots. Tim Bickmore, an Associate Professor at Northeastern University, working with students in the College of Computer and Information Science, has performed studies on the use of *relational agents* for healthcare purposes. Bickmore and his students are proving that patients prefer empathetic representations of nursing staff over real people for certain healthcare services such as medication compliance coaching and hospital discharge activities. That's because, to a large degree, these relational agents have been designed to show more interest, patience, and understanding than time-pressured staff can demonstrate. They never get tired, distracted, or interrupted. They never reply sarcastically, never question opinions, and never do anything overtly wrong. Patient satisfaction increases, therapy adherence and recovery improve, and human staff (who are dramatically more expensive resources) can be deployed elsewhere. Everyone wins, and that's just the beginning of what's possible.

YOUR ROBOT RELATIONSHIP

By creating robots that emulate human behaviors, UX designers are conveying human emotions. With frequent and positive interaction scenarios, social robots engage people further and build rapport. As the robot follows through on tasks, it earns trust. To build what seems like a real human connection, the recovery robot in our scenario learns things about you. It does little things wrong intentionally. It gets confused and asks you for help. It seems to "get" your sense of humor and it's quick with a joke. You might or might not be aware of it, but you are developing a relationship with the robot. It's helping you, and you are helping it. You might or might not realize that your robot was designed to get you to like it. And you do like it—a lot.

From this foundation of trust, robots can perform tasks that go well beyond being compassionate. Your recovery specialist didn't mention that the designer of your robot built in a number of features that have purposes not immediately apparent to you. The motion detectors that give your robot personality are also sensing and monitoring your activities, alerting hospital staff and researchers about your recovery status. They want to know how well you understand various instructions: do you pick up on the initial hints and nudges or do you need a more commanding voice to take action? Your care team wants to know how often you comply with instructions, when, and why. And, as much as medical professionals care about you, they also must care about controlling costs and making smart expenditures. Hospitals want to avoid readmissions. Insurance companies want to reduce claims. Employers want their people back at work and Uncle Sam wants the income tax derived from a healthy and productive workforce.

Addressing both personal and cost-cutting needs, the recovery robot helps you connect to friends and family caregivers. He acts as your butler by helping out around the house. He's also your concierge, alerting you to issues that require your attention while deflecting everything else. He affords you the freedom to focus on recovery. He might engage a member of your family at a time when you need physical or emotional support that he (being only a robot) can't quite give. For example, suppose that your doctor has prescribed something to help you sleep or perhaps something to help take your mind off of whatever the nano-robots are investigating inside your body. Your recovery robot reminds you to take the medication or warns you if you are about to take the same medicine twice. He also sends status updates to the family member you and your recovery coach appointed. Each day-to-day interaction you have with your new robo-friend helps you get to know him a little better. He helps you communicate more easily and effectively to everyone involved. Even though you know it's a robot, the fact that he has proven himself to "know" you helps you to take him seriously. Because of his unlimited attention span and persistence as well as his access to people at the hospital and your family, your recovery is faster than if you'd had a home-health nurse visiting you each day.

In fact, because you know that your robot would never have malicious intentions, you come to trust it even more than some people you know. The robot's objectives, even if annoying, are all about your best interests. In addition, because the robot is clever, it can figure out ways to accomplish its objectives indirectly, if needed. What if your trusted robot was connected to your cable service and could say: "I am not letting you watch the baseball game until you replace the bandages on your incisions. Go ahead and try turning to channel 7... I dare you!" Or, when you miss multiple therapeutic tasks, your recovery robot could escalate the situation by contacting your recovery specialist. She beams in asking, "What's going on? Do you need more support? Do you need to watch the recovery video again?" The robot and the specialist gang up on you, and because you're embarrassed, you recommit to get back on track.

But your recovery robot isn't heartless. He knows when you need time to yourself. Clever programming sets interaction type and frequency to balance privacy and therapy needs. It appears as though your robot can be reasoned with, just as you'd expect to be able to do with a human. These thresholds, behaviors, and tactics are all designed into the robot: an orchestration of human-to-robot interaction along with human-to-human interaction, mediated by a robot.

Because the designers of your recovery robot know that people nurture what they love, and love what they nurture, they designed your robot to ask for your help frequently, cultivating a sense of partnership. The robot's dependence upon you as a caregiver also improves your own well-being. You not only trust the reliability and fact-based tasks he performs, but also the subtle, more ambiguous advice or decision-making functions your recovery robot can offer. However, you don't follow its advice blindly, nor does it pretend to be omniscient. Because your recovery robot can express a degree of confidence while offering advice, through body language or other nonverbal cues, the interaction feels more like dialog than simply giving and receiving information. There is communication, interpretation, and discussion. During the course of your recuperation from surgery, the recovery robot seems less and less like your old preconception of "robot." He actually seems nuanced, sophisticated, and social. He is smart, spontaneous, and knowledgeable—almost self-aware—and that's when you also realize that somewhere along the line, you began referring to him as "he," not "it."

QUESTIONS TO CONSIDER

Industrial designers often view the development of a design language as a compelling challenge. This is because a design language must be prospective: a set of visual conventions that might be applied to future products by other designers—like designing the DNA, not the thing itself. Human-robot interaction designers face an even greater challenge, along a similar vein: how do you design the robot's behavior for tasks that are not yet known? In other words, doing the task might be the easy part; designing the way the task is completed in cooperation with people or other robots is the real objective. Depending on the application, designers might want to consider the following questions:

1. Should the robot have its own personality? Or, does it need to reflect individual personalities of human counterparts they represent? Should it be some combination of the two?

2. How should the robot share its evolutionary point on the machine-learning scale? Is it already highly intelligent (an expert) or still in a passive, learning mode (a student)? How should that degree of sophistication be personified by the robot to help people know how to interact with it?

3. At what point might an expert robot seem arrogant? How can it teach people in the most constructive way?

Sherry Turkle, Professor of the Social Studies of Science and Technology in the Program in Science, Technology, and Society at MIT writes, "for artificial companionship to become a new normal, we have to change ourselves. We may think we are only making robots but really we are remaking human values and connections. We change ourselves as we get ready for them."

Me Robot? On Becoming Robotic

Let's return to your healthcare scenario to illustrate another direction in which robots and UX design is headed. To further accelerate your recovery, a custom-fitted physical therapy exoskeleton is strapped to your body. This smart, powered appliance does not immediately seem like a robot, but it is.

Your exoskeleton is a relatively simple model. It attaches to your leg and pelvis to improve recovery from your knee surgery. You wear this device to regain your balance, strength, and flexibility. Because it's smart, the exoskeleton appliance measures your capabilities and provides the appropriate level of assistance in perfect synchronization with your care plan. It is set to the limits of your physical and psychological potential to minimize your recovery time. Unlike your therapy-buddy robot, the exoskeleton's interaction style and use experiences are designed to drive you to do things for which you don't believe you are ready. The voice of the interface is much more like a drill sergeant. Its sensors and cameras are making judgments to control how much pain you feel, correcting physical therapy regimens in real time. As much as you dislike this robotic appliance, you know you're lucky to be rehabilitating that limb. Others in the hospital were being outfitted with full robotic prostheses that replace the limbs they lost.

Robotic exoskeletons already exist in research labs and some are starting to become available for commercial use. Cyberdyne's hybrid assistive limb, known as HAL, was developed in conjunction with Tsukuba University in Japan. It is designed both as support to people with physical disabilities, but it can also expand capabilities beyond the power range of the normal human body. In the scenario we described above, your robot has governors that simulate your physical capabilities before the accident. The robot won't let you behave like a bionic man. However, exoskeletons such as HULC developed from work at the University of California, Berkeley, by Ekso Bionics and now Lockheed Martin are being developed to give soldiers superhuman load carrying capabilities. Designing robots to match typical human ergonomic parameters is easy to support. But creating superpowered humans is a different matter altogether. As military experiments become military issue equipment, it's only a matter of time before these technologies find their way into the commercial equipment market, and then the consumer product markets. What use experiences should limit designs? If the idea is to enhance human capability, how far should enhancement be allowed to go?

Up to this point we've only discussed accommodating appliances that can be removed from bodies—another self-applied limit. But, what should happen if a person wants to replace a working system with a better artificial system? Why be limited by old-fashioned anthropometrics? Longer, more flexible arms might be nice. Stronger arms sound good, too. Arms that are much longer and much stronger might make someone perfectly suited to a certain job. It is easy to imagine supermen in bodyguard roles or military special operations.

As this branch of the UX tree becomes a reality, there will be serious social and moral issues to address. Yet, the issues we will have to address in the future won't end with physical systems. Remember, we defined a robot as "one or more sensors that provide data to a processor." Well, in the area of neuroprosthetics, one of the primary processors is the brain.

The trajectory toward becoming "bionic" began with passive assistive devices some time ago: hearing aids, augmented reality glasses, stair-climbing wheelchairs, etc. With the development and insertion of cochlear implants inside the body to "create" hearing, some of us have already become cybernetic organisms—part biological, part machine. The United States Defense Advanced Research Projects Agency (DARPA) has its Revolutionize Prosthetics program. DEKA Research is working on its Luke arm (yes, it is named after Luke Skywalker of *Star Wars* fame), and Johns Hopkins Applied Physics Lab has diverse project teams. These are only three of the numerous groups working on neuroprosthetic devices. In all these projects, patients receive sensory stimulus from electromechanical sensors in a robotic device that can allow them to see, hear, feel, and even manipulate objects in their environments. By feeding the patient's brain with electrical signals (feedback) and harvesting the electrical signals generated in the brain (the user's intent—electrical signals we call thoughts), these robotic limbs are being naturally and accurately controlled by their users. So, when we can install panels of electrodes in the motor cortex of a person's brain to relay thoughts about movement to a robotic replacement for a missing limb, it is relatively easy to imagine the desirability of creating active and productive cybernetic organisms (for example, as a way of restoring the bodies of wounded soldiers).

Into the Future

Technological Singularity, as theorized by Kurzweil and Vinge, will occur when artificial intelligence will have progressed to the point of a greater-than-human intelligence. Depending upon how "intelligence" is defined, this has already taken place in some arenas. With the ability to super-stimulate the brains of partially robotic people, it will be difficult to predict how that will change human experience.

In the near future, UX designers (working as scientists and engineers and UX professionals) will make neuroprosthetic assistive devices smarter, easier to use, and more available. Designers will give users new capabilities. What these users do with new capabilities will be partially governed by the rules we create for acceptable and unacceptable behaviors. How are we going to get ready to make that level of decision for an individual? For a population?

Your Robot: Consider Nielsen, Maslow, and Aristotle

UX designers from any of the backgrounds we've identified can take some comfort in the fact that they will have time to think through the big moral and societal questions posed in this chapter. There will be many situations for which technology selection or cost targets will limit a design's potential. But, sooner than we probably expect, designers will need to address tough questions about access, control, capability, as well as moral issues. Lacking discipline-wide standards by which to work, designers must look to adjacent fields for inspiration and guidance.

On a tactical level, human-computer interaction (HCI) offers heuristic principles, as originally described by Jakob Nielsen in the 1990s, that can be extrapolated to human-robot interactions (HRI). In this update of Nielsen's heuristics, we substitute "system" with "robot," and "user" with "person."

Visibility of robot status
Keeping people informed of the robot's status, intentions, confidence, time to chat, and so on.

Match between robot and the real world
Use human terms and behaviors rather than "robot" terms and behaviors.

User control and freedom, error prevention
Providing an emergency exit, or way of correcting the robot when needed ("undo" and "redo").

Consistency and standards
Follow real-world conventions rather than imposing new platforms or constructs that are unfamiliar.

Recognition rather than recall
People should not have to remember information from one part of the dialogue to another.

Flexibility and efficiency of use
Make novice and expert modes of use equally available.

Aesthetic and minimalist design

Be concise, to avoid clouding relevant information with irrelevant or rarely needed information.

Help and documentation

Make reference materials easily available when needed, germane to the scenario of use or interaction.

Skills

Support and enhance the person's skill and knowledge, not replace them (except in cases when that is an objective of the robot's design).

Pleasurable and respectful interaction

Interactions with the robot should enhance the quality of the person's work/life, treat the person with respect, and offer artistic and functional value.

Although robots were initially valued for their ability to accomplish dull, dirty, dangerous, or difficult jobs, they have progressed to higher-order jobs. Robots should be able to respond to all of Maslow's Hierarchy of Needs:

Physiological needs

- Value: doing dirty jobs we don't want to do ourselves

Safety and security

- Value: doing dangerous jobs

Love and belonging

- Value: unconditionally positive dialogue and attention span

- Expectation: social robots, providing meaningful and personal interaction

Self-esteem

- Value: helping people build awareness of capability

- Expectation: anticipating human needs and addressing them in a mature, constructive way

Self-actualization

- Value: performing more sophisticated procedures on behalf of the doctor

- Value: assisting the patient in making a strong recovery and getting their life back on track

- Expectation: robot becoming self-aware enough to project its own degree of confidence in decision-making

- Expectation: robot assessing its own role and gravity in the human-robot relationship; is it trusted, why or why not

- Expectation: Singularity principle—best-of-robotics and best-of-humanity working together in as yet unimagined ways

We can also reference Aristotle's thinking on persuasion, appealing to our desire for credible, logical, and emotional interactions. If we believe robots can effectively communicate and facilitate learning, robots should be designed with a combination of these very human attributes to create personality and increase their effectiveness.

Credibility (ethos)

People have credibility based on their pedigree and past performance. Robots will need to be designed to provide ways of expressing their credentials, verbally and nonverbally. They will need to anticipate questions such as "Just how smart are you?" and "Why should I trust you?"

Logic (logos)

As robots become more autonomous, the sources they reference for their actions and recommendations might be questioned. Designers will need to consider ways of reflecting the logic tree, thought patterns, and source materials that lead to the robot's actions or recommendations. How designers decide to interpret that material for their human audience is a design question in and of itself. Building information and communication methods that are logical, credible, and understandable by the user is a critical design task.

Emotion (pathos)

Emotional appeal is a catalyst, if not a requirement, to the adoption of robots in general. Designers must provide the right stimulus to trigger desired human responses. Designers must design the language, behavior, tone-of-voice, and every other aesthetic element that can be interpreted. Aspirational qualities of the design (such as what my robot says about me and my work) also play a significant role in adoption. Designers must ask themselves, "How does the user or organization want to be perceived as robots play roles that humans used to?"

While asking and answering questions like those proposed above, wise designers won't simply pursue the ideal robot-to-human interaction; they'll think more systematically to define which human-to-human relationships their robot can facilitate. Imagine healthcare experiences in which doctors', nurses', and administrators' primary roles are your cognitive, emotional, and spiritual well-being. Robots designed to take care of routine and even complex tasks can clear the way for people to connect more deeply. They can monitor and interpret information in the environment and deliver that data to the human caregivers so that they treat you more empathically. Robots will assist caregivers in their human-to-human care interactions; that is, if designers decide to address this opportunity. Robot-enhanced human empathy, connection, motivation, belonging, love—why shouldn't this be our design goal?

Conclusion

In a world of increasing specialization, robot UX designers will hail from very wide-ranging backgrounds: from social science to library science, mechanical engineering to graphic design, software development to film-making. Thinking and designing holistically will require robot design teams to blend expertise and skills in new ways. Well-directed modern movies require hundreds of specialists to work in concert to relate a relatively simple, linear, predefined story. Robots by contrast will be telling deeply personalized stories to different audiences with different needs, simultaneously, and over long periods of time. The design of robots will require even greater collaboration among many more human (and robotic) contributors.

If we want to distribute the future more evenly (and effectively and safely), we must build interdisciplinary understanding and skill sets like we've never built before. Although technology will be an important enabler to robots taking on higher-ordered functions, there are historical lessons that can help guide the most appropriate implementation and evolution of these technologies. From King Zhou, reportedly experiencing the *uncanny valley* 2,400 years ago, to Aristotle's recipe for persuasive communications, to more widely accepted UX principles, interactions with robots will be most successful and meaningful when they support the social conventions of the cultures for which they are designed.

[17]

Tales from the Crick: Experiences and Services When Design Fiction Meets Synthetic Biology

MARCO RIGHETTO AND ANDY GOODMAN

Design Fictions as a Speculative Tool to Widen the Understanding of Technology

The primary purpose of this chapter is to propose a role of design as a tool for investigation, used as a speculative means to materialize tales of possible futures. The scenarios that will be taken into consideration are founded on two premises: first, slowly but constantly we are moving from an overconsumption-driven society to a service access–driven one; second, the progress in the field of synthetic biology (a brand new genetic engineering) resembles the historical path of digital and electronic technologies from the 1970s, where only technical experts were allowed to intervene.[1]

Design is going to be used as a tool to break this barrier and bridge the gap between science, technology, and society at large. Using real scientific achievements as a starting point, we can think about synthetic biology not as an abstraction but in fictional scenarios relevant to our

---

1 Synthetic biology is the design and construction of biological devices and systems for useful purposes. Schmidt, Markus (2012). *Synthetic Biology: Industrial and Environmental Applications* (3rd ed.). Weinheim, Germany: Wiley–Blackwell. pp. 1–67. ISBN 3-527-33183-2.

It is an area of biological research and technology that combines biology and engineering, thus often overlapping with bioengineering and biomedical engineering. It encompasses a variety of different approaches, methodologies, and disciplines with a focus on engineering biology and biotechnology. Folliard, Thomas. "What is Synthetic Biology?" SynBioSoc. Retrieved 1 March 2013.

day-to-day experiences. Putting the issues in real context, we can materialize an aesthetic of these new possibilities, understand them, and discuss the ethical landscape. These technologies have the power to entirely change industries and industrial procedures.

Furthermore, what if these technologies were part of our daily lives? What if we could actually generate and grow our genetically modified object at home as easily as it is possible to print 3D objects today? The economic and social structures would change dramatically when synthetic biology will be woven into the fabric of everyday life. What role would money and intellectual property play in a world of "living things"? With such fragmented and homemade product generation, what would be the role of brands?

The scenarios that will be presented in this chapter will not only contemplate the direct manifestations of synthetic biological (or, *synbio*) objects, but will also ponder their side effects produced along the way.

The Building Bricks of the Debate

This discussion is not intended to provide answers; it's purpose is to set the scene for debate, investigating and presenting hypothetical life cycles of products and services, and identifying design paraphernalia to better visualize the ethics and aesthetics of not-so-distant fictions.

In this new environment, objects become multifunctional frameworks in which even matter can be programmed and change its behavior and properties.[2] Along with the ability to deform into different shapes with different functions, objects will be personalized so that automated customization down to the individual unit will coexist with mass manufacturing processes. Still, true personalization, wherein the objects around us are completely adapted to our needs, is a distance away.

One possible way to bridge this gap is with biology. We are fast approaching a world in which synthetic biological *organ objects* begin entering our everyday life. Craig Venter, entrepreneur and scientist, managed to create the first cell whose DNA was entirely synthetic (meaning that it didn't previously exist in nature) and watermarked it with an email address. In a nutshell this was possible thanks to what is called

---

2 *http://bit.ly/1nTDfNB*

BioBricks (see Figure 17-1): standard DNA sequences of defined structure and function, which can be combined to form new life forms.[3] These elements cannot be patented, but the result or their combination can. These completely synthetic living organisms are grown within a protein-nutrient matrix and maintain their stable DNA with antibiotic agents, which can both be patented, as well.

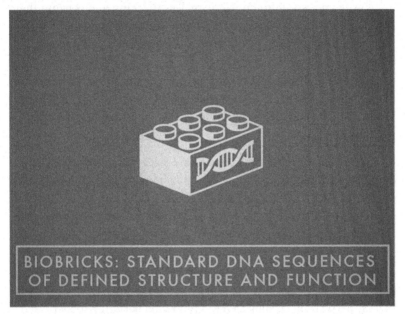

Figure 17-1. The building blocks of new life forms

Using these real scientific achievements as a starting point, we can think about synthetic biology not as an abstraction but in fictional scenarios relevant to our day-to-day experiences. We can bridge the gap between science and design, putting the issues in real context to understand the range of possibilities and discuss the ethical landscape. These technologies have the power to entirely change industries and

---

3 Every BioBrick part is a DNA sequence that is carried by a circular plasmid, which acts as a vector. Sleight, S. C.; Bartley, B. A.; Lieviant, J. A.; Sauro, H. M. (12 April 2010). "In-Fusion BioBrick assembly and re-engineering." *Nucleic Acids Research* 38 (8): 2624–2636. doi:10.1093/nar/gkq179.

These Lego-like building blocks are used to design and assemble synthetic biological circuits, which would then be incorporated into living cells such as Escherichia coli cells to construct new biological systems. "SynBio Standards –Bio Brick." Retrieved 27 March 2014.

industrial procedures. What if these technologies were part of our daily lives? What if we could actually generate and grow our organ objects at home in a even easier way that it is possible to print 3D objects today?

Synbio objects already can be patented, leading to all kinds of problematic scenarios. Genetics companies argue that it is their right to own these structures because they have invested heavily in research to identify and isolate them. Nevertheless, hacking and copying their structure is possible. On the other hand, the nutritional and antibiotics components that keep these objects alive will be scarce and actually quite difficult to replicate properly. For a scenario that features fragmented homemade production of synbio objects, what would be the role of brands? Perhaps they will patent these components, and probably our loyalty relationship with them would be based on the biological DNA they will produce.

In a world in which "living things" are widely common, it's easy to speculate that intellectual property and monetary value would play very different roles. If we stretch our minds enough, we can see that the synthetic biology has the potential to revolutionize the society at scale. Imagine the monetary system in this context. New currencies probably will be generated by a mixture of models, formulas, and generative diagrams of these DNA sequences, which would be traded according to their demand value. On the other hand, functionalities and intellectual properties will be subjected to a renovated bartering model. Such a dichotomic model will raise questions about how we will perceive value and price. Will finance still be possible? How would it evolve? What kind of social configurations could coexist in this future? Will we live in a mixture of global tribes based on DNA?

Rather than being judged by our possessions, the logos we wear, the cars we drive, or the teams we support, we might be divided up into groups possessing different genetic characteristics, some of which are rarer, cooler, and more expensive than others. This kind of division echoes racial segregation, but perhaps it will be more akin to fashion or to English soccer fans or American baseball fans wearing their team's colors and stripes.

CLOTHING AND FASHION: GOOSE-BUMP
COATS AND OTHER SYNBIO PERKS

Within this future, where nearly everything is biologically produced, we stretched our imagination to pursue concepts integrated in our daily lives. A fertile area would be the clothing industry, in which digital technology and fashion are merging in the work of designers such as Hussein Chalayan. Even more aptly, Suzanne Lee and others have already started working with textiles grown from synthetic organisms.[4] What if these technologies could merge together?

Possibly we will be wearing entirely biodegradable garments that we have grown ourselves. This doesn't mean the design aspect in fashion will become less significant: setting the parameters of how a dress grows will be just as skilled a job as drawing it. As in the other fields, models and shapes will be the focus of the new industrial processes in which an entire wardrobe of clothing could actually be supported by the same material, changing its shapes and properties according to the user's needs and environment.

Imagine a scenario in which you fly from a Chilean summer to a −30 degree Canadian winter. Normally, you would have to pack two sets of clothing. What if you could just buy a new set of features for your shirt in an airport vending machine, as illustrated in Figure 17-2? During the flight the molecules in the shirt would be reconfigured so that it grows into a warm coat. The coat might even get goose bumps in the cold weather causing the hairs on the fabric to stand up and provide even greater thermal insulation. These kinds of organic mutations would require a significant amount of time to happen. But, if we combine them with nanotech, responses to the environment could be instantaneous.

Clothing would change in response to the social environments the wearer is in, shifting color to become anonymous in a crowd or become the focus of attention, or changing shape to be appropriate to the social situation, to make her feel comfortable and confident, as depicted in Figure 17-3. This could happen quite seamlessly: a combination of gestures directly on the fabric, interlaced with our behavioral patterns and the data gathered from the environment. Sensors embedded into the

---

4 *http://www.ted.com/talks/suzanne_lee_grow_your_own_clothes*

garments would continually feed data back into the clothing so that over time it would become optimally adjusted to the wearer's needs. Fashion brands are already trying to envision this kind of future through their advertising.[5]

Figure 17-2. The goose-bump coat

THE MOVING DEFINITION OF NATURE IN A SYNBIO WORLD: THE AGRICULTURAL EXAMPLE

It is interesting to consider the industrial systems that would emerge from these new types of technology. Mass production of synbio objects would occur on a distributed and local level in biologically grown buildings. A large amount of nutrition would still need to be available on a global scale, though.

---

5 Lacoste with its "Polo of the Future," *https://www.youtube.com/watch?v=3olKLG6mzNk*.

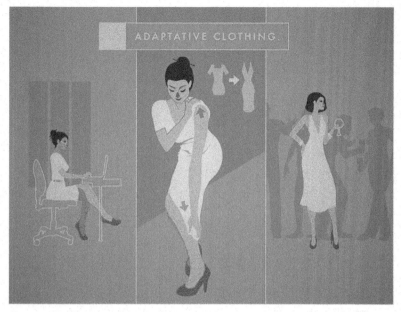

Figure 17-3. Clothing could change in response to the social environments the wearer is in

In this scenario, we envisage a new concept, *farmtories* (a combination of farm and factory, shown in Figure 17-4), in which agriculture and industrialization are subproducts of a combined process. Rather than buying in feed components for the growing ranks of products, raw materials would be extracted from cows' milk in a local ecosystem. When the products, grown from nutrient substrates, are no longer needed by users, they would be recycled back into feed for the animals. Everything would be localized; waste would be eliminated, as well as the fuel costs for transportation. A combination of grown bio-objects and 3D printing would yield a huge environmental and cost benefit.

In such a system, what if animals and plants could communicate to you exactly what they needed, and you could engineer them so that they would be perfect for your farm? What would be the iterative process that could bring us there, and to what extent would we accept it?

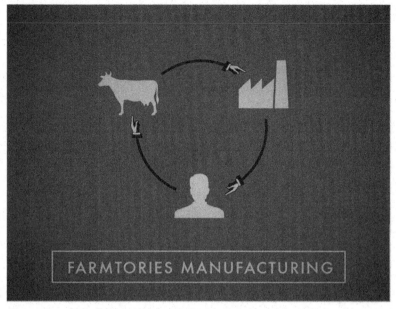

Figure 17-4. Agriculture and industrialization as subproducts of a combined process

That would bring *natural selection* back into the equation of industrialized farms. The main difference is that it would be a synthetic selection. Our current understanding of genetically modified foods and monoculture will be challenged by seeds and animals when sophisticated responses to the environment are engineered and therefore developed at a speed that is faster in order of magnitudes.

The encoding of information in DNA from living organisms engineered by using massive, automated studies that statistically match DNA changes to the conditions in which these organisms live will result in a system of "personalized organisms" that are tailored to the microenvironment in which they will grow.

One of the most interesting paradoxes of such a scenario is the anti-industrialization process that food and genetically modified objects could go through. In this sense, the mechanized harshness of current techniques of production, manipulation, and delivery of meats and vegetables could be reframed and diluted by the localization of breeding and growing. A hypothetical counter-culture of "naturalists" could emerge that will embrace these new technologies, as pictured in Figure 17-5.

Figure 17-5. Created by counter-culture "naturalists" who embrace these technologies

Healthcare Narratives: From Scenarios to Societal Debates

Fashion and agriculture are two sectors of society that might be affected by these new technologies in a rather short time span. Nonetheless, the domain that will see these technologies first adopted is going to be healthcare.

TREATMENT SCENARIOS

The application of gene therapy pursued for the past 20 years is yet another confirmation of the fertility of the sector. When digital and synbio technologies merge, the improvements for our health could be huge. The scale of interventions goes from performing current practices in a much less invasive way, to actually changing the way we cure diseases.

Microcustomized medical technology might be embedded in clothing for infants. These bio-bedclothes would be grown at home and integrated with diagnostic tools and genetic treatments in their fabric, as illustrated in Figure 17-6. While the child sleeps, they would "breathe in" the monitoring system, a cloud of nanoparticles that is gently being "exhaled" by the blanket. The cloud would contain a mixture of tiny digital and synbio agents, which enter the bloodstream of the child unnoticed and analyze it, looking for signs of disease. Automated analysis would trigger the creation of the appropriate treatment vectors, woven out of the DNA structure of the bedding. In this way, the entire procedure would be completely seamless for the patients: they might not even realize they had become ill and then been cured.

Figure 17-6. Microcustomized medical technology might be embedded in clothing for infants

SCENARIOS OF ENHANCEMENTS

It might soon become possible to extend our capabilities by implanting functionalities from other organisms into our own bodies. With the aid of bio hardware and software we would be able interpret, visualize, and understand inputs from previously unfelt phenomenon such as magnetic fields or sonar. Our brains are remarkably plastic, and it is not inconceivable that if you spliced mantis shrimp DNA into your own, you could learn how to perceive the world through all your new photoreceptors and be able to see polarized and hyperspectral light. Other useful animal qualities could improve our hearing, smell, balance, and coordination.

However, there are more dramatic ways of enhancing ourselves through genetic modification. On the one hand, is it plausible that the development of our society will lead to eugenics as a standard practice of giving birth? Within this context, will we try avoiding reproduction by persons having genetic defects or presumed to have inheritable undesirable traits? On the other hand, perhaps healthcare departments and insurance groups will be lobbying to avoid eugenics practices and instead go for post-birth treatments, to preserve their power and position in society.

A *Time* magazine article from July 2012 discusses recent research into people on the autism spectrum. This research discovered that some people who have been identified with exceptional levels of ability or genius have common traits with people with autism. It is a real concern that if we selectively remove the genetic propensity for autism in humans we will also unwittingly remove the tendency toward genius, as well. The correlation between specific genes and certain complex traits and characteristics, especially those that are related to the mind, is almost completely unexplored and it will be a long time before we have the correct understanding of how these traits can be amplified or reduced through genetic intervention.

In this engineered world, there is a fine line that marks the distinction between treatment and enhancements. Currently, viruses are used as vectors to treat genetic diseases such as hemophilia by delivering the correct copy of the dysfunctional gene into the cells, or even editing mutations into genomic DNA. What if we could extend our capabilities by delivering functionalities from other organisms and a way to interpret them? We are imagining the possibility to actually have the hardware and software to interpret, visualize, and understand colors that we cannot see, or even magnetic fields, such as turtles can. Will this lead to a rapid proliferation of new races or subraces within the human species? How would racism be perceived when scientifically and biologically "justified"?

A DEBATE ON WHAT'S FAIR

The potential to identify our own genome and compare it with a model human genome would skew the individual's relationships with state and private healthcare. By understanding the economic implications of specific genes and gene combinations in terms of developing diseases later in life, health insurance taxes and medical fees can be adjusted on a person-by-person basis. When genome sequencing, profiling, and modification have become the norm, government policy would be informed by a cost-benefit analysis produced by algorithms that constantly scrape and process this data. The danger of this is self-evident—would people with genetic issues be treated equally by the healthcare system? Predictive algorithms in financial services have proven to produce catastrophic results. Would we accept scientific prediction as authentic? Even so, which kind of ethical implication would this have?

A DEBATE ON WHAT'S LEFT

In this hypothetic scenario, how would it morally change our definition of segregation? Will people's choices be defined by their race and DNA characteristics—not only regarding health, but more broadly in terms of working possibilities and personal relationships? How will our perceptions of finding a partner change when we can know his/her genetic background? Will we still even search for a partner or will the human beings with the best sets of DNA become the primary reproducers? What is the sense of romantic love imagined as the result of a casual encounter? Will it became a casualty of biotech progress?

Living Objects: Symbiotic Indispensable Companions

Mankind has long dreamed and told stories of creating life, of imbuing inanimate objects with living force. We are hard-wired to see agency, the capacity for independent action, in all things, from rustling shadows in the jungle to terrifying silhouetted shapes in our childhood bedrooms. Our mythologies are littered with tales of made and enchanted creatures: golems, familiars, Frankenstein's monster, risen up from the mud or built from spare parts. It is a compelling narrative and speaks of our desire to control the living world and escape death. Now that we have the technology to actually create life, it is interesting to daydream about the forms this life might take and the uses we put to it. Think about the emotional reactions that were created by such devices as the Tamagotchi or Furby.

Our intrinsic desire to imagine a soul where there is none brought these inanimate lumps of plastic and nylon vividly to life. We have speculated about a new kind of companion, intelligent, connected to the network, malleable, and made from nanocomponents that could grow over time. Even more strikingly, it would be solely and intimately yours as it would have some of your DNA inside it. Its learning algorithms could predict what you wanted before you even knew you wanted it. It could deliver totally customized education, entertainment, healthcare, and advice zeroed in on you and your capabilities. It would be a lifelong companion given to you at birth and decommissioned when you die.

Unlike in a Cronenberg film, these bio-machines would not be literally plugged into our bodies—nothing as icky as that—but they would be fundamentally symbiotic with their owner. The form they take would morph over the years from a baby's pacifier, to a doll, then perhaps a hairband, bracelet, or some other kind of talisman. Small and intimate, the owner would carry or wear it next to their skin, its warm surface gently pulsing with life, soothing, reassuring, and guiding them. Using color, shape, sound, texture, and vibration, it would communicate in a multitude of different ways; the link with the owner would almost feel psychic at times. One thing to guard against would be keeping it safe; think about the panic you feel today when you lose your smartphone, multiply that by a thousand, and you might get close to imagining what it would feel like to lose your synthetic biological companion.

[18]

Beyond 3D Printing: The New Dimensions of Additive Fabrication

STEVEN KEATING

Additive fabrication, often referred to as 3D printing, is the construction of objects by adding material. This stands in contrast to subtractive methods, which involve removing material by means of milling or cutting. Although additive fabrication and 3D printing are thought of as synonymous, additive fabrication encompasses a far broader range of construction, and new dimensions are on the horizon, inspiring innovation across scales and applications. For instance, can you print a full-scale building? How can we structurally engineer color and alter on the nano-scale? If trees grow additively, can biology be designed for fabrication?

What are these new dimensions for 3D printing? How are they defined? The future areas for additive fabrication span along *spatial* (how the material is laid out in space/geometry), *material* (how new materials can be used and integrated with other constituents), and *temporal* (how materials/geometry can change through time) dimensions, and discussions in this chapter along with examples from our research will highlight novel design potentials in these areas.

MIT and the Mediated Matter Group: Previous and Current Additive Fabrication Research

In our lab, the Mediated Matter Group at the MIT Media Lab (led by Dr. Neri Oxman), we explore how these new additive dimensions can push the future of design. Our research focuses on digital fabrication and its intersection with biology, both for inspiration and for production. We strongly believe the next revolution lies in digital biology and how to control the processes across scales—both from the top down and from the bottom up. This can range from new material printers, combining manufacturing techniques (for example, 3D printing combined with milling), and looking beyond 3D printing as we currently understand it for the next generation of additive methods for enhanced speed, efficiency, and resolution. My doctoral work on these topics has resulted in one of the world's largest mobile digital construction platforms (with a robotic reach of over 80 feet diametrically), research into some of the smallest 3D printing systems (nano-scale, two-photon printers), and development of biological fabrication using growth systems of synthetically designed cells.

Using these newly developed techniques, the expanding limits of additive fabrication are beginning to be explored, and the hints at novel approaches for design are becoming apparent. Biology offers a glimpse into the possibilities for the future: in self-propagating algorithms, responsiveness, integration, and material sourcing. Biology can benefit from additive fabrication for generation of custom tools such as novel microfluidics. In addition, we can design biology as the tool itself. As synthetic biology begins to establish itself, we are excited by the new additive potentials for biologically tuned materials, integrated growth structures, and even living products.

The Dimensions of Additive Fabrication

Additive techniques hold the main benefits of shape complexity (internal feature geometry and spatial property distribution), digital control (the ability to repeatedly produce, edit, and tune via a computer), and distributed fabrication (single-machine factories hold the potential for fabrication on-site). However, the three areas often viewed as problematic in 3D printing provide a good analysis framework—with the main focus on the spatial dimension:

Spatial dimension limitations
Can printed objects scale to construction scales and nanometer scales?

Material dimension issues
Will printed objects accommodate multifunctional material properties?

Temporal considerations
How can additive fabrication techniques scale in responsiveness, speed, and sourcing?

Through the exploration of these additive fabrication dimensions, the current benefits and problems surrounding 3D printing will be viewed in a design light. In addition, these directions in additive research will detail the fascinating design potential for users, both new and current. From printing buildings, to making nano-scale machines on your desk, to growing the next synthetically designed biological products—the future is looking strong for additive techniques.

SPATIAL DIMENSIONS
In the past decade, the field of additive manufacturing, specifically 3D printing, has grown significantly in industry usage, technological developments, and consumer popularity. Although the first patents for 3D printing date back to the early 1980s,[1] increases in computer-aided design (CAD) software, availability of lower-cost fabrication systems, and new material options have recently spurred the field into new applications.

However, 3D printing has been limited to a small product footprint, with the typical 3D print volume limited to under a few cubic feet. This size limitation is due to the difficulty of making a large machine function at scale, printing time (small objects often take up to a day to print), and material considerations (cure mechanisms and stability). However, this dimension limitation is not permanent. Both on the macro and micro level, new additive techniques are poised to disrupt existing industrial techniques for construction and micromechanical fabrication through novel features, material integration, and customizability.

Macro-scale dimension
Since Henry Ford's automobile assembly line, inventors and futurists have proposed different ways to automate large-scale construction techniques. Residential construction is a challenging task to automate due to its considerable scale, one-off designs, and varying environmental conditions and requirements. The first significant attempt occurred in

---

1 Hull, C. Apparatus for production of three-dimensional objects by stereolithography. Patent No. 4575330, 1984.

1917 with Thomas Edison's patent on single-pour concrete housing.[2] Edison proposed a novel system by which a large single reusable metal mold could be used to cast concrete houses, including furniture, indoor accessories, and even pianos all made with concrete. However, the prototype molds proved to be far too complex with expensive molds consisting of over 2,300 pieces and the project became a well-documented failure.

Current modern research efforts into large-scale 3D printing have resulted in several projects such as Contour Crafting and 3D Concrete Printing.[3] These projects use direct extrusion of cementitious material using a gantry mechanism (a mechanical framework support system) to move the extruder along to print walls. Even though these projects have successfully printed large objects, full building-scale structures have not yet been achieved, due to several challenges, particularly due to the material limitations of direct concrete extrusion. These limitations, including integration, geometrical restrictions on production (limited to curvature only in the horizontal plane), and layer strength, have garnered significant attention and focus over time, and as a result, the future has become brighter for such large-scale digital fabrication.

Digital construction platform

A new approach we are currently pursuing involves building a mobile digital platform capable of on-site design, sensing, and fabrication of large-scale structures. The system combines a large hydraulic boom arm and a smaller electric robotic arm, as illustrated in Figure 18-1. Through the control of both arms, the system enables digital fabrication processes at architectural scales capable of spanning buildings. As a result, the system, referred to as a Digital Construction Platform (DCP), opens up new opportunities for on-site sensing, design, and fabrication research.

---

2 Edison. Apparatus for the production of concrete structures. Patent No. 1326854, 1917.

3 Khoshnevis, 2004; Lim, Buswell, Le, Austin, Gibb, & Thorpe, 2012.

Figure 18-1. The Digital Construction Platform comprises a six-axis KUKA robotic arm mounted to a five-axis Altec hydraulic boom arm

The DCP utilizes a mobile system capable of a large physical reach and high load capacity that enables new modes of in situ construction. The platform design was motivated by the need to generate a flexible system capable of implementing various kinds of large-scale digital fabrication approaches including additive, subtractive, and assembly techniques. An extended stationary reach and large hydraulic arm make large load capacities possible; the smaller electric arm affords high degrees of access and accuracy. Furthermore, a mobile system allows for fast setup times and ease of repositioning.

Compared with existing construction platforms, hydraulic boom arms are much more flexible to digitally manipulate from a stationary position. However, these boom arm systems typically lack the precision required for automated fabrication techniques. The DCP is designed around a hydraulic boom arm with an added robotic arm effector for the spatial compensation of temporal oscillations to achieve increased precision and ease of access.

Informed fabrication

The current system we have built utilizes a truck platform, an Altec boom arm, and a KUKA robotic arm to provide a lift capacity of 1,500 lbs (boom-arm mount) with a manipulation capacity of 20 lbs (small arm). The six-axis KUKA robotic arm is mounted on the end of a two-axis hydraulic jib on the three-axis boom arm, as demonstrated in Figure 18-2. The system uses a KUKA arm controlled via a custom Python script package, enabling real-time control via the Robot Sensor Interface (RSI) package.

Figure 18-2. The range of motions for the DCP large (five-axis boom) and small (six-axis KUKA robot) arms are shown through long-exposure photography

With real-time sensing and actuation, new design possibilities can be achieved based on environmental conditions, process data, and material goals. For the DCP, this ability is critical to operation to integrate site conditions into the system. The controls system is designed as a feedback loop based on current data from magnetostrictive sensors, rotary encoders, and inertial measurement units. The coupling of input and output fabrication capabilities of a robotic arm allows for a system capable of producing objects that incorporate environmental data. This use of environmental feedback to directly inform and influence fabrication holds many potential new avenues for design and manufacturing. We use the term *informed fabrication* to refer to this combination of environmental sensing and fabrication (Keating and Oxman, 2012).

To enable the variation of material properties with any castable material while providing enhanced speed, we created a new technique based on formwork (see Figure 18-3). Akin to a mold, formwork makes it possible for any castable material to be poured inside, providing benefits of wide material selection, fast production, and monolithic cast strength. Similar to insulated concrete forms, leave-in-place insulating formwork can be 3D printed for castable structures. By using a fast-curing BASF polyurethane material, layers of foam can be printed into formwork and also provide thermal insulation to the final structure. The process, termed *Print-in-Place construction*, is designed for on-site fabrication of formwork for castable structures, such as concrete exterior walls and civil infrastructure (Keating and Oxman, 2013). The process can also be rapidly integrated into current building strategies and regulations because the Print-in-Place construction method aligns directly with the traditional mold-based insulated concrete form (ICF) technology. After the mold is printed, conventional methods and regulations that apply to ICF construction can also be applied to the Print-in-Place process.

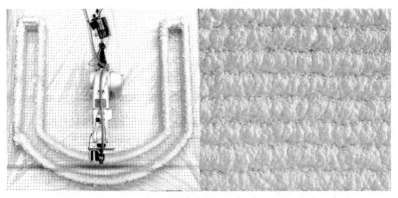

Figure 18-3. Additive fabrication tests using polyurethane spray foam with a KUKA six-axis arm (left) produced test insulative formwork samples with consistent and tunable layer heights (right)

In addition to additive printing, Print-in-Place utilizes secondary milling techniques to improve surface finish and reduce manufacturing time. The resulting resolution from a cast structure inside a printed and milled mold is shown in Figure 18-4. Furthermore, subtractive processes, combined with embedding objects (such as rebar or tie structures) in the printing process, enable creation of complex details such as windows, wiring areas, and embedded sensor integrations.

Figure 18-4. Combining additive and subtractive processes in a compound end effector (right) facilitates fast build times and high resolutions, as seen in the cast structure produced from a printed and milled mold

The proposed method will have comparable energy, strength, and durability benefits over insulated concrete formwork construction. Importantly, it also aims to tackle the safety, design, speed, environmental, energy, and financial issues currently plaguing the residential construction industry.

Benefits of digital construction

A compelling benefit of digital construction is its potential to significantly decrease the number of injuries and deaths in the construction industry by eliminating many of the dangerous and laborious tasks of manufacturing a building. Traditional construction methods are unsafe, slow, labor intensive, costly, and damaging to the environment. According to the United States Bureau of Labor Statistics, 4 out of 100 full-time American workers in 2010 were injured or contracted a work-related illness, and 802 total annual American fatalities were reported. This is the largest number of deaths in any sector, making construction one of the most dangerous professions in the country. The significant decrease in building time and labor proposed here through the use of automated methods is expected to greatly reduce costs and improve safety in an otherwise inefficient and hazardous field.

3D printed buildings would also have structural benefits and could be built more easily than traditional buildings. Although ubiquitous due to their simplicity and low cost, rectilinear buildings are actually weaker and more dangerous due to stress concentrations. Curvature improves structural integrity, but curved shapes are extremely challenging to form using traditional methods. With additive fabrication, creating curved structures is as simple as designing them on a computer, with which architects can create more stable, unique, and versatile structures. Imagine what buildings would look like in the future if the total cost were completely independent of the shape and merely tied to the cost of raw materials. The potential economic impact could range in the billions and all with the ability to digitally back up your house structure, to boot!

Additionally, automation facilitates highly detailed process control, as demonstrated in Figure 18-5—both in building specifications and in scheduling. Parameters such as wall properties and construction time can be controlled and precisely predicted. By removing human error and variation, civil engineering calculations can be much more accurate, allowing for a house to be built to exact structural and thermal specifications. Automation of the building process also eliminates the scheduling difficulties of having multiple contractors on a jobsite at the same time in addition to saving construction time and, consequently, labor costs. Time calculations based on prototype test conditions estimate that the mold for a typical one-story house with 10-foot walls and a perimeter of 170 feet could be printed in approximately 8 hours. Having accurate time prediction is very useful for planning purposes and ensuring a project finishes on time.

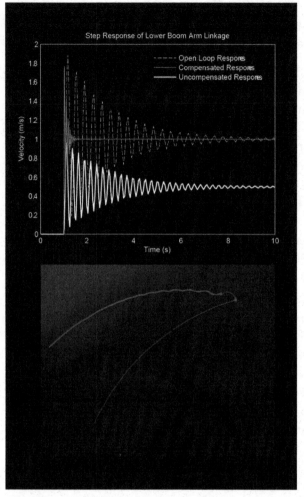

Figure 18-5. The control model (top) for the DCP compensates for robotic arm oscillations (bottom); a simulation of open loop, compensated, and uncompensated response from the control model is demonstrated (top); control model work conducted in collaboration with Nathan Spielberg and Will Bosworth

Future work entails further detailing the mechanical and sensing systems, material testing, and investigations into multiplatform collaboration with swarm construction techniques. Finally, we aim to design and construct a full-scale architectural pavilion using the DCP system in the near future (Figure 18-6). We believe this is a new growth area for 3D printing and look forward to digital fabrication encompassing digital construction.

Figure 18-6. Computer renderings of potential uses for the DCP showing on-site fabrication (left) and a sandwich structure for potential future printing (right) (image: John Klein)

Micro-scale dimension

On the other side of the spectrum, micro-scale 3D printing has significant applications in micromechanical devices, optics, and research. However, the current micro-scale limitations include material restrictions, warping and inaccuracy, and speed. Accessible one-photon 3D printing has become a key driver in biological and medical research, including printing tissue scaffolds and microfluidic devices.

Commercial optical 3D printers commonly use stereolithography techniques with z-stage resolutions on the order of 10–100 microns, with x-y minimum feature sizes around 100 microns (for example, Formlabs Form 1, Figure 18-7). These types of printers use one-photon absorption to trigger polymerization of a resin. Positioning of the light source and resin depend on the specifics of the printer and common methods such as galvanometers to steer a laser beam, inkjet deposition of resin, or projection-based systems. Standard one-photon absorption systems usually use UV-curable resins, which require average continuous wave optical power around 100 mW. Typical print times for a 5 x 5 x 5 cm part with these commercial stereolithography printers are around 10 hours, and the current cost can be as low as a few thousand dollars.

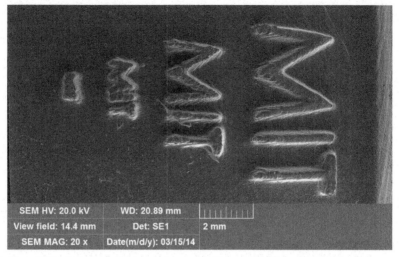

SEM HV: 20.0 kV	WD: 20.89 mm	⊥⊥⊥⊥⊥⊥⊥⊥⊥⊥
View field: 14.4 mm	Det: SE1	2 mm
SEM MAG: 20 x	Date(m/d/y): 03/15/14	

Figure 18-7. Scanning electron microscopy image detailing a resolution test print from a Formlabs Form 1 printer (image: Dr. James Weaver)

Meanwhile, advances in two-photon polymerization have helped realize applications that require high resolution on the nano scale. In contrast to one-photon printers, two-photon polymerization systems function via nonlinear optical absorption to achieve a smaller polymerization voxel unit. Two-photon absorption occurs when two photons are simultaneously absorbed by a molecule to allow an electron to jump to a higher state. This is a third-order process in which higher photon densities are required for two-photon absorption compared to one-photon absorption (linear process). For fabrication, a system typically uses either a pulsed femtosecond or a nanosecond laser operating at double the absorption frequency of the light-curable resin. The latter requires that the laser is tightly focused into a bath of resin, with the focal point being where the two-photon absorption primarily occurs. This generates a small voxel of polymerized resin, typically around 100–500 nm in size. Such systems (such as printers made by NanoScribe) are capable of submicron resolutions, but are limited by speed and positioning capability to under 1 mm object size typically. The print time for a 1 x 1 x 1 mm object on a NanoScribe printer is around 50 hours. In addition to the limitations on speed and size, cost is another barrier; commercial two-photon systems such as these start around $500,000.

Work done in collaboration with Will Patrick and Christian Landeros has focused on the limitations of both one-photon and two-photon printers. Our group has taken steps in developing a combination system to take advantage of the two systems' inherent strengths: fast one-photon polymerization for larger areas and precise two-photon polymerization for small features where needed. We believe the future of 3D printing with this system scales down to the nanometer and will facilitate micromechanical features on product-scale devices, such as structural color, sensing, and actuation mechanisms.

The integrated one- and two-photon polymerization system we designed and built uses an optical setup similar to a fluorescent microscope, as depicted in Figure 18-8. In our configuration, we used two different lasers: a blue diode laser for one-photon polymerization, and a Nd:YAG laser for two-photon polymerization. Early results are promising and show improvements for reliability, measurement data, and the potential to improve resolution based on material monitoring (see Figure 18-9). The work has taken key steps in the direction of coupling the relatively low cost and high speed of one-photon 3D printing with the nano-scale precision of two-photon printing in a combination system. With these advancements, we set the stage for the development of a 3D printing system capable of closing the gap between submicron and centimeter scales. The area of digital fabrication on the small scale continues to push boundaries, allowing for novel structural color fabrication, micromechanical devices, and advances in metamaterials.

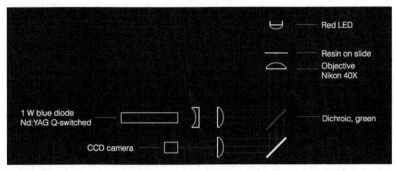

Figure 18-8. Schematic diagram of the combination one- and two-photon 3D printing system; note that the mechanical actuation system, comprised of a stepper motor stage with a piezoelectric stage, is not detailed in this schematic (graphic: Will Patrick)

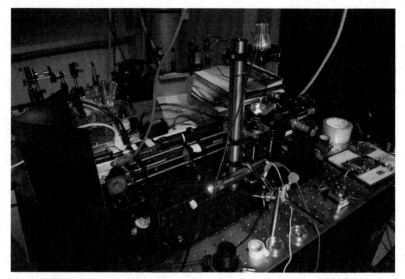

Figure 18-9. Experimental setup showing the combination one- and two-photon printing system with the 1W blue laser in the process of curing material; designed and built in collaboration with Will Patrick and Christian Landeros

Microfluidic devices

Our work in micro-scale printing is motivated by exciting opportunities for using optical 3D printing in biological applications. Microfluidic devices are used in chemical and biological applications to perform fluid reactions using internal channels on the order of 1–1000 microns.[4] Typical microfluidic devices are generated by using top-down lithography techniques, but additive manufacturing holds exciting potential in this field for fast turnaround, complex internal features, and multimaterial structures. In particular, we are exploring printers such as the Formlabs Form 1 and the Stratasys Objet500 Connex to create microfluidic devices. We have demonstrated the first 3D printed microfluidic valves made from both single and multiple materials (Figure 18-10).[5] Similar to integrated circuits, microfluidics hold potential for miniaturizing biological and chemical reactions for a variety of medical and product devices.

---

4 Whitesides, G.M. 2006.

5 In collaboration with Dr. David Kong, Will Patrick, and Maria Isabella Gariboldi.

Figure 18-10. Microfluidic devices are additively fabricated using a Stratasys Objet500 Connex printer in both single material (top) and multimaterial modes (bottom)

MATERIAL DIMENSIONS

Another important area in additive fabrication is material selection. Currently, commercial printers exist for a wide variety of materials, ranging from thermoplastics, optical-cured polymers, ceramics, metals, biomaterials, and even food. These printers use a selection of different techniques for solidifying the material, such as thermal, optical, and chemical curing methods.

Multimaterial printing

Currently, most printers still function with a single primary material. In the future, however, multimaterial printers will become the standard rather than the exception that they are today. For commercial printers, the small subset of multimaterial printers are limited to mainly optically cured photopolymers. Stratasys is a leader in this field and its top printer models presently can print using a mixture of three resin types, in addition to support material used for generating overhanging features. These multimaterial machines use inkjet deposition heads and can print mixtures of the three selected resins to allow for gradient material properties. The material gradients can vary in properties such as stiffness, color, and translucency. A relevant example using the Stratasys Objet500 Connex3 printer is a recent chaise lounge designed by Dr. Neri Oxman and Dr. W. Craig Carter, as illustrated in Figure 18-11. It was based on the functional goal of an acoustically quiet orb. As seen in the lower portion of the figure, gradients of color and elasticity were designed to inform the aesthetic and acoustical properties of the chair. The printer uses a 16 μm voxel (volumetric pixel) size to accommodate spatial variations throughout the printed parts. The chaise lounge uses a milled wood back panel for support and is an example of combining both additive and subtractive fabrication modes.

Material tunability

Mass manufacturing commonly assembles single material parts in post-production. In contrast, digital fabrication and multimaterial additive techniques are beginning to introduce specificity, customization, and material integration into product design. This concept, referred to as *tunability*, makes it possible for designs to be adapted to their functional goal or environment. Instead of assembling single materials discretely, 3D printing can produce graded material properties with tunable characteristics such as color, density, and stiffness. In the previous chaise lounge example, the functional goal was acoustical. For the environmental case, we used sensed data alongside design algorithms to create a computational model. Another example is seen in a customized 3D printed helmet for a specific person's head, designed by a team led by Dr. Neri Oxman.[6] As opposed to a mass manufacturing approach based on a generic user, 3D printing enables tailored, highly customized design both in terms of geometry and material property variation. For the helmet, user data from a medical head scan allowed for the external geometry and internal material distribution of the head to be

---

6 Design team for the Minotaur Head with Lamella included Dr. Neri Oxman in collaboration with Stratasys, Dr. W. Craig Carter (MIT), Joe Hicklin (The Mathworks), and Turlif Vilbrandt (Symvol, Uformia).

mapped, as presented in Figure 18-12. The helmet was designed and 3D printed with variable stiffness properties on a Stratasys Objet500 Connex 3D printer. The helmet model is algorithmically generated to provide a geometrical fit that provides different elastic responses corresponding to the layout of tissue and bone in the user's head.

Figure 18-11. The Gemini Acoustic Chaise was 3D printed on a Stratasys Objet500 Connex3 3D printer and mounted on a CNC milled wood back (Le Laboratoire). Designed by Dr. Neri Oxman in collaboration with Stratasys and Dr. W. Craig Carter (MIT). Image credit: Michel Figuet (top) and Yoram Reshef (bottom).

Through these gradients of elasticity, the helmet provides improved function and feel. In this sense, 3D printing introduces a new era of customized fit and functionality for individual users and environments. The final helmet is printed on the Stratasys machine and is exhibited as the *Minotaur Head with Lamella*.

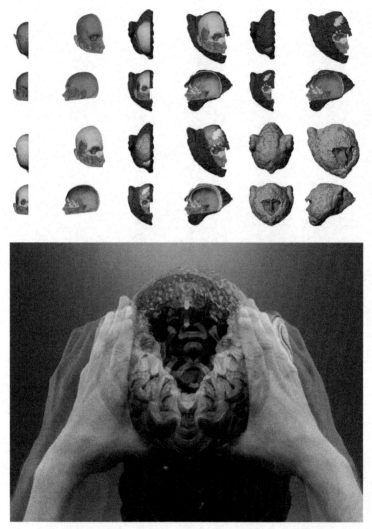

Figure 18-12. Minotaur Head with Lamella. From the Imaginary Being series, Centre Pompidou (Paris). 3D printed by Stratasys with variable stiffness properties on a Objet500 Connex 3D printer. Designed by Dr. Neri Oxman in collaboration with Dr. W. Craig Carter (MIT), Joe Hicklin (The Mathworks), and Turlif Vilbrandt (Uformia). Photo credit: Yoram Reshef.

The future of 3D printing is moving toward increased control of multi-material printers. In time, additional printing techniques will be developed or converted to output multiple materials. Multimaterial printing control allows for functional gradient properties to accommodate functional goals and environmental data. For now, the field is limited primarily to optically cured polymers. These polymers work well for prototypes, but due to the higher cost, long-term stability issues, and material properties, additional material types is a forthcoming challenge and will be developed in future technologies. We believe multi-material metal/thermoplastic printers, digital electronics printers, and biological material printers are on the near horizon.

TEMPORAL DIMENSIONS

The final dimension of additive manufacturing is the temporal regime, which affects both the fabrication process and the resulting product behavior. In comparison to mass manufacturing methods, current 3D printing techniques are slow, and build trays often require in excess of a day to finish a single part. In contrast, traditional mass manufacturing techniques such as molding, stamping, and casting are carried out in seconds to minutes. Looking toward the future, we expect the temporal dimension to be exceedingly important in new product development and processes.

Printing processes will become much faster in the future and will begin to challenge mass manufacturing techniques because of its inherent advantage in producing complex geometry, customization, and integration benefits, as discussed in the previous sections of this chapter. To achieve higher print speeds, the serial print process (print head) can move faster, print a larger bead size, and/or utilize parallel processes. Unfortunately, resolution is often inversely proportional to speed due to the total tool path length, thus limiting the 3D printing process to slower speeds for detailed parts at scale. However, biology excels in two areas—scale and adaptation—and growth mechanisms offer possibilities for additive techniques that surpass the conventional limits.

Digital biological fabrication

Turning to the exponential growth and parallelization capacity in biology, we are excited by the potential that biological materials offer for printing. The common *Escherichia coli* cell can replicate itself, along with all its internal complexity and high resolution, in approximately

20 minutes (genetically engineered strains of *E. coli* can approach doubling times much faster, currently down to 11 minutes). The concept of parallelization, in which individual fabrication units fabricate larger systems, is a powerful technique that biology applies to enable speed, robustness, adaption, and responsiveness. Applying the scaling laws, it is easy to imagine the vast potential for biological growth systems to be combined with digital controls and materials. In our work, we are exploring parallelization through large-scale fabrication with biological growth systems and digital controls.

Beginning in 2012, our group started studying silkworms, organisms that produce silk cocoons used for the world's silk supply. Viewing the silkworms (*Bombyx mori*) in a framework akin to miniature 3D multimaterial 3D printers, scaffolding template experiments were conducted by the team led by Dr. Neri Oxman.[7] These experiments revealed silkworm motion patterns and provided scaffolding guidelines to produce flat sheets of silk as opposed to cocoons (the silkworms still metamorphose outside the silk into moths; the cocoon is for protection from predators). Using this data, a digital controls model was developed and a robotically constructed scaffold was produced to provide spatial information to the silkworms. 6,500 silkworms were placed on the scaffold and over the course of two weeks the silkworms layered the scaffold with silk in the geometry constructed by the digital controls model. When the scaffold was removed, the final Silk Pavilion was exhibited in the MIT Media Lab lobby, as shown in Figure 18-13. The Silk Pavilion, with its massive parallelization of additive fabrication, serves as an excellent example of the power-scaling potential for biology. By extension, looking around a common room and noticing the bulk of natural materials (for example, wood, cotton, and food), the potential for controlling biological growth models is very exciting.

Although existing biological organisms are impressive in their capacity to engage spatial and temporal growth and material variation, we are also intrigued by the potential to design biology itself through synthetic biology methods. These methods focus on genetic engineering through designing the gene pathways with logic structures analogous

---

7 Silk Pavilion team led by Dr. Neri Oxman with Mediated Matter's Markus Kayser, Jared Laucks, Jorge Duro-Royo, and Carlos Gonzales Uribe—in collaboration with Dr. Fiorenzo Omenetto (Tufts University) and Dr. James Weaver (Wyss Institute, Harvard University).

to electrical and computer engineering. Using the biological equivalents (using transcription factors) of logic gates (such as AND, NOT, and OR gates), genetic circuits can be designed and constructed within organisms.

Figure 18-13. Scanning electron microscopy images detail a typical silk cocoon, and the observed spinning patterns are highlighted in false color generated by surface orientation (top); the Silk Pavilion on display in the MIT Media Lab (bottom) (photo: Dr. James Weaver [top], Steven Keating [bottom])

In the future, what would wood look like if it were optimized for structure, color, homogeneity, speed of growth, and so on? Could we have living products? Cell phones that are half-biological and half-digital? Houses that can replicate or materials sourced from the air like plants? The new field of synthetic biology designs genetic biological functions for engineering solutions. Synthetic biology is an exciting area with serious potential to revolutionize not only medicine, but also fabrication and computation. The thoughts seem infinite, although we are just at the beginning of the science, tools, and capabilities to design basic synthetic biological systems.

The beginning building blocks of synthetic biology are emerging, as new science from the last decade has created designs for genetic circuits akin to logic gates. These genetic circuits are designed gene pathways made from materials such as deoxyribonucleic acid (DNA) and ribonucleic acid (RNA) that program certain chemical actions from cellular organisms. From these basic logic gates, the goals of genetic circuits and computation are starting to emerge in scientific research by leading biologists in the field. As a research group, we are just in the first stages of getting our feet wet in the area, but we are enthused and look forward to a future of growth, temporal responsiveness, and hybrid systems with digital components.

Current research in our group in the area focuses on fabrication systems and mechanical means of combining top-down digital controls and bottom-up biological growth. Early work has generated inkjet distribution heads for printing cells, genetically modified cell lines for tunable biofilm growth, and mathematical models for using light to trigger fabrication gene pathways in cell lines for potential 3D printing techniques (see Figure 18-14).[8] In the future, we believe 3D printers will function with biological resins capable of complex parallelized growth with responsive temporal and spatial properties.

---

8   Work performed in collaboration with Will Patrick and Dr. David Kong.

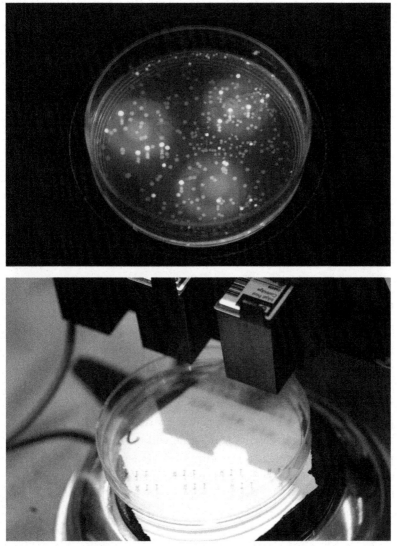

Figure 18-14. Genetically engineered Escherichia coli cells with a fluorescent tag (top); a biological print head using inkjet nozzles to print living cells onto substrates (bottom)

While these are very early predictions, we look forward to the future of printing living materials and believe that the capabilities in all of the dimensions discussed in this chapter—spatial, material, and temporal—hold the future for vast scaling potential, material/energy sourcing, and responsive products, as illustrated in Figure 18-15.

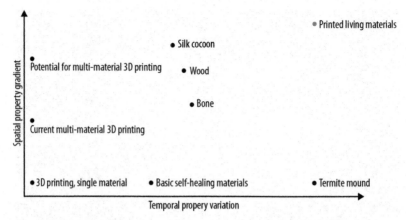

Figure 18-15. An overview chart detailing the spatial and temporal variations possible with different materials systems (work in collaboration with Will Patrick)

Conclusion

The future for new dimensions in additive manufacturing holds promise for novel design processes and industrial applications. Starting with spatial control, the scales of 3D printing are continuing to expand on both the small and large scales. In the coming years, we will see infrastructure made through automated additive techniques. Buildings printed, assembled, and dynamically measured will create responsive architecture. Conversely, the nano-scale will begin to merge with the product-scale through novel printing techniques such as two-photon absorption curing. We will see the development of a multitude of applications empowered by these new nano-scale machines, ranging from structural color, to on-product mechanism arrays, and widespread sensors/interfaces.

Spatial limitations are just one frontier—new printed materials and graded properties hold potential for design to move beyond combining standardized parts. With current optical printers capable of dynamically mixing base materials to print in multiple materials, products can be customized to design environments. Gradients of stiffness, translucency, and density have made possible a new language of monolithic design in which integration offers significant benefits in functionality, efficiency, and ease of fabrication. Moving forward, the research direction of multimaterial printers will progress with more materials such as composites, ceramics, and metals. Research work is pushing the materials dimension toward active electronic properties, such as printable circuit boards, integrated digital sensors, and batteries. For designers, the ability to create complex products is becoming simpler, faster, and accessible. At the moment, this complexity is defined as shape/material sophistication, though it will continue to grow into electronics, at-scale manufacturing, and in the more distant future, biological complexity.

Ending on a biological note, design is often inspired by natural organisms. Current research directions predict a future of design in which organisms themselves can be designed. Although current 3D printing techniques are limited in the temporal dimension (print time) due to speed/resolution/geometric scale, biology has found solutions through growth and adaptability. Turning to synthetic biology, the concept of a digitally controlled (top-down), biologically designed (bottom-up) fabrication system holds mesmerizing potential for fast growth of significantly complex systems. Even though the field of synthetic biology is still in its infancy and there is enormous work to be done, encouraging examples of grown bricks, tunable biofilms, and designed biological calculators hint at the design capabilities. The concept of a biologically grown house, self-healing vascular networks in our products, and integrated electronics with biology are exciting ideas for future focus. Overall, the possibilities of combining digital controls, logic, and memory with the biological power of scaling, resolution, paralleling, and material/energy sourcing are limitless.

We are excitedly enthused by the potential to explore new dimensions of 3D printing in spatial scale (construction-scale and nano-scale), material possibilities (multimaterial gradient properties), and temporal considerations (parallelization and biological combinations). The future for additive techniques is bright and we look forward to continued developments in the field.

ACKNOWLEDGMENTS

The work explored in this chapter focused on recent research from our university lab group, Mediated Matter, and my doctoral work on introducing new scales in fabrication. It was conducted with a number of colleagues and associations that deserve acknowledgements and kind thanks. The presented work was conducted with the Mediated Matter Research Group, led by Dr. Neri Oxman, at the MIT Media Lab. The Digital Construction Platform project was funded with support from the NSF EAGER Grant (Award No. #1152550) and technical/material support from Altec Inc and BASF Corporation. Thanks to Nathan Spielberg (MIT), John Klein (Mediated Matter), Grant Sellers (MIT), David Boger (Altec), and Marc Schroeder (BASF) for their work with the Digital Construction Platform. The research into combination one- and two-photon printing systems was conducted with Will Patrick and Christian Landeros, with special thanks to Max Lobovsky (Formlabs) and Dr. Peter So (MIT). The Silk Pavilion project, led by Mediated Matter's Markus Kayser, Jared Laucks, Jorge Duro-Royo, Laia Mogas Soldevila, and Carlos Gonzales Uribe, was in collaboration with Dr. Fiorenzo Omenetto (Tufts University) and Dr. James Weaver (Wyss Institute, Harvard University). Multimaterial printing work including the Gemini Chaise Lounge and the Minotaur Head with Lamella was conducted with Stratasys Ltd. Collaborators on these multimaterial prints led by Dr. Neri Oxman include Dr. W. Craig Carter (MIT), Joe Hicklin (The Mathworks), and Turlif Vilbrandt (Symvol, Uformia). The microfluidic printing work was conducted with Dr. David Kong, Will Patrick, and Maria Isabella Gariboldi. We would also like to thank the Center for Bits and Atoms and the Synthetic Biology Center, specifically Dr. Tim Lu and Dr. Ron Weiss, for providing fabrication facilities and technical support. Special thanks are due to both of my doctoral advisors, Dr. Neri Oxman and Dr. David Wallace, the undergraduate research assistant team led by Nathan Spielberg, and friends and family.

REFERENCES

Bonwetsch TF Gramazio, et al. *Digitally Fabricating Non-Standardised Brick Walls.* ManuBuild, 1st International Conference, Rotterdam, 2007.

Edison T. Apparatus for the production of concrete structures. Patent No. 1326854, 1917.

Gramazio F., Kohler M. *Digital Materiality in Architecture*, Lars Müller Publishers, 2008.

Hull C. Apparatus for production of three-dimensional objects by stereolithography. Patent No. 4575330, 1984.

Keating S. *Renaissance Robotics: Novel Applications of Multipurpose Robotic Arms Spanning Design Fabrication, Utility, and Art.* M.Sc. Thesis, Mechanical Engineering, Massachusetts Institute of Technology, 2012.

Keating S., Oxman N. *Immaterial Robotic Fabrication*. Proceedings of RobArch: Robotic Fabrication in Architecture, Art and Design, 2012.

Keating S, Oxman, N. Compound fabrication: A multi-functional robotic platform for digital design and fabrication. *Robotics and Computer-Integrated Manufacturing* 2013;29(6):439-48.

Khoshnevis B. Automated construction by contour crafting—related robotics and information technologies. *Automation in Construction*. 2004;13(1):5-19.

Lim S, et al. Development in construction-scale additive manufacturing processes. *Automation in Construction*. 2012;21(1)262-8.

Whitesides GM. "The origins and the future of microfluidics." *Nature*, Vol. 442, 2006.

Become an Expert at Becoming an Expert

LISA DEBETTENCOURT

"So, the first project we want you to work on when you get here is the user experience redesign of a genetic variant database and clinical reporting software," he said over the phone.

I swallowed hard and thought, "What the hell am I getting myself into?"

Before I even began at my new position as the Director of User Experience at Involution Studios, a boutique software design firm in Arlington, Massachusetts, I found myself planning my strategy for how I could quickly refresh my outdated understanding of genetics and learn about the technologies that were now used to sequence DNA. I had two weeks to prepare for the project while wrapping up my then-current job designing 3D modeling software for architects and engineers.

I knew this was the way of life at a design studio: creating wildly different tools and products, for a variety of clients across a number of industries, and in rapid succession. But I was really looking forward to it. I knew I would be repeatedly diving headfirst into new projects and domains while striving to understand the client's business, technology, workflows, and user context to creatively solve real problems. Although I'd always taken the time to deeply learn the domains and technologies of every product line and company in my career—from digital imaging, to automotive systems, to medical devices, to ecommerce, to civil engineering, and architecture—I usually had a runway to build up the breadth and depth of knowledge I needed, one project at a time. As a designer on an in-house team, successive projects in the same domain provided many opportunities to expand my comprehension. In this role, I knew I wouldn't have that luxury.

After that phone call, I took a step back and realized that over the years, I had been employing (and improving) a small set of strategies and methods for quickly coming up to speed at a new company, or on a new project, that enabled me to become more effective sooner. I recognized that this lightweight framework was flexible enough to be applied in shorter bursts, such as within a design agency setting, and I could have success with it there, as well. I felt a little bit better.

I believe that designers cannot be successful if they do not understand the business, technology, and subject matter of which their designs serve. Therefore, I want to share a framework that I've created, which practitioners can use to quickly gain expertise in new domains or technologies. In this chapter, I discuss why this practice is critical to thriving as a designer in the coming waves of emerging technology.

Into the Fire

In 1995, I graduated college and went to work in digital photography. It was an emerging technology at that time, and no one knew if it was just a fad or a massive disruption in the making. Because I was an avid photographer and color-science nerd, I was captivated by the idea of what digital capture and imaging could do for photography. Only five years prior, in 1990, Kodak had launched the first professional digital camera for photojournalists: the DSC-100. They partnered with Nikon, put a 1.3-megapixel imaging sensor and electronics in the Nikon F3 camera body, and then sold it for $13,000 (in 1990 dollars).[1] That same year, Adobe Photoshop version 1.0 was also released.[2]

After graduation I began working for Leaf Systems out of Westborough, Massachusetts, a company that had launched the "DCB1,"[3] a camera attachment that could turn a traditional film camera into a high-resolution digital camera, a year after the introduction of the DSC-100. The DCB1 was quite different from the DSC-100; it used a 4-megapixel

---

1 http://en.wikipedia.org/wiki/Kodak_DCS-100

2 http://www.storyphoto.com/multimedia/multimedia_photoshop.html

3 http://www.epi-centre.com/reports/9304cs.html

imaging sensor, was designed to only be used with a medium or large format camera such as a Hassleblad or Sinar 4 x 5, and could only be used in the studio tethered to a custom PCI board installed in an Apple Macintosh. Also, it sold for $36,000 (in 1991 dollars)—without the camera.

The industry was buzzing with the excitement from all the opportunity and change happening in digital imaging. Rapid advances in storage technology, optics, DSP circuits, CCD and CMOS[4] sensors, and lithium-ion batteries,[5] plus the formation of JPEG and MPEG standards culminated into the perfect storm in which digital photography could explode. Additionally, eight industry giants—and fierce competitors— came together to form the International Color Consortium (ICC)[6] and establish color management standards so that any digitally captured, rendered, or printed image would appear the same regardless of software, display technology, operating system, paper, or ink. I was designing most of the features of the digital cameras I worked on as well as the editing and management software that accompanied them, and I was proud to be a small part of the seismic shift that was happening in the world of photography at that time.

Everything was advancing, and it was all happening at once.

Digital photography quickly morphed from a technology only available to professionals into what we see it today: a prevalent and ubiquitous technology used for documentation, communication, and selfies.[7] Imaging sensors continued improving, DSP[8] algorithms became more accurate, color and image quality improved, and electronics grew smaller and faster, prompting more digital cameras to come to market every week. New markets were forming as innovative form factors evolved and never-before-heard-of features popped up. Every company was trying to outdo every other one.

---

4 Charge-coupled device and complementary metal-oxide semiconductor

5 http://en.wikipedia.org/wiki/Lithium-ion_battery#From_commercial_introduction

6 http://en.wikipedia.org/wiki/International_Color_Consortium

7 To give you a sense of how much has changed in 20 years, the iPhone 5S that launched in September 2013 includes a camera component, which has an 8-megapixel sensor. It is selling at Walmart for $49. The current model of the Leaf studio camera now has an 80-megapixel sensor and is still selling at around $36,000.

8 Digital signal processing

Who would win the battle to own the digital camera market? The race was on.

In the mid-1990s, two other massively disruptive technologies were also in their infancies: the Internet and the mobile phone. Of course, my friends, colleagues, and I had our own wild ideas about what could happen, and we regularly talked about what products and services we thought would emerge at the intersection of these three technologies. We talked about how "it would be so cool if you could take a picture and send it to someone with your phone. Or post it directly to a website." We imagined buying everything online by looking at beautiful product shots. We even talked about our refrigerators recognizing an empty milk carton and placing a replacement order with our grocery store directly (still waiting for that one!). But, we could not even begin to fathom just what this mashup of technologies would ultimately mean for people, our relationships with one another, and society as a whole.

I was lucky to have contributed to the creation of a number of digital cameras, both professional and consumer, as a designer *and* domain expert. I knew the science of color and imaging and the technology of cameras and CCDs. I knew the industry of photography and I had a good design sense. I was, as *Dictionary.com* defines it:

> Expert [n.] A person who has some special skill or knowledge in a particular field; specialist; authority.

Eating the Elephant

As the digital photography field matured and became commoditized, I directed my career into the design of other complex (and sometimes emerging) technologies. However, that posed a new challenge: diving headfirst into a new industry or trying to learn the intricacies of a new technology can be incredibly overwhelming. There is so much to learn; how could I possibly learn it all or even know where to start? I felt inadequate. If I never studied it in college, how would I ever know if I was learning the right things? I knew I was going to be working around people who knew the subject matter inside and out, and I would constantly be left in the dust. How could I possibly catch up?

If I was going to grow as a designer, I had to embrace the emotions. They were real. But I couldn't let them stop me.

Emerging technologies can be very complex systems that contain many moving parts. Often, these parts are rapidly evolving and it can be hard to feel like you have a grasp on the state of any of them at any given time to be able to begin designing a desirable product or worthwhile service. That's OK. You typically don't need to be up-to-date on everything, but it is helpful to attempt to acquire a general historical sense of how things came to be, what trends are actively unfolding, and what the trajectories are for the future.

How do you eat an elephant?
One bite at a time.
—AFRICAN PROVERB

At the beginning of a new project, no one expects you to show up fully versed in all the lingo and domain knowledge. Thus, you can quickly break down the framework for understanding the subject matter and becoming an "expert" into three main components:

1. What you need to know

2. Where to find it

3. When to stop

Let's explore each of these in more detail.

WHAT DO I NEED TO KNOW?

What do you already know? I'm sure that there are some things in, around, or about the subject that you already know and might not even realize it. Even if the emerging technology space you're about to set foot in is the most revolutionary, groundbreaking, never-seen-before amazing thing, it *emerged* from somewhere so there is still a decent likelihood that you can take advantage of some transferrable knowledge. Take 3D printing technology, for example. Its current state is an evolution of high-end stereolithography for rapid prototyping, which was invented in the 1980s,[9] and large format three-dimensional printing, which itself was derived from technology used in inkjet printers and patented by MIT in the 1990s.[10] The same can be said for the Internet of Things and sensor networks. Before the Internet of Things, there

---

9 http://www.google.com/patents/US4575330
10 https://www.google.com/patents/US5340656

was the Internet, mobile devices, sensors, and microprocessors. Even genetic engineering and DNA synthesis is only possible because of the discovery of DNA, the history of traditional plant or animal breeding, and Sanger sequencing, developed in the 1970s.[11] The point is, there is likely some body of valuable knowledge you already have buried in your memory somewhere about these technologies that you can dust off and use.

The real question you need to answer is, "Is my knowledge still relevant or useful?" I mean, my high school biology might have been 22 years ago (yikes!) but I can tell you that what I learned then was definitely helpful during my research into genetic testing because it provided the scaffolding for supporting new and more complex concepts and details. Genetics hasn't fundamentally changed in the past two decades, we just know more—a *lot* more. So, that double helix I first learned about in 1989 was still relevant, but it certainly wasn't enough.

What's the project?

At the beginning of a new design project, especially in a topic unfamiliar to you, it's most important to align your efforts of learning to the goal of the project and to identify what you need to know to most effectively help you get there. In other words, create a smaller elephant. Here you ask yourself, "Is my goal as a designer to build something new or to evolve something that already exists?" The answer to this question helps you scope what you need to know, where you should look for information, how deep you should go into each of those areas, and when you should stop. The genetic variant database project I worked on was a major redesign of an existing product, so I had something to study and work with. Compare that to when I was working on the first consumer digital cameras, there was no product to iterate on so we were designing from scratch.[12]

Next, you should identify the users and business goals, and roughly map the ecosystem in which the new product or service will live. This is basically answering the questions, "What problem is it solving, for

---

11 *http://en.wikipedia.org/wiki/Sanger_sequencing*

12 You can argue that both consumer film photography and other digital cameras were on the market prior to the ones I worked on, and therefore this was not a V1.0 product. Although that is true, the company I worked for had never built any before; we were working with a blank slate and building a V1.0 product for them.

whom, and in what context?" This will frame your research efforts and help you to avoid diving down too deep into the domain details. As you begin to get into the weeds, you can simply step back and answer the question, "Is this relevant to the project?" If not, even though the information might be quite interesting, drop that line of research and move on for the sake of expediency in climbing the expertise curve.

Finally, identify what are, or might be, this product's competitors. Who else is working on products or services like the one you are working on, and what kinds of approaches are they taking? (The client or project team can help you here.) This will help you understand how others are solving the same or similar problems as you are, what variations of technologies they are using or feature sets they have developed, and what the limits and benefits are of those approaches.

Because these projects are about designing how people will use technology to achieve their specific goals within a domain, the expertise you should have plus the expertise you should look to build lies in the blue region depicted in Figure 19-1.

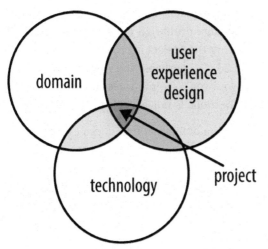

Figure 19-1. Designers should be experts in their field, and learn enough about the domain and the technology to execute the project successfully

If you are a user experience (UX)/product designer, you are already an expert in your craft or you are at least expert enough to have been asked to work on the project at hand. That leaves two things you'll need to understand in your quest for expertise for the project: the domain you'll be working in and the technology used within it. At the introduction to the project, you should spend a little time brainstorming what you'll need to research in each area. You should also create a section in your notebook for capturing and defining new domain-specific terminology you come across, which you'll refer back to throughout your project.

What's the domain?

In Figure 19-1, "domain" and "technology" are the variables in the diagram that need to be defined for the project. You might not think that doing this explicitly is very helpful, but it will help you focus on exactly what information you need to research and direct you to where you might find it.

Let's take the domain to start. You might think, "Well, I already know the domain I'm working in." Ok, fine. Just take five minutes to write it on paper and ask yourself these two questions: 1) is this topic going to provide the information I need to directly help me with my project, and 2) do I have enough time to adequately explore this topic? If you have only a day or a week to rapidly familiarize yourself with the domain while planning and beginning the project itself, it will help you recognize if you've gone too broad. Or, perhaps, you might have narrowed your focus so much that you won't see the forest for the trees. If the answer to either of those questions is no, go back and try again.

Getting specific in defining the domain at first doesn't mean that you have to strictly maintain your attention on that area alone for the duration of the project. You will likely wander beyond it as you pick up the scent of information that you know is relevant to your design project or your overall understanding of the subject. It just allows you to prioritize learning what is most impactful at the beginning, and then you can fill in details around that knowledge as you progress through the duration of the project.

In starting the genetic variant database project, the domain I ultimately chose to understand was DNA replication because that is the biological process when errors or "variants" occur in DNA, and the product tested for those. I originally thought genomics should be the domain I would research, but after a quick scan of Wikipedia, I immediately realized that it was far too broad and that I'd never get to the point of having enough of the right information, quickly enough, to be effective in designing something useful. Genetics was also too broad and would have left me winding down paths that were, while interesting, not all that useful in actually getting my project done. The DNA replication topic covered enough theory that I learned what I needed about genetics to understand the context of the project and targeted the specific processes for which I'd need to design the database interface.

Although defining a specific domain is important to defining the scope of your area for research, getting too specific is also detrimental to your ability to gain expertise in the subject. It is a delicate balance to strike at the beginning. You don't want to limit yourself so much that you end up working in only the weeds and missing out on higher-level concepts, theories, and trends. Had I only explored genetic testing for cardiomyopathy and the other specific diseases for which the tool was programmed, I would have certainly missed out on learning about advances in detecting other diseases and how certain technologies— beyond the scope of the tool and project I was working on—were aiding that. That kind of insight—how others are solving similar problems— can help you rethink how you structure your high-level design. And, if the company decides to branch out into other areas in the future, they wouldn't have to go through another application redesign because the information architecture had been structured in such a way as to be extensible and scalable enough to support additional functionality.

What's the technology?

The next thing I recommend doing is naming and writing down what primary technologies you'll be working with in your project. In many cases, this is far easier than defining the domain, but it is still important. Keep in mind that there is a possibility that you might find yourself a bit overwhelmed with all the various technologies involved with, or supporting, the project so, as I mentioned earlier, the important thing is to identify only the primary ones that are directly related to your project.

Again, identifying what technology you'll be working with in the project will help you to focus on what information to search for and what to filter out. For example, in my genetic variant database project, the technologies involved in the process included the hardware for the sequencing of the DNA, the IT infrastructure to manage, process, and store the massive quantity of data that resulted from the process, the analysis tools developed to determine whether a variant was present, and the national database of variants, as well as the software I was working on that tracked patient test results and disease data. To be successful in designing the software, it was clear that learning the inner workings of a Next Generation DNA sequencer would add no value; however, had I been working on the user interface that people used to drive that piece of hardware, it would have been essential. In this case, I felt that it was helpful for me to know about the sequencer at a high level; for example, where and roughly how it was used in the testing process, what testing method or methods it replaced, and what it was capable of doing.

In looking back at the digital camera projects, we were targeting the consumer photography market with the goal of displacing film with CCD or CMOS sensors and bringing to market a series of simple point-and-shoot digital cameras that didn't require the knowledge of f-stops, shutter speeds, focal lengths, or even ISO values. During the process of developing the cameras, it was incredibly tempting to try to keep up with all of the changing technologies every day, but the one I needed to understand deeply was just the sensor technology. For that project, my diagram looked like that shown in Figure 19-2.

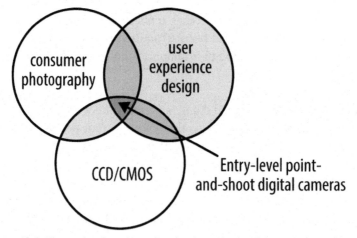

Figure 19-2. Target the domain and technology that really matters to your project

Parlez-vous français?

Now that you've identified what the domain and primary technology are for the project you're working on, you need to think about how you will gather information. For that, I believe that if you want to learn anything about any domain, technology, process, method, and so on, you must *take the time and effort to learn its language.*

The beginning of wisdom is to call things by their proper name
—CONFUCIUS

Learning the terminology, jargon, idioms, slang, and acronyms regularly used within a domain or technology is truly the decryption key to unlocking the knowledge within them. The language creates the scaffolding upon which you will build understanding and insights around processes, workflows, rationale for existing systems, cause-and-effect relationships, and so forth. How else will you effectively communicate with the engineers, scientists, fellow designers, and business people also working on the project if you don't understand what they're saying or can't share your thoughts using words they understand? This mantra is true regardless of whether you're embarking on a design project for an emerging technology or a mass market product. You need to have the tools to communicate effectively and that means learning the language.

In the case of technology, when I say language, I don't mean the programming language. I don't suggest you have to go learn C#, Python, or Java to be able to understand what an emerging technology can do or how it works. Although it's great if you do happen to know those languages, it's not a prerequisite to understanding the emerging technology for which you'll be designing.[13]

A lingo-to-English dictionary

If you understand how valuable it is to learn the vernacular to facilitate your rapid rise to expertise, you need strategies to actually learn it. My suggestion is that when you begin a design project, create a separate notebook or section of the notebook you're using for the project and dedicate it to capturing all of the lingo you encounter. (Evernote is a

---

13 Unless, of course, you're designing a UI for a new programming language toolkit. Then, by all means, learn the language, too.

great digital tool to use for this.) Then, during the project, write down every word, phrase, acronym, slang, jargon, reference, concept, method, or other terminology you encounter and don't understand, think you might understand but aren't completely sure, or want to understand more deeply, and take the time to add the definition or sketch an example of the term in the notebook.

Carry this notebook with you at all times.

Add to it, edit and update it, and review it regularly.

You'll find that this notebook will be invaluable to you as you will be constantly referring to it for help and reminders of what terms mean or how to use them. You might also find yourself adding color, additional explanation, or examples of use to the entries you have in there. In some cases, I have added little sketches to help me understand what certain terms were. I also found that some terms took longer to embed into my vocabulary than others. For example, throughout the genetic variant database project, terms I had to continually go to my notes for were phenotype, exome, SNP and dbSNP, and allele. Even though in some cases I was encountering them almost daily, they just wouldn't stick.

Eventually, as you progress through your project and better understand the domain and technology, your notebook will become less and less necessary to you. The information within it will have become second nature and you'll quickly find yourself spouting TLAs,[14] jargon, and idioms regularly without thinking about it. Congratulations! You're beginning to become an "expert"! From this point, your rate of learning will increase exponentially as you quickly add more and more details to fill the gaps in your understanding.

WHERE DO I GO FOR MY RESEARCH?

Now that you've established boundaries on what you need to know about the domain and technology to become an "expert" in the project, and prepared your notebook to capture the custom language you will be encountering throughout it, you need to think about where to go to get the information you need. Although it's tempting to just go straight to Google, type in some search terms, and let your "fingers

---

14 TLA is a three letter acronym for Three Letter Acronym.

do the walking," as the old advertisement used to say, you should take some time to plan how to find better and more relevant sources for the information you need.

There are three main ways you'll be regularly exposed to domain knowledge, technology expertise, and unique lingo while you're on the project, and coincidentally these happen to also be the three main sources you'll use to gain expertise: People, Product, and Publications.

People

If you don't have this already, you should quickly establish good relationships with the people on the project team. They will be your go-to sources for helping you understand the project, domain, and technology better by providing you relevant information you need to know quickly and easily. These folks can also introduce you to other people or resources in the organization that can also help you. Identify a triad of primary go-to people for the project, domain, and technology and help them help you. These are whom I call, respectively, the Business Maven, the subject matter expert (SME), and the Dev.

The Business Maven will help you understand who the users/customers are, what problems and pain points they believe those people have, what market segment the business is serving, and who they believe is their competition. The Business Maven will help ensure that the product or service you design meets their business goals. The SME is the person on the team who knows the subject or industry inside and out and can answer your questions, clarify your misunderstandings, and fill in your knowledge gaps. Finally, the Dev is the person on the team (typically a developer or a development manager) who knows the technology inside and out, and can answer questions about the technology stack, software or hardware capabilities and limitations, implementation details, and interdependencies within the product.

At the very beginning of a new project, there is a relatively short window during which you have carte blanche to ask "dumb" (in other words, basic) questions. Ask them early and often during this phase to any and all of your go-to people, and feel free to preempt the questions with, "OK, I have a dumb question..." The further along into the project you get, you'll be more comfortable with the material, the questions you ask will become more complex, and you'll begin to feel like and establish yourself as the design-domain expert with the team. It also holds, however, that you will be able to get away with asking fewer and fewer basic questions the further you are in the project without appearing like you haven't invested the time in learning the material, thereby losing credibility and respect.

A lot of new and unique terminology you encounter and capture in your notebook will originate from the project team. You will, of course, come across a lot of terms in your research, but because the team will be using them in context of their product and organization, they might use alternatives of some of the words that you won't find predominantly used elsewhere. For example, one of the most commonly used terms in genetics is "mutation," which means there was a mistake in the DNA replication process. The company I was working with preferred to use the term "variant" in their applications and processes—a more neutral sounding word—as they asserted that not all mistakes resulted in disease or a negative result, which the term "mutation" tended to infer.

Product

If there is an existing product that you will be either redesigning or to which you'll be adding new functionality, you're going to want to get your hands on it, in whatever form it currently is, to explore, use, and understand. Now, I'm not talking about running formative user feedback sessions or usability tests here. I'm talking about *you* using it *yourself* and becoming intimately familiar with it, including any help documentation that is provided with it. Even if it is barely functioning, tedious to use, and buggy as hell, you have to do it. You won't be shooting for Gladwell's 10,000 hours,[15] but you should be using it as often as possible at the beginning, if not daily, and continuing to use it throughout the project.

To begin, you are probably going need some kind of support from the team such as getting a test login or a test account set up. You might even be required to sign up on a schedule to use a prototype during an allocated time. This is common in hardware development where prototypes are being built out in mechanical and electrical engineering labs

---

15 In Malcolm Gladwell's book, *Outliers*, he repeatedly discusses how success or expertise comes with upwards of 10,000 hours of practice.

and teams can reserve time to use and test them. Here is where knowing the people on the team is quite helpful; ask your Dev for how to get access. He will point you to the process or the people who can help you.

It can certainly be interesting if there is no existing product for you to take advantage of. You will obviously have more to work with if there is one, but you can still learn quite a bit from using prototypes. If even those don't exist, see if the technologies that will be incorporated into your product are being used in other products inside the company you are working with and try to get your hands on those. There might be a proof of concept you can get a demonstration of too. Also, spend time researching what other companies are doing in that same space and how they are doing it.

When you do have an existing product to work with, you will want to approach getting to know it in two ways: temporally and in depth. Learning the step-by-step workflows to perform specific tasks and achieve certain objectives will help you design more elegant solutions or introduce automation and reduce steps in the process. Ask your SME for tutorials or Getting Started guides to help you with that. Dive deep into important areas of the product to understand more thoroughly how things work, what cause-and-effect relationships exist within the system, where the interdependencies are, and how functionality is compartmentalized.

You can choose to do these independently of one another—for example, workflow first and then deep dives—or simultaneously; there isn't really a best practice I recommend. Sometimes, busting through a workflow quickly and circling back later makes the most sense and other times diving deep is more relevant. I've also found myself mid-workflow where some behavior or action catches my attention and then I dive down into trying to figure it out. Do what feels most comfortable to you.

Publications
When you're not meeting the team, capturing and defining lingo, using the technology, asking "dumb" questions, or doing other design process–related things, you'll need to be researching and reading literature about the domain you identified earlier in the process that is historical, theoretical, academic, procedural, or technical in nature. So, where do you start?

First RTFM.[16] Or Help. You know, if there is any. Get your hands on materials from the Business Maven or any marketing folks on the team. Ask for release notes and PowerPoint slide decks. Even white papers or tech specs are helpful to better understand the technology you're working with. Read them, highlight terms or concepts that you need to define, and put them in your notebook. I find that the information in these internal documents is incredibly useful because it helps you understand the company's goals and their ideas for how they want people to use the technology they're building. You can gain an enormous amount of insight into the company, the market they are serving, and how they want to build and use technology to get there.

Secondly, ask your SME and your Dev for reading recommendations: appropriate books, trade magazines, and relevant and useful websites that might help you come up to speed faster. Limit the request by asking for the top two or three in each category that they think would be appropriate for someone like you coming into it fresh; remember you need to come up to speed quickly, not write a PhD dissertation.

Lastly, and only once you've gone through these steps and begun to create a good foundation of knowledge to build upon, you should feel confident in using the Internet effectively to fill the gaps in that knowledge and connect your existing dots. Jumping on Google, which is probably your first instinct when you start a new project, is not something I recommend doing until you know specifically what you need to find out. We all know that Internet is a huge time suck but, if you know what exactly the information you need to track down is, you will be much more efficient and effective during time online, thereby enabling your move up the expertise curve quickly.

STOP!

So, how expert is expert enough? There seems to be a point on the learning curve (see Figure 19-3) at which the rapid rate of increase finally levels off. This leveling off allows for peak performance (at that level) and efficiency in designing creatively and innovatively for the project.

---

16 Google it.

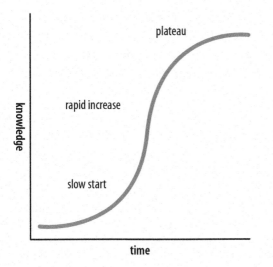

Figure 19-3: The learning curve of knowledge over time

I believe that there comes a point on the curve—somewhere around the plateau—at which you know so much about the domain that you begin to move away from being an impartial pillar of people-centered design and toward designing for maximum efficiencies in the domain and technology. At this point, you've become too much of an expert; you understand the system too well and are losing your ability to clearly distinguish between what is good for the people who will use the product you are designing and what is easiest for those who are building it.

This is when you find yourself supporting feature creep, designing workflows that are just a little bit too arduous or complex and justifying it by claiming that the users are "experts themselves," or even writing off user complaints as coming from those who "just don't get it" or who "need more training." Don't get me wrong, it's very important to balance ease-of-use and supporting user goals with the cost of implementation but, when the balance tips in the direction of the latter, you've become a superuser and you need to stop.

The duration of the plateau is likely dependent on a number of factors such as the complexity of the technology, the nature of the domain, and your own prior knowledge.

There are a few ways you can inject new thinking into your process and get back your focus on the user when this happens. You can't fix what you don't acknowledge, so assess the situation and recommit yourself to returning to creating a solid set of designs for the user. If the project hasn't ended yet you could do the following:

- Find inspiration from technological change in other domains, not just the one in which you are working. Read up on other emerging and evolving technologies and learn how people are changing their lives on a daily basis with them through online publications such as *Wired, Fast Company*, the *New York Times*, or the "Science and Technology" section of the *Economist*. Read about socioeconomic challenges. Explore Kickstarter for ideas.

- Research what some local startup incubators are doing. Go to local tech meetups. Get outside of your comfort zone and see what else is going on.

- Visit customers or beta users. Listen to what they have to say. Watch what they do. Ask them what they might do differently or what they need. You don't need to run any formal feedback sessions for this, just send an email, pick up the phone, schedule a Skype session, or drop by for a visit.

- Meet with the marketing team (if there is one) or your Business Maven and ask questions about the market, what else the end users are asking for, or where they think the business is going.

If you're working for an in-house design team and the project is coming to an end or has already concluded, look for another project to work on with a different technology or in a different domain. You might need to do a little political engineering to get yourself transferred or assigned to a different project but, if something else seems interesting to you, you should try. Longer term, you might need to think about moving on. Besides helping you grow as a designer, this will provide an opportunity for the organization you're currently in to bring in new blood and fresh thinking. Unless you know—or think you know—that you want to be working in that domain or with that technology for the next 20 years and potentially become an SME yourself, spending too much time in one domain could limit your career path from ever designing beyond that domain.

Obviously, if you're in an agency setting, this is less of a challenge because new projects come in regularly and you can get yourself assigned to one.

Onward

Before reading this chapter, your first instinct when beginning a new project with a new technology in an unfamiliar domain might have been to immediately jump over to your computer and surf Google until your eyes bled. It makes sense: we've learned that this oracle can tell you where to find anything you want to know—and then some. However true this is, by doing this you're diving headfirst into the abyss without a life line. Without having a sense of where you're trying to go or what you're trying to learn, you'll soon be drowning. And when you have to "become an expert" quickly, you don't have any time to waste.

Now, you have a better strategy to approach any new design project and feel confident that you can gain expertise in the domain and technology swiftly. You can use this framework to easily identify what you need to learn, where and how to get the information, and when to stop. You know to leverage the terminology for identifying things you need to understand, find the key people within the team who can help you, and use the existing product or technology to build your understanding. Finally, you know how to strategically utilize the Internet for additional literature research and fill gaps in your knowledge.

With practice, and whatever tweaks that need to be made along the way, this framework can serve you throughout your career, whether you work in startups, established companies, academia, or design agencies. You can use it for projects large and small, monumental or miniscule. I hope that you'll adopt it and adjust it to your needs. And please feel free to share with me how it works for you at *lisa@debettencourt.com*.

[20]

The Changing Role of Design

DIRK KNEMEYER

On the Impact of Emerging Technologies

At every point in human history, there are "emerging technologies." However, it is only at certain, critical moments that the confluence of emerging technologies dramatically alters the ways in which we live and the environments in which we live. We are in the midst of one such moment. To better understand it, we should understand other important markers of world-changing impact caused by emerging technology.

The printing press was a singular technology that permanently changed us from a species of near-ignorance to one that today has remarkably high levels of learning, education, and understanding. More than just being smarter, we were able to pursue higher-quality and more civilized lives in an increasingly universal way that previously was the domain of a privileged few. It is, in my opinion, the most important single technology that can be attributed to a specific time and person. This one machine took us from a species of relative ignorance and shocking inequality to one of knowledge, insight, and understanding.

The emerging technologies of today, a burst of advances crossing many fields without one being particularly dominant, is very different from the printing press. This dynamic shares more in common with the Industrial Revolution. Building from the enlightenment of the Scientific Revolution—just as we now are building from the enabling technology that is the Internet—dozens of technologies blossomed across a wide front of intellectual and practical concerns and in close proximity to one another. Together they created new structures and systems that gave rise to a world that is much more similar to our world today than that of just 50 years before. Manufacturing processes moved us from a largely agrarian existence and spawned the modern city. The steam engine made continental travel and transportation an easy—if technologically miraculous—practice. Harnessing electricity removed from us the yoke of the natural circadian rhythm while providing a power source that shaped the twentieth century. These are just a few among dozens of other important and contributory advances, both large and small.

History identifies the Industrial Revolution as having taken place roughly between 1760 and 1840. It is worth noting that, when the founding fathers of the United States ratified the first constitution in 1789, the Industrial Revolution was in full swing. Yet, they reflected almost nothing of the Industrial Revolution itself, nor of the new world it was about to enable. They rode around on horses, wore powdered wigs, lived on family farms, kept slaves, and generally led the same sort of privileged lives their English ancestors were living 500 years before. Less than 100 years after that first constitution, the world would not resemble that which they knew. Not only did the change happen quickly, not only was the change massive in breadth and scale, but even though they were in the middle of its happening—30 years after the now-acknowledged beginning of that period—none of them had the slightest idea how different the world to come was going to be.

This is the moment that faces us today. Our era, however it comes to be known many decades hence and after things are settled and decided, began with the Internet. While the technology dates back to the mid-twentieth century, the likely demarcation point will be in the 1980s or early 1990s, when access became available to the general consumer. Now, 20 years later, the emerging technologies of 2014 exist thanks to the Internet as a tool, but they reside in dozens of scientific fields and commercial markets. Since the general availability of the Internet, we've mapped the entire human genome. We've taken computers from being room-sized specific-purpose devices to something that fits in the palm of your hand as general purpose devices that a majority of American adults own and use heavily each and every day. We've developed computers that can defeat humans in chess and television game shows; cars that can drive themselves; space tourism; and synthetic limbs that propel Olympic-caliber athletes. The list goes on and on. All of these advances—some of which are seminal and others that are more incremental—are products of this interconnected time enabled by the Internet.

Yet, as remarkable as these things might be, we can't see the world to come yet. In 50 years, will I be a 90-year-old cyborg, able to continue living a vibrant life thanks to replacing my decaying natural matter with synthetic parts? Will our living spaces be smart, interactive, digital homes that relegate drywall, plaster, and brick to the category of quaint remembrances from a bygone era? Will massive desalination plants ship fresh water from our oceans to people around the world, rendering obsolete those old concerns about the decreasing supply of fresh water? Will our great grandchildren be the product of genetic selection and usher in what will be a new race of perfected and optimized humans? Many of these ideas sound like they are out of science fiction. Yet, the emerging technologies of today make each of these things possible, if not likely, within the next 50 years. We cannot truly imagine what *that* world will look like, imagining all of these technologies and dozens more we are not even able to see. They will change the world at a scale comparable to the Industrial Revolution.

We're at the beginning of it all, a remarkably exciting time of discovery and intellectual adventure. And, it is one that readers of this book have the opportunity to help shape.

THE CHANGING ROLE OF DESIGN

This century, with the proliferation of the Internet in general and the shift from thick to thin software applications in particular, technology has spurred a seismic shift in the very function and meaning of being a professional designer. Specifically, the role of designer has lurched from that of artist or author to that of facilitator and translator. Today, people who professionally use some permutation of the title "designer" in the professional creation of digital products and services are more likely to have a liberal arts degree than they are to have attended design school. Twenty years ago this would have been heretical; today it is the standard.

This shift from designer as creator to designer as facilitator is only going to accelerate in the emerging technologies–fueled decades to come. It is akin to the shift in academic knowledge and research over the past 100 years. Until the 1920s having a single academic author on an important research paper was the norm. This changed because the complexity of more advanced scientific knowledge moved beyond the point where a single individual could independently contribute meaningful new knowledge to the overall body. Indeed, as the years pass, the list of authors generally attached to significant new scientific research grows longer and longer. Due to the nature of scientific inquiry becoming increasingly complex and built on the foundation that preceded it, this is a trend that will only accelerate as time passes.

Considering now the world of digital products, even 20 years ago devices were relatively unsophisticated. They shared far more in common with the antique computers that would fill an entire building of the 1950s than the smartphones most of us have today. Since then, massive improvements in a litany of modest technologies—from battery power, to LCD screens, to random access memory (RAM), to hard drive speed and size—have come together with advances in material science to result in a device that is remarkably advanced compared to the devices of just a decade ago. If you were to consider this in a vacuum, this is a truly momentous advance; yet, what is really intriguing is that it is only an infinitesimal example of progress within the context of all the emerging technologies converging at the moment.

We have robotics crashing together with synthetic biology crashing together with these same handheld digital devices. Engineers dedicate their careers to expertise in just one of—or perhaps even a subset within—those fields. How are we to envision the potential of those combinations? From whom and how are we to take someone else's vision and design as the best possible solution to exploit the opportunity? Who will take an existing solution bringing these things together and redesign it comprehensively to make it better, and how are we to take that? These are the challenges posed to designers, and they are being framed in contexts of compounding complexity.

Do you consider yourself a professional designer who could be considered an expert in the field of robotics? Are you an expert in materials science? How about handheld digital products? Are you a subject matter expert in synthetic biology? If your answer to all of these was yes, the world is your oyster and at some point in the near future you should have the opportunity to simply print money, owing to how desirable you will be in the job market; congratulations to your heirs. For everyone else—who I'm imagining is all of us—this quandary outlines the essential challenge: how do we become suitably expert in the fields relevant to the domains that will produce the most interesting and lucrative future opportunities?

I went into software design in 2004. That largely meant designing user interfaces. It did not take me more than a couple of years to develop legitimate expertise in that field. Yet, the lack of complexity inherent in those challenges from 10 years ago is almost laughable from where we are today. Hardware design was explicitly separate and outside the reach of my influence; today the integration of software and hardware is a first-order concern. Vertical contexts had to do with domains and users; today, they relate to advanced technologies and sophisticated scientific influences. Even though these differences might not seem significant as words on the page, they are vast. Vastly vast!

Today, those differences have had minimal impact upon the designer or design process. There might be some additional context introduced. Designers and other people involved in the research, planning, and creationary process might be getting some education or trying to build some knowledge. But, it's guerilla at best and haphazard at worst. We are still flopping around in the same limited, narrow ways that worked well a decade ago but are now woefully behind the opportunity and challenge before us, one that increases in difficulty each day.

In the more distant past of hardware and software design, the engineers were the designers. The role of a dedicated designer had to do with user needs. Ergonomics and aesthetics came later. And it happened for a good reason: most engineers were terrible designers! The things that made them brilliant and exceptional as engineers did not translate into the skills that became the pillars of the supporting design disciplines. To have something that was both appropriately powerful and designed to maximum usability, usefulness, and desirability, it took more people and skills. Yet as challenging as these things so recently seemed, they are child's play compared to what is coming tomorrow. The question now is this: how do we anticipate and get ahead of this instead of spending the next decade thrashing around, missing opportunities, and making unnecessarily bad things?

Design Complexity and Emerging Technologies

There are two fundamental issues regarding the design of emerging technologies: the convergence of disparate technologies, and the increasing scientific and engineering complexity required to work with each of those technologies.

Famously, creation at Apple Inc. after the return of Steve Jobs in 1997 had been largely credited to Jobs or Jonathan Ive. Jobs was the hero of the masses, the visionary who saw the right confluence of technologies and market opportunity to make the iPod a phenomenon and follow that up with an entire decade of meaningful innovation. Jobs is thought of as an entrepreneur given the market success of Apple Inc., but he was more rightly an inventor in the ilk of Thomas Edison, if not a designer. Jobs excelled at not just looking across various technologies and identifying sweet spots, but tying those into the needs and desires of people. Jonathan Ive, a trained industrial designer, is more deeply knowledgeable in the materials science and engineering relative to actually having those products get made. The getting it done, the fit-and-finish, the vision-to-reality: these are the contributions of Ive. Together, Jobs and Ive made Apple the preeminent business case of the 2000s. And they did it by inventing, innovating, and making better stuff.

As we look to the future, there are two important things to note about the partnership that existed between Jobs and Ive.

First are the very different skills they brought to the table. Whereas dividing the labor into vision and execution is perhaps an oversimplification and not doing justice to the totality of either of their contributions, creation in emerging technologies will generally require similar bifurcation. It will be uncommon that any one individual has the broad cross-technology vision and insight into markets and cultures to imagine the correct future solutions on one hand, while also having the deep scientific and engineering knowledge to wrangle the vision into reality on the other. As such, their partnership serves as a guide for what next-generation creation—from A to Z—looks like.

Second is that people filling these same roles in the future will need to have dramatically more knowledge and experience than Jobs and Ive did. Although Jobs and Ive had knowledge of related fields such as computer hardware, software, and materials science, the exceptional advances of the future will require knowledge and experience that bring together diverse fields that are less initially synergistic or immediately obvious. Even though Jobs and Ive were able to author a world of portable music players, incrementally better computers, and exceptional handheld computing devices, it is unlikely that they—given their particular training and experiences—could have brought us the killer products that will arise from an understanding of the genome, synthetic biology, and handheld computers.

Whereas great design in the past was typically credited to a single vision—what is now often derisively referred to as "genius design"—we are in the midst of a decade-long trend toward highly specialized design teams that might or might not have strong, visionary leadership. These are your typical "UX teams," those that banded together within the cult of "human-centered design" and now continue to practice similar approaches while changing their self-description to better conform to the dogma of the day. This shift superficially seems to be the result of the increased complexity that software forces design to deal with. This is an easy myth to ascribe to, and one that is further comforting thanks to the so-called scientific approaches offered by metrics-based processes such as usability testing. However, in reality this shift is an issue of scale: there are so few strong, talented creative leaders that to get decent software done, larger teams of narrow talent were required.

This is certainly a fine solution to get around the lack of qualified talent, but in the process, we've lost sight of the reality that vision-driven design is both more efficient and ultimately effective than the assembly-line approach employed by most large organizations. The paradox, though, is that increasingly fewer people will be capable of delivering such leadership as the complexity of emerging technologies compounds. The suboptimal process of today, although not deserving of its role as the idealized structure for design and user experience, has provided models that will serve the new world well.

Design Trends for Emerging Technologies

I mentioned earlier that engineers used to design software user interfaces without the involvement of any designers. Get ready for more of that. Designers today lack deep knowledge and experience in the foundational scientific fields behind currently emerging technologies and, in most cases, even lack broad knowledge from which to apply a Jobsian vision to a good opportunity.

ENGINEERS AS VISIONARIES AND CREATORS

As they have in so many other fields before, the engineers will step in and provide their own product visions and designs, thank you very much. Sure, standalone "designers" will have some input into industrial design or user experience, but the big problem solving, the fun problem solving, the stuff that changes markets and reshapes the way we think about the world, is going to come from the people who understand what it is that is being crafted.

Everyone understands software as a user to some degree—or advertising, or handheld devices. We know what works for us and what does not, what we like and what we do not like. Expanded to genetics and synthetic biology, the interesting decisions will have already been made by the lead engineers. If I had a child in junior high school who was interested in creating things having to do with technology I would encourage her to go into an engineering field relating to emerging technologies—not design. From there, she can establish a beachhead toward the sort of deep and broad knowledge that will define the next generation of iconic business leaders and world-changing designers in the decades to come.

DESIGNERS AS ENGINEERS

When I founded Involution Studios, it was in partnership with Andrei Herasimchuk. For someone who came out of academia, advertising agencies, and web design shops (me...) this was like a university student learning Renaissance art from Michelangelo. Andrei dropped out of college to help build and serve as the designer for Specular International, an early computer graphics software company. Adobe Systems poached Andrei from Specular in 1995, where he became the first designer ever in the 13-year-old software company. Like virtually all software companies at the time, Adobe Systems had its design done by its engineers by default. Not only did Andrei design Adobe's key applications, he came up with the design strategy that resulted in the Creative Suite, a software bundle that enabled Adobe to crush its vertical competitors.

Back then, Andrei always had counter-cultural opinions that the rank-and-file disagreed with—loudly. That's because Andrei was interested in truth and progress, which often necessarily threatens the quiet status quo that envelops the simply mediocre in a blanket of security. Perhaps Andrei's most emphatic point was that the digital product designers of the future would have to code to stay relevant. This made perfect sense to me, and I joined him in treating this as a key tenet in our shared vision for the future of digital product design. At the time, we were ridiculed. Designers code? Heresy! Of course, a funny thing happened: 10 years later, designers are coding. It is not controversial; it is obvious. Instead of our being remembered as visionaries the new world we foretold carries on acting like everyone thought it was obvious in the first place. As if!

That evolution in digital product design—from designers as "designers only" to designers also being developing engineers—was inevitable. As industrial designers well know, you cannot competently create without a thorough understanding of the science and engineering underpinning what it is you are creating. As software design pulled so-called web designers from the shiny confines of their style-driven medium into a more complex and behavior-driven context, this became all too clear. Now, we are moving to digital experiences that synthesize with the most advanced fields of human endeavor. The requirements that pulled designers, artists, and stylists to take an interest in computer science and programming languages will pull the next generation into a far more diverse tableau of sciences that relate to biology, neuroscience, and the essential human condition.

ENGINEERS AS SCIENTISTS

See a pattern emerging? There is a long tradition of software engineers who have degrees in both computer science and the liberal arts. For example, my friend Soren Johnson has degrees in both history and computer science. This served him well in becoming one of the most successful computer game designers (as someone who both designed and engineered) of his generation, contributing to projects such as Spore and helming the fourth generation of the Civilization series. If fact, it is now dogma that to be a great computer game designer you must be engineering your games. Although this sort of background will remain a strong one for people in Soren's specific medium of computer games, the many software engineers involved in companies impacted by emerging technologies will need to have broader and deeper scientific and engineering training if they want to participate in architecture and design. Otherwise, they will be limited to being coders. There is nothing wrong with that; we will need millions of them in the world to keep up with the spiking demand of digital products and services.

But, if you want to be a leader, or just want to be someone who creates as opposed to implements, significantly more scientific knowledge is where it is at.

User Experience: Finding Its Level

The rise of *user experience* (UX) in the 2000s was the culmination of more than a decade's scrappy growth since Don Norman normalized the term as a professional at—ironically—Apple Inc. That growth was about formalizing and professionalizing the shift from engineer as designer, and visionary and/or designer as senior genius, to a systematized process with various specialties and a myriad of actors. Over the past 10 years, UX has shifted from being the clear unifying field of the software design intelligentsia to a ubiquitous concern that even CEOs will ask for by name. Yet, still fledgling in the greater scheme of things, it is only now, in 2014, that educational organizations that seem able to be sustainable for the long term are bubbling up in the United States to offer certification-style UX courses outside of academia.

During this same timeframe, UX became a synonym for "design" in the realm of digital design. In many cases it has replaced design: "We need UX!" is a common turn-of-phrase in software organizations. To what degree design is articulated within a software organization, it is usually framed as being UX. Design is reduced to the graphic design component that is part of a larger train of activities ranging from research to content organization to interaction architecture to user testing. In the process, design is relegated to the most tactical of concerns amidst a process which, even while now legitimated, exists on the fringes of business compared to more traditional and left-brained considerations.

How unfortunate! That the rise of a more procedural approach to design would reduce "design" to something so un-Jobs-ian or un-Ive-ian!

What is called design, and what the tasks happening around the intersections of science, engineering, and design are going to be called, I really have no idea. They will percolate up from those convergence points in serendipitous ways and have some meaning native to their context or the people responsible for them. UX will be a second-order priority and most likely broken into some pieces. For example research, a discipline often relegated to UX-like parts of an organization, is a highest-order priority, with application from the boardroom down to the most menial of concerns. As knowledge and insight become increasingly important to every aspect of a company, research will be elevated and expanded. With design coming from places far afield from the UX function, we will return to a more standard and sane conception of design relative to other priorities.

For its part, the most valuable long-term impacts of UX are likely to be procedural. The injection of design and UX into the core product process was a lubricant for engineering and product organizations broadly shifting to Agile development methodologies. Also, the model for assembly-line design as frequently practiced within UX will prove essential in the much larger and extended design teams of the future that synthesize more complex digital products. The lessons of how engineering and UX work together; how research, information architecture, and interaction design create synergy; how people with very different skills and ways of thinking can coalesce in cross-disciplinary ways to contribute to something far larger than would otherwise be possible. And even though UX should continue filling a functional role at the intersection of what is being created and the users of it, no one reading this should be surprised if "design" in a broader sense lives in a very different place.

The Future for Me, the Future for You

At 41 years of age, the opportunity for me to participate professionally in the future design landscape of emerging technologies has passed. My university training is not conducive to it. My family responsibilities do not afford me the luxury to try and accrue the significant additional knowledge required. And, it is not clear to me that I would try even if I could. However, as I've watched the confluence of emerging technologies in recent years I've thought about what I would like to be doing professionally if I could start over. Without question, the problem I would be most interested in helping to solve is developing artificial intelligence in the abstract, or robots in a more concrete manifestation, which fully replace the human brain. This is not an "if" pursuit for humanity; it is a "when." It is one in which I have a keen interest and, from the standpoint of behavioral psychology, insight.

To be the primary vision setter in such an endeavor I would need some significant degree of training in all of neuroscience, computer science, synthetic biology, behavioral psychology, and materials science. If this vision were to manifest in a robot as opposed to software, I would need training in robotics, as well. I would further benefit from hands-on experience being part of less sophisticated artificial intelligence systems—which nonetheless would be far advanced from what we have today—as well as the creation of some kind of physical products that integrated with or were built upon foundations of human biology. Although proper training, pure genius, and dumb luck—the last being the secret sauce behind more of the best technology companies than you might imagine—could potentially enable a young turk to be the visionary solving this problem, the complexity and perhaps even wisdom required to get it right will likely transcend what the inexperienced can do. After all, Steve Jobs himself could be dismissed as a glorified marketer... that is, until his second act at Apple, well after the gray was creeping in.

What do you want to create in the world? If it is technologically advanced, and you want to be on the vision side of things, get ready for a great deal more science and engineering than you might have once imagined. However, if you are content working on older technologies or prefer to be part of an implementation process as opposed to toward the frontmost visionary contributors, the good news is there is going to be plenty of work to go around for those who are smart, hard-working, and curious.

[*Appendix A*]

Companies, Products, and Links

Throughout this book, the authors have discussed a variety of companies and products to illustrate important concepts in and approaches to designing for emerging technologies. The following list of these companies and products, ordered alphabetically, contains relevant links to further information.

PRODUCT	COMPANY	URL
Ambient Umbrella	Ambient Devices	*http://www.ambientdevices.com/*
Arduino	Arduino	*http://www.arduino.cc/*
Areo	GameDesk	*http://gamedesk.org/project/aero/*
Athos Gear	Mad Apparel, Inc.	*http://www.liveathos.com/*
Baxter	Rethink Robotics	*http://www.rethinkrobotics.com/baxter/*
BioHarness	Zephyr Technology Corp.	*http://zephyranywhere.com/products/ bioharness-3/*
Bluetooth necklace	CSR	*http://www.csr.com/news/pr/2014/ bluetooth-smart-jewellery*
BodyMedia FIT	BodyMedia, Inc.	*http://www.bodymedia.com/*
CastAR	Technical Illusions	*http://technicalillusions.com/*
Davinci Systems	Intuitive Surgical, Inc.	*http://www.davincisurgery.com/ da-vinci-surgery/da-vinci-surgical-system/*
Digital Construction Platform	MIT Media Lab, Mediated Matter Group	*http://matter.media.mit.edu/tools/details/ boom-arm*
Drum Pants	Drum Pants	*http://www.drumpants.com/*
FitBark dog activity monitor	FitBark	*http://www.fitbark.com/*
Fitbit	Fitbit, Inc.	*http://www.fitbit.com/*

PRODUCT	COMPANY	URL
Fitbit Flex	Fitbit, Inc.	*http://www.fitbit.com/flex*
Flyfit Smart Ankle Tracker	Flyfit, Inc.	*http://www.myflyfit.com/*
FRIDA	ABB	*http://new.abb.com/products/robotics*
Galaxy Gear	Samsung	*http://www.samsung.com/us/guide-to-galaxy-smart-devices/galaxy-gear.html*
GlassUp	GlassUp	*http://www.glassup.net*
Google Glass	Google	*https://www.google.com/glass/start/*
HRP-4C	National Institute of Advanced Industrial Science and Technology (AIST)	*http://www.aist.go.jp/aist_e/latest_research/2009/20090513/20090513.html*
inFORM Dynamic Shape Display	MIT Media Lab, Tangible Media Group	*http://tangible.media.mit.edu/project/inform/*
iRobot 510 PackBot	iRobot Corporation	*http://www.irobot.com/For-Defense-and-Security/Robots/510-PackBot.aspx#PublicSafety*
iRobot 710 Kobra (formerly Warrior)	iRobot Corporation	*http://www.irobot.com/For-Defense-and-Security/Robots/710-Kobra.aspx#PublicSafety*
June	Netatmo	*https://www.netatmo.com/en-US/product/june*
Kompai	Robosoft	*http://www.robosoft.com/*
Kuka Control Panel	KUKA Roboter GmbH	*http://www.kuka-robotics.com/en/*
Leap Motion Controller	Leap Motion, Inc.	*https://www.leapmotion.com/*
LG Lifeband	LG Electronics	*http://www.lg.com/us/lifeband/index.jsp*
littleBits	littleBits Electronics, Inc.	*http://littlebits.cc/*
LMS400 Laser Scanner	SICK AG	*https://www.mysick.com/*
Lumo Back	Lumo BodyTech, Inc.	*http://www.lumobodytech.com/lumoback/*
LWR-5	KUKA Roboter GmbH	*http://www.kuka-labs.com/en/service_robotics/lightweight_robotics/*

PRODUCT	COMPANY	URL
M100	Vuzix	*http://www.vuzix.com/*
MakerBot	MakerBot Industries, LLC	*http://www.makerbot.com/*
MEMI smartbracelet	Two Tin Cans, LLC	*http://www.hellomemi.com/*
Meta AR	Meta Company	*https://www.spaceglasses.com/*
Metria IH1	Astutecare	*http://www.astutecare.com/metria-ih1/*
Mimo baby monitor	Rest Devices, Inc.	*http://mimobaby.com/*
Minotaur Head with Lamella	MIT Media Lab, Mediated Matter Group	*http://matter.media.mit.edu/tools/details/ minotaur-head-with-lamella*
Mio LINK heart rate wristband	Mio Global	*http://www.mioglobal.com/Mio-LINK-Heart-Rate-Band-Grey/Product. aspx?ProductID=14*
Montessori beads	Montessori Outlet	*http://www.montessorioutlet.com*
Montessori cylinder blocks	Montessori Outlet	*http://www.montessorioutlet.com*
Motion Math	Motion Math	*http://motionmathgames.com/*
Moto 360	Motorola	*https://moto360.motorola.com/*
Multisense-S7, 3D sensor	Carnegie Robotics LLC	*http://carnegierobotics.com/ multisense-s7/*
Myo Arm Band	Thalmic Labs	*http://www.thalmic.com/*
Nabu	Razer, Inc.	*http://www.razerzone.com/nabu*
nECG	Nuubo	*http://www.nuubo.com/?q=en/node/165*
Nike+ Fuelband	Nike, Inc.	*http://www.nike.com/us/en_us/c/ nikeplus-fuelband*
Notch activity tracker	Notch Interfaces, Inc.	*http://www.wearnotch.com/*
nVista HD	Inscopix	*http://inscopix.com/*
Nymi bracelet	Bionym, Inc.	*http://www.getnymi.com/*
Objet500 Connex	Stratasys Ltd.	*http://www.stratasys.com/3d-printers/ design-series/objet-connex500*
Oculus Rift	Oculus VR, LLC	*http://www.oculus.com/*

PRODUCT	COMPANY	URL
PC Robot	Parallax, Inc.	http://www.parallax.com/product/28992
Peak	BASIS, An Intel Company	http://www.mybasis.com/
Pebble Steel	Pebble	https://getpebble.com/steel
Pebble Watch	Pebble	https://getpebble.com/
PR2	Willow Garage	https://www.willowgarage.com/pages/pr2/overview
REEM-C	PAL Robotics	http://reemc.pal-robotics.com/en/
RefView 2.0, Fanuc Robot programmer interface	Thinkbot Solutions	http://www.thinkbotsolutions.com/
Robonaut	NASA/General Motors	http://robonaut.jsc.nasa.gov/
Roomba 880	iRobot Corporation	http://www.irobot.com/For-the-Home/Vacuum-Cleaning/Roomba
RPVita	InTouch Technologies, Inc.	http://www.intouchhealth.com/products-and-services/products/rp-vita-robot/
Senseg FeelScreen	Senseg	http://www.senseg.com
Shine	Misfit Wearables	http://www.misfitwearables.com/products/shine
Sifteo Cubes	Sifteo, Inc.	https://www.sifteo.com/cubes
Silk Pavillion	MIT Media Lab, Mediated Matter Group	http://matter.media.mit.edu/ee.php/environments/details/silk-pavillion
SmartWatch	Sony	http://www.sonymobile.com/us/products/accessories/smartwatch/
Sproutling baby monitor	Sproutling	http://www.sproutling.com/
Tactus Intelligent Surface	Tactus Technology, Inc.	http://tactustechnology.com/
Totoya Creatures	Carnation Group	http://www.totoyacreatures.com/
UBR-1	Unbounded Robotics	http://unboundedrobotics.com/ubr-1/

PRODUCT	COMPANY	URL
UP	Jawbone	*https://jawbone.com/up*
UR5	Universal Robotics	*http://www.universal-robots.com/GB/Products.aspx*
Withings Pulse	Withings	*http://www.withings.com/us/withings-pulse.html*
WorkerBot	pi4	*http://www.pi4.de/english/products/pi4-workerbot.html*
YOXO	Play from Scratch, LLC	*https://playfromscratch.com/yoxo/*

[Index]

Rubin, Andy, 4
Runaround, 350

S

safety standard tests, toys, 238
safety systems, robotics, 143–154
Samsung
  Galaxy Gear smartwatch, 67–68,
    86
  Galaxy smartphone, 43
  Mahru research robot, 149
scale variety (design tenet), 16–18
Scanadu, 284
Schilling, Ron, 183
Schulze, Jack, 338
science, designers influence on
    scientific community,
    342–343
scientific complexity, emerging
    technologies, 431–433
scientific models, visualization
    design, 188–193
  creating model
    visualizations, 189–192
  simplicity and prediction, 192
  yt project, 192–193
screens (embeddables), 211–212
scrolling, gesture interaction case
    study, 52–54
scrubbing audio recordings,
    pressure-sensitive tablet
    computers, 266
S-curve, toy design, 239–241
SDL (self-directed learning),
    designing learning
    objects, 131
seasonal nature, toy industry, 238
Seeed, 127
self-actualization, robotics
    design, 362
self-directed learning (SDL),
    designing learning
    objects, 131
self-esteem, robotics design, 362
semi-automatic operation,
    microinteractions, 104
Senseg, 125
sensors
  extended human,
    embeddables, 219
  Lumoback posture sensor, 89

musical instrument design,
    262–264
PIR (Passive Infrared), 229
robotics, 151
toy design, 248–250
sensory augmentation, 215
separate visual field display, 102–103
Shaping Things, 313
Sharklet Safe Touch, 30
Sharklet Technologies, 29
shark skin, properties, 29
SICK, LMS400 measurement
    system, 146
Sifteo cubes, 128
Silk Pavilion, 398
silkworms study, parallelization of
    additive fabrication,
    398–399
Silly Putty, 247
size, full interactive display
    devices, 97–100
sketching with code, 226–227
Skillman, Sam, 192
skin indicators (embeddables),
    211–212
skin marks, history of, 209–210
skin-top computers,
    embeddables, 221
Skylanders: Spyro's Adventure, 244
Skytree, 198
Slippery Liquid-Infused Porous
    Surfaces (SLIPS)
    material, 30–31
SLIPS (Slippery Liquid-Infused
    Porous Surfaces)
    material, 30–31
SMALLab Learning, 130
Smarcos Project, 342
smartglasses (wearable
    technology), 69–71, 97
smart pointer, gesture interaction
    case study, 54–57
SmartThings, 298
smartwatches (wearable
    technology), 67–68, 97
SMBHs (super-massive black
    holes), 190
SME (subject matter expert), gaining
    domain knowledge, 419
social cues, robots, 351–352
social skills, robotics, 148–154

[*About the Authors*]

Stephen P. Anderson is a speaker and consultant based in Dallas, Texas. He spends unhealthy amounts of time thinking about design, psychology, and leading entrepreneurial teams—topics he frequently speaks about at national and international events.

Stephen recently published the Mental Notes card deck, a tool to help businesses use psychology to design better experiences. And, he's currently writing a book on "Seductive Interactions" that will explore this topic of psychology and design in more detail.

Prior to venturing out on his own, Stephen spent more than a decade building and leading teams of information architects, interaction designers and user interface (UI) developers. He's designed web applications for businesses such as Nokia, Frito-Lay, Sabre Travel Network, and Chesapeake Energy, as well as a number of smaller technology startups.

Stephen likes to believe that someday he'll have the time to start blogging again.

A German-born independent design consultant based in London, **Martin Charlier** is a designer with experience across new media art, industrial design, interaction design, and design research. His speculative design work has been awarded by the Royal Society of Arts, where he is also a fellow.

He has previously worked at innovation firm frog design, cutting-edge art collective rAndom International, and digital service design consultancy Fjord. While at Fjord, he was involved in the EU-funded Smarcos research project investigating design for the Internet of Things. With his broad range of design skills, Martin's focus is on holistic product and service experiences spanning the digital and the physical.

Acknowledgements For debating and challenging my ideas, I'd like to thank Anab Jain, Anders Mellbratt, Devraj Joshi, Freya Dobrindt, Jack Schulze, Matti Keltanen, Olivia Solon, Rachel Armstrong, Stuart Wood, and Tom Metcalfe.

Lisa deBettencourt is a specialist in design strategy with an extensive track record of turning insight into groundbreaking systems, products, and services that delight. She takes a holistic approach to understanding and unraveling complex problems and utilizes unique ideation and collaboration methods to lead teams in solving them creatively.

Lisa has worked with major companies to define, design, and develop distinctive—and often disruptive—user experiences. Ferrari, Bose, Autodesk, Walgreens, and Partners Healthcare are some who have entrusted her with crafting elegant designs for their new products. Recently, she has been working closely with smaller companies in the emerging and disruptive technologies space—genomics, 3D printing, healthcare, education, and Internet of Things—to help them jump the chasm from über-geek technology to desirable product that serves real human needs.

Lisa holds a MS in human factors in information design from Bentley University and a BS in imaging and photographic technology from the Rochester Institute of Technology. She is a cofounder of the Interaction Designers Association (IxDA) as well as the founder of its Boston chapter. She holds several patents.

Acknowledgments There is always something being invented, adapted, or repurposed in the tech space for new and interesting uses. A 3D printer that prints a trachea to save a baby's life. Drones mounted with high definition video cameras that capture amazing bird's eye views of unseen places. Self-driving cars to get a little more work done on the way to the office. The demand for smart, talented designers who can also work on these kinds of complex projects has never been greater and will only continue to grow. It is up to us to rise to the challenge and keep our skills sharp.

A big thank you to Jon Follett for convincing me to get my thoughts on how designers can quickly gain domain expertise out of my head and onto paper. It's one thing to have personal ideas and techniques, and quite another to try to assemble them into somewhat coherent sentences and put them out there for all the world to read. Jon's own writing is consistently thought provoking, fresh, and inspirational, and his work sets a high bar for comparison. I am thrilled to be a part of his project and to contribute to the larger design and emerging technology communities through this book.

Lastly and most importantly, a special thanks goes out to my husband Chris who helped me carve out the time to write this chapter, even when it disrupted our already full and hectic family schedule. I couldn't have done it without his support.

Jeff Faneuff was the Director of Software Engineering at Rethink Robotics during the development and launch of the groundbreaking Baxter humanoid robot for use in manufacturing and packaging. Baxter was named a 2013 Award Finalist by the internationally renowned Edison Awards. Jeff has more than 20 years' experience developing software and user interfaces including the fields of scientific computing, audio entertainment systems, and robotics. He led the team that developed the software user interface for the Bose Videowave TV, which received PC Magazine's Editors' Choice Award in 2011. He also coauthored patents and papers related to speech recognition. Jeff received his master's degree in electrical engineering from Worcester Polytechnic Institute and is completing an MBA in entrepreneurship at Babson College. He is currently the director of engineering at Carbonite, Inc, which is a leader in computer backup systems and business continuity solutions.

Acknowledgements   I'd like to thank my wonderful wife, Wendy, for her edits and patience. My colleagues at Rethink Robotics deserve credit for their insights, experiments, and pioneering efforts.

Jonathan Follett is a principal at Involution Studios where he is a designer, business lead, and internationally published author on the topics of user experience and information design. He has contributed to online and print publications including A List Apart, UX Matters, and *Beautiful Data: The Stories Behind Elegant Data Solutions*, published by O'Reilly Media.

Over his 15 year design career, he has contributed to beautiful, usable software for enterprise, healthcare, and emerging technology clients, from the Fortune 500 to the market leaders of the future. Jon is a classically trained pianist who dreams of one day having a family rock band with his two sons.

Andy Goodman is a futurist. He's been a digital native since 1994, when he wrote a documentary called *Secrets of the Internet*. Along with his love of digital, scientists inspire him: brilliant people who make discoveries that transform reality. Now, as one of the early pioneers of the service design industry, Andy helps transform the world's biggest brands through innovative design.

After spending years in the games and interactive television industries, Andy joined Fjord in London. He later founded Fjord's Madrid studio where he has led them to become one of the most sought-after design agencies in Spain, working with clients such as BBVA and Telefónica.

Andy is an expert in mobile and a frequent speaker at global conferences and events including TED, SxSW, IXDA, and DMI. When he isn't thinking about the future, he's in his own lab working on the perfect curry recipe.

Over the past two decades, **Camille Goudeseune** has authored and coauthored dozens of scholarly papers and book chapters on the topics of multimedia analysis and virtual reality. His programming experience ranges from Microsoft Word for DOS through opera CD-ROMs to real-time audio analysis and synthesis. He holds a B.Math., an M.Mus in piano, and a DMA in music composition.

Besides his 9-to-5 job managing high-end VR at the Beckman Institute's Illinois Simulator Lab, he moonlights weeknights as the lead programmer for the radio-control flight simulator FS One, and weekends as music director at St. Elizabeth of Hungary Parish in Thomasboro, Illinois.

Bill Hartman is the director of research at Essential, a design consultancy developing physical products, digital products, and service experiences. Bill's user-centered design contributions have inspired innovations in a range of industries. He is an expert in the fields of ethnographic research and collaborative design methods, humanizing technology in compelling and differentiated ways. His research and strategy work with clients such as Genzyme, Philips Healthcare, Sonos, Kohler, and GE, has identified new opportunities for design, catalyzing breakthrough product and service opportunities in a range of industries. He was formerly a director of user experience at Razorfish and an independent research and design consultant. Bill is also an adjunct lecturer at Bentley University's Human Factors and Information Design graduate program. He holds degrees from Davidson College and the Institute of Design in Chicago.

As Senior Industry Programs Manager with Autodesk, a leading provider of software, Erin Rae Hoffer, AIA, fosters the adoption of innovative approaches to building design and operations through industry research, presentations, and publications. An architect with 25 years' experience in technology and computer-aided design, Erin served as executive vice-president with the Boston Architectural College and was on the board of directors of the Boston Society of Architects as commissioner of technology. She led technology organizations for Harvard, MIT, and Tufts University. Erin received a masters in architecture from UCLA and an MBA from MIT's Sloan School of Management. She is a LEED accredited professional, is registered to practice architecture in California and is a Ph.D. candidate in Northeastern University's program of Law and Public Policy.

Acknowledgements For the flame under a simmering vision of the next era, I'd like to acknowledge Phil Bernstein and the Autodesk strategy team. Thanks to Jonathan Follett and Lisa deBettencourt for bringing the architects into the conversation.

Steven Keating is a mechanical engineering doctoral candidate at the MIT Media Lab's Mediated Matter group. He is invigorated by creativity, design, and maple syrup. An alumnus of Queen's University in Canada, he holds two bachelors degrees, one in mechanical and materials engineering, the other in film. Viewing diversity as essential to creativity, Steven's past research interests have ranged from photovoltaic fabrication, to archeological reconstruction, to novel forms of animation. At MIT, Steven is currently investigating new frontiers of digital fabrication and bio-inspired design. In his current graduate work, he has authored numerous peer-reviewed publications, holds multiple patents, and has been a lecturer for three MIT design and engineering courses.

Acknowledgements   Work explored in this chapter focused on recent research from our university lab group, Mediated Matter, and my doctoral work on introducing new scales in fabrication. The work presented in this chapter was conducted with a number of colleagues and associations that deserve acknowledgements and kind thanks. The presented work was conducted with the Mediated Matter Research Group, lead by Dr. Neri Oxman at the MIT Media Lab. The Digital Construction Platform project was funded with support from the NSF EAGER Grant (Award No. #1152550) and technical/material support from Altec, Inc., and BASF Corporation. Thanks to John Klein (Mediated Matter), David Boger (Altec), and Marc Schroeder (BASF) for their work with the Digital Construction Platform. The research on combining one and two photon printing systems was conducted with Will Patrick and Christian Landeros, with special thanks to Max Lobovsky (Formlabs) and Dr. Peter So (MIT). The Silk Pavilion project, led by Mediated Matter's Markus Kayser, Jared Laucks, Jorge Duro-Royo, Laia Mogas Soldevila, and Carlos Gonzales Uribe, was in collaboration with Dr. Fiorenzo Omenetto (Tufts University) and Dr. James Weaver (Wyss Institute, Harvard University). Multimaterial printing work, including the Gemini chaise lounge and the Minotaur Head with Lamella, was conducted with Stratasys, Ltd. Collaborators on these multimaterial prints led by Dr. Neri Oxman include Dr. W. Craig Carter (MIT), Joe Hicklin (The Mathworks), and Turlif Vilbrandt (Symvol, Uformia). The microfluidic printing work was conducted with Dr. David Kong, Will Patrick, and Maria Isabella Gariboldi. The Mediated Matter lab would also like to thank the Center for Bits and Atoms and the Synthetic Biology Center for providing fabrication facilities and technical support. Special thanks are due to both of my doctoral advisors, Dr. Neri Oxman and Dr. David Wallace, the undergraduate research assistant team led by Nathan Spielberg, and friends and family.

Brook Kennedy is an industrial designer concerned with design and *making* in the twenty-first century. With a combined interest in additive manufacturing and biologically inspired design, his work is focused on creating a foundation for a sustainable global innovation economy.

Dirk Knemeyer is a social futurist and a founder of Involution Studios. He has provided consulting, design, and technology to some of the best companies in the world, including Apple, Microsoft, Oracle, PayPal, and Shutterfly. Dirk's writings have appeared in publications such as *Business Week* and *Core77*. He has keynoted conferences in Europe and the United States and spoken at venues such as TEDx, Humanity+, and South by Southwest. Dirk has participated on 15 boards in industries including healthcare, publishing, and education. He holds a, MA in popular culture from Bowling Green State University and a BA in english from The University of Toledo.

Acknowledgements On behalf of the first world, thanks to the developing nations that allow explotative business practices and inhumane treatment of labor. It is on these exploits that the cheap materials and labor enable modern digital technology and its ruthlessly efficient "progress."

An assistant professor and director of product design at the University of Minnesota (UMN), **Barry Kudrowitz** received his Ph.D. from the Mechanical Engineering Department at MIT, studying humor, creativity, and idea generation. Kudrowitz co-designed a Nerf toy, an elevator simulator that is in operation at the International Spy Museum in Washington, D.C., and a ketchup-dispensing robot that was featured on the *Martha Stewart Show*. He has taught toy product design for more than 10 years at both MIT and UMN. You can find more information at *www.wonderbarry.com*.

Acknowledgements I would like to acknowledge toy inventors Jeff Freeland Nelson, Andrew Comfort, Dave Kapell, David Merrill, and Kurt Roots for their advice and feedback on this chapter.

Over the past 15 years, **Gershom Kutliroff** has held several positions in the computer vision and graphics industries, leading research and development efforts in the area of human-computer interaction. He is an inventor on more than 20 patents and patents pending. He was the CTO and cofounder of Omek Interactive, which developed hand tracking and gesture control technology (acquired by Intel in 2013). Dr. Kutliroff continues to pursue his interest in new paradigms of human-computer interaction as a principal engineer within Intel's Perceptual Computing group. He earned his Ph.D. and M.Sc. in applied mathematics from Brown University, and his B.Sc. in applied mathematics from Columbia University. Dr. Kutliroff is married with five children, but he still holds out hope to one day hike the Appalachian Trail.

Acknowledgements I would like to gratefully acknowledge the contributions of members of the Omek Studio in the many stormy, yet fruitful, discussions, and in the prototyping work that yielded the ideas discussed in my chapter: Eli Elhadad, Edna Nuama, Yinon Oshrat, Shahar Oz, Amir Rosenberger, Bar Shulman, and Doron Houminer.

Michal Levin is a senior user experience (UX) designer at Google and author of the book *Designing Multi-Device Experiences* (O'Reilly). In a UX career exceeding 10 years, she has designed a wide variety of experiences for web, mobile, and TV. In addition, Michal regularly mentors startups and speaks at international UX conferences.

Acknowledgements "Without change there is no innovation, creativity, or incentive for improvement. Those who initiate change will have a better opportunity to manage the change that is inevitable." —William Pollard

I would like to first thank all of you out there driving a change and embracing innovation. You've been an inspiration to me in writing my chapter.

Thank you, Mary Treseler, my editor at O'Reilly, for giving me the opportunity to contribute to this exciting book. To all my esteemed reviewers, thank you for your invaluable feedback. And finally, thank you my love for being you, and for all your support, love and encouragement along the way.

#ChangeIsComing

Matt Nish-Lapidus holds a degree in new media art and is a practicing designer, musician, and artist. His work has included everything from digital library catalogs, enterprise software, video games, and large-scale public installations. He spent the first few years of his career assisting international new-media artists, later moving into the design and technology industry.

Matt loves to debate about art, politics, music, and just about anything else. He leads a design team at Normative in Toronto, Canada, where he focuses on design practice development in a twenty-first-century studio. He currently serves as the vice president of the Interaction Design Association (IxDA), a global organization dedicated to the development of the interaction design practice.

Acknowledgements Thanks to my team at Normative, and especially to Matthew Milan for helping me solidify and evolve my ideas about design. Also, thanks to the entire IxDA and global design community that has been a constant support and for challenging me over the years.

Marco Righetto is an interaction and service designer, fascinated by the relationships between physical objects and digital services.

As a designer, he is devoted to those little big details that make an experience pleasurable, coherent, tuned, and successful. Besides the professional environment, he loves to explore the role of design as an enabler to understand new technologies and speculate on possible future scenarios.

The creative director of Involution Studios, **Juhan Sonin** is an emeritus of some of the finest software organizations in the world: Apple, the National Center for Supercomputing Applications (NCSA), and MIT. He has been a creative director for almost two decades with his work being featured in the *New York Times*, *Newsweek*, BBC International, *Billboard Magazine*, and National Public Radio (NPR). His designs have enjoyed installations throughout Europe and the United States.

Juhan is a recognized expert in design for health, process management, and security, providing consultation to the United States Department of Health and Human Services and the Department of Defense. Juhan's most recent paper, published in the *Journal of Participatory Medicine*, is

"Hacking Health: Designing for and Understanding My Health." The article details the experience of designing software for medical applications and the future of noninvasive diagnostics.

Scott Stropkay is a founding partner of Essential, a design consultancy developing physical products, digital products, and service experiences. He helps companies build better discovery processes, define innovation opportunities, and use design thinking skills to inform business strategy. His work has guided the selection and development of market leading products and services for clients, including Genentech, Philips Healthcare, iRobot, Mayo Clinic, and Procter & Gamble. Scott has worked in both corporate and consulting design capacities for more than 25 years. Before Essential, he led an integrated design, human factors, and interaction design team at IDEO. He was also a director of design at Gillette and a director of design at Fitch. He holds a bachelor of fine art in industrial design from the Cleveland Institute of Art.

Scott Sullivan is an experience designer at Adaptive Path in San Francisco, California. He has a background in visual design, theater, modern dance, creative technology, and interactive performance art. You can usually find him getting his hands dirty building things that might or might not have a purpose. Before joining Adaptive Path, Scott was a digital product designer at Involution Studios, where he was heavily involved in launching and evolving startups. He has experience designing products in the education, energy, finance, social media, and digital publishing industries.

Scott's goal is to create products that operate seamlessly in people's physical lives and utilize emerging technologies to make the invisible visible, which generally involves spending lots of time waving his hands around in front of sensors.

Hunter Whitney is a senior UX design strategist who has more than 15 years of experience consulting for a range of corporations, startups, government organizations, and nongovernment organizations. He has worked in many domains but specializes in health, medicine, and the life sciences.

He is the author of *Data Insights: New Ways to Visualize and Make Sense of Data* (Morgan Kaufmann). He has also written numerous articles about a range of subjects, such as data visualization, for various online and print publications including *UX Magazine*.

Twitter: @*HunterWhitney* Website: *hunterwhitney.com*

As the creative director of the Omek Studio from its inception in 2007, **Yaron Yanai** led all aspects of game and UX design. In this role, he spearheaded the studio's efforts to create compelling, next-generation usages that take advantage of cutting-edge human-computer interaction technologies. Previously, Yaron held several positions in the CG and gaming industry. Omek Interactive was acquired by Intel in 2013, and Yaron now pursues his vision of revolutionizing the way people interact with their environments within Intel's Perceptual Computing group. He is a graduate of Bezalel Academy of Art and Design.

Acknowledgements I would like to recognize the members of the Omek Studio for all of the productive discussions and the prototyping work which resulted in the ideas presented in my chapter: Eli Elhadad, Edna Nuama, Yinon Oshrat, Shahar Oz, Amir Rosenberger, Bar Shulman, and Doron Houminer.

Get even more for your money.

Join the O'Reilly Community, and register the O'Reilly books you own. It's free, and you'll get:

- $4.99 ebook upgrade offer
- 40% upgrade offer on O'Reilly print books
- Membership discounts on books and events
- Free lifetime updates to ebooks and videos
- Multiple ebook formats, DRM FREE
- Participation in the O'Reilly community
- Newsletters
- Account management
- 100% Satisfaction Guarantee

Signing up is easy:

1. Go to: oreilly.com/go/register
2. Create an O'Reilly login.
3. Provide your address.
4. Register your books.

Note: English-language books only

To order books online:
oreilly.com/store

For questions about products or an order:
orders@oreilly.com

To sign up to get topic-specific email announcements and/or news about upcoming books, conferences, special offers, and new technologies:
elists@oreilly.com

For technical questions about book content:
booktech@oreilly.com

To submit new book proposals to our editors:
proposals@oreilly.com

O'Reilly books are available in multiple DRM-free ebook formats. For more information:
oreilly.com/ebooks

O'REILLY®

Have it your way.

CPSIA information can be obtained
at www.ICGtesting.com
Printed in the USA
LVOW06s1744060917
547761LV00002B/7/P